COMPUTERS IN SOCIETY

Seventh Edition

Editor

Kathryn Schellenberg

Kathryn Schellenberg earned a Ph.D. in sociology from the University of Utah and is presently an independent researcher and consultant based in Guelph, Ontario, Canada. One of her areas of scholarly interest is the social impacts of technology, especially computing. She has conducted and published research on computer-related topics, including computer impacts on policing and how workers in high-tech "information" firms deal with change and uncertainty. She has also taught computers/technology and society courses at the Universities of Utah, Calgary, and Guelph.

A Library of Information from the Public Press
Dushkin/McGraw·Hill
Sluice Dock, Guilford, Connecticut 06437

*Visit us on the Internet—*http://www.dushkin.com/

The Annual Editions Series

ANNUAL EDITIONS, including GLOBAL STUDIES, consist of over 70 volumes designed to provide the reader with convenient, low-cost access to a wide range of current, carefully selected articles from some of the most important magazines, newspapers, and journals published today. ANNUAL EDITIONS are updated on an annual basis through a continuous monitoring of over 300 periodical sources. All ANNUAL EDITIONS have a number of features that are designed to make them particularly useful, including topic guides, annotated tables of contents, unit overviews, and indexes. For the teacher using ANNUAL EDITIONS in the classroom, an Instructor's Resource Guide with test questions is available for each volume. GLOBAL STUDIES titles provide comprehensive background information and selected world press articles on the regions and countries of the world.

VOLUMES AVAILABLE

ANNUAL EDITIONS

Abnormal Psychology
Accounting
Adolescent Psychology
Aging
American Foreign Policy
American Government
American History, Pre-Civil War
American History, Post-Civil War
American Public Policy
Anthropology
Archaeology
Astronomy
Biopsychology
Business Ethics
Child Growth and Development
Comparative Politics
Computers in Education
Computers in Society
Criminal Justice
Criminology
Developing World
Deviant Behavior
Drugs, Society, and Behavior
Dying, Death, and Bereavement
Early Childhood Education

Economics
Educating Exceptional Children
Education
Educational Psychology
Environment
Geography
Geology
Global Issues
Health
Human Development
Human Resources
Human Sexuality
International Business
Macroeconomics
Management
Marketing
Marriage and Family
Mass Media
Microeconomics
Multicultural Education
Nutrition
Personal Growth and Behavior
Physical Anthropology
Psychology
Public Administration
Race and Ethnic Relations

Social Problems
Social Psychology
Sociology
State and Local Government
Teaching English as a Second
   Language
Urban Society
Violence and Terrorism
Western Civilization,
   Pre-Reformation
Western Civilization,
   Post-Reformation
Women's Health
World History, Pre-Modern
World History, Modern
World Politics

GLOBAL STUDIES

Africa
China
India and South Asia
Japan and the Pacific Rim
Latin America
Middle East
Russia, the Eurasian Republics,
   and Central/Eastern Europe
Western Europe

Cataloging in Publication Data
Main entry under title: Computer Studies: Computers in Society. 7/E. "An Annual Edition Publication."
    1. Computers and civilization—Periodicals. 2. Computers—Periodicals. I. Schellenberg, Kathryn, *comp.* II.
Title: Computers in society.
ISBN 0-697-39304-6   303.4'834   ISSN 1094-2629

© 1998 by Dushkin/McGraw-Hill, Guilford, CT 06437, A Division of The McGraw-Hill Companies.

Seventh Edition

Cover image ©1996 PhotoDisc, Inc.

Printed in the United States of America

Printed on Recycled Paper

Editors/Advisory Board

Members of the Advisory Board are instrumental in the final selection of articles for each edition of ANNUAL EDITIONS. Their review of articles for content, level, currentness, and appropriateness provides critical direction to the editor and staff. We think that you will find their careful consideration well reflected in this volume.

Editor

Kathryn Schellenberg

ADVISORY BOARD

Staff

To the Reader

In publishing ANNUAL EDITIONS we recognize the enormous role played by the magazines, newspapers, and journals of the *public press* in providing current, first-rate educational information in a broad spectrum of interest areas. Many of these articles are appropriate for students, researchers, and professionals seeking accurate, current material to help bridge the gap between principles and theories and the real world. These articles, however, become more useful for study when those of lasting value are carefully *collected, organized, indexed,* and *reproduced* in a *low-cost format,* which provides easy and permanent access when the material is needed. That is the role played by ANNUAL EDITIONS. Under the direction of each volume's *academic editor,* who is an expert in the subject area, and with the guidance of an *Advisory Board,* each year we seek to provide in each ANNUAL EDITION a current, well-balanced, carefully selected collection of the best of the public press for your study and enjoyment. We think that you will find this volume useful, and we hope that you will take a moment to let us know what you think.

We can only guess at how the ever-increasing power, diversity, and pervasiveness of computers— especially *networked* computers—might affect the patterns of our individual and social lives. However, it is hoped that *Computer Studies: Computers in Society* will complement your technical understanding of these emerging technologies by acquainting you with some of the philosophical, economic, political, and social dimensions of the information society.

Contributors to the seventh edition of *Computer Studies: Computers in Society* represent a diverse range of backgrounds, and their collective writings highlight a wide spectrum of issues and views about how the information age will or ought to unfold. For the most part, their writing styles are very understandable and devoid of the kind of unintelligible technical jargon that can be a barrier to becoming informed about technological issues.

Because of its social focus, *Computer Studies: Computers in Society* is organized to reflect the major dimensions of society rather than various aspects of computing. The major themes of the book are the economy, community, politics, and conflict. Many of these themes are also examined in an international context. The final section looks at some of the philosophical challenges posed by emerging technologies.

Each article has been selected for its informational value, but "informative" does not necessarily imply correctness or validity. In fact, some of you may find that you strongly disagree with, or are even offended by, a position expressed in one or more articles—I may well agree with you. On the other hand, some may feel simply inspired by arguments that make others irate. *Computer Studies: Computers in Society* is meant to generate rather than answer questions on how computers will affect society. Hopefully, such queries will serve to clarify issues, broaden perspectives, provoke curiosity, and stimulate informed discussion of and participation in the computer age.

Readers can have input into the next edition of *Computer Studies: Computers in Society* by completing and returning the postage-paid article rating form in the back of the book.

Kathryn Schellenberg

Kathryn Schellenberg
Editor

Contents

Introduction

Two articles offer various visions
of the present and future
computer-networked society.

UNIT 1

The Economy

Five articles examine the
impacts of computer
technologies on global
manufacturing, the
business cycle, productivity,
and commerce.

The concepts in bold italics are developed in the article. For further expansion please refer to the Topic Guide, the Glossary, and the Index.

UNIT 2

Work and the Workplace

Four articles look at the latest in office automation, electronic networks in the workplace, telecommunity, computer-related injuries, and information overload.

The concepts in bold italics are developed in the article. For further expansion please refer to the Topic Guide, the Glossary, and the Index.

UNIT 3

Computers and Social Participation

Four articles discuss aspects of
social involvement and
interaction in a
computer-mediated society.

The concepts in bold italics are developed in the article. For further expansion please refer to the Topic Guide, the Glossary, and the Index.

vii

UNIT 4

Social Values: Ethics, Law, and Privacy

Five articles examine issues related to intellectual property, legally and ethically questionable use of computer networks, computer crime, the use and potential abuse of computer simulations in legal proceedings, and threats of privacy.

The concepts in bold italics are developed in the article. For further expansion please refer to the Topic Guide, the Glossary, and the Index.

UNIT 5

Politics and the State

Four articles explore the implications of computing and networking for disseminating political information, the electoral process, democratic choice, local tax revenues, totalitarianism, and electronic warfare.

UNIT 6

Technological Risks

Four articles discuss technological obsolescence, the threats posed by computer malfunction, and legal implications of flawed electronic information.

The concepts in bold italics are developed in the article. For further expansion please refer to the Topic Guide, the Glossary, and the Index.

ix

UNIT 7

International Perspective and Issues

Five articles examine issues related to the computer industry in Ireland, networking in China, software piracy in Singapore, the gap between rich and poor nations, and Third World development.

The concepts in bold italics are developed in the article. For further expansion please refer to the Topic Guide, the Glossary, and the Index.

UNIT 8

Philosophical Frontiers

Three articles in this section discuss a range of issues, which pose or may pose philosophical challenges for the computer age.

The concepts in bold italics are developed in the article. For further expansion please refer to the Topic Guide, the Glossary, and the Index.

Topic Guide

This topic guide suggests how the selections in this book relate to topics of traditional concern to students and professionals involved with computers in society. It can be very useful for locating articles that relate to each other for reading and research. The guide is arranged alphabetically according to topic. Articles may, of course, treat topics that do not appear in the topic guide. In turn, entries in the topic guide do not necessarily constitute a comprehensive listing of all the contents of each selection. **In addition, relevant Web sites, which are annotated on the next two pages, are noted in bold italics under the topic articles.**

TOPIC AREA	TREATED IN	TOPIC AREA	TREATED IN
Africa	32. Disconnected: Haves and Have-Nots	**Electronic Monitoring**	*See* **Privacy and Security**
Artificial Intelligence	35. Ghosts in the Machine 36. How Artificial Intelligence Fails *(41, 42, 43, 44, 45)*	**Encryption**	*See* **Privacy and Security**
Artificial Life	34. What's It All About, Alife? *(40, 45)*	**Ergonomics**	10. Working Out the Kinks *(11)*
Asia	30. Great Firewall of China 31. Singapore Sting *(38)*	**Ethics**	16. Law and Order Comes to Cyberspace 17. Who's Reading Your E-Mail? 18. Simulations on Trial 19. Invasion of Privacy 27. Fatal Dose
Children	13. Session with the Cybershrink 14. Computer Delusion *(27, 29)*		28. Liability for Defective Electronic Information 31. Singapore Sting *(19, 21, 23, 24, 25, 26, 27, 28, 29)*
China	30. Great Firewall of China	**Etiquette**	8. Ripple Effect of Computer Networking
Communications	4. New Business Cycle 7. Money in Electronic Commerce 8. Ripple Effect of Computer Networking 10. Working Out the Kinks 11. Overload *(5, 6, 9, 11, 18)*		12. Finding One's Own Space in Cyberspace *(16)*
		Europe	29. Birth of a Celtic Tiger *(39)*
Crime	7. Money in Electronic Commerce 16. Law and Order Comes to Cyberspace 17. Who's Reading Your E-Mail? 18. Simulations on Trial 31. Singapore Sting *(6, 19, 24, 25, 26, 27)*	**Globalization**	*See* **International Issues**
		Government and Politics	16. Law and Order Comes to Cyberspace 19. Invasion of Privacy 20. High Resolution, Unresolved 21. Digital Politics 22. Great Internet Tax Drain 23. Is Big Brother Hanging by His Bootstraps? 24. Warfare in the Information Age 29. Birth of a Celtic Tiger 30. Great Firewall of China *(24, 26, 28, 30, 31, 32, 33, 34)*
Economic Issues	1. Welcome to Cyberspace 3. Clicking onto Webzines 4. New Business Cycle 5. What Has the Computer Done for Us Lately? 6. Creating the People's Computer 7. Money in Electronic Commerce 22. Great Internet Tax Drain 31. Singapore Sting 32. Disconnected: Haves and Have-Nots 33. Role of Computer Networks in Development *(2, 3, 4, 5, 6, 7, 8, 9, 37, 38, 39)*		
		Hackers and Hacking	*See* **Crime**
		Health and Medicine	10. Working Out the Kinks 27. Fatal Dose *(11)*
Education and Training	6. Creating the People's Computer 13. Session with the Cybershrink 14. Computer Delusion 15. Campus of Our Own 32. Disconnected: Haves and Have-Nots *(23, 29)*	**Human Interaction**	1. Welcome to Cyberspace 2. Internet 8. Ripple Effect of Computer Networking 9. Virtually Working 11. Overload 12. Finding One's Own Space in Cyberspace

TOPIC AREA	TREATED IN	TOPIC AREA	TREATED IN
Human Interaction (continued)	13. Session with the Cybershrink 15. Campus of Our Own 35. Ghosts in the Machine *(1, 12, 14, 15, 17, 18, 29, 34)*	Networks and Networking (continued)	33. Role of Computer Networks in Development *(1, 2, 6, 10, 14, 15, 17, 18, 24, 25, 27, 31, 32, 33, 34, 37)*
Inequality	2. Internet 32. Disconnected: Haves and Have-Nots 33. Role of Computer Networks in Development *(17, 23, 29, 32)*	Office Automation	6. Creating the People's Computer 8. Ripple Effect of Computer Networking 9. Virtually Working 11. Overload 25. It's 10 O'Clock *(10, 12, 13, 14, 15, 17, 37)*
Intellectual Property	3. Clicking onto Webzines 16. Law and Order Comes to Cyberspace 17. Who's Reading Your E-Mail? 24. Warfare in the Information Age 28. Liability for Defective Electronic Information 31. Singapore Sting *(1, 3, 7, 16, 22, 23, 24, 26, 27, 28, 32)*	Philosophical Issues	2. Internet 34. What's It All About, Alife? 35. Ghosts in the Machine 36. How Artificial Intelligence Fails *(1, 40, 41, 42, 44, 45)*
		Politics	*See* **Government and Politics**
International Issues	7. Money in Electronic Commerce 16. Law and Order Comes to Cyberspace 20. High Resolution, Unresolved 23. Is Big Brother Hanging by His Bootstraps? 24. Warfare in the Information Age 26. Software's Chronic Crisis 28. Liability for Defective Electronic Information 29. Birth of a Celtic Tiger 30. Great Firewall of China 31. Singapore Sting 32. Disconnected: Haves and Have-Nots 33. Role of Computer Networks in Development *(6, 15, 24, 25, 26, 31, 33, 37, 38, 39)*	Privacy and Security	7. Money in Electronic Commerce 8. Ripple Effect of Computer Networking 17. Who's Reading Your E-Mail? 19. Invasion of Privacy 20. High Resolution, Unresolved 23. Is Big Brother Hanging by His Bootstraps? 30. Great Firewall of China *(6, 8, 24, 25, 26, 27, 28)*
		Productivity	4. New Business Cycle 5. What Has the Computer Done for Us Lately? 6. Creating the People's Computer *(4, 5, 9, 15, 17)*
Legal Issues	7. Money in Electronic Commerce 16. Law and Order Comes to Cyberspace 17. Who's Reading Your E-Mail? 18. Simulations on Trial 28. Liability for Defective Electronic Information 31. Singapore Sting *(6, 19, 21, 22, 23, 24, 27)*	Publishing	3. Clicking onto Webzines *(3, 7, 9)*
		Risks and Computer Reliability	25. It's 10 O'Clock 26. Software's Chronic Crisis 27. Fatal Dose 28. Liability for Defective Electronic Information *(35, 36)*
Networks and Networking	1. Welcome to Cyberspace 2. Internet 3. Clicking onto Webzines 4. New Business Cycle 7. Money in Electronic Commerce 8. Ripple Effect of Computer Networking 9. Virtually Working 11. Overload 12. Finding One's Own Space in Cyberspace 13. Session with the Cybershrink 15. Campus of Our Own 16. Law and Order Comes to Cyberspace 17. Who's Reading Your E-Mail? 19. Invasion of Privacy 21. Digital Politics 22. Great Internet Tax Drain 23. Is Big Brother Hanging by His Bootstraps? 24. Warfare in the Information Age 30. Great Firewall of China 32. Disconnected: Haves and Have-Nots	(The) Self	13. Session with the Cybershrink 35. Ghost in the Machine
		Simulations	18. Simulations on Trial *(20, 21)*
		Women (and Gender) Issues	12. Finding One's Own Space in Cyberspace *(12, 23)*
		Working and Employment	4. New Business Cycle 5. What Has the Computer Done for Us Lately? 6. Creating the People's Computer 8. Ripple Effect of Computer Networking 9. Virtually Working 10. Working Out the Kinks 11. Overload 17. Who's Reading Your E-Mail? 19. Invasion of Privacy *(10, 11, 12, 13, 14, 15, 17)*

Selected World Wide Web Sites for Computer Studies: Computers in Society

All of these Web sites are hot-linked through the *Annual Editions* home page: *http://www.dushkin.com/annualeditions* (just click on a book). In addition, these sites are referred to by number in the Topic Guide on the previous two pages.

Some Web sites are continually changing their structure and content, so the information listed may not always be available.

Introduction

1. Short History of the Internet—*http://ubicom.com/history.html*—Bruce Sterling begins with the development of the idea for the Internet by the cold war think tank, the Rand Corporation, and goes on to explain how computer networking works. Links to other sites and to further reading.

2. Livelink Intranet Guided Tour—*http://www.opentext.com/ livelink/ otm_ls_test.html*—Livelink Intranet helps companies to manage and control documents, business processes, and projects more effectively. Take this tour to see how.

The Economy

3. Cyber Cafe Hot List: Magazines and Webzines—*http://cyber-cafe/ lbzne.htm*—A list of links to electronic magazines.

4. Generation Techs—*http://www.incomeops.com/online/ contents9702/gentechs.html*—Generation X entrepreneurs are becoming industry giants before their thirtieth birthdays. With virtually no capital and less experience, they are at the helm of some of the technology industry's most innovative start-ups.

5. Integrated Information and Communication System—*http://www.kepco.co.kr/About/e-abt-j.htm*—On this page, an electric company, KEPCO, which is building an integrated information and communication system to deal with advancements made in the field of communication technology, tells what it has done, and what it plans for the future.

6. Mersch Online: Links zu Informationen uber E-Cash—*http://www.mersch.com/links/moneyzz.htm*—This page has a good series of links to other sources of information about E-cash.

7. Site Reviews: Webzines—*http://lofgreen.com/webzines.htm*—This is an Internet site that offers reviews and ratings of selected webzines.

8. The End of Cash (James Gleick)—*http://www.around.com/money.html*—An article, previously published in the *New York Times*, on June 16, 1996, discusses the obsolescence of cash.

9. Welcome to Industry Week—*http:///www.industryweek.com/—IW* is an interactive management resource, an online magazine that features columns, articles, and conference news.

Work and the Workplace

10. HW: The Homeworking Phenomenon: Looking beyond the Hype—*http:///www.homeworker.com/issue2/hype/hype.html*—*Home Worker* magazine talks with analyst Abhijeet Rane about the issues and challenges affecting home-based workers—and the keys to finding success.

11. STEP ON IT! Pedals: Repetitive Strain Injury—*http://www.bilbo. com/rsi2.html*—Here is an explanation of carpal tunnel syndrome and links to alternative approaches to the computer keyboard, plus links to related information.

12. Telecommuting—*http://www.iamot.org/~chiklink/453home/html*—Here is a description of telecommuting—the convergence of work, home, and family spheres—that is particularly directed toward women in the home.

13. Telecommuting Centers—*http://www.telecommute.org/tc.html*—Explore eight telecommuting centers and find out what they have to offer the person who wants to work closer to home.

14. Telecommuting Links—*http://www.ci.chula-vista.ca.us/telecomu. htm*—Links to research papers that deal with telecommuting as well as examples of projects.

15. The International Telework Association—*http://www.telecom-mute.org/index.html#place*—International Information about telecommuting, the alternate route to work, and links about issues and challenges of the virtual workplace.

Computers and Social Participation

16. The Core Rules of Netiquette—*http://www.albion.com/netiquette/ corerules.html*—Excerpted from Virginia Shea's book *Netiquette*. This is classic work in the field of online communication.

17. Virtual Community in Real Reality—*http://panizzi.shef.ac.uk/ community/virtreal.html*—A realistic, if biased, look at the effects on community involvement of expanded information technology. This is an abridged version of a paper printed in *Inventing the Future, Partnerships for Tomorrow,* January 1996, by Greg Smith.

18. WorldNow Online—*http://www.worldnow.com*—This broadcast network offers consumers retail shopping, travel help, classified ads, and local community-based programming similar to that found on television networks.

Social Values: Ethics, Law, and Privacy

19. AS: Frequently Asked Questions—*http://www.hackers.com/faq.htm*—At this Web site of Axis Security (AS), a hacking/security organization, the answers to what hacking is in hackers' own words can be found.

20. Computer Modeling and Animation—*http://www.visualdesigns. com/3dmain.htm*—Here is an example of computer-generated animation from a company engaged in this kind of production.

21. Computer Simulation and Animation in the Courtroom—*http://www.evidence.com/Articles/Animation-admissibility.html*—The new wave of computer simulation and animation in the courtroom is discussed by lawyer Richard Alexander. Links to related sites.

22. Copyright & Trademark Information for the IEEE Computer Society—*http://computer.org/copyright.htm*—Here is an example of how a publication on the Web is legally protected. The section on Intellectual Property Rights Information contains further information about reuse permission and copyright policies.

23. Cybertronics: The Geopolitics of Cyberspace—*http://www.channel. zerocom/meta/articles/geopolit.html*—Written by Blake Harris, this article is a detailed examination of the unique problems of cyber-

space. The author sees in the very nature of the information society a serious threat to the future of democracy.

24. Information Security and Privacy in Network Environments—*http://www.cypher.net/info/pub/clipper/ota_priv_sec.report*—Good discussion by OTA (Office of Technology Assessment) on the issues, including government security, the European Union approach, cryptography, and much more. For a list of many links with descriptive abstracts, use *http://www.cypher.net/info/pub/clipper/*.

25. Internet Privacy Coalition—*http://www.privacy.org/ipc/*—The mission of the Internet Privacy Coalition is to promote privacy and security on the Internet through widespread public availability of strong encryption and the relaxation of export controls on cryptography.

26. My Lock, My Key: Encryption Policy Resource Page—*http://www.crypto.com*—These pages are maintained for information about U.S. encryption export restrictions and the need for policy reform.

27. Safety and Security on the Internet—*http://host1.webgate.net/services9.html*—This site deals with software programs that help keep children from accessing pornography on the Net, plus other aspects of Web security, hackers, con artists, protection of privacy, and viruses.

Politics and the State

28. ACLU: American Civil Liberties Union—*http://www.aclu.org/*—Click on the Supreme Court's Internet decision, plus details of the case, *Reno v. ACLU*, ACLU's campaign to restore information privacy, "Take Back Your Data," and cyber-liberties and free speech for opinion on First Amendment rights as they apply to cyberspace.

29. Comstockery in Cyberspace—*http://arlo.wilsonhs.pps.142.or.us/comstock.html*—This discussion by Janet Murray of the use of the Internet in schools leads to Child Safety on the Information Highway, which has many links to parent/child/school issues.

30. Congress vs. Free Speech on the Internet—*http://www.info-nation.com/congress.html*—This is a general discussion by Chris Sandberg, an attorney who practices telecommunication and computer law, about Congress's position on the Internet.

31. Firewall-Cyberwar—*http://ns.annex.co.uk/software/cyberwar.html*—The U.S. military considers foreign attack on U.S. computer sytems a real risk. This article discusses the threat of this new kind of warfare.

32. Issues in Telecommunication and Democracy—*http://www.benton.org/Library/TeleDemocracy/working8.html*—This article, prepared under the aegis of the Benton Foundation, discusses the issues surrounding telecommunications in the twenty-first century and concludes that, if designed with care, the new age can help realize "the enduring democratic promise."

33. Patrolling the Empire—*http://www.csrp.org/patrol.htm*—Reprinted from *CovertAction Quarterly*, this article by Randy K. Schwartz details the plans of NIMA (National Imagery and Mapping Agency) for future wars by helping to fuse high-tech surveillance and weaponry, according to the author.

34. Riley Information Services: Living in the Electronic Village—*http://www.rileyis.com/publications/phase1/execsumm.htm*—The Impact of Information in Technology on Government is the subtitle of this online book. Shown is the executive summary. Seven other sections are equally pertinent. Explore this entire site by clicking back and forth for this book and its sequel, Phase II.

Technological Risks

35. Georgia Tech Year 2000 Millenium Bug Guide—*http://www.gatech.edu/year2000/*—An important Year 2000 site with links to many other sites that are concerned with the last-two-digit millenium bug, which concerns both hardware and software.

36. Yahoo-Computers and Internet: Year 2000 Problem—*http://www.yahoo.com/Computers_and_Internet/Year_2000_Problem/*—Excellent list of sources on the Year 2000 problems and possible solutions. Has search capability and links.

International Perspective and Issues

37. GUIDE International—*http://www.guide.org/*—GUIDE International is the premier IBM user group for the management and use of information technology. Click on "How to Align Quality Objectives and Business Strategies" for Table of Contents and abstract of this book.

38. India: New Software Opportunities—*http://www.3seblr.soft.net/indianit.html*—This is the site of the Indian IT industry, which is planning for enormous growth in software development plus increased interaction with European countries.

39. Mission Statement—*http://nautilus.netcmi.co.uk/company/mission.htm*—CMI's mission, as stated here, is to become Northern Ireland's most respected independent provider of computer services.

Philosophical Frontiers

40. Artificial Life Games Homepage—*http://gracco.irmkant.rm.cnr.it/luigi/lupa_algames_res.html*—This Artificial Life Games Homepage leads to many exciting adventures, for example, robot-related sites, alife (artificial life) games, simulators, and demo programming.

41. Computer Chess Feature: Kasparov vs. Deep Blue Rematch—*http://www.chess.net/computerchess.html*—A discussion of the historic rematch between Garry Kasparov and Deep Blue also considers how to work with artificial intelligence effectively.

42. CS327: Artificial Intelligence—*http://hamming.mathcs.carleton.edu/courses/courses_resources/cs327.html*—Link to facts about the book *Artificial Intelligence: A Modern Approach.*

43. IEEE Robotics and Automation Society Home Page—*http://www.acim.usl.edu/RAS/*—Information about robotics within the Institute of Electrical Engineers' RAS (Robotics and Automation Society), as well as links to other associations, government, industry, publishing, and university sources and sites.

44. Introduction to Artificial Intelligence (AI)—*http://www-formal.stanford.edu/jmc/aiintro/aiintro.html*—A statement of what AI is. Click on John McCarthy's home page for a list of additional papers.

45. WWW Resources—*http://alife.santafe.edu/alife/www/*—Start here to find links to many alife (artificial life) Web sites, including demonstrations, research centers and groups, and other resources.

We highly recommend that you review our Web site for expanded information and our other product lines. We are continually updating and adding links to our Web site in order to offer you the most usable and useful information that will support and expand the value of your Annual Editions. You can reach us at: *http://www.dushkin.com/annualeditions/*.

Introduction

We often read and hear these days about the computer or information revolution. The *Concise Oxford Dictionary* defines a "revolution" as a "complete change, turning upside down, [or] great reversal of conditions" as in the example of the Industrial Revolution. In a thought-provoking book titled *The Micro Millennium*, the late British computer expert Christopher Evans observed that the Industrial Revolution:

> brought about immense shifts in all aspects of society, affecting the individual, his family, his neighbors, his domestic and working environment, his clothes, his food, his leisure time, his political and religious ideals, his education, his social attitudes, his life-span, even the manner of his birth and death. (1979:ix)

Evans claimed not only that the societal impacts of computers would rival the effects of the Industrial Revolution but that we are not free to choose the future. He argued that when we began to apply these powerful new tools to the tasks of bettering our lives, we set in motion a process that took on an independent, unstoppable momentum.

There are those who scoff at the idea of being swept up in a revolution or at least dispute the claim that we have no control over the future. For instance, in his book *Personal Computer Book,* Peter A. McWilliams argued that while computers will have a dramatic impact on our lives, humans are in command of their own fate:

> For the most part, personal computers will prove their worth to the extent that they fit into your daily life, not

to the degree that you adapt your life to be more in step with The Computer Age. (1984:15)

Contradictory predictions about the implications of computing are not surprising since people operate from different premises about society and human nature. We need to keep this is in mind when we try to make sense of competing claims about the future. This is not easy because we are often unaware of our own assumptions about social life. Mostly, we just tend to take certain things for granted and believe them so strongly we simply assume other reasonable and intelligent people see things the same way.

However, if you believe people are fundamentally honest, generous, and altruistic, it is just as clear to someone else that people are basically greedy, self-interested, and manipulative. If you take it for granted that an orderly, stable society is the result of people cooperating and working toward the common good, there are others who would argue that power and coercion bind society together. If you are convinced people have free will to create the kind of society they value, others are more inclined to think that the nature of society is determined by forces beyond human will. And, if you believe "idealism" governs society, others are persuaded that we live in a "material" world.

The contrast between the views of Evans and McWilliams basically reflects the difference between how idealists and materialists look at the world. Those who feel that idealism and free will govern society are uncomfortable with claims that cultural, political, or religious ideals are shaped by technical innovation. They would argue that ideals come first and are the foundation of society. Technology's innovations are accepted or rejected depending on whether they harmonize with basic values. This assumption is implied in McWilliams's argument that computers are mere tools, which people are free to adopt or reject. Materialists, on the other hand, insist that new technologies need not support any basic belief system. They maintain that if a technology can provide real material benefits, such as greater wealth or longer life expectancy to society or to a powerful minority, it will be adopted. If some aspect of the technology clashes with society's values and ideals, then the values, not the technology, will be modified or abandoned. Clearly, Christopher Evans is in the materialist camp.

Social theorists and philosophers have debated for centuries over which of the competing social assumptions is valid. Like the rest of us, they continue to disagree about where the truth lies. The articles in this seventh edition of *Computer Studies: Computers in Society* do not put these issues to rest. But they do show us that technology and cultural ideals influence each other in complex, and sometimes strange, ways.

The articles that introduce this edition center on the potential implications of computer networking. Philip Elmer-DeWitt sets the stage by welcoming us to "cyberspace." He acquaints us with the information infrastructure that makes up cyberspace as it exists now and how it might look in the future. Elmer-DeWitt refrains from drawing conclusions, but he concedes that the model of cyberspace "may—just may—be a vehicle for revolutionary change."

In the following two-part article, several prominent social thinkers were asked to comment on the computing-information revolution. In the first report, the outspoken and controversial social critic Camille Paglia rhapsodizes over her view that "the era of digital technology is simply a continuation of the Enlightenment, that splendid rebirth of Greco-Roman science." Paglia sees greatly expanded personal liberties among the benefits of this transformation. In the second essay, Richard John Neuhaus, a Roman Catholic priest, is more skeptical about the potential extent of change and about how beneficial those changes will be. He argues, rather, that the high-decibel noises about a technological revolution . . . [tend to] confuse information with knowledge and knowledge with wisdom. And as for new liberties, Neuhaus reminds us that we will retain "inescapable responsibility for what we do and are."

Looking Ahead: Challenge Questions

If we discover that we really dislike some of the social changes that result from new technologies, can we discard our inventions or channel their effects to more desirable ends? Why or why not?

The ultralibertarian versus traditional ideals espoused by Camille Paglia and Richard Neuhaus underscore the diversity of values that exist in society. If we have a choice about which technologies are developed and how they are used, how could we resolve conflicts between groups with strongly opposing values and objectives?

Welcome to Cyberspace

What is it? Where is it? And how do we get there?

Philip Elmer-DeWitt

IT STARTED, AS THE BIG IDEAS IN TECHNOLOGY often do, with a science-fiction writer. William Gibson, a young expatriate American living in Canada, was wandering past the video arcades on Vancouver's Granville Street in the early 1980s when something about the way the players were hunched over their glowing screens struck him as odd. "I could see in the physical intensity of their postures how *rapt* the kids were," he says. "It was like a feedback loop, with photons coming off the screens into the kids' eyes, neurons moving through their bodies and electrons moving through the video game. These kids clearly *believed* in the space the games projected."

That image haunted Gibson. He didn't know much about video games or computers—he wrote his breakthrough novel *Neuromancer* (1984) on an ancient manual typewriter—but he knew people who did. And as near as he could tell, everybody who worked much with the machines eventually came to accept, almost as an article of faith, the reality of that imaginary realm. "They develop a belief that there's some kind of *actual space* behind the screen," he says. "Some place that you can't see but you know is there."

Gibson called that place "cyberspace," and used it as the setting for his early novels and short stories. In his fiction, cyberspace is a computer-generated landscape that characters enter by "jacking in"—sometimes by plugging electrodes directly into sockets implanted in the brain. What they see when they get there is a three-dimensional representation of all the information stored in "every computer in the human system"—great warehouses and skyscrapers of data. He describes it in a key passage in *Neuromancer* as a place of "unthinkable complexity," with "lines of light ranged in the nonspace of the mind, clusters and constellations of data. Like city lights, receding . . ."

In the years since, there have been other names given to that shadowy space where our computer data reside: the Net, the Web, the Cloud, the Matrix, the Metaverse, the Datasphere, the Electronic Frontier, the information superhighway. But Gibson's coinage may prove the most enduring. By 1989 it had been borrowed by the online community to describe not some science-fiction fantasy but today's increasingly inter-connected computer systems—especially the millions of computers jacked into the Internet.

Now hardly a day goes by without some newspaper article, some political speech, some corporate press release invoking Gibson's imaginary world. Suddenly, it seems, everybody has an E-mail address, from Hollywood moguls to the Holy See. Billy Graham has preached on America Online; Vice President Al Gore has held forth on CompuServe; thousands chose to celebrate New Year's this year with an online get-together called First Night in Cyberspace.

In Washington cyberspace has become a political hot button of some potency, first pressed during the 1992 presidential campaign by Al Gore and Bill Clinton, who rode to the White House in part on the promise that they would build the so-called information superhighway and route it through every voter's district—if not to his home. But the Clinton Administration lost the high ground of cyberspace, having, among other transgressions, come out on the wrong side of the privacy debate when it endorsed the Clipper Chip security device favored by its intelligence services. The Republicans were quick to grab the initiative. No sooner had incoming House Speaker Newt Gingrich taken office than he made his bid, staging a big press conference to unveil a new House computer system. At a Washington confab called "Democracy in Virtual America," attended by his old friends, futurists Alvin and Heidi Toffler, the Speaker talked expansively about wiring the world. "Cyberspace is the land of knowledge," proclaimed an information age Magna Carta issued in his name. "And the exploration of that land can be a civilization's truest, highest calling."

Corporations, smelling a land rush of another sort, are scrambling to stake out their own claims in cyberspace. Every computer company, nearly every publisher, most communications firms, banks, insurance companies and hundreds of mail-order and retail firms are registering their Internet domains and setting up sites on the World Wide Web. They sense that cyberspace will be one of the driving forces—if not the primary one—for economic growth in the 21st century.

All this is being breathlessly reported in the press, which has seized on cyberspace as an all-purpose buzz word that can add sparkle to the most humdrum development or assignment. For working reporters, many of whom have just discovered the pleasures of going online, cyber has become the prefix of the day, and

they are spawning neologisms as fast as they can type: cyberphilia, cyberphobia, cyberwonk, cybersex, cyberslut. A Nexis search of newspapers, magazines and television transcripts turned up 1,205 mentions of cyber in the month of January, up from 464 the previous January and 167 in January 1993.

ONE RESULT OF THIS DRUM ROLL IS A growing public appetite for a place most people haven't been to and are often hard-pressed to define. In a TIME/CNN poll of 800 Americans conducted in January by Yankelovich Partners, 57% didn't know what cyberspace meant, yet 85% were certain that information technology had made their life better. They may not know where it is, but they want desperately to get there. The rush to get online, to avoid being "left behind" in the information revolution, is intense. Those who find fulfillment in cyberspace often have the religious fervor of the recently converted.

These sentiments have been captured brilliantly in an IBM ad on TV showing a phalanx of Czech nuns discussing—of all things—the latest operating system from Microsoft. As they walk briskly through a convent, a young novice mentions IBM's competing system, called Warp. "I just read about it in *Wired*," she gushes. "You get true multitasking . . . easy access to the Internet." An older sister glances up with obvious interest; the camera cuts to the mother superior, who wistfully confesses, "I'm dying to surf the Net." Fade as the pager tucked under her habit starts to beep.

Cybernuns.

What is cyberspace? According to John Perry Barlow, a rock-'n'-roll lyricist turned computer activist, it can be defined most succinctly as "that place you are in when you are talking on the telephone." That's as good a place to start as any. The telephone system, after all, is really a vast, global computer network with a distinctive, audible presence (crackling static against an almost inaudible background hum). By Barlow's definition, just about everybody has already been to cyberspace. It's marked by the feeling that the person you're talking to is "in the same room." Most people take the spatial dimension of a phone conversation for granted—until they get a really bad connection or a glitchy overseas call. Then they start raising their voice, as if by sheer volume they could propel it to the outer reaches of cyberspace.

CYBERSPACE, OF COURSE, IS BIGGER THAN a telephone call. It encompasses the millions of personal computers connected by modems—via the telephone system—to commercial online services, as well as the millions more with high-speed links to local area networks, office E-mail systems and the Internet. It includes the rapidly expanding wireless services: microwave towers that carry great quantities of cellular phone and data traffic; communications satellites strung like beads in geosynchronous orbit; low-flying satellites that will soon crisscross the globe like angry bees, connecting folks too far-flung or too much on the go to be tethered by wires. Someday even our television sets may be part of cyberspace, transformed into interactive "teleputers" by so-called full-service networks like the ones several cable-TV companies (including Time Warner) are building along the old cable lines, using fiber optics and high-speed switches.

But these wires and cables and microwaves are not really cyberspace. They are the means of conveyance, not the destination: the information superhighway, not the bright city lights at the end of the road. Cyberspace, in the sense of being "in the same room," is an experience, not a wiring system. It is about people using the new technology to do what they are genetically programmed to do: communicate with one another. It can be found in electronic mail exchanged by lovers who have never met. It emerges from the endless debates on mailing lists and message boards. It's that bond that knits together regulars in electronic chat rooms and newsgroups. It is, like Plato's plane of ideal forms, a metaphorical space, a virtual reality.

But it is no less real for being so. We live in the age of information, as Nicholas Negroponte, director of M.I.T.'s Media Lab, is fond of pointing out, in which the fundamental particle is not the atom but the bit—the binary digit, a unit of data usually represented as a 0 or 1. Information may still be delivered in magazines and newspapers (atoms), but the real value is in the contents (bits). We pay for our goods and services with cash (atoms), but the ebb and flow of capital around the world is carried out—to the tune of several trillion dollars a day—in electronic funds transfers (bits).

Bits are different from atoms and obey different laws. They are weightless. They are easily (and flawlessly) reproduced. There is an infinite supply. And they can be shipped at nearly the speed of light. When you are in the business of moving bits around, barriers of time and space disappear. For information providers—publishers, for example—cyberspace offers a medium in which distribution costs shrink to zero. Buyers and sellers can find each other in cyberspace without the benefit (or the expense) of a marketing campaign. No wonder so many businessmen are convinced it will become a powerful engine of economic growth.

At this point, however, cyberspace is less about commerce than about community. The technology has unleashed a great rush of direct, person-to-person communications, organized not in the top-down, one-to-many structure of traditional media but in a many-to-many model that may—just may—be a vehicle for revolutionary change. In a world already too divided against itself—rich against poor, producer against consumer—cyberspace offers the nearest thing to a level playing field.

Take, for example, the Internet. Until something better comes along to replace it, the Internet *is* cyberspace. It may not reach every computer in the human system, as Gibson imagined, but it comes very close. And as anyone who has spent much time there can attest, it is in many ways even stranger than fiction.

Begun more than 20 years ago as a Defense Department experiment, the Internet escaped from the Pentagon in 1984 and spread like kudzu during the personal-computer boom, nearly doubling every year from the mid-1980s on. Today 30 million to 40 million people in more than 160 countries have at least E-mail access to the Internet; in Japan, New Zealand and parts of Europe the number of Net users has grown more than 1,000% during the past three years.

One factor fueling the Internet's remarkable growth is its resolutely grass-roots structure. Most conventional computer systems are hierarchical and proprietary; they run on copyright software in a pyramid structure that gives dictatorial powers to the system operators who sit on top. The Internet, by contrast, is open (nonproprietary) and rabidly democratic. No one owns it. No single organization controls it. It is run like a commune with 4.8 million fiercely independent members (called hosts). It crosses national boundaries and answers to no sovereign. It is literally lawless.

Although graphics, photos and even videos have started to show up, cyberspace, as it exists on the Internet, is still primarily a text medium. People communicate by and large through words, typed and displayed on a screen. Yet cyberspace assumes an astonishing array of forms, from the utilitarian mailing list (a sort of junk E-mail list to which anyone can contribute) to the rococo MUDS, or Multi-User Dungeons (elaborate fictional gathering places that users create one "room" at a time). All these "spaces" have one thing in common: they are egalitarian to a fault. Anybody can play (provided he or she has the requisite equipment and access), and everybody is afforded the same level of respect (which is to say, little or none). Stripped of the external trappings of wealth, power, beauty and social status, people tend to be judged in the cyberspace of the Internet only by their ideas and their ability to get them across in terse, vigorous prose. On the Internet, as the famous *New Yorker* cartoon put it, nobody knows you're a dog.

Nowhere is this leveling effect more apparent than on Usenet—a giant set of more than 10,000 discussion groups (called newsgroups) distributed in large part over the Internet and devoted to every conceivable subject, from Rush Limbaugh to particle physics to the nocturnal habits of ring-tailed lemurs. The newsgroups develop their own peculiar dynamic as participants lurch from topic to topic—quick to take and give offense, slow to come to any kind of resolution.

But Usenet regulars are fiercely proud of what they have constructed. They view it as a new vehicle for wielding political power (through mass mailings and petitions) and an alternative system for gathering and disseminating raw, uncensored news. If they are sometimes disdainful of bumbling "newbies" who go online without learning the rules of the road, they are unforgiving to those who violate them deliberately. Many are convinced that the unflattering press accounts (those perennial stories about Internet hackers and pedophiles, for example) are part of a conspiracy among the mainstream media to suppress what they perceive as a threat to their hegemony.

THE USENET NEWSGROUPS ARE, IN THEIR way, the perfect antidote to modern mass media. Rather than catering to the lowest common denominator with programming packaged by a few people in New York, Atlanta and Hollywood and broadcast to the masses in the heartland, the newsgroups allow news, commentary and humor to bubble up from the grass roots. They represent narrowcasting in the extreme: content created by consumers for consumers. While cable-TV executives still dream of hundreds of channels, Usenet already has thousands. The network is so fragmented, in fact, that some fear it will ultimately serve to further divide a society already splintered by race, politics and sexual prejudice. That would be an ironic fate for a system designed to enhance communications.

The Internet is far from perfect. Largely unedited, its content is often tasteless, foolish, uninteresting or just plain wrong. It can be dangerously habit-forming and, truth be told, an enormous waste of time. Even with the arrival of new point-and-click software such as Netscape and Mosaic, it is still too hard to navigate. And because it requires access to both a computer and a high-speed telecommunications link, it is out of reach for millions of people too poor or too far from a major communications hub to participate.

But it is remarkable nonetheless, especially considering that it began as a cold war postapocalypse military command grid. "When I look at the Internet," says Bruce Sterling, another science-fiction writer and a great champion of cyberspace, "I see something astounding and delightful. It's as if some grim fallout shelter had burst open and a full-scale Mardi Gras parade had come out. I take such enormous pleasure in this that it's hard to remain properly skeptical."

There is no guarantee, however, that cyberspace will always look like this. The Internet is changing rapidly. Lately a lot of the development efforts—and most

It's as if some grim fallout shelter had burst open and a

full-scale Mardi Gras parade had come tumbling out

of the press attention—have shifted from the rough-and-tumble Usenet newsgroups to the more passive and consumer-oriented "home pages" of the World Wide Web—a system of links that simplifies the task of navigating among the myriad offerings on the Internet. The Net, many old-timers complain, is turning into a shopping mall. But unless it proves to be a total bust for business, that trend is likely to continue.

The more fundamental changes are those taking place underneath our sidewalks and streets, where great wooden wheels of fiber-optic cable are being rolled out one block at a time. Over the next decade, the telecommunications systems of the world will be rebuilt from the ground up as copper wires are ripped up and replaced by hair-thin fiber-optic strands.

The reason, in a word, is bandwidth, the information-carrying capacity of a medium (usually measured in bits per second). In terms of bandwidth, a copper telephone wire is like a thin straw, too narrow to carry the traffic it is being asked to bear. By contrast, fiber-optic strands, although hair-thin, are like great fat pipes, with an intrinsic capacity to carry tens of thousands of times as many bits as copper wire.

It's not just the Internet surfers who are crying for more bandwidth. Hollywood needs it to deliver movies and television shows on demand. Video game makers want it to send kids the latest adventures of Donkey Kong and Sonic the Hedgehog. The phone companies have their eyes on what some believe will be the next must-have appliance: the videophone.

There is a broad consensus in government and industry that the National Information Infrastructure, as the Clinton Administration prefers to call the info highway, will be the broadband, switched network that could, in theory, deliver all these things. But how it will be structured and how it will be deployed are not so clear. For example, if cable-TV and telephone companies are allowed to roll out the new services in only the richest neighborhoods—a practice known as "cream skimming"—that could exacerbate the already growing disparity between those who have access to the latest information and the best intelligence and those who must be content with what they see on TV.

An even trickier question has to do with the so-called upstream capacity of the network. Everybody wants to build a fat pipeline going into the home; that's the conduit by which the new information goods and services will be delivered. But how much bandwidth needs to be set aside for the signal going from the home back into the network? In some designs that upstream pathway is quite narrow—allowing just enough bits to change the channel or order a zirconium ring. Some network activists argue that consumers will someday need as much bandwidth going out of the home as they have coming in. Only then can ordinary people become, if they choose, not just consumers of media but producers as well, free to plug their camcorders into the network and broadcast their creations to the world.

How these design issues are decided in the months ahead could change the shape of cyberspace. Will it be bottom up, like the Internet, or top down, like broadcast television? In the best case, says Mitch Kapor, cofounder (with John Perry Barlow) of the Electronic Frontier Foundation, we could collectively invent a new entertainment medium, one that taps the creative energies of a nation of midnight scribblers and camcorder video artists. "In the worse case," he says, "we could wind up with networks that have the principal effect of fostering addiction to a new generation of electronic narcotics."

If Kapor seems to be painting these scenarios in apocalyptic terms, he is not alone. There is something about cyberspace that sets people's imaginations blazing. Much of what has been written about it—in the press and on the networks—tends to swing from one extreme to the other, from hype and romanticism to fear and loathing. It may be that the near-term impact of cyberspace is being oversold. But that does not mean that real change isn't in the works. As a rule of thumb, historians say, the results of technological innovation always take longer to reach fruition than early champions of change predict. But when change finally comes, its effect is likely to be more profound and widespread and unanticipated than anyone imagined—even the guys who write science fiction.

CAMILLE
THE INTERNET & SEXUAL PERSONAE
PAGLIA

N SEPTEMBER 1991 I gave a controversial lecture, "Crisis in the American Universities," at the Massachusetts Institute of Technology. It was one of my first public appearances after the release the prior year of my first book, *Sexual Personae*, and I was attacking what we all now know as political correctness.

Amid the general tumult at the end—police officers had to control a crowd estimated in the thousands—a man came up to me at the podium and said, "Do you know you're all over The Well?" "What is 'The Well'?" I asked, taken aback. When his explanations still left me baffled, he promised to send some samples.

A week later, a thick printout arrived at my university office in Philadelphia. I brandished it at colleagues. "Look at this!" I cried. "Someone in Boston is talking about me to people in Tennessee, and they're all arguing with someone in San Francisco! What the hell *is* this?" We were completely mystified.

How fast modern society changes! Only five years later, the World Wide Web is a major cultural phenomenon that is everywhere in the news and is the subject of fierce political debate and ruthlessly competitive marketing. It is also rapidly revolutionizing the mental lives of young Americans in ways that will not be fully understood until well into the next century.

I owe the Internet a lot. It is significant that my arrival on the scene coincided with a sudden leap forward in the availability of this technology. I had vainly struggled for twenty years to get my writing published and my ideas heard. All at once, things inexplicably changed. *Sexual Personae*, a seven-hundred-page scholarly tome by an unknown author, quietly sold and sold until it became one of the biggest sellers in university press history. There was neither a publicity budget nor media coverage—the latter exploded a full year later.

The Internet, totally unknown to me, was spreading my ideas nationwide along a grapevine of dissenters and freethinkers who were tired of both the rigidities of American politics (then stuck in a sterile liberal-versus-conservative mode) and the censorship and conformism on campus and in femin-

ism. My libertarian philosophy, as well as my pro-sex, pro-art, pro-popular culture positions, struck a chord with the radical individualists and space cowboys who were the pioneers of the Net. This is an excellent example of how the new personalized technology has broken the tyranny of the East Coast literary and media establishment. Ideas can no longer be controlled by an incestuous elite or the accidents of geography.

The sixties generation to which I belong was motivated by much more than antiwar sentiment or back-to-nature romanticism. We were very futuristic; we were children of the machine who had been teethed on transistors. We grew up with television, had our ears glued to portable radios at the dawn of rock 'n' roll, and went to college with stereos just as rock went political. I may be the first intellectual whose system of thought was profoundly influenced by raptly listening to Jefferson Airplane's acid-rock sonic experiments on stereo earphones.

I love science and technology and despise the ignorant literary academics who claim that science is nothing but veiled ideology. The arts and sciences are integrated in my view of Western culture, as it began in ancient Egypt and Greece. The problem with old leftism is that it has never honestly admitted the liberating effect of industrial capitalism. Thanks to technology, women have achieved economic independence for the first time in history. And thanks to mass media, the young inhabit their own extended community and are no longer oppressed by their parents' values and tastes. The Industrial Revolution has enormously benefited mankind: Most people used to be trapped in small, isolated villages, working constantly for survival, and suffering the totalitarianism of tribal life.

HE ERA OF DIGITAL TECHNOLOGY is simply a continuation of the Enlightenment, that splendid rebirth of Greco-Roman science currently vilified by the callow, word-obsessed poststructuralists and their postmodernist pups. I look for revelation not to that overrated nerd, Michel Foucault, but to *Star Trek*, our prophetic, multicultural saga of a universe where men and machines live in beautiful, elegant intimacy. As a teacher for twenty-five years, however, I am well aware of the worrisome aspects of the shift away from the Gutenberg printed book. Students' attention span has diminished, and their interest in complex texts is vanishing. The computer professionalizes the production of prose but also removes its subtleties of voice and style. And Internet communication is so easy and instantaneous that it can degenerate into childish impulse.

Ultimately, the computer represents the expended consciousness that my generation dreamed of and mistakenly tried to achieve through drugs. It will never supplant the brain, since so much of human creativity springs from direct experience and emotional highs and lows, which pass into our roiling subconscious. The exhilaratingly lawless Internet is like a carnival map of the soul, as shown by the ever mushrooming, perversely exotic discussion groups. The long effort by feminist zealots to ban the porn trade has failed. The Internet proves that the sexual imagination cannot be policed: Shut it down in one place, and it will bubble up somewhere else.

The Internet is democratic to the point of anarchy, but we must make sure that everyone has equal access to it, which means increased funding for public education. Right

> **I love science and technology and despise the ignorant literary academics who claim that science is nothing but veiled ideology.**
> −Camille Paglia

now, white middle-class students have an unfair career advantage because of their more technologically well-equipped homes. Finally, while the Internet surely facilitates international understanding and information sharing, there is no doubt that wherever it goes, it takes Westernization with it, which may mean an inevitable loss of irreplaceable native traditions.

Camille Paglia is a cultural critic, feminist, and libertarian. She is professor of humanities at the University of the Arts in Philadelphia. Her third best-seller is Vamps and Tramps.

PRIVATE LIFE

RICHARD JOHN
THE INTERNET PRODUCES A GLOBAL VILLAGE OF VILLAGE IDIOTS
NEUHAUS

I WRITE THIS WITH A PEN and legal pad at a vacation redoubt in the wilderness of Quebec, far from the computers, Internet, and email urgencies that keep my New York office in incessant commotion. This strikes me as a good place to nurture a healthy skepticism about a digital revolution that will presumably transform the human condition, for better or worse. Of course there are very significant quantitative changes in the storage and retrieval of information, and in the rapidity of calculations. Much less impressive is the capacity for simulation and projection. It is limited by a program's inability to anticipate *infinite contingency*—the mark of the real world beyond the most sophisticated of virtual realities.

We have not been here before or done precisely what we are doing now. A healthy skepticism does not deny what is new in our circumstance. It does remember the hype that attended the advent of, for instance, the railroad,

the telegraph, the airplane, radio, and television. Each in its time was a revolution that titillated a neophiliac culture. Was it only a few years ago that people who styled themselves futurists commanded celebrity attention? What was then the future has not been kind to them.

For some time I worked for the Carnegie Council on Ethics and International Affairs. Andrew Carnegie bestowed on the organization, originally called the Church Peace Union, several million dollars to be used in abolishing war. In a letter to the trustees (which I keep on my office wall), Carnegie assured them that, because of the great changes in communications and commerce, war would be abolished sooner than people believed. He therefore solemnly enjoined the trustees to give the remaining funds to the deserving poor. That was August 1914, when the world blew up. The deserving poor are still waiting.

Whether one is impressed more by the continuities than by

the discontinuities of history is, in part, a matter of temperament. But temperament is not unrelated to wisdom. High-decibel noises about a technological revolution derive from, and pander to, a mind-set that confuses information with knowledge and knowledge with wisdom. I am struck by the number of ads claiming that some new computer widget contains as much (or three or ten times as much) information as all thirty volumes of the *Encyclopaedia Brittanica*. So when was the last time you read the thirty volumes of the *Brittanica*?

Divorced from the cognitive structure that is knowledge and the reflectively internalized knowledge that is wisdom, information makes us dumb. It is a distraction—from the Latin verb *distrahere*, which means to draw away, disperse, or squander our capacity for thought. Today the poor of the urban underclass are said to suffer from radical dependency. The person who begins and ends the day with television, all-talk-all-the-time radio, or hitting the Web sites is cognitively crippled by a comparable dependency. Such people are burdened by an overload of opinions, but they have no opinions, meaning reflective judgments, that are truly their own. They cannot know what they think since they have not heard the latest thought and, by definition, never will.

A news station back in New York has the slogan "Something is happening right now, and the sooner you know about it the better." Anybody who believes that is terminally dumb, as in cognitively comatose. Another station declares, "Give us twenty-eight minutes and we'll give you the world." That is about the size of the world in which those who believe it are fated to live. Partisans of the digital revolution protest that the Internet, for instance, is interactive, not passive. But to the extent it is geared to quantity and speed of communication, it is interactive vacuity, a reciprocal fix to keep thought at bay, producing a global village of village idiots.

Fortunately, not nearly so many people are plugged in with the intensity that is commonly claimed. One of the happier consequences of the proliferation of sources of information and advocacy is the reduced influence of the establishment media. The political effect of that, however, is evident chiefly in the revival of radio, which is hardly cutting-edge technology. Claims that technology will assure a democratic future are also greatly exaggerated. There are probably more computers and faxes in China today than there were in Russia before the Soviet Union was toppled, yet China remains a dictatorship. Hong Kong is as technologically advanced as any place in the world, but will soon come under the Chinese tyranny. Politics trumps technology.

The human factor remains central, with an enduring capacity for good and inclination to evil. Adam blamed Eve, and we've been trying to evade moral responsibility ever since. The human project has been declared captive to sundry masters—magic, astrology, scientific revolution, economic determinism, and on and on. Technology is the latest fetish of moral evasion. Technology made me do it! The constant is the human factor. In the words of Jesus: "For out of the heart come evil thoughts, murder, adultery, fornication, theft, false witness, slander" (Mark 7: 21–22). The most avant-garde science fiction or high tech futurology, whether utopian or dystopian, draws on the moral and spiritual categories found in the first chapters of Genesis. It would be foolish to say that nothing has changed since then, but the exaggeration of change is an unchanging device for excusing ourselves for what we do and who we are.

The *Forbes ASAP* editors ask if or how advancing technology affects our relationship to the Absolute, to God. Certainly the renewed interest in the connections between brain, mind, and consciousness is stimulated, in part, by the prospect of artificial intelligence. Technology is important also in exploring the irreducible complexity of the microcosmic that opens a window to wonder at the macrocosmic. Elaborate messages in the smallest of cells force questions about who or what might have put them there, leading thoughtful scientists to reconsider the possible answer. "In the beginning was the Word" (John 1:1). Science, which must always be the enemy of mystification, is breaking out of its materialist mystifications that have obscured the fact that creation exists in and from and toward mystery. No offense intended, but theologians and the wiser philosophers and scientists have always known this. So has the illiterate peasant at his prayers.

There are very practical implications. In his 1991 encyclical on economics and freedom, *Centesimus Annus* (The Hundredth Year), Pope John Paul II notes how transistors and chips underscore the truth that the human mind is increasingly the most important economic resource. I have reservations about George Gilder's enthusiasm for the technological transcendence of matter—for we are, thank God, embodied souls—but he is onto something important.

So, yes, there may be something like a revolution under way. But expectations should be tempered by a skepticism informed by our memory of the hype that attended alleged revolutions in the past, and by a keen awareness of our inescapable responsibility for what we do and are.

Richard John Neuhaus, a Roman Catholic priest, is president of the Institute on Religion & Public Life, based in New York. He is also editor in chief of First Things *magazine and writes often for the* Wall Street Journal *and* National Review.

The Economy

The inventions we call computers and other information technologies are having a major impact on the production, distribution, and consumption of goods and services in society. In other words, they are transforming the economy. Because the economy is tied to nearly every facet of social and political life, this transformation will have some very far-reaching consequences—not all of which will be universally beneficial. In this unit, five articles look at the relationship between new computer-based technologies and just a few areas of economic activity.

Technologically advanced societies like the United States and Canada are postindustrial economies. That is, the bulk of economic output and employment is derived from services rather than from manufactured goods—especially services that revolve around the creation, collection, analysis, interpretation, and delivery of information. For society as a whole and for its individual members, access to accurate, timely information is vital to well-being. Try to imagine day-to-day survival without easy access to such ordinary information as schedules, prices, and telephone numbers. Businesses and government would screech to a halt without a relatively smooth and continuous flow of masses of reliable information.

Some of the more traditional information sources include the print media—newspapers, journals, and magazines. Computers have played an important role in the publishing industry for decades and that role is growing with online magazines. In "Clicking onto Webzines," Herb Brody explains that the new genre of magazines on the Internet can do much that their printed cousins cannot, such as including links to other information sources, providing sound and video, and supporting structured online forums. But, webzines have some "growing up to do" and though they are much cheaper to publish than conventional magazines, their financial success is far from certain.

The economic importance of other sectors of the communications and computing industry is emphasized in "The New Business Cycle." Here, Michael Mandel reports that, like the railroad industry in the last century and the housing and automobile industries of the last several decades, the high-technology sector is now a driving force behind economic growth. However, high-tech industries are volatile and a downturn here could have serious consequences for employment, investment, and growth for the economy as a whole. Thus, the growing importance of this sector should receive special attention from economic policy makers.

The following articles paint a different picture of the economic impact of computing. In "What Has the Computer Done for Us Lately?" Louis Uchitelle argues that despite major investments in new technology, America is "still waiting" for a surge in productivity. In part, the problem may stem from difficulties in measuring the computer's real contributions to economic growth, but it may also have to do with counterproductive features such as "junk e-mail and electronic solitaire." Michael Dertouzos also asserts that computers have not fulfilled their promise when it comes to productivity. In "Creating the People's Computer," this prominent computer scientist cites a number of design faults that lead to computer misuse and abuse, and he offers suggestions on how to make machines serve human needs instead of the other way around.

The economy provides the means to acquire goods and services, but French social scientist Émile Durkheim (1858–1917) pointed out that economic interests make people friends one day and enemies the next. Economic exchange cannot work unless parties agree on the terms of trade, and trust each other to fulfill their obligations—perform the labor, deliver the goods, pay the agreed price. Until rules governing exchange, property rights, and security are set and enforced, cyberspace will remain risky.

The final article in this section deals with the new electronic payment systems. Patiwat Panurach discusses bene-

fits, risks, and implications of digital cash, electronic funds transfer, and Ecash in "Money in Electronic Commerce: Digital Cash, Electronic Fund Transfer, and Ecash."

Looking Ahead: Challenge Questions

Do you think that as the "information age" advances, people will become more dependent on others for their basic needs or more self-reliant? Defend your answer.

Is the information explosion making us more informed as individuals? Are workers, parents, consumers, or voters, more knowledgeable than in the past? Does it matter? Explain.

Some historians have observed that major changes in mechanisms of economic exchange tend to result in power shifts in society. What effects do you think the move toward electronic money will have on the power of government, corporations, and other groups in society and on individual members?

CLICKING ONTO
Webzines

Collecting, selecting, and refining the stories that go online, Web-based magazines are transforming the Internet experience. But these embryonic publications don't yet fully exploit the new medium's potential—and their financial viability is in question.

HERB BRODY

HERB BRODY is a senior editor of Technology Review.

IT couldn't last. Ever since bursting into popular consciousness in the early 1990s, the World Wide Web kept growing chaotically. Universities had Web sites. Companies had Web sites. Individual families had Web sites. Any organization that didn't have a Web page seemed to be labeling itself a relic. But after the initial flurry of clicking around, most visitors to the Web wanted something to sink their teeth into. After awhile, grainy pictures of half-full coffeepots in England just didn't cut it anymore. Oh, sure, if you poked around enough you could find a brilliant essay or collection of digitized art or clever interactive game. But it was every surfer for him or herself. Although a breed of Net users reveled in this chaos and unpredictability, many people who logged on found the Internet about as fulfilling as wading through a warehouse full of pages ripped from student notebooks.

It is amid this mess that Web magazines have risen to popularity in the past year. A visit to *Salon*—a webzine of reviews and essays founded by expatriates from the *San Francisco Examiner's* arts section—guarantees a few snappy essays on life, culture, and politics in the '90s by name-brand writers. Enter the electronic portals of Microsoft-owned *Slate* and you can eavesdrop on a high-minded debate among policy wonks about the political and economic issues du jour. Tap into *Hot Wired* for spicy and often abrasive commentary about the medium itself.

In editorial direction, webzines buck the trend in print publications, where success has recently accrued mainly to specialty titles, especially those that give advice on how to live and what to buy. Advertising dollars flow into these publications, attracted by readerships presumed to be in a buying or self-improving frame of mind. Two of the wealthiest people in America—Patrick McGovern and William Ziff—made their fortunes peddling computer magazines. The new breed of webzines, by contrast, appeals to readers less with buying advice than by projecting an attitude. They do this in the form not of practical articles of the sort that fill the bulging pages of computer and "lifestyle" magazines but with compendiums of commentary—essays, cultural critiques, political analysis.

A magazine on the Internet can do much that its printed cousin cannot. Articles can include links that readers click on to find additional information. Previously published stories can be read as easily as this week's issue. Webzines can enrich their stories with sounds and video. Web publications can create structured online forums where readers can debate among themselves—and with the magazine's writers and editors—the ideas presented in the magazine's articles. Material online can be updated as needed, incorporating new information and correcting errors.

Overall, the dozens of webzines differ from each other as drastically as the array of titles on a conventional newsstand, ranging from the sassy countercultural rant-rags such as *Suck* (which devotes much of its space to bashing other webzines) to the sober and establishmentarian *Intellectual-Capital* to the New York artsiness of *Word*. The quality can be quasi-*New Yorker* literary or just-past-amateur. Designs

The strength of webzines as a new medium will depend on how well they take advantage of the interactive features that are uniquely possible online.

also vary greatly, from gray *Slate* to the self-conscious hipness of *HotWired*, with its gonzo icons and pages saturated in the neopsychedelic, Day-Glo colors that its print sister, *Wired*, inflicts on its readers. But a look at the top tier of webzines—including *Slate*, *Salon*, and *HotWired*—reveals most of what these publications are doing well, poorly, or not at all.

Follow That Link

A typical webzine invites the visitor not so much to study its text but to hop around within it, clicking on icons and highlighted phrases to see where they lead. In this exercise, the act of reading is submerged beneath the drive to explore. Pages are riddled with convenient electronic tunnels. The experience is less like reading a magazine than strolling through a bookstore or library, where you will expect to look at a lot of titles but may come out having actually read little.

A computer screen is not the best way to do extended reading. Thus it's not surprising that webzines favor short pieces. Print magazine feature articles (like this one) typically run 4,000 words or more. In *Slate*, *Salon*, and other webzines, a typical article is 1,000–1,500 words. These pieces may whet the intellectual appetite or stir up ideological fervor among those already in agreement with a writer. But because staffs are small and budgets low, and because the Web puts a premium on rapid production of new material, the stories generally lack the thorough reportage that makes for the most fulfilling reading experience—and that changes people's minds.

The strength of webzines as a new medium, then, depends on how well they take advantage of the interactive features that are uniquely possible online. Many webzines are still groping for how best to use the new technologies. Most of these publications amount to words on a screen—a vertical, glowing rendition of the magazines people have been reading for decades. Despite their multimedia cachet, webzines typically contain a smaller concentration of photographs, illustrations, and charts than one would find in a printed publication.

What webzines do provide are links to related information. The quality of these links varies widely. *Slate* takes particular care in its compilation of links. A recent article about how ballot initiatives in Arizona and California regarding the medical use of marijuana could affect the war on drugs, for example, links to the text of the referendums

and to documents from organizations arguing pro and con. It is one-stop shopping for political information.

A well-compiled set of links can make a webzine worth visiting. By January, the Oakland school board's controversial decision to formally recognize black English as a distinct language—Ebonics—had been pretty well hashed over in the media. But accompanying *Slate*'s article on the topic were links to a detailed synopsis of the decision put out by the Oakland Unified School District. Here the reader could find out without the filtering of reporters and commentators exactly what course of action the school board was recommending—a particularly helpful service in this case, given widespread confusion about the school board's intent. For historical context, the reader could hop to a 1972 article by University of Pennsylvania linguist William Labov that provides scholarly underpinning to the Oakland decision.

Links can also give readers a handy "reality check" that pressures writers and editors to get their facts straight. Dan Kennedy, a media critic for the printed *Boston Phoenix* and for *Salon*, explains: "I like to think I'm a careful reporter when I'm writing for print, but in *Salon* I really have to get it right."

But many webzine links seem thrown in with little thought and even work against a story's theme. A *Salon* essay convincingly decries the reduction of Martin Luther King, Jr., to a "safe" icon of both the right and the left. The writer worries that for many people, King has become just a reason for a holiday and an "I Have a Dream" sound bite. Oddly, however, the article provides only two links—one to a photo of King making that speech, the other to the full text of the stirring address. This article thus perpetuates the narrow perspective that it critiques.

The presence of links changes the character of reading. A highlighted word tempts the reader to click—where will it lead? The webzine page becomes a platform from which to dive into the roiling waters of the Internet. Each link is like a little exit door, and if the pastures are richer on the other side, online grazers will be lost. For this reason *Slate* and some other webzines gather up their links and put them at the end of articles rather than permitting them to interrupt the flow of reading.

Editors of any publication strive for quality control. Links represent a kind of surrender on this front. Not only is the linked-to site beyond an editor's control, but so are the sites that *it* links to, and that each of those sites links to, and so on throughout the Net. With each hyperstep away from the webzine's site, the possibility multiplies that a reader will encounter unchecked or unsavory pages (or pages that have disappeared). One *Slate* story about body piercing, for example, provided a link to a site that prominently featured links of its own—to pornographic pages. Such missteps are probably unavoidable in a medium as big and uncontrolled as the Internet.

Bad links are worse than no links at all, if only for

1. THE ECONOMY

the deflating feeling of expectations dashed. A provocative essay in the webzine *Suck*, for example, pointed out that with operations like *Wired* magazine and America Online hitting bad patches and laying people off, the defiant "geek culture" that had been contemptuously thumbing its nose at management was finding itself having to be more circumspect: having even a bad job was at least a job. It is not hard to find "dozens of people swapping enthusiasm for misery," said *Suck*—and highlighted this last sentence to indicate it was a hyperlink. But the link led to a newsgroup called alt.angst—an online bellyaching extravaganza filled with diatribes about atheists, Bill Gates, and many other pet peeves. A search through hundreds of recent postings found none discussing job anxiety.

Talk Amongst Yourselves

Some of webzines' most interesting interactivity involves conversations among selected people on an assigned topic. *Slate*, for example, features a "Committee of Correspondence"—a panel of four or five people who post every day for a week on a given subject. Messages often respond to points made in the previous day's submissions by the other panelists. The Committee of Correspondence operates under the gentle nudging of economist Herbert Stein, who frames the question on the first day, and then weighs in on every subsequent day to summarize what the other participants have been saying and to ask new questions.

The power of *Slate*'s panels lies in the credibility of the participants. The webzine has managed to assemble groups of thinkers who know what they're talking about and write well (or are the beneficiaries of fine editing by the *Slate* crew), and who refrain from turning political issues into personal attacks. For an Internet discussion, that's a rare triple whammy. A panel arguing the merits of a balanced-budget amendment, for example, included Jim Miller of George Mason University, director of the Office of Management and Budget from 1985 to 1988; Robert D. Reischauer of the Brookings Institute, director of the Congressional Budget Office from 1989 until 1995; Robert Shapiro of the Progressive Policy Institute, an economics adviser to the Clinton administration; and Sen. Paul Simon (D-Ill.). *Slate*'s contribution was not in giving these analysts a spotlight—they are for the most part the same talking heads that appear on Sunday TV political shows—but in constructing a forum where they can respond to one another's arguments and move beyond the glib answers that television often fosters.

In another *Slate* feature, two people engage in a long-term correspondence with each other on a provocative subject. The "Dialogs" column has grappled with whether there is a God and whether divorce should be more difficult to obtain, and featured a highly charged debate between *Newsweek*'s Jonathan Alter and the *New Republic*'s

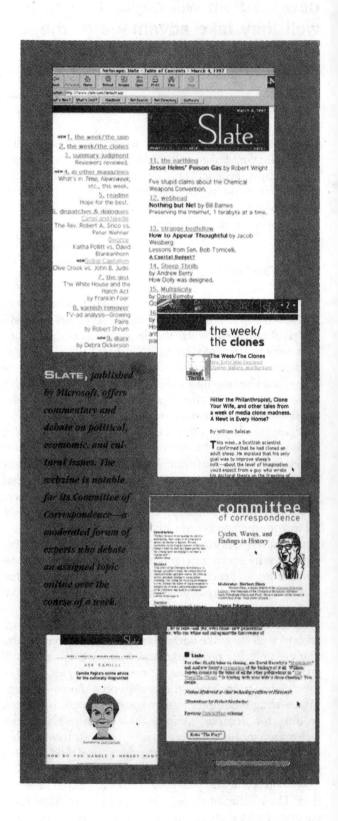

SLATE, published by Microsoft, offers commentary and debate on political, economic, and cultural issues. The webzine is notable for its Committee of Correspondence—a moderated forum of experts who debate an assigned topic online over the course of a week.

William Powers over whether the press is going too easy on President Clinton by underplaying the administration's scandals. While occasionally sparks fly, these debates are a good example of the kind of thoughtful and civil exchange often said to be missing from public discourse.

Even experts can become a bit cranky, of course. *HotWired*'s "Brain Tennis" feature—a week-long debate between two people on a technological issue—veers toward flaming, with flavorful put-downs such as this one from a spirited conversation about whether nanotechnology is more hype than substance: "To call this concoction a straw man is an insult to straw."

A webzine page peppered with links is not so much a document to read as a platform from which to dive into the roiling waters of the Internet.

Feed, more than other Webzines, constructs its panel discussions in the spirit of the Web's nonlinear structure. A selected group of people post short essays on a given topic. But reading through the forum you come across hyperlinks embedded in the text. Clicking here takes you to a response by one of the other panelists to the particular point being made in that specific sentence or paragraph. And within that response are other responses. Reading a *Feed* debate is like stepping into a hall of mirrors—the discussion swirls endlessly around in a manner that would be impossible to duplicate in print. *Slate* has started to use a similar style in its Committee of Correspondence.

Webzines also offer readers the opportunity to converse with one another online. Authors and editors occasionally wade in to join the stream of commentary and response. Democratic strategist and former Clinton campaign adviser James Carville, who writes a column of political commentary in *Salon* called "Swamp Fever," has posted frequently. So has novelist Anne Rice, who has published a series of diary entries in *Salon*. This kind of give-and-take occurs in print as well, of course, such as when a magazine appends an editor's or writer's response to a published letter from a reader. In webzines, however, the commentary can take on a life of its own and, without the delays of printing and mailing, the conversation assumes a more bantering, informal quality.

Print publications try to select and edit letters columns to roughly the same level of erudition and sophistication as the articles on which they comment. In webzines, however, this is not the case; reader forums are distinctly lower in intellectual power and cogency. Many contributors to these

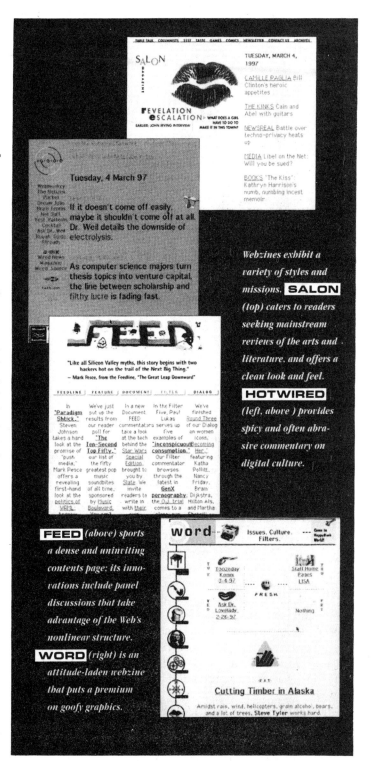

Webzines exhibit a variety of styles and missions. **SALON** *(top) caters to readers seeking mainstream reviews of the arts and literature, and offers a clean look and feel.* **HOTWIRED** *(left, above) provides spicy and often abrasive commentary on digital culture.*

FEED *(above) sports a dense and uninviting contents page; its innovations include panel discussions that take advantage of the Web's nonlinear structure.* **WORD** *(right) is an attitude-laden webzine that puts a premium on goofy graphics.*

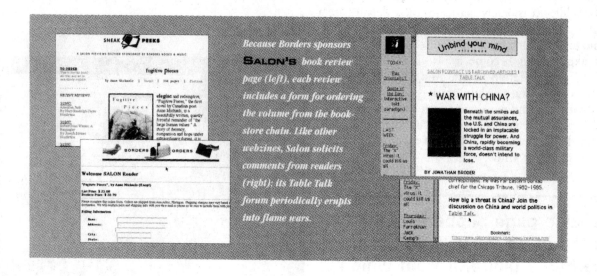

Because Borders sponsors *SALON'S* book review page (left), each review includes a form for ordering the volume from the bookstore chain. Like other webzines, Salon solicits comments from readers (right): its Table Talk forum periodically erupts into flame wars.

forums are curt, defensive, off-the-point, and have a tendency to substitute passion for intellect and knowledge. The moderator of *Salon*'s "Table Talk" spends much of her efforts "dousing waters on flame wars," admits David Talbott, *Salon*'s founder and editor.

Pictures and Sound

Some webzines are cautiously taking advantage of the Internet's multimedia capability. A *HotWired* article about Jimmy Carter, for example, provided a link to a 20-minute audio of a conversation with the former president, in which he expounded in his gentle Georgia drawl on his philosophical and religious views at far greater length than appropriate to quote in the article. To hear the interview requires RealAudio software, which its creator, Progressive Networks, offers free over the Web.

The interview is one of a series that *HotWired*'s "Netizen" section has run. In others, civil rights leader and ambassador Andrew Young has talked about affirmative action and Chinese human-rights activist Harry Wu has spoken of his experiences in a Chinese labor camp. Listening to Wu's tense voice and elegant statement, for example, one senses his pain and his passionate ideals for a better future in a way that a transcript of the interview could not convey.

Unlike listening to an interview on radio or watching it on television, the Web's audio capabilities allow the user to pause the playback, back up, or skip forward. Oddly, given that such interview tapes are essentially "free" content whenever a webzine covers a story, neither *Slate* nor *Salon* offers such audio features. Their hesitation stems partly from the low quality of sound. Ears accustomed to CDs and FM radio may find Web audio a step back in time. The warbly sound resembles, at best, a strong AM radio station, and often is more akin to that of a shortwave broadcast from overseas.

Webzines use video sparingly. *Slate*, for example, accompanies each movie review with a brief clip from the film. Unfortunately, technical quality is poor. The webzines have to trade off picture quality against transmission time, and choose speed. Not only are the images low resolution, but small as well, typically occupying a rectangle about 1 by 2 inches in the middle of the screen. Longer segments of video that would look sharper and occupy a larger portion of the screen are technically possible but would take impractically long to transmit. As it is, these 30-second video nuggets take a long time to download—for a computer chugging along with a 14.4 kilobit-per-second modem, the download will chew up typically 15 to 20 minutes, *Slate* warns.

Sometimes, however, this constraint makes little difference. Take *Slate*'s Varnish Remover column, which analyzes television ads. The Web reader can click on a link to download the video of the entire ad, not just an excerpt. During the presidential campaign, the column was devoted mainly to political TV commercials; now it has moved on to the kind of product ads that fill the screens in nonelection years, including Everready batteries and Levi's jeans, as well as two product categories—liquor and condoms— that recently were the subject of first-time-ever TV ad campaigns. The ability to view the ads and read the commentary at the same time gives this feature an almost scholarly value.

Multimedia links can also provide historical context. A *Slate* article by historian Michael Beschloss about the political problems that bedevil second-term presidents, for example, links not only to the Gallup poll's quarterly public-approval ratings for every president since Eisenhower but also to audio clips from two infamous moments in Richard Nixon's aborted second term: the "I am not a crook" passage from a speech he made while the Watergate scandal was unfolding, and his resignation address. The medium makes such additions uniquely possible; television delivers pictures without the intellectual depth that text provides; print cannot bring events back to life.

Lost in Space (and Time)

Browsing the current webzines yields the impression that no one has completely figured out how best to adapt a print tradition to electronic form. Simple matters such as knowing how to get from place to place and knowing whether an article is old or new seem to stymie the designer; a zine surfer must acclimate to different interfaces at every electronic publication.

Some differences are cosmetic; *Slate*'s maroon, gray, and white color scheme stands in sedate contrast to *Hot Wired*'s highly contrasting colors (a different glowing hue every day) and *Word*'s melange of moving images. Some entries into the field have yet to master Web basics. *Intellectual-Capital*, which comes off as a weighty magazine of political and economic issues, has not yet figured out that long tables of contents on the home page are difficult to penetrate.

Webzines spawned by the print magazine establishment sometimes reveal unhelpful allegiance to print conventions. *Slate*, for example, assigns "page" numbers to articles. The idea is to make readers feel that they can navigate the way they do in print. But Web surfers don't generally think of online material as numbered pages, and this system seems anachronistic—as if Henry Ford had built a set of reins into the dashboard of the Model T. (*Computer-Mediated Communication Magazine* numbered its pages when it started up three years ago, says founder and editor John December, but abandoned the system because the numbers seemed arbitrary in a nonlinear medium.)

If *Slate* errs by trying to be too printlike, the opposite tendency mars *Word*, a New York–based lifestyle webzine. In *Word*, nothing stands still; the graphic images dance and shimmy, usually without any particular meaning. The table of contents looks like something from *TV Guide*, with six fine-print listings of articles arranged in columns under inscrutable department titles like "habit," "gigo," "pay," "machine," and "desire." Graphical paraphernalia seem goofy; a gallery of animated dancing toilets, for example, adorns a page of self-described stupid jokes.

Salon and *Hot Wired* have probably devised the most fully Web-like sites. *Salon*'s main page presents links to the webzine's departments: "Sharps & Flats" (music reviews); "Newsreal" (commentary on the news); "Media Circus" (media criticism); "Sneak Peeks" (book reviews) and "Taste" (food and wine). Clicking on one of those choices brings up a page with content divided into compartments, known as "frames." The main frame contains the article of the day; along the left-hand side of the screen a narrow vertical frame presents an index of every article in that department for the past month, any of which you can read with a click.

Different webzines have different approaches for displaying articles that are too long to fit on a single screen. *Slate* delivers an entire article at once, no matter how long it is, allowing readers to scroll up and down through it much as they would flip through the pages of a long article in a printed publication. *Salon* and *Hot Wired*, on the other hand, often present articles in segments. A *Salon* essay analyzing the prevalence of libertarianism on the Net, for example, leads off with the first 500 words, along with a link to click on to get the 2,500-word balance of the piece. *Salon* breaks other articles into multiple, equal-sized chunks, with no apparent logic to guide the partitioning.

Webzine designers face a dilemma. The surest way for any Web site to draw traffic is to change the content frequently—nothing feels as stale as an unchanged Web site. Too much churn, however, confuses a print-oriented reader.

> **The best online panels bring together thinkers who know what they're talking about, write well, and refrain from making personal attacks. For the Internet, that's a rare triple whammy.**

Magazines as we have come to know them are defined by the issue date that anchors them in time; cover images and other cues help readers recognize what's new and what's old. And once an issue is read, it can be consigned to the trash or storage pile. Webzines treat time more cavalierly. It's not immediately apparent when you have already read something, so you find yourself revisiting the site in search of fresh material. And sometimes a label of "new" on the contents page indicates only a small addition to a department rather than an entirely new piece. *Slate* took a helpful step toward anchoring its articles in time by offering, as an option, a contents page that sorts articles by date.

The ease of dipping into a webzine's archives of past articles further muddies the reader's place in time. With last week's or last month's articles only a couple of clicks away, webzine sites make it about as easy to tap into their well of previously published material as their current issue. It is as if *Time* magazine came to the mailbox every week with a 100-pound box of carefully indexed back issues. The most current edition loses some of its primacy when stacked against all that history.

The best webzines are finding ways to update their material often while acknowledging many readers' preference for discrete "issues" pinned to a particular day or week. *Slate*, *Salon*, and *Hot Wired*, which change at least some of their content every weekday, all send out weekly e-mails summarizing the articles "now playing" at their sites; these notices go to all who have signed up for these webzines' (free) alert services. The e-mail contains hot links that allow recipients to jump immediately to read the piece that the blurb describes.

Who's Paying the Bills?

Most of the cost of publishing a conventional magazine goes to buy paper, operate the printing presses, and distribute the finished product through the mail and to newsstands, according to Christopher Harper, a journalism professor at New York University. A webzine incurs none of these. At first blush, therefore, any revenue that a webzine can produce "seems like free money," says Michael Mooradian, an analyst at Jupiter Communications, a market-research firm specializing in new media. *Salon*, which was launched in November 1995, began with one-tenth the capital that would have been required for a comparable national print magazine, asserts *Salon* founder David Talbott.

Nevertheless, whether webzines' unique attributes will lead to financial success—and hence long-term survival—remains an open question. Writers, editors, and computer programmers don't work for free. *Slate* has a staff of about two dozen, according to publisher Rogers Weed; *Salon*, says Talbot, is put out by 18 people. Thus maintaining a high-quality webzine requires a substantial flow of income from somewhere. The big webzines are still running on the momentum of their deep-pocketed founders—with Microsoft bankrolling *Slate*, and Apple Computer and Adobe Systems supporting the launch of *Salon*.

Print magazines make money in two basic ways: selling copies to readers and selling readers to advertisers. Neither source of revenue translates very well onto the Web. Internet users, steeped in an ethic of free information, are loath to pay for anything other than hooking into the Net itself.

Slate's saga shows that the day when webzines will charge for subscriptions seems, if anything, to be receding into the hazy future. When Microsoft launched *Slate* last June as a free service, the company warned that the deal was only temporary. Starting in November, *Slate* readers were going to have to pay $19.95 per year for the privilege. As November approached, however, *Slate* backed down. Access would continue to be free until February 1997, Microsoft announced, because the company had been unable to perfect the software needed to keep billing records. Cynics scoffed at that explanation, suspecting that Microsoft's real concern was a potential drop in readership.

And indeed, in January, Slate postponed this financial day of reckoning yet again—this time indefinitely. "Maybe in the future," wrote *Slate* editor Michael Kinsley, "people will happily pay for access to premium sites" on the Web, as they pay now for premium cable channels. But Kinsley acknowledged that with the possible exceptions of pornography and

> "We couldn't convince ourselves that people lust for political and cultural commentary the way they lust for sex or money."— *Slate* editor Michael Kinsley, announcing that the webzine would remain free.

financial information, that day has not arrived. "Even in our headiest moments," he continued, "we couldn't convince ourselves that people lust for political and cultural commentary the way they lust for sex or money."

The analogy with cable TV is telling, says David Card, an interactive services analyst at the market-research firm International Data Corp. Premium channels like Home Box Office didn't really take off, he says, until free TV and basic cable channels were glutted with very-low-quality programming. Only then were millions of people willing to pay for a service that they had been receiving for free. There is still plenty of valuable and entertaining material on the Web that costs the user nothing, Card contends. As long as that is the case, webzines will find subscription sales a tough path.

Web surfers have at least another year of free reading, analysts say. The only online publications that will be able to charge for access are those with gold-plated brand names that command an instant audience, says Jupiter's Mooradian. The *Wall Street Journal* has already begun charging for access to its online interactive edition; *Barron's* and ESPN might similarly get away with levying such fees for their financial and sports information.

Meanwhile, most webzines are trying to make ends meet by tapping into the explosively growing market of Web-based advertising. Companies spent $55 million on Web ads in 1995 and $260 million in 1996, according to Mooradian at Jupiter. The total is expected to top $1 billion this year. Web advertising has great allure because readers can do more than simply gaze at a picture or read the copy—they can also click through to the advertiser's page, where they can request more information, download trial versions of a software product, or place a credit card order.

Such advertising appears in two basic forms: long-term sponsorship of a webzine's department, and banner ads that appear on the top of pages anywhere in the webzine. A successful example of a sponsorship is the relationship between *Salon* and Borders, the national bookstore chain. In return for sponsoring *Salon*'s book review page, Borders gets a sweet prize: reviews are accompanied by links to the bookstore's order forms. Click on the order form, fill in a credit card number and address, and within days the item arrives at your door. The bookstore, in turn, prints excerpts from

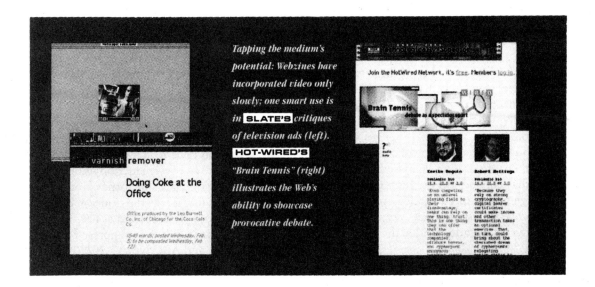

Tapping the medium's potential: Webzines have incorporated video only slowly; one smart use is in SLATE'S *critiques of television ads (left).* HOT-WIRED'S *"Brain Tennis" (right) illustrates the Web's ability to showcase provocative debate.*

Salon reviews on the bookmarks that it gives away to customers. Judging from *Salon*'s often-critical reviews, this cozy relationship has not seemed to compromise the webzine's editorial integrity.

Still, webzines may have difficulty surviving on advertising dollars. A print magazine sells ad space by promoting the demographics of its readers. While publications like *Slate* and *Salon* attract an upscale audience—*Salon,* for example, claims that its readers have a median household income of $80,000—this profile does not stand out in bold relief from the Internet as a whole, which is still largely an affluent preserve. "*Slate* and *Salon* have great demographics, but on the Internet that's no big deal," says Mary Doyle, a new-media analyst at the market-research firm IDC/Link in New York. It therefore makes more sense for a company to place ads in sites that millions of people surf by—the Netscape home page, for example, or one of the major search sites such as Yahoo and Infoseek. In fact, Doyle says, webzines will skim off only a small fraction of the total Web ad revenue; 1996 advertising revenue for all webzines totaled a mere $13.5 million, she estimates, puny compared with the $61 million spent on ads at search sites.

Mooradian of Jupiter counters that webzines do have special appeal. A company selling Scotch, he says, is not going to find a general-purpose Web page very attractive as an advertising site, since so many Net users are under the legal drinking age. "A company like that is going to be much more likely to put an ad on *Slate* than on the Netscape home page," Mooradian says. And *Salon*, which claims a readership that is 50 percent female, should attract advertisers who would otherwise dismiss the Web as an inappropriate medium.

Advertising is a numbers game, and Web sites are still struggling to come up with the solid numbers advertisers want—namely, how many people visit a site. One way is to have readers register. All the top webzines require registration to enter their forum, or to sign up to receive e-mail notification of what is in the webzine. Such registration is free to the user and gives the webzine its most reliable tallies of how many people are reading it. *Slate*, for example maintains about 15,000 people on its e-mail list. The webzine also claims that 50,000 to 60,000 different people visit the *Slate* site "on a semi-regular basis." *Salon* says more than 27,000 people have registered for its "Table Talk" forum. These are small numbers by magazine publishing standards; if advertisement is to sustain webzines, the companies placing the ads will need to believe that the Web is providing an added benefit beyond what they could get in print. An advertiser needs to be convinced, for example, that buying space on a webzine will do the company more good than an ad that reaches the same number of people in print.

Other streams of income are also possible. *Word*, for example, licenses some of its articles to companies who want to liven up their own corporate Web pages. The Net access and web-page-design company that owns *Word*—ICon—also rakes in consulting fees for dispensing advice on how to set up an attention-getting Web site. *Word* functions as a promotional tool for its parent company and therefore does not need to make money in its own right.

Growing Up

Webzines face a tough battle in establishing themselves as a viable medium. They are certainly nowhere near usurping the place of print publications (not a goal that they espouse in any case).

Technological innovations are arising faster than

webzines incorporate them. RealAudio has been available for two years, yet few webzines offer sound links. The reason lies partly in the low quality of Net access that most people have. Only about one U.S. household in five has a modem, and that will rise to about one in four by 1999, according to E-land, a company that compiles Internet usage data. And a substantial number of these modems crawl at 14.4 kilobits per second. At that speed, downloading graphics—not to mention sound and video—is an exercise in finger-drumming tedium, leading to more frustration than gratification.

Looking into the future, some predict the convergence of webzines with print. Picture an ultra-lightweight, ultraslim computer display that connects to the Internet and that receives data through a high-speed wireless transmission. This tablet would prove almost as portable as a print magazine but would offer all the added value that the online publications provide.

Journalistically, webzines have some growing up to do. The dearth of original reporting forces the webzines to establish identities, say some commentators, not by delivering information but by striking poses—*Suck* as an arbiter of what is good in Net journalism, *Slate* with its inside-the-beltway, know-it-all punditry, *Salon* with its literary pretensions. The need to keep readers on a page instead of hopping off through a hyperlink leads writers and editors to indulge in a kind of substanceless edginess. "The problem with these publications is that they're nothing but attitude," complains media critic Kennedy.

At the same time, the new media do provide a chance to make a clean break from print journalism, which the public has harshly criticized for flaws ranging from an obsession with violence to overreliance on information handouts by government officials and corporations. "The Web's great adventure is that it puts the reader in control," says NYU's Harper, whose present status as new-media scholar comes after a 20-year career as reporter for Associated Press, *Newsweek*, and ABC News's *20/20*. "The Web isn't the end-all and be-all, but it does gives us a wonderful opportunity to reexamine how we tell stories."

THE NEW BUSINESS CYCLE

It used to be housing and autos. But now, high tech rules.
And a stall there could stagger the economy

MICHAEL J. MANDEL

Six years into the economic expansion of the 1990s, and the living is easy. Almost 3 million jobs have been added over the past year alone, and consumer confidence is soaring. Company coffers are brimming with profits, the stock market is in the stratosphere, and inflation is actually falling.

Perhaps best of all, to many it seems the good times can go on for years. That old bugaboo of capitalism—the business cycle—has been tamed, according to today's conventional view. Rather than experiencing the booms and busts of old, the economy is on a steady growth path. Companies are avoiding past excesses, using computers and improved communications to manage inventories better and to boost workers' productivity. "Information technology has doubtless enhanced the stability of business operations," said Federal Reserve Chairman Alan Greenspan in his Feb. 26 testimony before Congress. His biggest worry? An overheated stock market.

But it is not the stock market or inventories or even inflation that will determine how long this expansion will last. Nor will auto sales, housing starts, or any of the traditional cyclical indicators give the first warnings of an impending recession, as they did in 1979 and 1989.

Instead, there is a new business cycle, tied to the health of the high-tech sector. Riding a wave of technological optimism, the computer, software, and communications industries have grown at a pace far exceeding the rest of the economy over the past three years, helping to extend the expansion.

But this exuberance has a price: With high tech having grown so big, the economy is now vulnerable to a high-tech slowdown in a way that was never true before. And there are already troubling signs of weakness in those industries that, if prolonged, could foreshadow a wider slump—as well as a steep decline in the stock market.

The distinctive character of the new business cycle raises the odds of policy mistakes. Like generals fighting the last war the Fed seems to be focusing on traditional cyclical indicators, such as retail sales, new-home starts, and industrial production, that have all been upbeat recently. These are "still what drives the business cycle," says Fed Governor Laurence H. Meyer. Meanwhile, semiconductor shipments and other measures of high-tech growth hardly are mentioned by Greenspan and other policymakers, despite their economic importance.

"The Fed needs to look not just at inflationary measures but also at what part of the technology cycle we are in," says G. Dan Hutcheson, president of VLSI Research Inc., a Silicon Valley research firm.

Over the past year, fully one-third of GDP growth has come from information technology, propelled by the Internet

---

Certainly there is little doubt that high technology has replaced the traditional cyclical industries as the main driving force for growth. In the past three years, the high-tech sector has contributed 27% of the growth in gross domestic product, compared with 14% for residential housing and only 4% for the auto sector. Over the past year, a stunning 33% of GDP growth has come from information-technology industries, propelled by everything from the Internet boom to the rise of direct-broadcast satellite television (chart, "The High-Tech Sector . . . ").

1. THE ECONOMY

The unique nature of an expansion led by high technology explains why the U.S. has been able to sustain a lower unemployment rate with faster growth and less inflation than economists ever believed possible. Despite strong demand and rising wages for programmers, network technicians, and other high-tech workers, inflationary pressures are counteracted by constantly falling prices for such products as computers and communications equipment. Meanwhile, with the rest of the economy growing at a meager 1.8% annual rate, the demand for workers outside of high tech has not been strong enough to drive up wages. A BUSINESS WEEK analysis shows that real wages for nonsupervisory workers outside high tech have risen by just 0.3% in the past year, hardly enough to trigger inflation.

But the business cycle has not disappeared. To the contrary: High technology is more volatile than the automobile industry, with the biggest swings driven by new technologies (chart, "Spending on Computers Swings Dramatically"). When the new-product pipeline temporarily slows, as it did in 1985 and 1989, demand can fall sharply. But a hot new technology, such as the Internet, can send sales skyrocketing just as suddenly. "Every time we thought something about our business was less cyclical," says Andrew S. Grove, chief executive at Intel Corp., "the next cycle was bigger than the earlier one."

There's another factor that could compound the impact of the tech cycle: High tech has grown so large and important that there's a feedback loop to the rest of the economy. When times are good, fast-growing high-tech companies throw off money that fuels general prosperity, which in turn sustains the demand for high-tech products. An expanding high-tech sector spends big dollars on everything from advertising to new buildings to cleaning services. High-tech profits boost stock prices, making investors more willing to spend. And rising wages and bonuses for high-tech workers finance the pur-

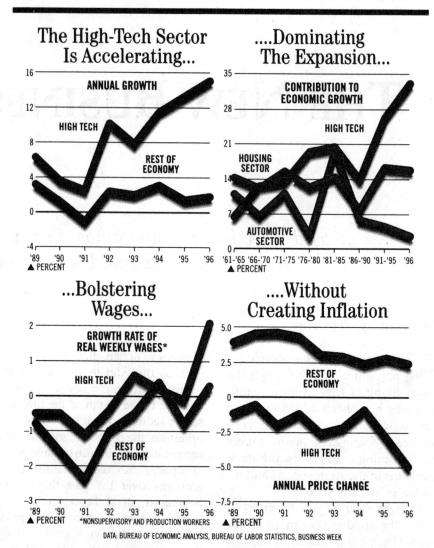

DATA: BUREAU OF ECONOMIC ANALYSIS, BUREAU OF LABOR STATISTICS, BUSINESS WEEK

chases of new cars and homes. Indeed, high-tech jobs and industries have accounted for roughly 20% to 25% of the real wage and salary growth over the past year according to new BUSINESS WEEK calculations, making them the key support for consumer spending.

But if and when things turn sour, look out. Information technology—now the single largest line in many corporate capital budgets—will make a tempting target for cost-cutting if the product cycle slows, or if the rest of the economy should slip because of, say, a Fed rate hike. Inventories are lean, and with 3.5 million jobs eliminated since 1989, Corporate America has squeezed most of the fat out of its workforce. Next time the economy slows, the only way tight-pressed companies can save money will be to delay nonessential info-tech projects. "Our industry used

to be immune from the business cycle," says Eric A. Benhamou, CEO and chairman of 3Com Corp. "We're no longer flying under the radar. There's just too much money being spent."

The downside of the new business cycle could have dramatic consequences for employment, investment, and growth. In Silicon Valley, in Boston, and in other high-tech hotbeds across the country, a multitude of software companies are staffing up in expectation of 20% annual growth, hiring hordes of programmers, testers, and technical writers who would not be needed if high-tech sales slowed. "It's a speculative bubble," says Larry Kimbell, director of the UCLA/Anderson Business Forecasting Project, "and there will be a lot of very disappointed people" when the boom slows.

If profits drop sharply enough, most high-tech companies would have to curtail new-product development and the construction of factories. Venture-capital finds, now going begging, would dry up. As the breakneck pace of technological change slowed, buyers would have less reason to upgrade immediately to the next generation of computers or software, dampening demand even more. "If our rate of innovation slowed, and the buying momentum consequently lessened, presumably that could have repercussions on the whole economy," says Grove.

A slowdown in high tech could hold dire consequences for the stock market. From 1993 to the end of 1996, high-tech stocks have been the market leaders, pulling other sectors along with them. Over that three-year stretch, high-tech stocks have produced blistering annual returns of 35%, compared with 20% for the S&P 500. The surge in tech stocks has given many of them sky-high price-earnings multiples on the expectation of soaring future growth. An unexpected slowdown in high-tech demand could send those stocks tumbling, knocking the rest of the market from its record levels.

FALL-OFF. There are some signs that such a high-tech slowdown may already have started. For one thing, tech stocks, as measured by the Morgan Stanley High Tech Index, are down 15% since mid-January. For

Trouble May Be Brewing

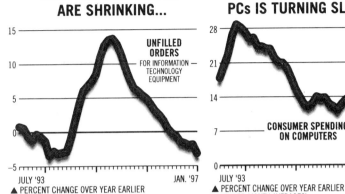

HIGH-TECH BACKLOGS ARE SHRINKING...

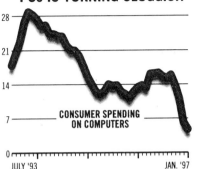

...AND DEMAND FOR HOME PCs IS TURNING SLUGGISH

UNFILLED ORDERS FOR INFORMATION TECHNOLOGY EQUIPMENT

JULY '93   JAN. '97
▲ PERCENT CHANGE OVER YEAR EARLIER (THREE-MONTH AVERAGES)

CONSUMER SPENDING ON COMPUTERS

JULY '93   JAN. '97
▲ PERCENT CHANGE OVER YEAR EARLIER (THREE-MONTH AVERAGES)

DATA: COMMERCE DEPT.

another, demand for high-tech equipment is weakening. Chip sales dropped by 3% from December to January and are down 14% from a year earlier, according to a Mar. 13 report from the Semiconductor Industry Assn. Government figures show consumer spending on computers rising at its slowest rate since 1992, while unfilled orders for information-technology equipment are shrinking for the first time since 1994. "We knew retail was slow, but now the corporate side—where most of the money is made—is showing signs of weakness as well," says Robinson-Humphrey Co. analyst Robert Anastasi, who follows computer sales. Adds Richard C. O'Brien, economist for Hewlett-Packard Co.: "We think we're in the late stages of a business cycle, and we're exhibiting the lower growth rates you'd expect," because of lower capital spending.

Of course, this high-tech slowdown may turn out to be a blip in a remarkable upward trajectory. Cheaper computers from Compaq Computer Corp., Packard Bell NEC Inc. and others could stimulate demand at the low end of the market. The Internet may continue to open up a range of new applications. And even an extended high-tech pause may be cushioned if global demand rebounds.

But even if high tech is the future of the economy over the long run, that does not preclude a bumpy ride along the way. In many ways, this period resembles the second half of the 19th century, also a time of massive investment in a new technology: the railroads. From 1869 to 1893, the miles of rail track quadrupled, and rail shipping costs dropped dramatically, opening up large parts of the country for manufacturing and commercial agriculture. The railroads themselves consumed much of the U.S. steel and coal production and accounted for almost 20% of all investment. Overall, the railroads' expansion fueled an economy that grew an average of 5% annually.

GROWING FORCE. But the long-term growth in this period conceals two sharp downturns, both linked to the railroads. The panic of 1873 was caused largely by railroad overexpansion, leading to a slew of railroad bankruptcies and an abrupt decline in new investment. And the mini-depression that started in 1893 was greatly aggravated when over-built railroads curtailed the construction of new tracks.

Like the railroads in the late 19th century, high tech is the leading sector of the economy. The Information Revolution started in the mid-1970s, when the price of computing power began to plummet. But until recently, high tech simply was not big

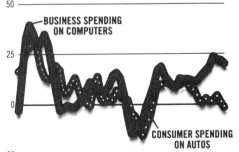

Spending On Computers Swings Dramatically

BUSINESS SPENDING ON COMPUTERS

CONSUMER SPENDING ON AUTOS

'83 '84 '85 '86 '87 '88 '89 '90 '91 '92 '93 '94 '95 '96
▲ PERCENT CHANGE OVER PREVIOUS YEAR (TWO QUARTER AVERAGES)
DATA: COMMERCE DEPT.

enough to influence the economy. From 1983 to 1993, high-tech spending in dollars grew no faster than the rest of the economy.

But over the past three years, the high-tech sector has skyrocketed while the rest of the economy has slowed down. High tech, as measured by BUSINESS WEEK totaled some $420 billion in 1996 (box). Consumers and businesses now spend $282 billion in the U.S. on information technology hardware alone, making it larger than any of the traditionally cyclical sectors such as autos and construction. That's 17% more than U.S. purchases of new motor vehicles and parts, 49% more than spending on new homes, and 168% more than commercial and industrial construction.

The clout of the high-tech sector shows up clearly in the labor market. Help-wanted ads plead for project managers, systems analysts, and help-desk technicians. Meanwhile, companies' continuing need for assistance with their computer systems has created a bull market for the management consulting industry, which is adding jobs at a rate of more than 40,000 per year. "We're experiencing 40% growth in the information-based consulting area," says Roger Siboni, deputy chairman and chief operating officer of KPMG Peat Marwick.

All told, there are more than 9 million workers now in the high-tech sector. Each new job creates additional jobs across the economy, generating a "multiplier" effect. Historically, manufacturing was thought to have the biggest multiplier effect in the economy, which is why it played such a big role in business cycles. The expansion of an auto plant, say, would ripple through the economy, boosting hiring at steel mills and other

JUST HOW BIG IS HIGH TECH?

How big is the high-tech sector, and how fast is it growing? The government's economic statistics, it seems, are still stuck back in the days when smokestack industries ruled supreme. But an analysis by BUSINESS WEEK shows the importance of high tech to the economy.

Take the job market first. According to BUSINESS WEEK's calculations, there are 9.1 million workers in the high-tech sector (table). In part, this total is based on the government's published numbers, which provide data on employment in such industries as software and semiconductors.

But the jobs within the high-tech industries are not the whole story. These days, most companies, from airlines to steelmakers, employ large numbers of programmers, network technicians, and other high-tech personnel. To count these workers, BUSINESS WEEK analyzed unpublished data from the Current Population Survey, the government's main source for employment figures. Adding these workers boosts the total by some 60%.
DOWNSIDE. The same calculation shows that the number of high-tech jobs rose by 4.9% in 1996, vs. a 2% increase in the rest of the economy. Wages also grew faster in high tech, according to our analysis of published and unpublished government data. The combination of more jobs and rising pay leads to the conclusion that high-tech jobs contributed roughly 20% to 25% of the growth in real wages and incomes in 1996.

On the output side, high tech's contribution to GDP totaled $420 billion in 1996, up 15% from 1995 (table). These figures are based on BUSINESS WEEK's new inflation-adjusted data series for high tech using the Commerce Dept.'s chain-weighting procedure. (Increases in computing power are captured by the inflation adjustment.)

But there's a downside to high tech's new preeminence. Anyone who is familiar with Silicon Valley knows that computers and related industries are given to booms and busts. To reveal this volatility, we constructed a data series showing high-tech spending without any adjustment for inflation or for increases in computer power. This "nominal" series is the number of dollars flowing through high-tech companies, measuring the resources they have to hire workers and to purchase goods. Nominal growth exhibited wide swings in the 1980s and early 1990s, including 1989 through 1991, when high-tech spending lagged behind other sectors.

This analysis demonstrates just how different the past few years are from what went before. From 1983 to 1993, nominal high-tech spending rose no faster than overall GDP. Only since 1993 has high tech accelerated far ahead of the rest of the economy, making it large enough to be the prime mover of the business cycle.

By Michael J. Mandel in New York

A Better Measure of the Sector

JOBS

1996 EMPLOYMENT (MILLIONS)

CORE INDUSTRIES
Computers, software, and communications — **3.8**

ASSOCIATED INDUSTRIES
High-tech sales, repairs, and a portion of management consulting and temporary agencies — **1.8**

REST OF THE ECONOMY
Programmers, network technicians, and other high-tech workers — **3.5**

TOTAL HIGH-TECH JOBS — **9.1**

DATA: BUREAU OF LABOR STATISTICS, BUREAU OF ECONOMIC ANALYSIS, BUSINESS WEEK

OUTPUT

MAJOR HIGH-TECH COMPONENTS OF GDP	HIGH-TECH SECTOR BILLIONS OF 1996 DOLLARS*	
Business and consumer spending on computers, peripherals, and communications equipment; net exports of information technology; consumer spending on telephone service and cable television; investment in telecom structures	1988	$215.7
	1989	229.2
	1990	237.2
	1991	243.2
	1992	268.0
	1993	289.1
	1994	322.3
	1995	365.0
	1996	420.3

*CHAIN-WEIGHTED

suppliers. Since factory workers were well paid, jobs would be created at nearby stores and even construction companies to supply and house the new workers.

There's growing evidence, however, that high tech may now have a larger multiplier effect in the U.S. than traditional manufacturing industries such as autos. As U.S. manufacturers have become more efficient, an expansion in output no longer requires massive hiring at factories. And with suppliers increasingly spread out in Mexico, the Far East, and Europe, the impact of an increase in auto sales, say, is diffused globally.

By contrast, creating a new chip design or a new software program is a labor-intensive effort that relies almost exclusively on well-paid domestic workers. A study of Microsoft Corp.'s impact on the Washington state economy showed that each Microsoft job created 6.7 new jobs in the state, compared with a 3.8 multiplier for Boeing Co. The difference? Almost $800 million in stock option income for Microsoft workers in 1995, the year of the study. These dollars spill over in the form of increased purchases of such things as cars and homes. In addition, Boeing outsources a lot of the work on each plane. As a result, "Microsoft spends three to four times more per person in the local economy than Boeing does," says Richard S. Conway Jr., the Seattle-based economist who conducted the study.

High-tech jobs tend to pay well—and salaries are rising—even the jobs that aren't so glamorous. Bureau of Labor Statistics data show that weekly wages for production workers in the communications-equipment industry rose by almost 7% in the past year, while earnings for nonsupervisory workers in the software and computer services industry rose by almost 5%. Intel distributed $620 million in profit-sharing and bonus money to its more than 40,000 employees for 1996.

Despite strong growth, an expansion driven by high tech is less likely to spur price inflation. In a tradi-

tional business cycle, prices would rise and productivity growth would slow as factories hit their capacity limits. But high-tech industries, such as semiconductors and software, are different. Creating a program or a microprocessor requires a big investment. But then the cost of actually producing the chips or software for sale is relatively low. The result is a virtuous circle: Rising demand drives average costs down, making it possible to charge lower prices and boosting demand even further.

OPTIMISM. How long can this high-tech expansion continue? Technology companies are banking on a continuing stream of new and improved products to fuel growth well into the future. "With lower costs and more advanced technology, you can do applications that weren't economically possible before," says Benjamin Anixter, vice-president for external affairs at Advanced Micro Devices Inc. At the bottom, falling prices may pull in new demand. The latest low-priced computer from Compaq, for example, "is selling extremely well to customers we didn't sell to before," says Robert A. Gunst, CEO of retailers Good Guys Inc., based in Brisbane, Calif.

Most growth forecasts are upbeat. Venture-capital firm Hambrecht & Quist predicts that the number of PCs sold in North America will rise by 17% in 1997. Looking further out, Gartner Group Inc. projects that spending on hardware and software will rise by about 8% annually for the rest of the decade.

Yet the history of the information-technology industries is anything but smooth. The biggest high-tech downturn in the past two decades came in 1985, when demand petered out just before the introduction of Intel's 80386 microprocessor. And in the first half of 1990, another product transition helped drive down business spending on computers even before the start of the recession of 1990–91.

Now, the industry may be facing another pause. With orders falling off, there is no obvious "must-have"

product on the horizon to stimulate demand, as the Internet did. Intel's much-ballyhooed Pentium MMX chip is turning out to offer only a minimal improvement in speed for existing software. "It hasn't set the corporate world on fire," says Anastasi. "Usually, new products create a lot of excitement, but that hasn't happened yet." High-definition TV, which will eventually create enormous sales, will not hit the airwaves until 1999, while the low-orbit satellite systems that promise a wealth of new applications are nowhere near ready.

DANGER. The dominant role of high-tech spending gives a bigger meaning to any drop-off in demand. An economy is vulnerable to a downturn when it develops "imbalances," to use Greenspan's term—that is, when one sector or industry expands too fast. For example, consumer spending and office construction far outpaced the rest of the economy during the 1980s. So when the recession came in 1990, these sectors crashed, making the downturn much worse.

With business spending so much on technology, it's a logical place to cut or postpone if times get tough

Now, high tech faces the same danger. Over the past three years, business spending on information-technology gear has risen by almost 45%. Meanwhile, spending on labor has risen by only 19%. Even if information technology has become a strategic asset for many businesses, its very size makes it a logical place to cut or postpone when times get tough. "After all," says Paul Saffo of the Institute for the Future, "you can only defy gravity if you're small."

Much of the planned increases in information spending can be deferred if the economy softens. Consider KPMG Peat Marwick. It is planning to spend $250 million over the next three years on information technology, more than double its historic spending pattern. Out of that, there's little flexibility in $150 million, but the remaining $100 million is more variable, says Siboni. "Building Web-centric information systems might become less critical."

The changing nature of corporate info-tech spending at companies will make it easier to make quick cuts. Rather than hiring a large internal staff of programmers, companies are relying on temporary workers and outside consulting firms, which can be easily sloughed off during tough times. At temporary-worker giant Manpower Inc., the division that supplies technology workers is growing at 40% per year.

Small businesses will not be reluctant to hold off spending if the economy turns down. "I have a lot of control over what I buy," says Josh Moritz, CEO of DMTG Inc., a small New York-based advertising firm. "I can delay purchases or buy used machines."

Consumers have even more reason to cut back during recessions. Over the past three years, the amount of money spent on home computers has risen by 55%, far in excess of income growth. Most consumers do not need a new computer. Instead, like autos, they buy the newest model if they can afford it. "A dominant force in the PC world is becoming consumer markets and hype," says William G. Rosser, a Gartner Group analyst. "That means you're more likely to see cycles like other consumer industries."

If and when the cutbacks come, they will not be confined to computers and software. Instead, the downturn is likely to spread to the telephone and networking industries as well. When the phone system was used mainly for voice calls, demand for lines was driven by population growth. But more and more, investment by phone companies is driven by the need for additional phone lines for computers and more capacity for data connections rather than basic voice service. The sudden prominence of the Internet, for example, forced Ameritech Corp., the Chicago-based telephone company, to boost its capital spending by $100 million to $200 million in 1996, to keep up with the need for more lines.

"PAYBACK." To be sure, there are forces that could prevent a high-tech downturn from happening anytime soon. Intel and Microsoft, the giants of personal computing, are investing hundreds of millions to create new products and to help other companies do so. "If the cycle is pointing down or is softer, then the only thing we can do to cope with that is to pump up our products," says Grove.

High-tech executives are also counting on competitive pressure forcing corporations to continue spending on information technology even in a recession. "The payback customers get from our products is very clear, very justifiable," says Mark Eppley, chairman of Traveling Software Inc., a Bothell (Wash.) maker of software for remote access. "Our business is growing very fast—independently of the economy."

A decline in U.S. sales could be cushioned by growth in overseas sales. Telecom deregulation in Europe may open the floodgates for cutting-edge computers and communications gear, where U.S. companies excel. Developing countries represent a huge untapped market that will become increasingly important. "There's a growing middle class in India, and it's as large as all of France," says Donald Macleod, chief financial officer at National Semiconductor Corp. "That's where the long-term opportunity lies."

But relying on global demand is no panacea. North America still makes up almost half the global market for computers, software, and peripherals. The latest data show chip sales falling faster in Asia than in the U.S. And growth in Japan and South Korea is expected to slow in 1997, according to DRI/McGraw-Hill forecasts, with Europe's economies still sluggish. In areas such as Japan, Germany, and France, "our business is still in most people's terms reasonably good," says John T. Chambers, CEO of Cisco Systems Inc. "But it's not good in Cisco terms."

Closer to home, the growing importance of high-tech poses new problems for economic policymakers such as the Fed. The tools of monetary policy—interest rates—do not work very well on high tech. In particular, it matters more whether compelling new products and technologies are available. When high-tech industries are riding a technology wave, they can power their way through slowdowns in the macroeconomy, no matter what the Fed does. "Whether the interest rate is 7% or 9% doesn't matter when you're growing at 30% per year," says AMD's Anixter.

So far in this expansion, the country has been lucky. The surge in high tech in 1995 and 1996 came just when autos and housing turned sluggish. But now the rest of the economy is turning up, judging from recent data. As a result, forecasters are raising their projections of growth in the first quarter to 3% or more, leading to speculation that the Fed will soon boost interest rates.

But ignoring the health of the information technology industries can produce bad policy. With order growth for computers and semiconductors having slowed noticeably, the economy may be far weaker than the traditional indicators make it seem. This raises the possibility that a rate hike by the Fed could be a serious mistake at this point.

Is a high-tech-led recession inevitable? Hardly. But for the first time, it's possible, and the odds are rising. The new business cycle is alive and well in Silicon Valley.

With Andy Reinhardt in San Francisco and bureau reports

What Has the Computer Done for Us Lately?

LOUIS UCHITELLE

At the end of the 19th century, railroads and electric motors were expected to transform America, making a young industrial economy far more productive than any seen before. And they did. At the end of the 20th century, computers were supposed to perform the same miracle.

They haven't.

Computers do wonderful things. But in purely economic terms, their contribution has been less than a transforming force: they have failed to bring back the strong growth that characterized so many decades of the American Century. By that standard, they have been a disappointment.

"It is a pipe dream to think that computers will lead us back to a promised land," said Alan Krueger, a Princeton University economist.

The issue is productivity. Those who look to computers for economic miracles, and there are many, insist that measuring their contribution only in dollars misses the less tangible improvement in quality that computers have made possible. But quality is often in the eyes of the beholders rather than in their wallets.

Through decades of invention and change, productivity has been measured as the amount of "output," in dollars, that comes from an hour of labor. A worker who makes 100 pencils in an hour, each valued at 50 cents, produces $50 of output. And the more output from each of the nation's workers, the greater the national wealth.

Or, put more broadly, productivity is the amount of output in dollars that comes from various "inputs," not only a worker's labor, but the tools he or she uses to carry out that labor: a machine or a computer or a wrench or an air conditioner that makes work more comfortable in summer. People work faster or concentrate better, and that shows up quickly in tangible output.

By this definition, the output resulting from the computer revolution of the last 25 years has been disappointing. Computers have, of course, contributed to productivity and economic growth. But that contribution has failed to register in Government statistics as the kind of robust catalyst that made the 1950's and 1960's such prosperous years.

If computers have fallen short of expectations, that would help ex-plain an apparent paradox that has puzzled economists and policy makers for two decades: how rapid technological progress and a booming stock market took place during a period of sluggish economic performance—sluggish, that is, relative to earlier decades.

America is all wired up—and still awaiting that big surge in productivity.

One possibility is that the statistics are wrong. A panel of economists came to this conclusion in a report to Congress last week, suggesting that growth has actually been quite robust but that this fact has been obscured by overstating the amount of output lost to inflation. This happened, the panel hinted, partly because the beneficial economic role of computers was not correctly taken into account. Some price increases that registered as inflation should really have registered as increases in output from computers.

Like Light Bulbs

But there is another explanation. Perhaps the computer is one of those inventions, like the light bulb early in the century, that makes life much better without adding as much to tangible national wealth as appearances might suggest. That is because, while the light bulb allowed factories to operate night shifts and students to study more easily, the measurable result was less impressive than the great improvement in the quality of life that the electric light bulb made possible.

Given the computer's ubiquity and convenience, should the calculation of productivity and wealth be changed to give more dollar value to the conveniences the computer has wrought?

That kind of recalculation has not been done over generations of technological change, largely because convenience is too hard to quantify and translate into dollars. Too often, convenience increases consumption more than production. With computers, "most of the recent use has been on the consumption side," said Zvi Griliches, a Harvard economist. "The time you waste surfing the Internet is not an output."

Others take a broader view. Children using home computers for schoolwork—gathering data from the Internet, for example—become better students, they say. In time, that will translate into rising workplace skills and greater measurable output. But it hasn't yet, and standard practice dictates that the nation wait until it shows up in the numbers before proclaiming the computer's great contribution to productivity.

"People have high expectations of this happening overnight," said

Nathan Rosenberg, an economic historian at Stanford University. "Computers are a major innovation, but absorbing so great an innovation involves many changes in work practices and behavior."

Useless Power

Right now, much of a personal computer's power goes untapped, or is employed in low-output tasks like sending and sorting through junk E-mail, compiling electronic Rolodexes and playing solitaire in the office. Harnessing a computer's spectacular ability to deliver and manipulate information is not easy. Edward McKelvey, a senior economist at Goldman Sachs, offers a hypothetical illustration:

Instead of more efficient production, the office of the 1990's has junk E-mail and electronic solitaire.

A consultant who charged $50 an hour 10 years ago to forecast trends in the economy now has a powerful desktop computer at his fingertips, feeding him information that in theory should make his forecasts more accurate. But he still charges clients $50 an hour because the forecasts, despite the computer, are not more accurate. Perhaps the consultant might never get that good at forecasting, even with a computer, or perhaps he will become so adept at extracting data from its depths that his forecasts will begin to hit the bull's eye. And that accuracy would allow him to raise his hourly fee, or "output," to

$70 an hour, a handsome improvement in his productivity.

There are other problems. The automated teller machine, for example, illustrates how measurable productivity has failed to respond fully to computer investment. A half-dozen machines installed in a bank's lobby permit the bank to cut its teller staff by half. That is clearly measurable productivity. The bank's income, or output, from bank transactions remains unchanged, but the input in teller hours goes down. The idled tellers can shift to other income-producing activities, perhaps becoming loan officers.

To make the productivity rate continue rising, however, the bank must continue cutting teller hours as it installs more A.T.M.'s. Instead, the next machines go to a dozen outlying neighborhoods, so that customers can bank at odd hours, almost at their doorsteps, or verify the balances in their checking accounts, something they did not bother to do very often before A.T.M.'s. That is convenience. Most banks don't charge extra fees for this convenience. If they had no neighborhood A.T.M.'s, then customers would have found themselves forced to use the machines already installed in the lobbies in their banks.

"The question is, how much would you have been willing to pay in fees for the convenience of having that neighborhood A.T.M. if the banks refused to furnish them otherwise?" said Erich Brynjolfsson, an economist at the Massachusetts Institute of Technology's Sloan School of Business. "That would then enter into measurable output."

Through a survey, Mr. Brynjolfsson tried to calculate what additional amounts Americans would pay for hundreds of conveniences that computers make possible. He came up with a total of $70 billion in additional output. That would add only one-tenth of one percent to the national wealth, which is the value of all the goods and services produced in the United States in a year—hardly enough to get economic growth back to the rates (at least 3 percent a year) that were characteristic of the 1950's and 1960's.

A Little Help

Still, computers and software in all their various forms make an important contribution. The national wealth—also known as the gross domestic product—has risen at an annual rate of less than 2.5 percent, on average, in recent years. That includes a contribution of roughly four-tenths of a percentage point from computers and their trappings, according to the calculations of two Federal Reserve economists, Stephen D. Oliner and Daniel E. Sichel. Manufacturing and the telecommunications industry have benefited especially from computerization.

But why haven't computers lifted the overall economy the rest of the way back to 3 percent growth? One reason is that they represent only 2 percent of the nation's capital stock, which is all the existing machinery, equipment, factories and buildings that business uses to produce goods and services.

By comparison, railroads in their heyday represented more than 12 percent. And they became the tool for opening up frontier lands to agriculture, and to new cities and industries. At the same time, electric motors, replacing steam, gave the nation a much more flexible and efficient source of power, and made possible the assembly line. The output resulting from railroads and electric motors became enormous.

Perhaps there is some set of conditions, having no direct connection to computers, that must develop before American productivity and economic growth can return to the old levels—conditions like greater demand for the potential output from computers, or hegemony again in the global economy.

Or perhaps, as some economists say, we should lower our expectations.

Creating the People's Computer

*One of the nation's foremost computer scientists, exasperated by the
unfriendliness of today's computer systems, suggests what designers can do to
make machines serve human needs—rather than the other way around.*

MICHAEL L. DERTOUZOS

*Michael L. Dertouzos is the director of MIT's Laboratory
for Computer Science.*

It is a few days before Christmas. I am out shopping at a well-known upscale department store in the Greater Boston area. I take nine items to the cash register. The cashier passes her magic wand over each package to read the bar code, and the impact printer rattles away as it prints a description and price for each item. I am getting ready to pull out my credit card when the woman turns to the cash register beside her and, horror of horrors, starts keying in the exact same information manually, reading the numbers off each package in turn.

She is on package number six when I clear my throat conspicuously and, with the indignation of a time-study specialist, ask her why in the world she is duplicating the work of the bar-code reader. She waves me to silence with the authority of one accustomed to doing so. "Please, I have to finish this," she says politely. I tell her to take her time, even though my muscles are tightening up and my brain is engaging in vivid daydreams of punitive acts.

She finishes the last package, ignores my pointed sigh, reaches for a pencil, and . . . starts all over again! This time she is writing in longhand on the store's copy of the receipt a string of numbers for every package; I am so shocked by this triple travesty that I forget my anger and ask her in true wonder what she is doing. Once more she waves me to silence so she can concentrate, but then obliges: "I have to enter every part number by hand," she says. "Why?" I ask, with a discernible trembling in my voice. "Because my manager told me to," she replies, barely suppressing the urge to finish her sentence with the universal suffix

"stupid." I could not let this go. I called for the manager. He looked at me knowingly and said with a sigh, "Computers, you know."

I told him that this looked a bit more serious than that, and he proceeded to explain in slow, deliberate phrasing that the central machine didn't work, so a duplicate had to entered by hand.

"Then, why enter it at all into the computer?" I ventured hopefully.

"Because it is our standard operating procedure, and when the central machine comes back, we should be in a position to adjust our records for inventory changes." Hmm.

"Then why in the world is she both keying in the numbers *and* entering them with the bar-code reader?" I countered.

"Oh. That's the general manager's instruction. He is concerned about our computer problems and wants to be able to verify and cross-check all the departmental entries."

I quietly walked out, stunned.

After I got over my shock at the absurd waste of time this store's procedures caused for the cashier— and me—I began to marvel at how the great promise that computers would improve human productivity is more easily discussed than implemented. Indeed, the topic of whether computers are raising human productivity has generated a great deal of controversy. Technology detractors will point to such encounters and say, "See, computers don't help us." And it's true that information technology does hurt productivity in some cases; it takes longer to wade through those endless automated phone-answering menus than it does to talk to a human operator. If technology is not used wisely, it can make us less productive instead of more so.

But computers can also be incredibly helpful. Used properly, they help ring up prices faster, track inven-

From MIT's *Technology Review* magazine, April 1997, pp. 20-28. Adapted from *What Will Be: How the New World of Information
Will Change Our Lives* by Michael L. Dertouzos. © 1997 by Michael L. Dertouzos. Reprinted by permission of HarperCollins
Publishers, Inc.

tory, and handle price changes. Productivity will rise in the Information Age for the same reason it did in the Industrial Age: the application of new tools to relieve human work.

Some people dismiss productivity concerns, arguing that computers make possible things we couldn't do otherwise. Certainly that is true, as the World Wide Web, special effects in movies, and credit cards have shown us. But to ignore the computer's fundamental ability to help humans do their brain work is at best perverse and at worst irresponsible. Productivity is the yardstick by which socioeconomic revolutions are measured. That was the case with plows, engines, electricity, and the automobile. If there is to be a true information revolution, computers will have to repeat the pattern with information and information work.

As we try to anticipate how computers might be used in the twenty-first century we are bombarded with unparalleled confusion and hype—a faster Web/Internet, network computers, intranets, cyberspace, 1,000 video channels, free information, telework, and much more. To my thinking, this future world can be described simply and crisply as an "information marketplace," where people and their interconnected computers are engaged in the buying, selling, and free exchange of information and information work.

Many issues surround the information marketplace: the technology of its underlying information infrastructures; its uses in commerce, health, learning, the pursuit of pleasure, and government; and the consequences of these new activities for our personal lives, our society, and our history. Here we will focus on a small but crucial aspect of this rich ensemble—ensuring that tomorrow's information marketplace will help us in our eternal quest to get more results for less work.

MISUSED AND ABUSED

Let's begin by examining a series of "faults "—ways in which computers are misused today because of either technological or human foibles. The first step toward improving our productivity will be to correct these faults. Next, we'll explore how to begin automating human work through computer-to-computer exchanges. The final and perhaps most vital step will be to make computers truly easier to use.

• *The additive fault:* The ridiculous duplication of effort that I ran into at the department store happens often and in many different settings. We'll call this failure the additive fault, because in these cases people are doing everything they used to do before computers plus the added work required to keep computers

happy or to make people appear modern. In anybody's book, this is a mindless productivity decrease. It should be stopped cold in whatever setting it raises its ugly head. And while we are at it, let's recognize this particular problem is not caused by technology but by our own misuse of technology.

• *The ratchet fault:* Some time after my encounter with the cashier, the same gremlins that seem to run ahead of me to set up challenging situations must have surely visited the airline clerk I encountered at Boston's Logan Airport. When I handed him my ticket to New York and asked him to replace it with one to Washington, D.C., he said, "Certainly, sir," and bowed to his terminal, as if to a god. As a seasoned observer of this ritual, I started recording his interactions. Bursts of keystrokes were followed by pensive looks, occasionally bordering on consternation, as with hand-on-chin he gazed motionless at the screen, trying to decide what to type next. A full 146 keystrokes later, grouped into 12 assaults demarcated by the Enter key, and after a grand total of 14 minutes, I received my new ticket.

What makes this story interesting from a productivity perspective is that any computer-science undergraduate can design a system that does this lob in 14 seconds. You simply shove your old ticket into the slot, where all its contents are read by the machine. You then type or speak the "change" command and the new destination, and you get the revised ticket printed and shoved back in your hand. Because 14 minutes is 60 times longer than 14 seconds, the human productivity improvement with such a box would be 60 to 1, or 6,000 percent!

Imagine requiring people to digest an 850-page manual to operate a pencil. We laugh at the thought but accept it readily in the case of a word-processing program.

Something is terribly wrong here. People run to buy a new computer because it is 20 percent faster than the one they have, and we are talking here about a 6,000 percent improvement. So why aren't the airlines stampeding to build this box? For one thing, if they did this for every one of the possible requests, they would have to build a few thousand different boxes for each terminal. All right then, why don't they reprogram their central computers to do this faster? Because that would cost a billion dollars. Why? Because the airlines have been adding so many software upgrades and changes to their systems that after 20 years they have built up a spaghetti-like mess that even they cannot untangle. In effect, they cannot improve their system without starting from scratch.

We'll call this the ratchet fault of computer use because it's like a ratcheting tire jack: every time a new software modification is added the complexity of the system rises, but it never comes down unless a precipitous event, like a total redesign, takes place. This problem is more a consequence of inadequate technology than of unsound human practice. If we had a software technology that could let us gracefully update our systems to suit our changing needs while maintaining their efficiency, then we wouldn't be in this bind.

• *The excessive-learning fault:* One-tenth of my bookshelf is occupied by word-processing manuals. Add the manuals for spreadsheets, presentations, and databases, and they easily fill half a shelf. Because I use graphics and do a bit of programming, I need a few more manuals. This brings the total length of my computer guidebooks to one EB—one (printed) Encyclopaedia Britannica. We'll simply call this the excessive-learning fault—the expectation that people will learn and retain an amount of knowledge much greater than the benefits they'd get from using that knowledge. Imagine requiring people to digest an 850-page manual in order to operate a pencil. We laugh at the thought, but we accept it readily in the case of a word-processing program. I have little doubt that the first half of the twenty-first century will be spent getting rid of fat manuals and making computers much easier and more natural to use.

• *The feature-overload fault:* Bloated is perhaps a more accurate adjective to describe the feature-packed programs hitting the market in the late-1990s. Vendors do so in part to cover their bets and to be able to charge higher average prices. Buyers are fascinated by the potential uses of their computers and value their prerogative to command their machines to do thousands of different things. Of course, in practice they end up doing only a few tasks and forget what features they have bought or how to use them. A top-selling "suite" of office software comes on a CD-ROM or 46 diskettes that require half a day to load into your machine. This is not productive. And it is caused by us, not technological weaknesses. Consumers and corporate executives should declare birth control on the overpopulation of excessive and often useless features.

• *The fake-intelligence fault:* My car has a fancy phone that was advertised as "intelligent" because when it makes a phone connection it automatically mutes the volume of the car radio to ensure a quiet environment. I found this feature delightful until one afternoon when I heard a good friend being interviewed on the radio. I immediately called a mutual friend so she could listen along with me over the phone and share in the excitement. This, of course, was impossible, because the phone muted the radio and I couldn't override it. Welcome to the fake-intelligence fault. It crops up in many situations where a well-meaning programmer puts what he or she believes is powerful intelligence in a program to make life easier for the user. Unfortunately, when that intelligence is too little for the task at hand, as is always the case, the feature gets in your way. Faced with a choice between this kind of half-smart system and a machine with massive but unpretentious stupidity, I would opt for the latter, because at least then I could control what it could do.

PRODIGY seized control of my computer, informing me it would take a few "moments" to download some new software. I could do nothing to stop it from "helping" me in its own murderous way.

As users striving to improve our productivity, we must always ask whether a new program offers enough value through its purported intelligence to offset the headaches it will inadvertently bring about. And suppliers of these ambitious programs should endow them with a Go Stupid command that lets users disable the intelligent features.

• *The machine-in-charge fault:* It is 2:00 a.m., and I just got home. My Swissair flight from Logan was canceled because of trouble in the motor controlling the wing flaps. Some 350 passengers whose plans were thwarted were bombarding every available clerk at the airport. I abandoned that zoo, rushed home, switched on my computer, and tried to connect to the Easy Sabre do-it-yourself airline-reservation service offered by Prodigy to search for an alternative ticket for a morning flight out of either Boston or New York. I had to find out before going to sleep if this was possible. But before I had a chance to enter a single keystroke, Prodigy seized control of my screen and keyboard. It informed me that to improve my system's use of its online services, it would take a few moments (meaning a half-hour minimum) to download some improved software.

There was nothing I could do to stop Prodigy from "helping me" in its own murderous way. A meager piece of anonymous software was in full control of this situation, while I, a human being, was pinned against the wall. Meanwhile, I knew that with each passing minute, another of those frantic nomads at the airport would take another of the rapidly vanishing seats on the next morning's few flights. I gladly would have used software that was several generations old to get my job done sooner. I felt I was drowning in shallow surf from a stomach cramp while the lifeguard on the beach was oblivious to my screams because he was using his megaphone to inform me and all the other swimmers of improved safety procedures.

This is exactly the same fault that requires precious humans to spend valuable time executing machine-level instructions dispensed by hundred-dollar automated telephone operators, with their familiar "If you want Marketing, please press 1. If you want Engineering . . ." A good part of this machine-in-charge fault must be attributed to human failure in allowing such practices to continue without objection, but programmers must also take some of the blame. They often deliberately commit this fault because it's simpler, therefore cheaper, to program a computer to interrogate the user and not let go until all questions have been answered in one of a few fixed ways than to allow the user to do any one of several things with the assurance that the computer will pay attention.

> *I have tried for years to interest sponsors and researchers in a project that would eliminate the need for people to essentially beg permission from a computer's software just to turn the machine on or off.*

Of course, interactions controlled by the machine are not always undesirable. A mistaken command by you to erase everything inside your computer should not be casually executed. However, 95 percent of the overcontrolling interactions on the world's computers don't involve such grave situations. The sooner these software crutches vanish and the user is given control, the sooner machines will serve humans rather than the other way around.

• *The excessive-complexity fault:* I am at my office, it is almost noon, and I discover with considerable panic that I forgot to retrieve from my home computer the crucial overheads I need for an imminent lunch meeting. No sweat. I'll call home and have them shipped electronically to my office. As luck would have it, though, the only one home is the electrician, but he is game. "Please turn the computer on by pushing the button on top of the keyboard," I say. He is obviously a good man, because I hear the familiar chime through the phone. During the two minutes the machine takes to boot up, the electrician asks why the machine doesn't come on instantly, like a light bulb.

I refrain from telling him that I share his consternation. For three years I have been trying to interest sponsors and researchers in a project that would address this annoying business in which a human respectfully begs permission from a computer's software to turn the machine on or off. Instead, I explain that the machine is like an empty shell and must first fill itself with all the software it needs to become useful. "Okay," I say, "pull down the Apple menu and select the Call Office command," which I had providentially defined some time back. He complies, and I hear my home modem beeping as it dials my office modem. On the second ring I hear the office modem next to me answer. We are almost there, I muse hopefully.

"Do you see the message that we are connected?" I ask.

"Nope," he responds. Another minute goes by and he reads me an alert message that has appeared on my home computer's screen. I know what happened. The modems latched correctly and can send signals to each other but for some unknown reason the software of the two machines cannot communicate. I ask him to hold while I restart my machine. Like many people, and all computer professionals, I know that restarting with a clean slate often solves problems like this one, even though I have no idea what actually caused the problem.

As I guide the electrician through rebooting my home computer, I get angry, because these problems would be reduced if my office computer were calling my home machine rather than the other way around. But my home machine has only "remote client" software, meaning that it can call out but cannot receive calls. This distinction between clients and "servers" is a residue of corporate computing and the time-shared era's central machines, which dispensed lots of data to the dumber terminals. The distinction must vanish so that all computers, which I'd coin clervers, can dish out and accept information equally, as they must if they are going to be able to support the distributed buying, selling, and free exchange of information that will take place in the information marketplace.

When my home machine has again booted up, we go through the modem dance once more, and this time the software latches. I ask the electrician to select the Chooser command and click on the Appleshare icon and then to click on the image of my office machine. Now he needs my password, which I give him promptly. He reports activity on his screen that I interpret as success. I tell him how to locate the precious file I need and send it to me. In two and a half more minutes the overhead images arrive safely in my machine. I thank the electrician profusely and send the images to my printer now filled with blank transparency sheets, and I've got them. I arrive at the meeting 30 minutes late.

Why couldn't I simply give my home computer in one second a single command like "Send the overheads I created last night to my office" and have them arrive three minutes later? Fellow techies, please don't tell me it can be done with a different kind of machine or a different operating system, macros, agents, or any other such tools, because I know and you know better. This simple act just cannot be carried out easily and reliably with today's computers.

As system designers we must begin the long overdue corrective actions against the excessive-complexity fault by simplifying options, restricting them, and, most important, reversing a design point of view rooted in decades-old habits. We should tailor computer commands and options to user's needs, rather than tailoring them to existing system and subsystem needs and expecting users to obediently adapt. We must do for computer systems what we have done for cars—get away from giving people controls for the fuel mixture, ignition timing, and the other subsystems, and give them a steering wheel, a gas pedal, and a brake for driving the car.

ELECTRONIC BULLDOZERS

One of the biggest roadblocks to building an effective information marketplace is the inability of interconnected computer systems to easily relieve us of human work. This is because today's networked computer systems have no way of understanding one another, even at a rudimentary level, so they can carry out routine transactions among themselves. Yet the potential for automating information work is huge—one-half of the world's industrial economy comprises office work, suggesting how huge this new socioeconomic movement could be. To offload human brainwork, we must develop tools that let computers work with one another toward useful human purposes. I call the tools that will make this possible "automatization" tools to distinguish them from the automation tools of the Industrial Revolution that offloaded human musclework.

Today we are so excited by e-mail and the Web that we plunge in with all our energy to explore the new frontier. If we stop and reflect for a moment, however, we will realize that human productivity will not be enhanced if we continue to use our eyes and brains to navigate through this maze and understand the messages sent from one computer to another. Imagine if the companies making the first steam and internal combustion engines of the Industrial Revolution made them so that they could work together only if people stood beside them and continued to labor with their shovels and horse-drawn plows. What an absurd constraint. Yet that is what we do today—expend a huge amount of human brainwork to make our computers work together. It's time to shed our high-tech shovels and build the electronic bulldozers of the Information Age. That's what the automatization tools are all about.

Achieving some basic degree of understanding among different computers to make automatization possible is not as technically difficult as it sounds. But it does require one very difficult commodity: human consensus. One simple way to achieve automatization is to use electronic forms (e-forms), where each entry has a pre-agreed meaning that all participating computers can exploit through their programs. Suppose that I take 3 seconds to speak into my machine the command, "Take me to Athens next weekend." My machine would generate the right e-form for this task and ping-pong back and forth with the reservation computer's e-form before finding an acceptable date and class and booking the flight. Since it would have taken me 10 minutes to make an online reservation myself, I could rightfully brag that my productivity gain was 200 to 1 (600 seconds down to 3 seconds), or 20,000 percent!

Thus we can imagine that in the information marketplace, common interest groups will establish e-forms to specify routine and frequently recurring transactions in their specialty, whether those entail buying oranges wholesale or routing around x-rays among different medical departments. If the members of such a group can agree on an e-form, especially one that represents a laborious transaction, then they will achieve substantial automatization gains. Computer programs or people interested in doing that kind of business would be able to look up the agreed upon e-form and use it in their computer, toward the same gains but with much less effort.

Quite a few computer wizards, and people who are averse to standards, believe that common conventions like e-forms resemble Esperanto, the ill-fated attempt to create a universal spoken language among all people. They argue that attempts at shared computer languages will suffer the same ills. Instead, they advocate that the only way our computers will get to understand each other will be by translating locally understandable commands and questions among their different worlds, just as people translate between English and French.

This argument is faulty because shared concepts are required even in translating among different languages. Whether you call an object *chair* or *chaise,* it is still the thing with four legs on which people sit. It is that shared concept base, etched somehow in your brain, that makes possible a common understanding of the two different words in English and French. Without it, no amount of inter-conversion can lead to comprehension, simply because, as in the case of computers, there is nothing in common on either side to be comprehended.

If we can form a consensus within and across specialties concerning the most basic concepts computers should share, then even if we end up with different languages and dialects, software developers will be able to write programs and ordinary users will be able to write scripts that install useful computer-to-computer automatization activities—searching for information on our behalf, watching out for events of interest to us, carrying out transactions for us, and much more.

GENTLE-SLOPE SYSTEMS

Automating computer-to-computer transactions and fixing problems in present computer systems are good steps toward making computers and the information marketplace serve us. But designing systems that are inherently easier to use is the really big lever. I believe that this endeavor will consume our attention for a good part of the next century.

In the last decade, anyone who has uttered the phrase "user friendly" in my presence has run the risk of physical assault. The phrase has been shamelessly invoked to suggest that a program is easy and natural to use when this is rarely true. Typically, "user friendly" refers to a program with a WIMP interface, meaning it relies on windows, icons, menus, and pointing along with an assortment of pretty colors and fonts that can be varied to suit users' tastes. This kind of overstatement is tantamount to dressing a chimpanzee in a green hospital gown and earnestly parading it as a surgeon. Let's try to penetrate the hype by painting a picture of where we really are with respect to user friendliness and where the true potential for ease of use lies.

It is sometime in the late 1980s. A friend approaches you, excited by his ability to use spreadsheets. You ask him to explain how they work. He shows you a large grid. "If you put a bunch of numbers in one column," he says, "and then below them put the simple command that adds them up, you will see their total in the bottom cell. If you then change one of the numbers, the total will change automatically." The friend rushes on, barely able to control his exuberance: "And if you want to make the first number 10 percent larger, you just put in the cell next to it the simple command that multiplies it by 1.1." His expression becomes lustful: "Do you want to increase all the numbers by 10 percent? Just drag your mouse down like this, and they will all obey."

He takes in a deep breath, ready to explode once more, when you stop him cold. "Thank you. Now go away," you say. "You have taught me enough to do all my accounting chores." This is how millions of people today use their spreadsheet programs like Microsoft Excel and Lotus 1-2-3. They hardly know more than a tenth of the commands yet they get ample productivity gains.

You are happy with your newly acquired knowledge until one day you discover that you need to do something a bit more ambitious, like repeat over an entire page all the laborious operations you have set up but with a new set of initial numbers. Perplexed, you go back to your friend, who smiles knowingly and tells you that you must now learn about macros. His explanations are no longer as simple as before, and you just can't get the spreadsheet to do what you want. This is where most of the millions who use spreadsheets give up. But instead you fight on, eventually mastering the mysteries of the macro. It's really a computer program written in an arcane programming language that replaces you in commanding the spreadsheet program to do things you would have done manually.

You sail along for the next six months until you develop the need to do an even more ambitious task that involves designing a human-machine interface that will make your program more useful. You go back to your friend, who tells you that you have become too good for the limited capabilities of this spreadsheet application, and that you must now learn how to use a real programming language like C++. Unaware of what lies behind these three innocent symbols but unwilling to give up, you press on. This costs you your job, because you must now devote full time to a colossal new learning endeavor. Yet you are so enamored with programming that you don't mind. In fact, you like the idea. Two years later, having harnessed C++ and a few more programming languages and operating systems, you begin a career as a successful independent software vendor and eventually become wealthy.

This happy ending cannot hide the barriers that you have had to overcome along the way. You decide to graph the effort you expended versus the ability you gained. The result is a line starting at the left and moving along to the right. There is a long slowly rising portion and then a huge hill where you had to learn a lot of new stuff in order to move further right. Then there are more slowly rising lines and more huge hills, like a mountain chain where each new mountain gets higher. You wish that someone would invent an approach with a gentler slope, one where you get ever-greater returns as you increase your learning effort, without the impossible cliffs that you had to climb. I predict that such "gentle-slope systems," as I like to call them, will appear and will mark an important turning point of the Information Age.

The gentle-slope systems will have a few key properties. First and foremost, they will give incrementally more useful results for incrementally greater effort. They will be able to automate any activity you do that is repetitive. They will be graceful, in the sense that incomplete actions or errors on your part will result in reasonable degradations of performance rather than catastrophes. Finally, they will be easy to understand—no more complicated than reading a cookbook recipe.

CONCEPTUALLY CHALLENGED

One reason it is difficult for nonprogrammers to tell computers what to do is that the software systems that surround us are preoccupied with the structure rather than the meaning of information. We can program them to do anything we want, but they are unaware of the meaning of even the simplest things we are trying to do. Let me illustrate.

It takes me 17 seconds to say to a programmer, "Please write me a program that I can use to enter onto my computer the checks I write, along with the categories of each expenditure—food, recreation, and so forth. And do this so that I can ask for a report of the checks that I have written to date, listed chronologically or by category."

I have given this assignment several times to different people. Master programmers invariably decline to play and tell me to go buy this program because it's commercially available. Good programmers will say they can meet the request in a couple of hours—and end up taking a day or two to develop a shaky prototype. Inexperienced programmers will say cockily that they can write the program in a few minutes as a spreadsheet macro—and are generally unable to deliver anything at all. The company Intuit, which devel-

oped the very successful Quicken program that does this job and more, took two years and many millions of dollars to develop, test, document, and bring to market.

Why can I "program" a human being to understand the above instruction in 17 seconds, while it takes a few thousand to a few million times longer to program a computer to understand the same thing? The answer surely lies in the fact that humans share concepts like check, category, report, and chronological, while computers do not. The machine is so ignorant of these concepts that programmers must spend virtually all of their programming time teaching the computer what they mean. If, however, I had a computer that already understood some of these "concepts," then I might be able to program it to do my job in a very short time. This is an important way in which computers could increase our productivity in the twenty-first century: by being made to better understand more human concepts in better ways.

For computers to be truly easier to use, technologists will have to shift their focus away from the twentieth-century preoccupation with the structures of information tools like databases, spreadsheets, editors, browsers, and languages. In their early stage, computers became ubiquitous because this focus allowed these common tools to be used equally in thousands of applications, from accounting to engineering to art. Yet that same generality is what makes them ignorant of the special uses they must ultimately serve and ultimately less useful than they should be—much like a dilettante jack-of-all-trades.

What we need now, to boost utility further, is a new breed of software systems like a spreadsheet that an accountant can easily program and that already "understands" higher-level repetitive tasks like setting up charts of accounts, doing a cash reconciliation, and pulling trial balances.

Freed from the tyranny of generality, these specialized programming "environments" will rise toward offering a lot more of the basic information and operations of their specialty. The time has come for computer technologists to abandon the "generalist" orientation that served people well for the first four decades of the computer era and shift their focus from the structure to the meaning of information.

EVERYONE A PROGRAMMER

The biggest promise of the Information Age is the great and still unrealized potential of tailoring information technology to individual human needs. Today's applications programs are like ready-made clothes—one size fits all. So most are ill-fitting, and we have to contort ourselves to improve the fit. Another potential outcome of this practice for business is that if every company used the same set of canned programs, they would follow more or less the same procedures, and no company would stand out against the competition. Shrink-wrapped, ready-made software is good enough for the state of information technology at the end of the twentieth century. But it won't be as good in tomorrow's information marketplace.

> *We invented writing to communicate better with one another. Tomorrow we'll need a means to communicate better with our electronic assistants.*

Great gains will be achieved when individuals and businesses can bend and fashion information tools to do exactly what they want them to do, rather than bending themselves to what the tools can do. This quest for customizable information tools with specialized knowledge will be no different than the current trend toward customized manufacturing. It could well be that by the close of the twenty-first century, a new form of truly accessible programming will be the province of everyone and will be viewed like writing, which was once the province of the ancient scribes but eventually became universally accessible.

This isn't as absurd as it sounds. We invented writing so that we could communicate better with one another. Tomorrow we'll need to communicate better with our electronic assistants, so we'll extend our "club" to include them as well. Everyone will then be a "programmer," not just the privileged few. And none of them will be conscious of it. In fact, this is already happening on a small scale among the millions of people who use spreadsheets and who would be very surprised to learn that they are programmers.

When I say people will program, I am not talking about writing the detailed code and instructions that make computers run. That will still constitute the bulk of a software program and will indeed be created by professional programmers, who will fashion the many larger building blocks that we will use. Each individual's "programming" will account for a very small fraction of the software code, maybe 1 percent. But it will be the crucial factor that gives the program its specificity. It will be like building a model railroad; you don't make all the track or engines or cars, but you do arrange the pieces to create your own custom railway patterns.

We can increase the usefulness of our machines in the emerging information marketplace by correcting current human-machine faults, by developing automatization tools, and by creating a new breed of gentle-slope software systems that understand specialized areas of human activity—and that can be easily customized by ordinary people to meet their needs. Pursuing these directions should get us going on our quest, which I expect will last well into the twenty-first century, to harness the new technologies of information for the fulfillment of ancient human purposes.

Money in Electronic Commerce:
Digital Cash, Electronic Fund Transfer, and Ecash

Driven by inherent weaknesses in traditional paper-based payment methods, networked companies and their customers around the world now have at least three pervasive electronic options to move the numbers between their online accounts.

Patiwat Panurach

ROBERT NEUBECKER

THE extraordinary growth of international interconnected computer networks and the pervasive trend in commerce of using these networks as a new field for business operations is stimulating demand for new payment methods. These new methods must attain unprecedented levels of security, speed, privacy, decentralization, and internationalization for digital commerce to be accepted by both consumers and businesses. This article analyzes three such electronic payment methods:

• The generic, widely used electronic fund transfer
• The proposals for a digital cash standard
• The real-world technology called Ecash

These methods are examined in terms of the dynamics of transaction clearance; the effects on money supply and the macroeconomy; their classification in terms of money and cash; and the comparative viewpoints of monetary authorities, financial institutions, and consumers. This article does not go into detail on the myriad encryption systems, protocols, algorithms, and other technical matters concerning the new systems. These are all secondary aspects of electronic payment. Electronic payment systems are simply logical evolutionary steps that began with recognition of the limits of bartering. The need to pay for transactions is the root of all electronic payment systems.

Electronic Fund Transfer

THE electronic checking system for electronic payments has been in use since the late 1960s. For many consumer end users, electronic checking and electronic payment are the same thing, although the assertion does not apply in all cases. Electronic checking uses the existing banking structure to its fullest potential by eliminating paper checks. Electronic fund transfer and electronic checking are synonymous. Electronic fund transfer is an extremely varied system. Examples include:

- Paying university fees through the banking automatic teller machine (ATM) network,
- Paying telephone bills through monthly bank account deductions, and
- Large-value(ranging from thousands to millions of dollars) interbank overseas fund transfers.

Conceptually, electronic checking, and almost all electronic payments, involves three agents—the buyer, the seller, and the intermediary. The buyer initiates a transaction with the seller, and the seller demands payment. The buyer then obtains a unique certification of payment (the virtual equivalent of a check) from the intermediary. This certification (in electronic form) debits the buyer's account with the intermediary. The buyer then gives the certification to the seller and the seller gives the certification to the intermediary. The certification credits the seller's account with the intermediary. Schematically, the transaction is like a conventional checking transaction. But when conducted electronically, the certification is an electronic flow documented by the intermediary. Most important, delivery of the certification, transfer of the certification, and debiting and crediting of the accounts occur almost instantaneously. If the buyer and seller don't use the same intermediary, some standardized clearinghouse system between intermediaries is used, usually coordinated by the country's central bank (for domestic transactions) or by a third country (for international transactions and when the third country's central bank is a trusted authority).

Since electronic checking is essentially checking, it can be analyzed as if it were conventional checking. Payments made via electronic checking would be conducted without cash and paper. Instead of sending a check or paying at a counter, the buyer would initiate an electronic checking certification via computer or point-of-sale terminal. If such a transaction is done as a substitute for paying cash, electronic checking could substantially reduce the transaction's demand for money. Instead of carrying wads of cash, consumers could initiate an electronic fund transfer

at precisely the moment of the purchase. In essence, such a payment system is not electronic checking but electronic cash. But if electronic checking becomes a substitute for conventional checking, the speed of the transaction would increase. From an economic standpoint, there is no difference in the dynamics of the checking process between electronic and normal checks, aside from the transaction cost reductions in paper handling.

Electronic checking provides a number of advantages over paper checks:

Saved time. The instantaneous updating of account balances allows all financial players more financial flexibility. There is no clearing period for transactions to be finished, allowing large cost reductions and more opportunities in cases of large-sum arbitration, while giving even normal consumers and savers a great deal of financial freedom. Time savings are also considerable. Checks no longer have to be cashed and purchased at bank branches.

Reduced costs for paper handling. Universities are not overwhelmed with paper checks at the beginning of each term; banks aren't faced with unmanageable lines of people every payday; governments don't need large check printing and mailing facilities; fewer trees are cut.

No bounced checks. Being virtually simultaneous, receipt of the certification and debiting and crediting of accounts ensures that no certification is made without the funds to back it up. Such payments could be done through an automatic confirmation of account status before the certification is issued. This operation is similar to the verification of the credit limit before credit card transactions are finalized, except it can be done on the buyer's side.

Flexibility. Electronic fund transfer is an extremely broad and generic field, used, in various forms, worldwide. Transactions range from small-value retail-level withdrawals through ATM networks to international large-turnover networks, like the Clearing House Interbank Payments System (CHIPS), an international payments clearing system set up by some of the largest New York commercial banks, now consisting of a network of more than 115 depository institutions around the world. CHIPS handles an average of 182,000 transactions a day worldwide, valued at $1.2 trillion.

Electronic checking bypasses the physical weaknesses of paper checks, although it is still, in essence, a check. A critical weakness of checks is privacy, since transactions must pass through the banking system. Moreover, the banking system is obligated to document the details of every transaction passing through it to comply with federal regulations governing documentation of electronic funds transactions, namely Regulation E, which implements the Electronic Funds Transfer Act of 1979 (15 U.S.C. 1693). But what is to prevent a bank from selling or leaking such information to third parties, like marketing researchers and governments, risking the possible loss of personal civil liberties? Such was the case of Winai La-onsuwan, formerly known as the Buddhist monk Yantra Amarobhikku, whose alleged illicit adventures in an Australian brothel were documented through American Express receipts [6]; such evidence was critical in his being defrocked. An even more frightening scenario would be if governments demanded access to or control over electronic checking transactions or electronic checking records. What would prevent governments from, say, compiling lists of people who bought blacklisted books or patronized blacklisted businesses? Electronic fund transfer systems could conceivably be a tool for Big Brother to gain control over individual lives. As payment systems using electronic checking become more pervasive, is it necessary to sacrifice the privacy and undocumentability associated with cash?

Digital Cash

Many groups and individuals feel that cash itself still has a role as an electronic payment system. But digital cash—the electronic equivalent of paper cash—would have to reflect the consumer's view of cash's essential characteristics:

Anonymity. The buyer would pay the seller. Nobody, except the seller, would know the identity of the buyer or the details of the transaction. In cases where the buyer was using a sufficiently sophisticated pseudonym system, not even the seller would know the identity of the buyer. Aside from the personal records of the two agents, there would be no record of the transaction's having taken place. The certification of payment would be the payment. There would be no immediate transfer between accounts that banks could analyze to discern the exact flow of funds.

Liquidity. Digital cash would have to be accepted by all concerned economic agents as a payment method. For example, in the global Internet, true digital cash would involve a significant proportion of Internet merchants' accepting digital cash for digital cash to be more than electronic play money. In pilot projects, there must be a large threshold of affiliated merchants willing to accept digital payment for the system to succeed.

On the institutional side, digital cash has many advantages over existing fiat money (paper money and coins), mainly involving the physical weaknesses of fiat cash. First, cash is at high risk of robbery; it

must be kept in secure vaults and be guarded by security guards. The more cash is held, the greater the risk and the greater the investment in security. Second, cash has high transport costs. Because physical mass is proportional to the amount of cash held, large amounts of cash are difficult and expensive to store and move. It has been estimated that the handling costs of transporting cash in the U.S. amount to more than $60 billion a year [4]. Last, the advent of high-quality color copiers and counterfeiting methods make government stores of cash insecure. It is widely documented that counterfeit currency is used as a weapon of economic war, with the goal of destabilizing national economies and governments [6]. Digital cash can take many forms, including prepaid cards and purely electronic systems:

Prepaid cards. Buyers can buy prepaid cards that are accepted by special sellers. For example, self-contained phone cards (such as those used in Asia and Europe) act as surrogates for coins in paying for public phones. The weakness of phone cards as digital cash is liquidity; no one would accept a phone card for the payment of a meal. Electronic toll-road payment systems suffer the same weakness. Recent pilot projects conducted in Australia by Visa International show more promise. Prepaid and rechargeable cards are accepted at the point of sale of a variety of merchants. Furthermore, to increase the system's acceptability, Visa subsidizes the cost of point-of-sale terminals. It is now possible to pay for a beer at the bar and a hotel bill with the same card [4]. Incorporation of digital cash functions into multipurpose smart cards, announced by MasterCard, involves a card that conforms to the latest standard from the EMV (Europay, MasterCard, Visa) consortium and includes dynamic public-key authentication. Such multipurpose smart cards potentially allow many functions, such as subscriber identity modules (SIMs) for Global System for Mobile Communications (GSM) phones, ATM transactions, encryption/decryption, and digital cash.

Purely electronic systems. Purely electronic digital cash would be devoid of explicit physical form, making it useful for network and Internet transactions in which the buyer and the seller are in physically remote locations. The payment would take place through electronic deductions of digital cash from the buyer and its transmission to the seller. The actual transfer of digital cash is usually encrypted by either public-key or private-key encryption systems

> Instead of carrying wads of cash, consumers could initiate an electronic fund transfer at precisely the moment of the purchase. In essence, such a payment system is not electronic checking but electronic cash.

so that only the intended recipient (the seller) can actually use the cash. However, institutional constraints, like U.S. export restrictions on advanced encryption systems, might impede the acceptance and practicality of digital cash. Furthermore, methods of ensuring anonymity must be in place so that fully electronic systems are not turned into variants of electronic checking systems.

In its various forms, digital cash is not always cash. If, for example, a financial institution were to issue digital cash, the creation of digital cash could be considered a withdrawal from that financial institution. Similarly, the financial institution would be obliged to credit user accounts for deposits of digital cash. The digital cash would not need real funds to back it up, other than a legal reserve limit for the original deposits. Digital cash could be considered cash in calculations of the money supply. Therefore, when currency includes cash, coins, and digital cash:

$$M1 = \frac{1 + (currency/deposits)}{LRR + (currency/deposits) + (excess\ reserves/deposits)} \times MB$$

where M1 is the money supply, LRR is the legal reserve limit on bank lending, excess reserves are any nonobligatory reserves banks do not lend out, and MB is monetary base.

Withdrawing digital cash increases the ratios of currency/deposits and excess reserves/deposits, thus reducing the amount of deposits the financial institution has available for extending loans and reducing any dynamic effects on the expansion of the money supply.

If, on the other hand, a nonfinancial business were to issue digital cash, such issuance would simply be a purchase of one unit of digital cash with one unit of fiat cash. It could be backed up only by the willingness of merchants to accept digital cash as a unit of payment and not by any insurance (like the Federal Deposit Insurance Corp. [FDIC], the government agency that insures depositors' bank funds in the U.S.) or reserves. This nonbank type of digital cash is inherently riskier for the consumer than bank-issued digital cash. It is actually more like coupons than cash. Furthermore, redeeming fiat cash for non-bank-issued digital cash does not affect the monetary conditions of the economy. Buying digital cash does not affect the money-creation process; there is no decrease in the economy's capacity for loan creation and money supply creation.

> As payment systems using electronic checking become more pervasive, is it necessary to sacrifice the privacy and undocumentability associated with cash?

Ecash

Now consider a real-world example of electronic payments. Ecash is an electronic payments system developed by the Digicash Co. of Amsterdam, The Netherlands, and is currently being implemented by the Mark Twain Bank of Missouri in the U.S. As of March 1996, another implementation of Ecash was initiated by the Merita Bank of Finland, but for the sake of consistency, only the Mark Twain Bank version is analyzed.

To undertake transactions, both buyer and seller have to have deposits in the Mark Twain Bank's WorldCurrency Access accounts. Access accounts are conventional checking accounts, insured by the FDIC but do not pay interest or have a fixed maturity period. Buyers must instruct the Mark Twain Bank to transfer funds from their WorldCurrency Access accounts into their accounts' Ecash Mint. Funds in the Mint are no longer deposits in the bank, and they are not insured. The Mint acts as a personal buffer account. At any time, buyers can order their computers to remotely interface with the Mint and withdraw funds from the Mint into the hard disk drives on their personal computers. The format of the funds is now completely electronic—a series of zeros and ones cryptographically secure and unique. It might be useful to consider the funds in the Mint and in the buyer's hard disk as being in an electronic wallet.

To make the payment, the buyer encrypts the appropriate amount of Ecash with a suitably secure encryption protocol and sends the Ecash to the seller. The Ecash can be sent to the seller by any data communications medium (e.g., email, ftp). Ironically, Ecash can even be saved onto a disk, printed onto paper, and the printed copy or disk sent to the seller. Sellers receive the Ecash and, after decrypting it, store it in their own computers. This can then be sent to the Mint and transferred into the seller's WorldCurrency Access account. The net result is a decrease in the buyer's funds and an increase in the seller's.

Ecash is private. Although the Mark Twain Bank maintains records for each Ecash withdrawal and deposit (to comply with banking laws), it is impossible for the Bank to trace any subsequent uses of that Ecash. Lack of traceability is due to the fundamental specifications of the Ecash system, which is based on asymmetric public-key cryptography [2]. Specifically, it uses the RSA cryptographic system from RSA Data Security, Inc. with a key size of 768 bits. Such key size is not a maximum; it can be increased by the issuing bank. Besides being untraceable and anonymous, Ecash provides nonrepudiation; any disputes between a buyer and seller can be unambiguously resolved. Nonrepudiation of transactions can also be a fundamental factor in the success and security of payment systems [1]. But although Ecash is purely electronic and is easily copied, it is impossible to use any Ecash twice because any Ecash must be verified with the Mark Twain Bank's database as never having been spent.

Given its nature, Ecash must be considered cash from the monetary standpoint. Ecash withdrawals from the user's account are leaks from the money-creation process, just like cash withdrawals. If a user's WorldCurrency Access account had $100 in it, and $50 is withdrawn as Ecash, only $50 (minus any legal reserve limit and excess reserves) could be lent out to other borrowers. Conversely, a $50 Ecash deposit would give the Mark Twain Bank $50 (again, minus legal reserve limit and excess reserves) to lend out.

Monetary Implications

Now consider some tendencies in all types of electronic payment. First is the long-term trend to increase the velocity of money flow in the national economy. As the growth of the credit card industry (actually a subset of electronic fund transfer) shows, increased convenience of payment is a significant factor in increasing the number of payments made. As electronic payments become more widespread and increasingly available to the consumer, we might expect a similar long-term trend of increased price level for goods and services in the economy and for increased economic growth through increased velocity of transactions. Also, the disembodiment of cash tends to create illusions as to its value. Transforming money from bills in your wallet into charged electrons on your hard disk is probably a greater abstract leap than the transformation of gold coins to fiat currency. As another evolutionary step in the development of money, we might expect consumers to reexamine their conceptions of money, cash, and value. Another significant impact is revealed by research into the roots of interest-rate margins in the money market. For example, Citicorp, one of the largest banks in the world, has claimed that around 40% of the interest charged on a consumer finance loan represents branch delivery and management costs. Such costs could be reduced substantially with increased adoption of electronic means of payments. This implies that the interest differentials in the money market could be dramatically reduced with adoption of consumer electronic payments, spelling drastic changes for the structure of the banking industry.

Standards, Competition, and Acceptance

Comparing these three electronic payment systems and their impacts, it should be noted that no single system is best. Which system is adopted depends largely on the details of the transaction and the needs of the people conducting the transaction. On the consumer side, survey data shows the single most important factor is wide acceptance of the system [7]. Thus, it may be that any system, whether formally standardized and secured or not, could gain market dominance and remain in that position by virtue of its being the ad hoc standard. Sellers would use it because most customers use it; customers would use it because most sellers use it. The main channel for competition among payment systems would be not in the cost of the system, but in gaining exclusive rights to the point of sale of a large number of merchants. This environment would make electronic payments widely available in a relatively short time but would not exactly be conducive to diversity or technologically innovative systems. This scenario would be analogous to the entrenched triopoly of Visa, MasterCard, and American Express in the credit card market.

An alternative to this situation might be the wide adoption of an open standard electronic payment system. If such a system were adopted, all intermediaries would jointly adopt an interoperable system, whereby the client of one system could transparently conduct transactions with any other seller whose intermediary uses the same system. Transparent transactions would be similar to the openness and competition in Thailand's ATM banking system, where the two ATM consortiums (ATM Pool and BankNet) support an open transactions system. The holder of a Bangkok Bank ATM card can withdraw money from, for example, a Thai Farmers Bank ATM.

Such an open electronic payment system would have several advantages over a proprietary electronic payment system:

Choice. Users could be given greater choice among financial intermediaries and their services. Since there could be several intermediaries vying for the same open market, they would have to use a policy of differentiation. Such a structure would bring about a monopolistic competition type of market—the market for open standard electronic payments. Hopefully, this differentiation would be to the benefit of the users.

Policy. Government policy implementation would be less ambiguous. Generally, the fewer heterogeneous systems there are to regulate, the more effective government policy would be on each system. Such relationships occur because each system would need a specific interpretation of the applicable laws. Since in most nations, the legislative process can't quickly enact new laws, the applicable laws tend to be arcane and controversial. Combined with the constrained capacity of the state, this lag might cause an ambiguous period of years before systems are finalized. The ambiguity during this period can kill off enthusiasm for new systems, leading confused consumers to adopt ad hoc methods or to return to conventional paper methods of payment. It could also lead to market distortions, as shortsighted governments could give anticompetitive concessions to single firms.

Simplicity. Open standard electronic payments systems would provide a consistent payment method from the user's side, where consistent interfaces are synonymous with system efficiency. Survey data [7] shows that simplicity is the second most important aspect in an electronic payments system. Thus, consistency in terms of transaction dynamics and interface of an open standard could contribute to the wide adoption of the open system.

Despite the advantages of open standard electronic payments systems, it is also likely that a variety of standards could simultaneously gain market acceptance. A heterogeneous market would not grow through conventional price competition but rather by seeking niches in the market. For example, it is highly likely that some form of electronic cash system will gain a market niche due to its unquestionable privacy. Besides the easily targetable markets of such socially deviant products as pornography, it would also gain acceptance from users uneasy with the fact that each of their transactions would be documented by the banking system. Fear of such information getting into the hands of bosses or governments would probably cause users to move to a more private system. An example of such concern for privacy is the case of the Clipper chip, where the perceived threat of U.S. government intrusion into personal communications is being publicly resisted.

Other niches might include government-subsidized systems for the payment of various state benefits. For example, an advanced virtual food stamp system has been implemented in New York City [8]. Grocery stores with a high proportion of food-stamp-using customers are required to install electronic payment systems at the point of sale. These customers can buy their groceries without cash, allowing an automatic transfer of funds from their food stamp account to a grocery's account. This system reduces long lines at government offices, eliminates the black market in redeeming food stamps for cash, and significantly reduces the shuffling of paper by all parties. This system is used by 500,000 recipients and is reportedly favored over the old system by 94% of them.

Conclusions

As for any new technology, it would be impractical to view the status of electronic payments as clearly defined. Ambiguities exist in both the technological and institutional realms. Technological constraints include the insecurity of some types of payment systems, especially in the area of anonymity. Institutional constraints include government regulations that may cripple the growth of electronic payment systems even before they take off. Also, reluctance of existing financial institutions to adopt new payment technologies due to lack of investment funds can be a considerable hurdle, especially in countries with underdeveloped financial institutions. Probably most crucial, however, is the role of consumer acceptance in catalyzing system adoption. Although the technol-

> **T**ransforming money from bills in your wallet into charged electrons on your hard disk is probably a greater abstract leap than the transformation of gold coins to fiat currency.

ogy has existed for decades to implement many systems, they have just begun to permeate the lives of ordinary consumers. The number of merchants (as of Jan. 1 1996) accepting Ecash is less than 100, according to Digicash's own registries. Card-based electronic cash systems have been implemented only in pilot projects in a handful of cities around the world. Nevertheless, the trends of modern commerce, driven by the weaknesses of traditional payment systems, point to the eventual rise of electronic payments. Electronic payments might not completely replace traditional systems, but there is plenty of room to grow.

References
1. Anderson, R. Why cryptosystems fail. *Commun. ACM 37,* 11 (Nov. 1994), 32–41.
2. Chaum, D. Security without identification: Transaction systems to make Big Brother obsolete. *Commun. ACM 28,* 10 (Oct. 1985), 1030–1044.
3. Levy, S. The end of money? *Newsweek* (Oct. 30, 1995), 62–65.
4. Levy, S. E-Money (that's what I want). *Wired 2,* 12 (Dec. 1995) http://www.hotwired.com/wired/2.12/features/emoney.html
5. Pincus, M. Econo-Terrorism. *Real World Intelligence Alert* (1995) http://www.lookoutpoint.com/look/econo.html
6. Police asked to examine credit card pay slips. *Bangkok Post 50,* 55 (Feb. 24, 1995), 1.
7. Weiler, R. M. Money, transactions, and trade on the Internet. MBA thesis, Imperial College, London, England, 1995 http://graph.ms.ic.ac.uk/results
8. Wood, J. C., and Smith, D. S. Electronic transfer of government benefits. *Federal Review Bulletin 77,* 4 (Apr. 1991)

About the Author
PATIWAT PANURACH is a student in the Faculty of Economics at Thammasat University in Bangkok, Thailand. **Author's Current Address:** BE Program, Faculty of Economics, Thammasat University, 2 Prachan Road, Bangkok, 10200, Thailand; email: pati@ipied.tu.ac.th.

Work and the Workplace

Whether we work and the kind of work we do affects our standard of living, our social status, our self-image, and even our sense of moral worth. With large-scale technological change, the nature of work is correspondingly altered. In this process, new jobs are created, while others become obsolete and disappear.

During the Industrial Revolution, many people, most notably Karl Marx (1818–1883), predicted that mass unemployment and hardship would result as machines displaced human labor. What actually happened is that industrialization did render many jobs obsolete, but many more jobs were created. According to U.S. census records, there were only 323 different occupations in 1850; today there are thousands of job specialties in technologically advanced countries. The National Occupational Classification of the kinds of jobs performed by Canadians, for example, lists about 25,000 occupational titles. And rather than causing impoverishment, wages and living standards have risen immeasurably. Moreover, social reforms such as a shorter work week, paid retirement, and prolonged schooling for the young have eased competition for jobs and afforded workers more time for personal and educational pursuits.

The contemporary work scene is not without problems, however. As Marxist scholars would correctly point out, many jobs require little skill and offer low wages; some are dangerous. Even in some of the most advanced nations, too many people are unable to find work at all. And as computing technologies enter the workplace at an accelerating pace, a pervasive worry is that many jobs could be eliminated. Automation and offshore production have already cost thousands of manufacturing jobs, and the same forces threaten some clerical jobs as well. There is further fear that the number of new jobs that are created will be fewer than the number lost. And there are concerns that existing jobs will be deskilled and that newly created jobs will be in low-skill, low-pay fields.

Optimists, on the other hand, predict that, overall, future jobs will be more skilled, more satisfying, and better paying than jobs are now. In a recent Canadian study, researchers found that white-collar workers tended to think computers have led to increased job skills and made their work more challenging and interesting. Still, there is no question that computers make a lot of jobs much easier (and more dull and more routine as a result). To cite just one example, supermarket cashiers now need only a fraction of the skills that were required before bar code scanners became common.

The articles in this unit highlight other dimensions of the "good news/bad news" effects of computing on work. For example, by having employees work away from the office, companies can save millions of dollars on office space. But some of these savings are lost if employees have difficulty making the psychological and social adjustments to being separated from coworkers. Marc Hequet describes some of those adjustments from a personal perspective in "Virtually Working: Dispatches from the Home Front." As he points out, "telecommuting can be great. But it isn't great for everybody. Even if it's right for you now, it might not always be right for you."

As Bob Filipczak explains in "The Ripple Effect of Computer Networking," computer communications systems can also have both positive and negative consequences. They can increase employee involvement in decision making, or can make it harder to build consensus and thus lead to information overload. Jay Stuller expands on the problem of "Overload." A glut of electronic messages can lead to gridlock that has negative implications for individual workers and organizational productivity.

Another kind of overload is addressed by Catherine Romano. In "Working Out the Kinks," she reports that computer users are among a growing number of workers at risk

of developing "repetitive strain injuries," and she discusses the causes, symptoms, costs, and prevention of RSIs.

Looking Ahead: Challenge Questions

Regardless of what is technologically feasible, is it a good idea for most white-collar workers to work in "virtual offices"? Why or why not?

When we hire the services of highly trained professionals such as physicians and lawyers, what we are "purchasing" is their scarce, valuable, expert knowledge. We now see that an increasing amount of this expert knowledge is being packaged in easy-to-use "do-it-yourself" computer programs. What are some positive and negative implications of do-it-yourself medicine, law, accounting, or other services normally provided by professional experts?

THE RIPPLE EFFECT OF COMPUTER NETWORKING

BOB FILIPCZAK

Bob Filipczak *is staff editor of TRAINING Magazine. His e-mail address via MCI Mail is Sproskin.*

The computer network your company installed is more than a simple change in the way employees communicate. The impact may dramatically affect the way they work and think.

I n the beginning, it was a simple concept. You have a computer and your co-worker has one, too. Both are useful tools, but what if you could share information between the two? What if you could get these computers to talk to each other across distances? What if....

...and then there was light!

Without further notice, we were networked. Companies began to connect computers with cables, using network software to help the machines send information across the lines. Later, the networks connected PC's with file servers, essentially big hard drives that could be a central storehouse for programs everyone in the company used.

What business needs drove all this networking? There are probably as many rationales as there are organizations, but the simple desire to be more effective and get more work out of fewer people is the best all-purpose explanation. Others include the need to preserve the consistency of data and improve information sharing among headquarters and field-office employees.

One of the first byproducts of computer networking has been an increase in the speed of communications. Electronic mail (e-mail), document sharing, central data bases of information, and computer forums where people can discuss topics with each other in real time have all resulted from connecting computers to networks. All change the way people communicate, and changing the way people communicate within a company produces reverberations we are just beginning to understand.

Lee Sproull, a professor of management at Boston University, and Sara Kiesler, a professor of social and decision sciences at Carnegie Mellon University in Pitts-

burgh, recognized some of the ripple effects of computer communications two years ago. In *Connections: New Ways of Working in the Networked Organization,* a book that examines some of the cultural implications of the computer-network revolution, Sproull and Kiesler write:

"Communication can't be separated from who is in charge of the giving, receiving, content, and use of what is communicated. Information control is tied to other forms of power and influence. When we change information control using technology, we also change the conditions for other control relationships in the organization."

So aside from the increase in efficiency, we're now beginning to see the ramifications of those changes in communication and information control. These changes are what Sproull and Kiesler call "second level" effects of computer networks—the unforeseen ways people use the technology.

The Wall Street Journal and *Fortune* magazine use terms like "flattened hierarchies," "empowerment" and "teamwork" to describe the second-level effects of computer networks. Because employees are using networked computers to get access to important information, and sometimes important people, they start to ask questions about their limits. If, for example, your department can gather and crunch its own budget numbers because of the network, is there any reason to wait for the accounting department to do it? Or, if your employees don't like the new vacation policy, is there any reason they can't send the CEO electronic mail saying so?

Some of these changes appear to be no big deal. Others appear to have far-reaching implications, especially in a traditional corporate hierarchy. Either way, your computer network is making its mark on your corporate culture. And some of the changes may not be what the company had in mind when it invested in networking technology.

IF YOU'VE GOT THE TIME

So what are we really talking about here? In the future, computer videoconferencing may become a reality, but right now networks simply allow users to send files to other people and exchange e-mail. Even by using computer networks for those simple tasks, however, employees have begun to alter the way they accomplish their work.

For example, a friend who works for a computer company in Minneapolis used to make multiple journeys each month to Des Moines, IA, to help another division of the company work out its computer problems. When the Iowa division "got on" the network, my friend could go to Des Moines every morning if he had to and never leave his office.

On its face, that looks like a simple first-level efficiency outcome: It reduces travel time, for instance. But the immediacy of his consulting over the network also improved his service to the Des Moines division. He is available *all the time*. His availability to other divisions and co-workers is just one of the ripples that will translate to changes in work styles across the company. It seems obvious that this kind of change in work styles is bound to have some impact on an organization's culture, although there is considerable disagreement over whether computer networks will produce dramatic cultural change.

At the heart of the discussion about the ripple effects of e-mail and computer networks is what computer techies call "asynchronous communication." In practical terms, it means you don't need all the people involved in the communication to be available at the same time. In a phone conversation, for example, two or more people must be on the line at the same time to achieve communication. (With voicemail and answering machines, even this condition is becoming superfluous, but that's another story.)

With e-mail, communication is sent by one party at a time, usually at the convenience of both parties, and it's sent instantaneously. Since there's no time lag in sending and receiving e-mail, the only time-dependent factor is the convenience of the e-mail recipient. Clearly, a conversation over e-mail takes longer than face-to-face discussion, so urgent communication probably will remain the province of meetings or phone calls. But how much of our interoffice communication is *that* urgent?

Subordinates, real experts, women and minorities are less reticent in a computer discussion.

Assuming time and communication are among the scarcest resources in most organizations, e-mail addresses both shortages.

It's also important to take convenience into account in the e-mail equation. Say, for example, you need to ask your boss a question but it doesn't demand an urgent reply. If you send it over e-mail you won't forget to ask it when she gets back from her battery of meetings. Because she can answer it at her convenience, she may be able to give you a more complete answer and consider it more carefully. In this case, the communication of information is improved because it is asynchronous.

So far, the same could be said of putting a Post-it Note on her door or dropping a memo into her in-basket. But what if others might be able to address the question or benefit from the answer? An electronic distribution list can be an effective way to broadcast a question or concern to scores of people or even the whole company. In the hands of a CEO, this potential for immediate and widespread distribution becomes a new tool for communicating to employees.

Of course, in the hands of a front-line employee with a chip on his shoulder, the same tool can create problems.

A FORCE FOR DEMOCRACY?

E-mail and computer networking have the potential to flatten traditional hierarchies, but the impact depends on the company. Most experts agree that, in a hierarchical company with rigid chains of command, a network is not going to do much to make the company more egalitarian—at least in the short term.

"You don't stand up and announce, 'We're going to install a network and henceforth everyone will communicate openly and democratically across the organization,' " Sproull tells TRAINING. On the other hand, she says, the democratization of computer-networked workplaces is inevitable.

In *Connections,* Sproull and Kiesler make a powerful case for the long-term, hierarchy-flattening power of e-mail conversation. In most cases, they examine the impact on meetings of conducting business electronically vs. face to face. Their findings might be a little scary—if you're a command-and-control type.

First off, status tends to be negated in an electronic meeting, whether it's conducted over e-mail or in real time (with everyone meeting simultaneously on the network and typing their suggestions and responses). In face-to-face meetings, people with higher status tend to dominate the discussion—whether or not they are the most knowledgeable on the subject. In electronic meetings, according to Sproull and Kiesler's research, contributions to the discussion tend to be more equal. Moreover, subordinates, real experts, women and minorities are less reticent in a computer discussion.

Sproull and Kiesler describe the democratizing effect of the technology in a study they conducted with some executives: "When groups of executives met face to face, the men in the groups were five times as likely as the women to make the first decision proposal. When those same groups met via computer, the women made the first proposal as often as the men did."

The authors traced similar results among graduate students teamed up with undergraduates to solve problems. Even when the undergraduate clearly knew more about a subject, face-to-face communication negated that expertise. Electronic meetings leveled the playing field between the two groups.

An outcome-focused person might rightfully ask whether the quality of the solutions was any better when the discussion was more democratic. Sproull and Kiesler say yes. The quality of decisions, solutions and products produced by a group communicating through computer networks was significantly better, according to their findings.

Yet many disagree that computer networks are going to change corporate cultures or knock executives out of their ivory towers. John Mueller, a technical writer in San Diego and co-author of *A Hands-On Guide to Network Management,* has set up networks for a lot of companies. He disagrees that a network will tend to flatten a company that isn't already evolving toward more open communications.

THE ELECTRONIC WATERCOOLER

The communication taking place on the computer networks in your company—people discussing movies and exchanging recipes using electronic mail—is really nothing new. Since before the first watercooler appeared in the first office, social interaction at work has been a fact of life. But when watercooler conversations move onto the computer network, all kinds of interesting things can happen.

First, and most important, informal conversations among employees are no longer limited to just a few people. Only so many people fit around a watercooler, but an e-mail distribution list is practically limitless.

"What happens invariably when I install a network is that the break room starts emptying out. And management gets super happy for at least a month or two until they figure out what's going on," says consultant John Mueller, author of *A Hands-On Guide to Network Management*. What's going on, of course, is that those dedicated employees sitting at their desks are assembled around an electronic watercooler. You'll be hard-pressed to

figure it out by looking, however. When they're working they're sitting in front of the computer and tapping on the keyboard. And when they're talking to each other about going out after work, they're doing exactly the same thing.

Some companies are less concerned about informal conversations than others; some even encourage the free exchange of ideas (and chitchat) via company-sponsored electronic bulletin board systems (BBSs). A BBS is similar to e-mail, but messages are available to everyone who has access to the system. When you write something on a BBS, it can be read by anyone who logs on to that area of the network.

Companies set up BBSs for a variety of purposes. IBM, for instance, has had a BBS for software developers for years. It gives programmers a place to discuss problems where peers can chime in with solutions. At Lotus Development, an informal BBS called Soapbox allows employees to post anything they want. Russ Campanello, vice president of human resources, says discussions range from "what to do with leftover cafeteria food"

to searching for a good computer dealer in Cambridge, MA, to speculation about why Digital Electronics Corp. used pentium chips in its new computer.

Some BBSs dedicated to a specific subject wither as employees' interest in the topic declines, says Steve Riley, a systems analyst for Ashland Chemical in Columbus, OH. He advises putting a termination date on most BBSs so people know they have a limited time to contribute. A BBS dedicated to discussion of your new corporate vision, for example, should terminate by the date the vision is supposed to be completed.

Lee Sproull, a professor of management at Boston University and co-author of *Connections*, says some internal BBSs can thrive for longer than three months, but they must be dedicated to topics that attract lasting attention. The one topic that stands the test of time, she says, is food. A BBS dedicated to restaurant reviews and recipes can keep employees' attention longer than just about anything, although systems dedicated to information about a company's competitors can last just as long.—**B.F.**

The contention that e-mail gives line employees more access to top executives is a fallacy, he says. If the company doesn't have a culture of open communication, few employees are going to bypass official lines of communication and go straight to the top. Even if they do, top managers will often stop reading their e-mail if they're inundated with gripe mail. When they stop reading and responding to e-mail, it sends a pretty clear message to the rest of the company that certain kinds of communication are not welcome.

Mueller also has seen some companies try to use a network to monitor individuals' work and reinforce the hierarchy. When that happens, he says, employees who think Big Brother is watching will likely avoid the network altogether, a reaction that defeats the purpose for investing in the network in the first place. "In companies where the Big Brother approach is used," he says, "the network doesn't work."

Paul Breo, owner of Chicago-based Infochi, a computer-network consulting

company, agrees. "If [companies] use it as a whip or to harden a structure that might not have been good in the first place, then the whole networking process is going to be a failure, at least in terms of the human element," he says.

Sproull, however, stresses the long-term effects of computer communications. She and Kiesler outline four principles that a company should establish to make a network effective.

• The network should be available to everyone, not just the techies.

• There should be a spirit of open communication and flowing information so everyone can offer something and get something from it.

• The company should provide diverse computer forums to enable people to work together.

• The company should establish incentives and policies that encourage the exchange of information.

In this kind of climate, write Sproull and Kiesler, the long-term effects of democratization through computer networks will

unfold. In the absence of these principles, the changes will take longer, Sproull says, but they will still evolve.

David Daniels, a senior consultant with Metropolitan Life, a New York-based insurance company, agrees with Sproull's prediction of the long-term effects. We are just beginning to see the impact of computer communications, he says, but it will include a gradual opening of the corporate culture.

Sheldon Laube, national director of information and technology for Price Waterhouse, the New York-based accounting and consulting firm, puts a different spin on the debate. A computer network will definitely change a corporate culture, he says, but not the underlying corporate values. His argument goes like this: The corporate culture is a reflection of the way people in a company work. Groupware (software that allows document sharing and electronic meetings) and e-mail undeniably change work styles, but company values are deeper than the surface culture. And values are very difficult to change, assuming you want to change them at all. For example, your company may value customers above all else, and a computer network probably won't change that. But if front-line employees have better access to accounts and can answer customer questions faster and with more confidence, then the employees' sense of empowerment (in other words, the culture) could change.

FLAME MAIL

Sproull and Kiesler are not unequivocal boosters of electronic communications, despite some of the evidence they cite. Other experiments they've done reveal some of the disadvantages of e-mail in terms of communication, reaching consensus and information overload.

The first drawback they mention is that as an informal mode of communication, e-mail is a double-edged sword. For some reason, e-mail feels more casual to users than either written or face-to-face communication. It encourages people to write short, concise and pointed communiqués that tend to cut through bureaucratic mumblings and the ambiguities of business jargon. You may not consider that a problem, but this informality has also given birth to the phenomenon of "flame mail."

Flame mail or flaming are terms that were coined to describe the terse, angry, insulting or threatening tone of many e-mail messages. Flame mail occurs on public electronic bulletin board systems (BBS) or between employees on e-mail systems within a company. Sproull and Kiesler pinpoint a variety of reasons for the incendiary nature of flame-mail messages, and many of them are inherent disadvantages of e-mail and computer communications.

> 'When you get a zinger,
> sit back
> and let it age
> a day or two
> before you zing
> them back.'

Because computer communication is primarily text-based—i.e., written words—people don't have any of the additional clues that make up a face-to-face or telephone conversation. There's no tone of voice, gesture or facial expression to fill in communication gaps, so people often use more expressive language. That crescendo of expressive language can be interpreted as an indication of strong emotions, something generally frowned on in a business environment. In other words, some "flame mail" isn't really very flame-like at all. It's just perceived as unusually blunt in relation to the more formal tone of traditional business correspondence.

The cause of more aggressive flame mail can be traced partly to what Sproull and Kiesler refer to as the ephemeral nature of computer communications. It's generally agreed that the written word is more formal than the spoken word, but because there is no physical record of e-mail (i.e., paper) people seem to attach less importance to it. Consequently, they are more likely to "flame."

Mistakes in e-mail etiquette are easy to make because it's a new medium and the rules are still being written. Daniels tells of the time he wrote an e-mail message to a co-worker and, by mistake, used the caps lock on his keyboard. Because the whole message was in capital letters, the recipient thought Daniels was angry. He got back a response asking, "Why are you shouting at me?"

Rick Rabideau, an Atlanta-based consultant and expert on computer collaboration in work groups, says flame mail tends to generate more flaming unless someone breaks the cycle. "When you get a zinger, sit back and let it age a day or two before you zing them back," advises Rabideau. This computer equivalent of counting to 10 should take some of the venom out of responses.

Oddly enough, consensus building may be another casualty of computer communications. In face-to-face meetings, the 80-20 rule often applies: 80 percent of all the talking and input comes from 20 percent of the participants. Precisely because electronic meetings tend to level the playing field in terms of hierarchy, you get more input from more people. Moreover, the participants are less likely to back down from their opinions if they don't see their bosses glaring at their suggestions. Consequently, reaching a consensus via e-mail can be a laborious and frustrating process. When Sproull and Kiesler tried to test the consensus-building properties of electronic communication, they had to abandon the experiment when participants got so caught up in arguing that no consensus was reached.

Information overload may be the most productivity-busting aspect of computer-network communications. Once a network is installed, line workers may have immediate access to almost anyone in the company. That's when a kind of volcano effect can spew out over managers and top executives. Without social barriers to upward communication, the CEO of a good-sized company might receive 50 e-mail messages a day. E-mail usually just lands in a manager's desktop computer in a lump. Everything from recipes for a new dessert to someone interested in selling a concert ticket to notification that his performance-appraisal forms are due in two days can pile up in a manager's e-mail in-box, with no way to separate the important from the fluff.

Sure, managers can just stop reading all e-mail to avoid this pitfall. One professional confessed that the CEO of his company has a computer on his desk but never turns it on; there's not much chance that anyone sends that executive electronic mail. On the other hand, if people don't read their e-mail in the interests of saving time or preventing information overload, they defeat the purpose of using a computer network to improve communications.

A better solution is the use of computer-network filters, what *The Wall Street Journal* terms "bozo filters." If you want to eliminate e-mail correspondence from known "bozos," you can program the software so mail originating from certain individuals never gets delivered to your mailbox. In a kinder, gentler work environment, however, filters can also prioritize your e-mail so it doesn't arrive in one enormous lump. A filter, for example, can ensure all mail with your supervisor's name on it lands at the top of your list.

Lotus Notes, a popular groupware program that lets people share all kinds of information and e-mail correspondence, has a sophisticated filter, or "agent," that organizes e-mail into folders. Therefore, computer tips from the training department land in one folder and missives from the board of directors land in another. Notes can even search your mail for strings of words and prioritize them that way. If, for example, you're working on a project to develop an aperture flywheel gramis with a vacuum gasket, you can have all e-mail that contains that string of words sent to the same folder.

An easier way to prevent important mail from getting buried in an information avalanche is to train employees in how to use e-mail effectively. Russ Campanello, vice president of human resources for Lotus Development, says his company not only built Notes, it also uses the software on a day-to-day basis. His simple solution to losing important mail within a pile of random e-mail deposits is to tell employees to include the words "action request" on the subject line. That way, he separates information that's nice to know from the stuff asking him to do something.

If you're going to use a filter to screen out mail, instead of just prioritizing it, you also run the risk of losing any important information a bozo might send you. Rabideau says we are still a few years away from a truly intelligent filter that can read your messages and make a judgment call on whether you need it or not. He also suggests that employees should be informed if you're using a filter to screen mail. "On one hand you're telling them 'I'm open, please send me messages,' but on the other hand, 'I have my bozo filter and am screening them out.' It's a little contradictory," admits Rabideau.

OUT IN THE BOONDOCKS

Some advantages to computer-networked communication go deeper than just better communication, not the least of which is the ability to connect with "peripheral" employees—those who are located away from company headquarters. Sproull and Kiesler cite several studies that indicate that computer communication boosts the morale of these employees and helps them feel more in touch with the rest of the company.

This is precisely what General American Life Insurance, a St. Louis-based insurance provider, had in mind when it decided to upgrade its computer communication to Notes, says Larry Connor, group administration vice president. General American's sales reps around the country could access headquarters via a network set up years ago, but it was a cumbersome, inefficient system and field reps hated to use it.

Consequently, Connor's department was constantly dealing with field employees who didn't send policies to headquarters in a timely manner. Using Notes not only cut in half the time it took reps to enter the information into the computer network, it also decreased the number of clarifying questions Connor's employees had to ask reps.

Connor's group has just five new-business coordinators and, under the old system, they were continually swamped with phone messages from sales reps. Because these coordinators now spend less time clearing up ambiguities, they are more available—by phone and computer—to help sales reps with more important is-

sues. Moreover, the scarce new business coordinators can broadcast answers to frequently asked questions throughout the network.

Price Waterhouse's Laube, a peripheral employee himself, agrees that a good computer network is a morale builder. Because the chairman of the company uses e-mail to deliver messages to employees, everyone gets important information at

How's that again? Employees who use e-mail are more loyal?

the same time. In the past, Laube's California office workers might wait a week before a memo from headquarters got to them. Now the chairman can send instantaneous messages—whether important policy changes or wishes for a happy new year—to every Price Waterhouse office in the world.

The worldwide computer network also creates another advantage for Price Waterhouse's peripheral employees: virtual teams. Now, through electronic document sharing and videoconferencing over the network, a team can include the best people for the job no matter where they are located, says Laube.

Nevertheless, he cautions, computer networks do not obviate the need for face-to-face communication. "I live in California, and the senior executives are in New York. When it comes time to review my budget, we don't do it over e-mail," says Laube.

His warning is echoed by others: E-mail cannot replace face-to-face meetings. It can, however, make meetings more efficient because all participants can arrive completely informed about the agenda and updated on any new developments.

Another effect that Sproull and Kiesler discovered as they researched computer communication was an increase in compa-

ny loyalty among employees. How's that again? Employees who use e-mail are more loyal? In a study of employees of a city government, they found that over 90 percent routinely used electronic mail. Furthermore, Sproull and Kiesler write: "We discovered that the more [employees] used it, the more committed they were to their employer—measured by how willing they were to work beyond the requirements and hours of their jobs, how attached they felt to the city government, and how strongly they planned to continue working for the city." The researchers also discovered that the relationship between workplace loyalty and computer communication was stronger in employees who worked later shifts, another finding that bolsters the argument that e-mail strengthens the commitment of peripheral workers.

Sproull and Kiesler's analysis of computer-network communication uncovers many "second-level" effects on organizations. But they posit that any new technology has at least three levels of impact on society—and that with computer communication, we've only just begun to see the effects of Level 2.

What happens when organizations go from LANs (local area networks) to WANs (wide area networks) like Compuserve, America On-Line, MCI Mail or the Internet? According to the newly formed Internation Internet Association (IIA), the Internet adds a million users to its ranks every month. Max Robbins, IIA's executive director, says about 99 percent of the additions to the user base in the last three years have come from the business sector.

It's one thing when employees can access top executives via e-mail. What happens when employees can access professional peers over the Internet? And what happens to a company's trade secrets when these discussions heat up? No one has answers to these questions yet, but a little forethought about the costs, benefits, and far-reaching implications of computer networks is probably in order. Clearly, the networks set up in companies all over the country are more than a tangle of cables and software. These computer networks are changing the way employees communicate, and that changes everything.

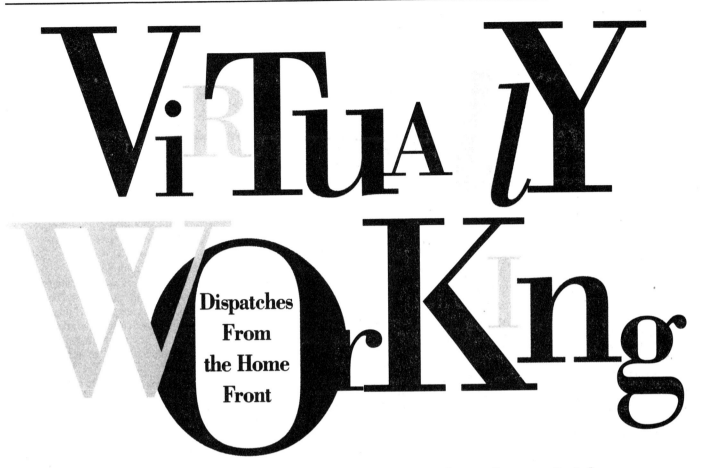

VIRTUALLY WORKING

Dispatches From the Home Front

Sure telecommuting works—because people who know how to do it have learned to deal with the dirty little secrets.

MARC HEQUET

Marc Hequet *is special projects editor of TRAINING Magazine.*

This will be too nice a day to work. I can already tell that from the early sun sifting through the drapes. But I'm working here at the dining room table. And I'm going to keep working. Across the room the big speakers roar out Franz Liszt's creepy old "Fantasia and Fugue on '*Ad Nos, Ad Salutarem Undam*' in C minor." The devotional groans of the bass pedals on the Geneva Cathedral's organ rattle the leaded glass in my buffet cabinet windows. Sometimes I can write when it's like this.

Liszt downshifts about six gears to adagio, and the dog jingles to her feet, thumping the carpet, scratching herself somewhere. You know the type. Big and ugly for a miniature schnauzer. Abject but crafty. Too much fur on her face and not enough on her skinny rat legs. The neighbor kid says she looks like a goat.

This particular animal has piddled on the carpet somewhere, sometime, and on humid days you still remember a thing like that. I'm remembering it now.

The thumping stops. I can't see the dog. But I know she's looking at me. She probably wants to go out. When doesn't she? She's been out already. I'm writing. Who cares? Does she have dog food in her dish? I paw at my laptop keys. I'm writing. Never mind. Fresh water? I take a peek. Yes. Now I'm writing again. No, I'm not writing. I'm playing cabana boy to my rat-goat dog.

This is telecommuting. Virtual work. Two-dollar names that mean I'm working at home and there's a computer involved. It's very nice. *Ad nos salutarem undam,* indeed. Whatever that means. The "Fantasia and Fugue" is based on Meyerbeer's 19th century opera about 16th century religious passions, about Reformation Anabaptists preaching the urgent necessity for adult rebaptism in order to be born again, as in the Gospel of John. Must have been quite the opera, Meyerbeer.

OK, so now I'm reading record covers instead of writing. But it's apt in this case: By the year 2000, more than 60 million people—half of American workers—will do some kind of work at home, says *Investor's Business Daily.* IDC/Link, the Manhattan research firm that tracks the phenomenon known as telecommuting, says the annual work-at-home numbers rose 7.6 percent to 39 million households in 1995.

That's a lot of born-again workers getting their baptism of fire in the big, ongoing job reformation known as virtual work. And you've heard latter-day corporate Anabaptists urgently preaching why telecommuting is needed. It cuts corporate expenses for office space, it saves commuters gas and mass transit fares, it reduces pollution and the need for public spending on transportation. And the experts claim that telecommuters, away from the distractions of the office, are up to 40 percent more productive.

SHREDDED HEART

In Connecticut, Diane Siroky is working at home, too, and it's even nicer there than it is in my vibrating, dog-soiled dining room. She's reminded just how nice it is every time she phones the office and hears a New York City siren in the background.

From a third-story office window in her Fairfield County colonial two hours outside the city, she can see long-limbed show horses stilt-legging through their paces on the 18-acre place across the road. Over the phone, as the horses lope, the sirens of the city wail past the building where her peers labor deep in the frantic ambience of Manhattan. The sound-over is eerie, otherworldly.

Siroky likes it at that office in the city, to which she reports (from time to time) as senior account executive for Makovsky & Co., a public relations firm. But she loves her home office with its pastoral vista, the horses, the trees.

Her four-day workweek up there in Fairfield County is just right. She shuts herself into her office and steels herself to ignore her 2- and 3-year-old daughters even when they cry. They're with the nanny, and nanny will know what to do.

It shreds a mother's heart, though. "When I hear crying I want to go and I don't," Siroky repents. "Doesn't that sound *terrible?*" The woman of steel stays put and works.

Siroky finds herself toiling even during off-hours, doing phone records and other paperwork, because she wants billable hours strictly focused on clients. Her husband, a chemical salesman, says the at-home overtime is OK, Siroky explains. It's worth it because they don't have to juggle taking their daughters to day care.

Once or twice a month Siroky goes into Manhattan for meetings or training sessions at the Makovsky office. "When I'm there it's energizing," she muses. "I miss the spontaneous ex-

change of ideas, the interaction with my peers. I really do like being there. I think, 'Gee, this would be terrific to work here in the city.' Then I come back to reality and realize all the benefits I have working at home." Those horse vistas again.

TURF WARS AND BACKWATERS

Well, thanks for the idyll, lady. I want your job. And your house. You can keep the kids. But how do you expect a poor working journalist to make hay out of your bucolic tranquility?

Telecommuting is getting a lot of positive play in the media. Telecommuting can be great. But it certainly isn't great for everybody. Even if it's right for you now, it might not always be right for you. And regardless of how attractive it might look going in, you'll have to do some serious planning.

Now I'm writing on what we call the balcony, a glorified second-story mop porch, about 6 feet by 10, overlooking the back yard. It's a little like being in a tree house. A line of looming catalpas runs down one boulevard. Blue spruce taller than houses tower in the neighbor's yard across the alley. Oak and elm and one bright yellow sunburst locust fill in the background. Front and center is a Russian olive I planted myself. Robins dive-bomb from its branches for bugs in the compost heap below.

A hotheaded male cardinal runs this turf, rocketing bright red after martins, starlings and blackbirds, whistling defiance from wherever he perches. In the distance, alone and splendid, *Ardea herodias*, the great blue heron, wings its way with prehistoric, ungainly dignity not far above the treetops, shuttling between hot, still backwaters along the river.

Is this a great way to work or what? Sure it is, except for one thing: I'm not working. I'm watching birds.

What does Jan Sherwin see out the window of her home office in Middlesex County, MA? "I see quite a lovely view of backyard lawn and a tree." What kind of tree? "A beech tree," says the NYNEX Corp. process reengineering director. "And some birds." What kind of birds? Sherwin quickly cools on the subject. "When I'm working," she says, "I don't spend a lot of time

looking out the window."

Telecommuting is a great way to do a job. It's very productive. You can blow off the soul-corroding hours of commute time, the grueling bus and train rides, the freeway Richard Petty wanna-bes who'll cut you off and leave you for dead.

For Kathie Blankenship, telecommuting is psychotherapy, two days of healing for three of commuting. She works at home two days a week to skip a 50-mile, sometimes two-hour drive from Danville, CA, to her job as communications vice president with Smart Valley Inc., a Santa Clara, CA, nonprofit trade association.

BUNNY SLIPPERS

"For me it's the only way to keep my sanity," she says. "I put on my bunny slippers. I walk to my office. I sit down at the computer and I do correspondence, thinking, phoning. When I drive back into work the next time I have a better state of mind."

Telecommuting lets you escape the standard office distractions—meetings, interruptions, the mad search for the missing file, the executive mood swings, the hotheaded turf battles, the corporate mating dances and posturing.

Telecommuting lets you work early and late, saving some in-between time for family—doctor visits, ball games, the occasional moments with the kids that if you miss they're gone forever and you'll never even know you missed them.

I have telecommuted and worked remote for years, and I will personally make the claim here and now that I can go virtual and be productive with anybody, anytime, from any room in my home including the bathroom, from any motel or church basement or beer joint in continental North America. Try me and see if I can't.

That said, let's tell the other truth about telecommuting. Because you see, virtual work has a rank underside.

DIRT AND WHISPERS

When you telecommute you're invisible. What does that do to your career? You're missing some or all of the workplace dirt, the little whispers that can mean so much: Who's in the doghouse? Who needs cheering up? Who's plotting

This dog has piddled on the carpet somewhere. On humid days you remember a thing like that.

Is this a great way to work? Sure, except for one thing: I'm not working. I'm watching birds.

for the job you might want? Do you even know about the job you might want?

You're missing the moments when somebody down the hall is in the right place at the right time to go partners with you on some little scheme to advance both your interests. You're blowing chances to look good in front of the right people. Burke Stinson, public relations manager with AT&T Corp. in Basking Ridge, NJ, puts it bluntly. "If the boss doesn't see you," Stinson says, "you lose suck-up opportunities."

When you move from a downtown office cubicle into your family den, you're loaning the company part of your house to hold down its overhead. Are you getting a cut of the avoided costs? No. You're saving the company money on tech support by doing most or all of your computer troubleshooting yourself. Are they grateful? No. You load your own software and train yourself to use it. Do you get paid extra? No.

In fact, maybe you took a demotion and a pay cut for the privilege of working remotely because the idea of a *manager* who isn't around the office is just too weird for most organizations to ponder. Whatever the money, whatever the status, you're working all hours, probably longer than you've ever worked before. Is it worth it?

Kim Keiser, public affairs administration manager for Champion International Corp. of Stamford, CT, says her peers confuse the days when she's telecommuting with the days when she's out sick or caring for a sick child. They call her at home as if she's on duty. "Kim, can you do this?" they ask. She sighs, "If I can get to it, I'll try."

When you *are* on duty at your home office, your peers may suspect the worst: They picture you kicking back on your sofa despoiling a box of Fanny Farmers and watching your favorite soaps. Then later, when you ask about the crisis at the office, they'll tell you acidly: "That's right. *You* weren't here when *that* broke."

Meanwhile you've been quietly skipping lunches, busting your hump, getting plenty of work done, and trying to decide how much longer you can stand it before you call your neighbor and

scream about his dog barking while you're trying to concentrate.

At the end of a long day the kids joyously tug you into their basement playroom because you promised them a game of Candyland. As long as you're back downstairs, right next to your office, you think, you might as well check your e-mail.

What then? Does the Candyland game ever happen? If it does, is your heart in it?

When you work at home, everybody in the family gets a piece of your office angst. They can't escape it and neither can you. Champion International's Keiser says she's trying to break her husband of a just-trying-to-be-helpful habit: When he happens to boot up their computer, the one they let the company use so she can do her work, he'll announce, "Kim, you have e-mail." "Oh, please," she scolds, "don't do that."

CHECKLIST FOR TELECOMMUTERS

- Establish a routine and follow it.
- Pace yourself. If you don't take breaks, you may find yourself dragging by 2:30 p.m.
- Become self-sufficient. It's not impossible to toss something on another person's desk, figuratively, when you're telecommuting, but it's harder.
- Be consistent with kids. Break protocol once, and they'll expect it every time. Office hours should be office hours, even if the little ones are bored with the baby sitter.
- Stay visible. Phone people. E-mail them. Ask team members to patch you in by speakerphone for scheduled meetings and even for impromptu meetings.
- Make sure you bring home more than enough work. Telecommuters tend to work faster at home than at the office.
- You say you're doing everything on your laptop computer and hauling it back and forth? Cool. But don't get cocky. What if you forget your power adapter at the office? Better have a spare at home, or plenty of battery capacity.
- Go buddies with somebody at the office to do legwork for you when you can't be there. When you need a paper document, your buddy can fax it. Or when you're trying to phone your boss about something urgent, but your boss is busy and isn't picking up, you need your buddy to go and flag the boss.
- Get a second phone line. It's not worth fighting with family members and fielding telemarketers' residential calls. Indeed, you might need a third line for fax and/or data so you're not missing calls when you're checking e-mail or going into a database.
- Don't have a fax machine at home? Locate a nearby fax service at a drugstore or copy center. In fact, locate one even if you do have a home machine— for the times when your fax goes down.
- Get to know your neighbors. Find out their names and phone numbers. When the local kids set up a lemonade stand under your window and start screaming their wares at the top of their lungs every time a car rolls past, it saves time just to call their parents instead of going out there and throttling them yourself.
- When the teenager across the street practices his guitar riffs at about 130 decibels with the windows open, call him up and let it ring. And ring. It might take half an hour, but sooner or later his fingers will get tired and he'll stop. Then he'll hear the phone.—**M.H.**

'If the boss doesn't see you, you lose suck-up opportunities.'

LOVE, NOT WORK

You finally curl up after the kids are in bed—then jump up to check whether that important call is in your voice mail. How does this affect your relationship with that woman you just left on the sofa? Did you catch the icy look, the light hiss of threadbare patience? "I'm from the old school," grumbles AT&T's Stinson. "My school says once you cross the threshold into your home, it's a place for relaxation, love, food. Not work."

Even if you have your own house in order, when you telecommute you have to deal with the neighbor kids' impromptu, prolonged bang-the-pots-and-pans parade while you're trying to find the six-figure mistake in the spreadsheet. The neighbors' sanding and sawing and remodeling never seems to stop. One day, unannounced, the jackhammers will be in the street first thing in the morning. The faucet will drip. The toilet will run. Always and forever, every window in the house will be open when it starts to rain.

More family time must make telecommuting worthwhile, doesn't it? Of course. But kids grow up. I left a staff job with another magazine years ago to free-lance so I could have more time with my then-toddler son. I'm delighted I did it. Wouldn't trade the memories for anything: toboggan rides to day care down the street, peanut butter and honey sandwiches after school. Then, too, there was the screaming in the back yard when he kneecapped a bigger kid with a baseball bat. All right, I thought I could work *and* watch my son that summer. I was wrong.

I still greeted him with milk and peanut butter after he got big and strong and didn't want to talk about his day in school anymore. At least I was there to unlock the door so he didn't have to kick it in if he forgot his key. But I had to ask him more than once to please turn down the volume of his thrash tunes so Daddy could finish work. And then Daddy would be going away for a while to check into an insane asylum.

BLOOD AND FIRE

You get the picture. By the time my son was 14, it was clear that me being

gone when he got home from school would probably be a good thing for both of us. I took this staff job. Now he can come home from school and play his Every Mother's Nightmare loud enough to make the neighbors' pipes shudder; from downtown, I can barely hear it.

Kids and telecommuting are a constant adventure. When you kiss the little darlings goodbye and close that door, it doesn't mean diddly. They know you're in there, and you know they know. You need discipline. You need rules. "When Mommy is in this room she is working and not to be interrupted," one NYNEX telecommuter tells her brood. "There are two exceptions. You may interrupt me if there is fire or if there is blood."

The standard advice is that when you're working at home you should *not* be taking care of kids. That's very good advice. But when you work at home just try and keep the kids out of the way. Asleep, awake, in or out of school or day care, kids always find ways to impose themselves.

Marina van Overbeek, workplace strategist with Cisco Systems Inc. of San Jose, CA, which makes networking systems for large-scale computer net-

works, says her 14-year-old leaves her alone when she's working at home. "He's at that stage in life where he doesn't want to have much to do with me anyway," she sighs.

But not the other one. "My daughter, who's 8, understands but doesn't always understand," van Overbeek says. "She will want me to get her a juice or come watch her do something or bring her a snack or generally be her slave."

Van Overbeek's solution: She farms out the youngster on days she wants to work at home, sending her to after-school care or to a neighbor's to play.

DOG DAYS

If anything is more incompatible with telecommuting than kids, it would be animals. You've heard the stories: The dog is accustomed to its romp and biffy break when its beloved master comes home at end of day, and said beloved master suddenly starts working at home two days a week, whereupon the dog's biorhythms get totally out of kilter and it puddles indoors. The cat prowling the desk and hacking hairballs into the printer. And so forth.

Emily Bassman, director of virtual

'I'm from the old school: Home is a place for relaxation, love, food. Not work.'

The golden retriever rambled over and laid a magnificent belch right into the speakerphone.

office development for Pacific Bell, tangles with three cats and two dogs while she's telecommuting at her home 18 miles from the San Ramon, CA, Pac Bell office. She could just close her home-office door to exclude the troop, she admits, but she likes the ventilation and she wants to listen to CNN on TV in the other room.

Trixie is a fool for love, and Bassman must patiently and repeatedly lift the persistent tabby down from the desktop. Bassman says her workaday phone mates take the barking in stride when golden retrievers Perry and Dolly announce the news that Federal Express is at the door. Still, Bassman is glad she was talking to a particularly understanding peer when an out-of-sorts Perry rambled over and laid a magnificent belch right into the speakerphone.

GETTING BUSINESSLIKE

Some companies lay down the law when it comes to home-front interruptions. American Express requires child care: Import a nanny or ship 'em to day care, just don't try to watch them yourself. And if you have an animal, it had better be a quiet one. "Our clients should not be calling in hearing dogs barking or children crying," warns Yee Jao, project leader for American Express' work-at-home travel agents. "We have the ability to monitor phone calls and screen."

Other companies are more lenient. Insurer ITT Hartford Group Inc. of Hartford, CT, doesn't require child care for telecommuters with kids. Can you work while the little nippers nap? Fine. "If the work gets done, there's not an issue," says Karon Moore, director of diversity (she runs the flexible-work program as well) for ITT Hartford Group.

How *should* companies approach the subject of telecommuting? Start at the beginning. Business is business, and the company should have a strategic business reason for letting people telecommute. That somebody simply might want to isn't a good enough reason, argues Kathleen Parrish, an engineering supervisor at Arizona Public Service Co. in Phoenix, who led a telecommuting pilot for her company.

The organization wants to save mon-

ey on office space? That's a business reason, but not necessarily a good one. Involuntary telecommuters can find a multitude of ways to be unproductive, at which point you'll have little choice but to bring them back to the office or replace them with raw recruits who'll probably have to spend some time in the office learning the ropes. Either way, the telecommuting scheme is a turkey.

One good business reason: Arizona Public Service was going to lose some of its hard-to-replace nuclear engineers if they didn't get less commute time and more time for families, says Parrish.

Another business reason would be productivity. Homely distractions notwithstanding, recall those expert claims that telecommuters still tend to be more productive than peers back at the office.

But the company must have clear measures in order to know how productive its telecommuters are. Arizona Public Service developed a software tool to record and analyze changes in the amount of time spent on productive work (vs. interruptions) as a function of work location, including home. Hewlett-Packard Co. measures call volume for its help-desk engineers who assist computer system administrators. HP software engineer Greg Schall of suburban Atlanta says his productivity jumped 40 percent when he began working from home.

MANAGING AIR

Supervisors must learn to manage these airy associates, these phone voices, these electronic wisps. How? Set objectives and check to see if they're met on time. That's just good management, after all. But is that really all there is to it?

Maybe not. "I think there's a lot of communication that gets missed talking over the phone," says Jim Donnelly, based in San Jose, CA, as general manager of AT&T Business Communication Services. "I think part of leadership is how you treat people—laughter, touch, kidding around. I think in a telecommuting environment it can become less personal."

When Donnelly himself telecommuted a couple of days a week for a month, some of the members on the nine teams for which he's responsible

started bickering, losing focus while they fought over side issues. Competitive people push things sometimes, and a few individuals weren't on their best behavior in the absence of the boss. Donnelly concludes that managers have to be there in the flesh for their people.

Other managers are trying to make it work from a distance. Vi Beaudreau, director of ITT Hartford Group's advanced-technology unit in Hartford, CT, had to learn how to supervise Marcia Tingley working at her home in Minneapolis.

"The hard part had to do with trust," says Beaudreau, "counting on one another to communicate the right thing, getting real clear for the employee." That takes some soft skills, a sensitive-'90s-kind-of-guy approach. "A traditional, hard-core, command-and-control manager," says Beaudreau, "probably should not try this."

Telecommuting keeps the boss from looking over their shoulders? Good, many will say. But they still want technical support, don't they? And when they telecommute, tech support can't sit with them and show them what to do. It can only talk to them on the phone.

Train telecommuters to be their own first-line tech support. Don't assume they'll figure it out. Not even computer-literate workers—not even computer workers—will know all they need to know about setting up hardware and installing and using software.

Computer-applications researcher Tingley considers herself pretty adept at software but finds an upgrade from Windows 3.1 to Windows 95 daunting. She's hoping for remote help. "I'm a little nervous about this situation," she confesses. "Technical support is very difficult to do from a distance."

NETWORK *THIS*

Some problems will be out of the company's hands entirely. Lisa Converse, who books IBM corporate travel as an agent with American Express travel services, took a demotion from supervisor to be able to telecommute five days a week from her Stratford, CT, home. But Converse had to wait for the phone company to send people

'Calm down, Kathie. Don't throw your PC out the window. You'll regret that later. Trust me. This will be OK.'

out not once but twice to get the lines right, and her equipment likewise required a long wait.

When her computer-link phone line died this spring, Converse and her help-desk guy had to turn to the phone company again to spot the problem in a relay. Back at the office, a worker can move from a crashed machine to one that's up. Not at home. Meanwhile, some telecommuters might be strapped for something to do.

Some home-front techno-conflicts will be a matter of personal choice. "People want to communicate with me via fax," says Cisco Systems' van Overbeek, "and I don't have a fax machine because I don't *want* a fax machine at home going off all the time."

One can get by without a fax, of course. Mary-Louise Houghton Polo, an operations manager with ITT Hartford Group, didn't have a fax at her Ivoryton, CT, home when she was called in on a crash project. She had documents faxed to a copy service a mile down the road.

Smart Valley's Blankenship, a Mac devotee, was switched to a PC at her home office when her employer started working exclusively in a PC environment. For those who can't sympathize, it's like this: When you live and breathe one environment long enough, when your fingers do the thinking for you, trying to get something done in the other environment is like trying to stuff a pterodactyl into a cement mixer.

When Blankenship crashed the new system, she stared out the window at her tranquil five acres of pine trees and manzanita, where the hummingbirds browse among the flowering bushes. It was 50 miles to work. That's two hours, California time. She was also staring at her swimming pool.

Blankenship got on the phone. "My computer has just crashed," she told Cyrus, the computer guy. "I'm at the point of throwing my monitor out the window, Cyrus. It will land in the pool. What should I do?"

"Calm down, Kathie," Cyrus told her soothingly. "Don't throw out your PC. You'll regret that later. Trust me. This will be OK."

This may be the most important point of all: Telecommuters need a Cyrus.

ARE WE BONKERS YET?

And not just a Cyrus. Virtual workers need some kind of hard-to-define moral support. Homo sapiens is a social creature. We want to be with others. We like it. We can't help it. That's how we're made. Sadie the collie may be a beloved companion, but she's no substitute for human contact. "I like talking to other people," says AT&T's Stinson. "When you're in your home office there's no give and take. How many ideas can you bounce off your cat?"

Staying busy is a good idea for telecommuters. Greg Schall works at his suburban Atlanta home as an electronic-messaging customer-support engineer for Hewlett-Packard Co. He has $12,000 worth of HP equipment in his spare-bedroom office: ISDN line for plenty of bandwidth; Unix workstation and a PC, both networked to an HP hub; fax and printer. When your company's help-desk folk need help, they call people like Schall. "I can do everything from home that I can do from the office," he says proudly.

Schall lives and works in Acworth, 33 miles north of Atlanta. Out his office window he sees his lilies—lemon lilies, day lilies, tigers. The software engineer spends nine hours a day worrying about other people's problems, but he typically spends the day by himself. Lunch might be leftover pizza. Most days Schall doesn't see anybody until his 13-year-old son Zachary comes home from school.

"You do get lonely sometimes," Schall volunteers. "I hesitate to add that as a problem or a challenge. But I know that with my scenario, being a single parent, it gets even lonelier than it might be otherwise."

Schall stays busy coaching and refereeing soccer with Zachary and tending his lily bed. He goes to the office once every two or three weeks, and his team of support engineers gets together for dinner every six weeks.

Is it enough? Some people can work like that indefinitely and love it. Others can't. "They are going to feel that their world has caved in on them," Sherwin of NYNEX warns.

Right now, though, HP's Schall is happy with his situation. He is taking the lead in pushing for more telecommuting in his unit.

So telecommuting works. Except when it doesn't. Personally, I'm having a counter-reformation with regard to telecommuting. I can't work at home so much anymore. A nervous Airedale across the street barks at pigeons and anything else that moves, including air molecules. Its piercing bellows echo between the tall old houses. And my teenager has juiced the speakers on the stereo. It was a school science project, so I couldn't complain. But now even "Moonlight Sonata" comes out so loud it strips plaster.

I'm glad I have a downtown office. It's a refuge of sorts. Not that I can write there either. But telecommuting is terrific. Try it sometime. Me? Next time I need to write maybe I'll check into a monastery.

Working Out the Kinks

Companies could reduce workers' comp claims and injuries if they paid attention to how employees are working. An ounce of prevention is worth a pound of cure where repetitive strain injuries are concerned.

CATHERINE ROMANO

At the top of the decade, carpal tunnel syndrome and a variety of ailments that fall under the umbrella of repetitive strain injuries were the hot topic. More and more office workers were experiencing the effects of RSI, something production and manufacturing workers had suffered from for years. (RSI can actually be traced back to 18th-century Italian clerks and scribes; a researcher described the cause of their ailments as "continuous sitting, repeated use of the hand and strain of the mind.")

In modern day, the perception was that computer usage was to blame for repetitive strain injuries, and since 70 percent of the population was expected to use computers by 2000, nearly everyone was at risk.

The subject garnered so much attention that there were more than 1,200 newspaper and magazine stories on repetitive stress injuries in 1993 alone—thanks in part to journalists who themselves were experiencing symptoms such as tingling, numbness, in the hands and fingers from sitting at their keyboards all day.

Three years later, much has changed and yet nothing has changed. Computer users are still at risk of developing RSI, but no more than any other group and actually less than workers in other industries. The Bureau of Labor Statistics reported that about 1,396 out of every 10,000 meat-packing plant workers are afflicted with RSI compared with 44 out of every 10,000 newspaper employees. Mentions of repetitive stress injuries in magazine and newspaper stories dropped in 1994 by more than 10 percent, and virtually no one spends time anymore discussing the best wrist rests to purchase.

Yet, despite the decrease in attention, RSI is still a problem. The Occupational Health and Safety Administration (OSHA) data reveals that in 1993 employers reported 302,000 upper-extremity repeated trauma cases, which primarily consist of carpal tunnel syndrome and shoulder tendinitis. In 1983, that number was only 22,700. Adjust those numbers to reflect the changes in the size of the employed population and that is a more than sevenfold increase in 10 years.

"It's more of a problem because more companies are using computer technology and trying to put new technology onto old furniture," says Dr. Rab Cross, the co-author of the soon-to-be-published *ErgoSense* (AMACOM, 1996). In addition, more people are using computers in their homes, perhaps at a laptop on the kitchen table or at a poorly designed computer workstation.

OSHA was even going to promulgate ergonomic standards to make it easier for the federal agency to levy fines against white-collar workplaces. The standards would have required evaluation of the workplace and individual work sites through injury or illness logs, an ergonomics-risk-factor checklist, a review of records for the previous two years and an identification of all ergonomic hazards. OSHA's proposal was put on hold because of congressional budget debates, and ergonomics continues to be covered under the general duty clause which requires that "every employer shall furnish to each of his employees employment and a place of employment which are free from recognized hazards which are causing or are likely to cause death or serious physical harm to his employees."

Some companies were troubled by the legislation because it is difficult to isolate the exact causes of work-related musculoskeletal disorders. It would be hard to create requirements backed by quantifiable information that OSHA inspectors would be able to enforce. "There is no data that says how many keystrokes per hour causes injury," says Bradley Joseph, corporate ergonomist for Ford Motor Co.

Repetitive strain injuries are defined as cumulative trauma disorder (CTD) resulting from prolonged, repetitive, forceful or awkward movements. RSI is actually a form of muscle strain or tendinitis, which is painful but not crippling. Carpal tunnel syndrome, a condition that is often incorrectly used interchangeably with RSI, is caused by pressure on the median nerve in the wrist. Surgery is often required to alleviate this debilitating condition. An example of the condition's severity: one writer, by age 26, was unable to drive a car, type or even

BRIEFCASE

After paying dearly for workers' compensation claims stemming from repetitive strain injuries, companies are realizing it's time to be proactive. Attention to ergonomics will avert lawsuits, workers' comp claims and employee injury—and make for more comfortable, and hence, productive, workers.

ronment can be modified so the task can be performed safely.

Others approach the situation with a bottom-line sensibility: These workers' comp claims are expensive. According to OSHA, work-related musculoskeletal disorders now account for one-third of all money spent on workers' comp, and it costs as much as $20 billion a year in direct costs. The Bureau of Labor Statistics reports that the median amount of time away from work due to repetitive motion injuries is six days.

write with a ballpoint pen because of carpal tunnel syndrome developed from keyboard use at work.

And while research has identified the major risk factors as force, frequency and posture, it has also clarified factors that can exacerbate the problems: diabetes, pregnancy, thyroid conditions, oral contraceptives, heredity and the individual's threshold for injury. "There is a highly complex set of circumstances which lead to injury," says Dr. Emil Pascarelli, professor of clinical medicine at Columbia University College of Physicians and Surgeons.

The complexity of the condition leads to an unfortunate reality—many of these problems are often misunderstood and misdiagnosed. According to Pascarelli, evaluation of such injuries is a time-consuming process that crosses medical disciplines to include general practice, occupational medicine and psychology. "Traditionally physicians tend to view problems in terms of their own specialty," explains Pascarelli. A thorough evaluation requires observing and videotaping a patient in a work setting, which is rarely done.

Cross agrees, "Patients go in with tendinitis and come out with carpal tunnel syndrome. There is a lot of overdiagnosis since a lot of people who see it and treat it are not accustomed to seeing a lot of it."

Worth the Cost

With companies cutting costs left and right, it makes sense that ergonomics would not make the top of the spending list, especially if there is even the slightest evidence that a patient's problem may not be as serious. But employers are seeing a different side to the situation.

Employers, at least the progressive ones, are recognizing that it's a problem worth fixing. Ergonomics managers—the existence of whom is a credit to the importance companies affix to the health and well-being of their employees—believe that improvements can be made by fitting a particular job to a person, rather than the person to the job. The principles of ergonomics are used to evaluate a job or task, a workstation, the equipment used or processes used to complete the task. The job or envi-

From Theory to Practice

Companies have approached the situation in a variety of ways, but the experts' consensus is that each situation must be looked at individually. "There's no magic bullet in ergonomics. You can't give them an adjustable chair and leave," says Ted Rooney, manager of employee health management at L.L. Bean.

"There's no magic bullet in ergonomics. You can't give them an adjustable chair and leave."

—Ted Rooney, L.L. Bean

Instead, L.L. Bean has created adjustable stations so that employees can change positions throughout the day—either at a sitting or a sitting/standing station. Individual workstations are designed with the height of the user in mind. "There is no one perfect ergonomic standard. The human wasn't meant to sit in one place continually," explains Rooney.

L.L. Bean's system works well with their 4,000 full-time employees, but the company cannot create such individualized workstations when its workforce doubles at peak times. It sets up temporary stations, which are not as adjustable as the permanent fixtures. Employees are assigned to a station based on their height. Even though these employees are temporary, L.L. Bean would still be responsible for their workers' comp claims.

To tie the program together, L.L. Bean appointed ergonomics representatives, hourly employees they train to be a resource to other employees. According to Rooney, L.L. Bean follows the tenets of TQM, one of which is involving the workers in the way work gets done. The system works well when combating one of the major problems associated with workplace injury—employees will work through the pain, without stopping to fix the situation. "We don't have to have a professional ergonomist or health nurse [nearby] if the person sitting next to them can help," says Rooney.

Rosemount Measurement Division, a subsidiary of Emerson Electric Co. in Eden Prairie, Minn., encourages already existing process-improvement teams to address ergonomics and safety. "They know their jobs better than anyone," says Tom Smolarek, senior ergonomics engineer. "Why have an outside team come in?"

These companies want employees to feel comfortable identifying problems—early prevention is cheaper and easier to correct. Rooney believes, "We make a big deal of not making ergonomics a big deal. We're hopeful that after a while you don't have to pay so much extra attention to it; it becomes the way you do business."

American Express Financial Corp. has certainly found this to be true. The goal, according to Nancy Larson, the company's ergonomics manager, is to "have ergonomics become incorporated into the culture." Sixty-five percent to 70 percent of employees change workstations yearly, and the company uses the moves as a chance to customize workspace and provide information and training.

Even small changes, such as having ergonomics training included in new-employee orientation, are paying off. Since her company started these programs, Larson reports that there have been fewer people taking time off and the claims they do have are less severe.

"Companies will show a good effect if ergonomics are done correctly," says Dr. David Rempel, assistant professor of medicine at the University of California at San Francisco. "There will be reductions in lost-time injuries, overall workers' comp, and improved employee satisfaction."

Witness Ford Motor Co.'s improvements. After Ford and the United Auto Workers formed a joint committee on health and safety and implemented programs to find and fix ergonomic problems, there was an 80 percent drop in cumulative trauma in one plant. That same plant, which Joseph admits represents a good ergonomic example, reduced its lost-time days from 1,870 to 554.

Joseph believes that correcting bad situations doesn't have to be expensive. Since Ford and UAW began keeping a record at one plant in 1990 to 1991, costs for fixing ergonomic problems have been approximately $2 million. But, he says, "on the prevention side, it doesn't cost you anything if you designed it right the first time."

Companies often make the mistake of believing that an ergonomic label means it is more expensive. You can buy a footrest for $25 or a forearm support for $40, rather than spending $5,000 redesigning the entire office. Off-the-shelf solutions can be very effective, and that is the first place employees look for fixes to ergonomic problems. Larson noticed a decrease in complaints once it made ergonomic supplies available through regular interoffice mail. What's more, no special requisitions are needed to get a wrist support or copy stand. "Try to fit the function of the job and add a little extra, adjusting it to fit the person," says Rooney.

This game plan also has its drawbacks, according to Dr. Rab Cross, who is not convinced you can upgrade an office without spending a lot of money. "After so many Band-Aids, it becomes an uncomfortable dressing," he explains. Good-quality furniture is a smart investment that can be amortized over a few years, says Cross. Timing is also key—replace old furniture or equipment with ergonomic equivalents.

The importance of buying new furniture is determined by management. In some cases, managers are reluctant to buy new equipment because they fear that if one person gets new furniture, everyone will demand equality. But in some companies, managers are getting accustomed to viewing the purchase of office furniture as a regular business expense. "Management may have been reluctant to spend $400 on a chair, but after they've done it a while, it becomes okay, a cost of doing business," says Smolarek.

Having the right equipment and furniture is a start, but the equation is incomplete without training. Not providing training, says Pascarelli, is akin to "expecting employees to play golf just by giving them a golf club."

A lack of proper training counteracts the benefits of even the best office furniture. "We had good equipment. Our furniture had adjustability," says Joseph. "But people didn't know how to use it." So Ford piloted an hour-long training program in which it coaches small groups on how to use the equipment. Employees can also borrow equipment to see if it fits their needs before ordering it.

Larson offers open ergonomics sessions so that employees with questions and problems have a place to address them immediately. That kind of timeliness is needed, as is individual attention to problems. Says Pascarelli, "You can't have a one-size-fits-all situation. People have different ergonomic needs."

For James Mendelsohn and his colleagues at Perdue Farms, instant and urgent communications has an almost incalculable value. The manager of marketing research and information for the Salisbury, Md.-based firm, Mendelsohn explains Perdue is a far-flung enterprise that deals in a perishable commodity. Thus, tools such as voice mail, e-mail, cellular phones, and beepers are like nerves that carry impulses, which in turn drive a timely distribution system.

This is especially important for Mendelsohn and Perdue. "As we say in our business," relates the poultry peddler, "you either sell it or smell it."

But in a lament that is increasingly common at large companies, those same tools are raising an electronic cacophony that's louder and more demanding than a henhouse at feeding hour. "When I'm faced with 50 e-mails and a couple of dozen voice mails, the chore is to sort out what's important from what's not relevant to my job," says Mendelsohn. "I find myself

Are you and your workers really coping with the glut of e-mail, voice mail, and faxes? Here's how others deal with it.

delsohn, "at times, I go home realizing I haven't completed any of the tasks that I'd planned for that day."

Welcome to the world of communications overload, an environment in which a torrent of messages pelts people like a relentless Seattle rain. As the intensity of the deluge grows, we're only beginning to feel the true effects of being soaked in a surfeit of information.

A variety of services and technologies have facilitated an explosion of rapid communications, be it carried by overnight express couriers, fax machines, voice mail, the Internet, the World Wide Web, e-mail, and other systems. Changes in organizational structures have also contributed to the exchange. Self-directed teams—an evolution facilitated by easy-access e-mail—have generated a tremendous need for fast, cross-functional communications. In turn, there are fewer supervisors to filter information and serve as gatekeepers, sending out what is essential and spiking the egregiously trivial.

As a result, corporations have undergone a *sociological* change.

Call it the Great Democratization of corporate com-

Overload

By Jay Stuller

spending an awful lot of time these days on electronic-communications overhead."

He has also discovered that the ever-mounting backlog of requests and FYI messages is compounded by the company's electronic scheduling system, a form of "groupware." On a computer, his colleagues can see when he's available; this makes it easy for them to schedule Mendelsohn into a chock-full day of cross-functional study-team and task-force meetings. "Even though I have the right to say no," he explains, "the system is a real facilitator for bringing disparate people with complicated schedules together. So I end up going to a lot of meetings." When he's away, internal and external message senders continue to play.

"After dealing with one unexpected message or request after another," says Men-

munications. For better or worse, these systems enable thousands of employees to function as individual publishers.

For large, complex, or multinational companies, the systems are essential. But thanks to the miracle of electronic mail, a typical manager may well boot up a computer, only to find a critical report or request for information encased by 15 FYI copies from study teams, each announcing they've completed a quality process step. Whoopee. In the backlog of e-mail that's growing faster than kudzu, Sally's latest joke about Anna Nicole Smith may be considered a must-read. Among the clatter and tangle, senior management occasionally gets in a word edgewise: The CEO might make an announcement about some huge new corporate strategy.

"This is not an 'information' problem, since

From *Across the Board,* April 1996, pp. 16-22. © 1996 by Jay Stuller. Reprinted by permission of the author.

From Kazakstan With E-Love

Arriving at the Tengiz field for his 28-day shift after 28 days at home in the United States, Charlie Auvermann came to dread one particular task. "My computer would be stuffed with hundreds of e-mails," says the public-affairs supervisor at Tengizchevroil (TCO), a joint oil-production venture between the Republic of Kazakstan and Chevron Corp. "Important messages would be buried among reports of lost wedding rings and power shutdowns that had happened two weeks before. It seemed like I'd spend a full day on e-mail triage, sorting out the critical from the trivial."

Auvermann wasn't alone in his frustration. TCO's 1,100 e-mail users—about 30 percent of whom are expatriates working 28-day rotations—were flooding each other with missives.

"Even as the use and costs of the system increased," says Auvermann, "we started to notice that communications gaps were developing, mainly because of the information clutter."

A small quality action team was formed to tackle this rather complex technological, behavioral, and organizational issue. The team's first recommendation: Remove the "All E-Mail Users" address from the system. Whenever message-senders had the slightest doubt about the relative importance of a message, "All Users" had turned into a first and last resort, ensuring the coverage of all bases.

"Today, just about anyone who wants to reach the entire organization has to go through our Information Communications Services help desk," Auvermann explains. "The team developed guidelines for these information gatekeepers, to help them sort out the relative importance of messages. And then the team developed alternate places in which to put various announcements."

One alternate is an electronic bulletin board linked to the e-mail system. It's the place to find general TCO announcements and the latest airline and bus schedules, but, most important, the information isn't forced upon users. In addition, the bulletin board includes a monthly electronic newsletter, with material of interest of the entire employee population.

The company also put up physical bulletin boards in cafeterias and other common areas. Says Auvermann: "The old tried-and-true really works for things that are important but aren't time-sensitive or limited to one audience."

For notices of power shutdowns, lost wedding rings, and the like, TCO set up a daily "sign-on bulletin board." That is, when e-mail users sign on at the start of each day, the screen shows a list of messages, with labels ranking their urgency. A message marked with INFO, for example, may be an explanation of an operational disruption or a description of a new security procedure. A message labeled QUICK means it is more urgent—say, a notice of bad road conditions—but not of lasting interest. "This way," Auvermann says, "people can quick-scan the notices at the start of the day, use the labels for triage, and get on with the rest of their work."

Removing the "All E-Mail Users" feature from the system took away the easiest message-sending option. Yet it forced TCO's people to think in terms of narrower target audiences. "There's been a real drop in common or junk mail," Auvermann observes. "People can still locate and use what they need. The system is by no means perfect. But we may be closing some of the communications gaps that form when you get too much disorganized information."**—J.S.**

just about any piece of information is important to someone in an organization," says Dave De Long, a research fellow with Ernst & Young's Boston-based Center for Business Innovation, who interviewed subjects at nine major companies for a paper on the topic. "It's a communications concern, because of the number of channels that are available and how many people use them. The recipients of the messages are starting to feel the impact of having 8,000 chefs in the kitchen."

The upshot, adds De Long, is more than an annoyance. "This is not a case of employees whining about hard work. The complaints I've heard come from the recognition that the overload has serious implications for organizational performance." In other words, De Long maintains that the load could evolve into a true productivity crisis—if it has not already gripped American workers by their throats.

Too Much of a Good Thing

At the most senior levels of management, this threat is barely flashing on the executive radar screen. "Senior executives are among the few in corporate America who still have secretaries and assistants who help filter and manage information," notes De Long.

However, since 1987, the number of secretaries employed in the United States has declined by more than a half-million. Replaced by voice-mail systems and computers with e-mail, this has saved costs. But as a result, it's the middle managers and professionals who are forced to handle an inundation of incoming requests, FYI copies of everything imaginable, stuff from shared data bases, and all the information that pours in from trade, profession, and industry sources.

With downsizing, many professionals need these tools to do the work that once required two or more employees.

This is quite wonderful from the current business standpoint. Instant access to all the data a knowledge worker could ever want—and tight links with co-workers, vendors, and customers—is an Information Age dream come true. It's part of why during the 1990s, nonfarm U.S. productivity has increased by 2.2 percent annually, double the rate of the past couple of decades, as measured by the U.S. Bureau of Labor Statistics. In 1996, those investments in information technologies are driving per-worker output to what could be a 3.5 percent gain over 1994.

"This is what's pushing American productivity ahead of the rest of the world," says management guru Robert H. Waterman. "When I visit companies in Europe or Japan, they simply don't have the information-technology systems that are comparable." Indeed, according to the International Data Corp., America has 63 computers for every 100 workers employed, including machines at home and in schools; Japan has but 17 computers for every 100 workers. We are riding the crest of a huge wave.

"The full use of the information highway is one of the things America does right," adds Waterman. "And I've yet to see communication overload hurt productivity at any of the companies I've consulted with. On the other hand, I do worry about the human capacity to absorb such an overwhelming amount of information, especially when several channels are full and flowing at top speed."

This is also true for workers who are already stretched to the thinness of phyllo dough. And as any surfer will attest, when you fall from the crest of a big wave, it has a nasty habit of pounding you straight into the sand.

"I know people who routinely get 50 to 100 e-mails per day, and some receive as many as 500," says De Long. "If you average a minute dealing with each one, the magnitude of the volume is obvious." To avoid a larger backlog of e-mails, voice mails, and the demands for responses, a growing number of workers are now taking defensive postures, leaving their

systems full. Still others simply dump the wheat along with the chaff.

"I interviewed the CFO of a large Silicon Valley company who'd just come back from a week's vacation to find 2,000 e-mails in his computer," recalled De Long. "He told me, and kind of sheepishly, that he'd erased all of them. 'If it's important,' he said, 'they'll get back to me.' A CFO can get away with this; a middle manager might end up in big trouble."

Such avoidance behavior is increasingly pervasive. Ever notice how colleagues leave voice mails at times when they know you're not around to answer calls? "It's even easier to hide behind e-mail," says Mendelsohn. "If someone doesn't want to be pulled into a dialogue, during which you might be asked to respond to even more requests, these systems provide protection. Now, I think e-mail is great for sending information to a large number of people. But I prefer the camaraderie and the give-and-take you get from personal interactions."

Superhighway Gridlock

The communications channels are embedded, systemic, and, on the whole, a great industrial plus. But if they continue to evolve without some modification in their use, says De Long, the overload creates a number of ticking organizational time bombs. "There are two broad issues," he explains. "The first is the personal impact on workers. The other is the way it influences the organization's ability to meet its goals and adapt to change."

Workers are using information technology to shift the time and place in which they deal with electronic messages. Increasingly, this is done at home, which no doubt warms the hearts of managers who need to get every second of work possible out of each employee.

Such shifting is just fine with the likes of Catherine Fanning, director of project information management for Johnson & Johnson's Pharmaceutical Research Institute in Raritan, N.J. "I'd be lost on Monday morning," Fanning explains, "if I didn't spend an hour or so on Sunday evening cleaning up my e-mail." But others are taking their responses and dedication to the extreme.

"When I give presentations on this subject," says De Long, "I ask people how many of them find themselves checking on voice mails after 10 p.m. About two-thirds of the hands go up. I worry about people who quickly shuffle young kids off to bed so they can log on to the company system. If it comes down to spending time on the Internet or with your daughter, the right choice ought to be self-evident."

Perhaps. But communications overload is starting to twist some fundamental values.

And from the coldest of business perspectives, well, tough luck, kiddies, Mom and Dad are busy. But the effects of the load also appear at the office.

De Long suggests that key value-added functions, such as sales and marketing, may fail to get a quick response from crucial but overwhelmed support functions. Strategic projects or change initiatives lose momentum or merely get lost in the clutter of communications. Because so many messages appear through so many channels, employees have a difficult time separating what is truly important from what is routine.

Longtime employees, observed De Long, are too busy to share vital knowledge with new hires about processes, customers, and the organization's history. Perhaps worst of all, senior managers who have adapted to the telecommunications environment are often distracted by an onslaught of requests, all of which appear urgent. This leaves little time to contemplate the larger issues that determine the course of their business and its future.

In fact, no one these days seems to get much time for reflection and learning. Workers have little chance to build their knowledge and skill bases—other than learning the nuts and bolts of yet another new communications system. "The tyranny of the urgent really is upon us," says Richard Hillebrecht, Apple Computer Inc.'s director, information systems & technology.

"I came in one Saturday hoping to do some planning-type work," he continues, "and ended up going 0-for-six hours doing nothing but answering leftover e-mail. During the working day, it does seem like the only 'learning time' that people now have is for instruction on yet another communications system."

Hours for deep analytical thought and reflection are indeed limited and perhaps no longer even prized. "In our culture," says Perdue's Mendelsohn, "if you're sitting in your office reading a book or paper memo, people look at you as if you're not working; the phone and computer is work. We've put a value on haste. But there are knowledge-based jobs in which what you learn from reading a book might be the most important thing you do all year."

In organizations that are operating at warp speed, that urgency makes everything, including trivial issues, seem important. While working terribly fast, employees still aren't getting as far as they can or should.

"We deliver about 1.5 million e-mails per day," says Bob Walker, Hewlett-Packard Co.'s vice president and chief information officer, "and most people in this company feel like they're getting all 1.5 million. Folks are constantly telling me, 'Bob, you've got to stop this.' The odd thing is that we've had a classic e-mail system for 12 years; we're supposed to be sophisticated in this area. And it's not as if people are sending information maliciously. When any employee sends an e-mail to colleagues, he or she is convinced that it's important."

However, HP is not about to stanch the flow of information. "Our longstanding belief is that we empower people by telling them what we want but not how to do it," Walker continues. "With all that autonomy, we've created a whole lot of opportunities for our people to interrupt each other."

A Question of Context

This raises another productivity issue, in that different working groups assign different priorities to various channels. This makes it difficult to spread essential information to all of a company's employees.

For example, an engineering division of a company might well consider e-mail the most important form of communication. Since it's the medium that carries critical items, each member of the group knows that a missive will be checked out and receive a response. But a design group might gravitate to voice mail or printed faxes as its priority channel; with this bunch, e-mails ring no bells. Neither way is right or wrong, but assuming that another group has the same priority as yours risks miscommunication.

"A division president gave his employees a 24-hour notice about a meeting to discuss a major reorganization," relates De Long. "A lot of people didn't see the message and missed the meeting. That started a considerable swell of employee gossip about the motives behind that 'last-minute' e-mail message."

What's more, for major change initiatives and corporatewide strategies, says De Long, senior management must identify and use a channel that all employees understand is priority. "If a major issue gets squeezed into the mass of messages," he explains, "its importance and meaning will be missed."

There are also profound and often-overlooked differences between the various channels. "We simply could not operate as a worldwide enterprise without e-mail," says Johnson & Johnson's Fanning. "With all the time-zone differences, it's the only way we can get things done." And as Mendelsohn of Perdue suggests, folks have become so comfortable with electronic mail that they're using it for nearly all communications.

But the most effective form of communication—the one with the greatest power, richness and value—is direct. Aside from the thoughts expressed in a face-to-face meeting, additional nuance and meaning are conveyed

> As for the CEO, he finally took himself off the e-mail system. "The guy was getting cc'ed with every 'cover your ass' memo written."

through tone, facial expressions, and body language. What's more, the listener has a chance to respond immediately, and a consensus is reached much more quickly than with other channels.

"A phone conversation is next down the list, followed by voice mail and finally e-mails," says De Long, who cites the example of a pharmaceutical research manager who had a problem with a certain formulation. "She needed to find a consensus among the people involved and started to send out an e-mail," he recalls. "But e-mail gets awfully public, and when you don't want leaks or are dealing with a sensitive subject, an e-mail is the last channel you'd want to use."

Yet another aspect of the overload is the inappropriate use of e-mail. Electronic mailboxes have turned into "cc hell," repositories for FYIs and other data put there by individuals mainly to show their colleagues and superiors that they're producing work.

De Long has found that e-mail messages often fail to contain information that lets the recipient figure out its importance. "And senders have this habit of burying action requests deep in lengthy items," he explains. "It then takes readers longer to recognize if they have to respond right away or have some time to act upon the request." And just as constantly ringing phones can make a worker who needs reflective time downright daffy, e-mails can be equally intrusive.

But it's a fact that in some corporate cultures, the number of e-mails one receives each day is the stuff of macho braggadocio. Microsoft employees, for example, have boasted of their e-mail load for years. (Despite repeated telephone requests, Microsoft offered no company officials willing to talk with *ATB* about this.) To help people manage the information glut, the techies at Microsoft have developed an "exchange server," a filtering mechanism that collects and delivers messages from all the various channels; with preprogramming, it can sort out the stuff the recipient

thinks isn't needed. It is, of course, a technical solution to the problem.

"That's crazy, just plain nuts," says Waterman. "Why even try to develop a technological solution to what is, fundamentally, a human behavioral problem?"

Probably because the techies can't help themselves.

A Case for Quiet Time

However, some firms are trying to deal with the overload at the behavioral level, to get employees either to send fewer unnecessary or pointless e-mail memos, or free them—albeit temporarily—from the tyranny of the urgent.

One of the most notable approaches is that of Computer Associates in Icelandia, N.Y. There, chairman and CEO Charles Wang ordered the company's e-mail system to be shut down from either 10 a.m. until noon or 2 p.m. to 4 p.m. "When it first happened, it was like quitting cigarettes," says Marc Sokol, the firm's vice president of advanced technology. "We had 9,000 very edgy employees. But as we got used to it, people found that they had time to think. We now like those periods when we can concentrate on tasks at hand."

As for Wang, he finally took himself off the e-mail system. "The guy was getting cc'ed with every 'cover your ass' memo written," says Sokol. "Now, if you want to meet with the CEO, go to his office or call."

Computer Associates may well write a computer application like Microsoft's Exchange to "take out stupid e-mails," says Sokol, "even though people shouldn't be sending them in the first place."

If enforced quiet time isn't enough, a company can always use financial disincentives. At Philadelphia-based SmithKline Beecham, the pharmaceutical firm's business units are charged fees based on the number and length of the unit's e-mail message. The company's manager for electronic messaging reports that the measure has produced a "dramatic falloff in the total number of messages," especially cc's and FYIs.

Perhaps the best way to tackle this growing problem is at the small work-group or individual level. Apple's Hillebrecht generally limits himself to one hour of e-mail per day. "You've got to take a defensive stance on your working time, because if you allow all the intrusions, you'll never get that time back."

Following the model of Computer Associates, divisions and smaller groups can set aside a couple of hours a day—ignoring e-mails and phones—just to deal with their primary tasks. "In companies where people have tried this," says De Long, "I've heard the same thing over and over. That quiet time is the most productive time of the day."

Hewlett-Packard is trying to package communications better. Explains Walker: "In the past, information was just pushed at people. Now we want to put it in repositories where people know they can find it if it's needed." And in defining the most important messages from senior management, HP makes use of its professional communicators.

"We have a magazine that's published eight times a year, with articles and essays that describe trends and strategies in an analytical way," says Walker. "It's old-fashioned. But what's in the publication are messages with substance. We also have 'Newsgrams' that go out over the e-mail. These are clearly labeled as having companywide significance."

Every organization has a communications channel that carries the most powerful symbolic value. For some companies it may be a worldwide teleconference featuring the CEO; for others, it's the company magazine; for high-tech firms, it might well be e-mail. "But senior managers had better know which channel is most effective," says De Long, "and they should use it wisely."

The democratization of corporate communications is an irreversible trend. The wealth of sharing information is, on the whole, a benefit to productivity. And fresh information will keep a business from smelling like week-old chicken—just so long as workers aren't suffocated in a pile of feathers.

JAY STULLER, who lives in San Francisco, is a frequent contributor to ATB. *His book* How to Love a PMSing Woman: When Timing Is Everything *is published by Bridgeline.*

Computers and Social Participation

According to classical French sociologist Émile Durkheim (1858–1917), a thriving society must provide its members with a sense of community or identity and belonging. In traditional societies, strong kinship ties and a shared religion provide a basis for trust and shared values. People have common life experiences; they work at the same occupations (farming, hunting, fishing) and face the same challenges of existence. Social norms and expectations are dictated by tradition.

In modern societies, however, social cohesion is harder to achieve. Though mass production results in an outward appearance of a homogeneous culture, other forces foster differences between people. Rather than a single unifying set of values and beliefs, there are countless competing moral and philosophical perspectives. Families have weaker ties with extended kinship groups. Individuals work in very diverse occupations. Differences in work and social position can make it difficult for people to identify with each other's needs and interests; they are often anonymous to each other as they go about their daily affairs.

Under these conditions, social cohesion can be eroded by factionalism or self-interested individualism. In his day, Durkheim felt that social problems such as crime, divorce, and suicide were symptoms of social disintegration and individual isolation. He was concerned with finding ways to reduce the alienation of modern life and reintegrate society. Today, many people are optimistic that information technologies can play a major role in achieving this goal. For example, computers have made it possible for many people with disabilities to participate more fully in many aspects of society, including the workplace.

On the other hand, some critics feel that some disadvantaged groups may be further marginalized by computerization. They argue, for example, that women have been largely excluded from influencing the shape of the information society as there are few women in computer science and engineering fields. Despite low visibility, however, women have made significant contributions to the development of computer hardware, software, and languages.

Others worry that pornography and other sexist content on the Internet is a barrier to women's participation in online communities. Amy Bruckman warns that it can be hard for men as well as women to find a comfortable space online but those who have an "open mind . . . may come across something good." In "Finding One's Own Space in Cyberspace," Bruckman describes some virtual "communities" that readers may want to join (or avoid) and explains how to create and shape an online environment that will bring together "birds of a feather."

Online networks allow for social participation and action on a very large scale. Environmental activists are using global networks to spread the word about creating a sustainable society. Another potential application of wide-scale networking is the online university—a project that has been proposed by several western U.S. states. A university that is not bound by physical space will offer many benefits, but it raises questions about what kinds of communities might exist in such an environment. In "A Campus of Our Own," Susan Saltrick focuses on two groups—faculty and students—and speculates about "how their roles, their behaviors, and their sense of belonging have been and will be affected by technology's advance." And, Todd Oppenheimer, in "The Computer Delusion," questions whether most uses of computers in schools really improve teaching and learning, and whether it makes sense for school districts to cut music, art, and physical education programs to make room for them.

Another article looks more closely at the effects of networking on the "self" and personal identity. Sherry Turkle, a leading scholar on the social implications of computing and a licensed clinical psychologist, is highlighted in the next essay, "Session with a Cybershrink: An Interview with Sherry Turkle." Turkle offers encouraging as well as disconcerting observations about computer networking and how people think about themselves and their role in society.

Looking Ahead: Challenge Questions

Compared to the traditional campus setting, in what ways do you think the experience of acquiring a college or university education could be enhanced or diminished in an online environment?

Do you think that cutting school programs (such as art, music, and physical education) in order to increase computer accessibility in the classroom is a good idea? Defend your answer.

Finding One's Own Space in Cyberspace

Far from being a monolithic entity, the Internet encompasses a rich assortment of communities. Net users who don't find an online society in which they feel comfortable can start their own—shaping the community's character to their liking.

AMY BRUCKMAN

AMY BRUCKMAN, a doctoral student in the MIT Media Laboratory, is founder of two virtual communities on the Internet: MediaMOO (for media researchers) and MOOSE Crossing (for children).

THE WEEK the last Internet porn scandal broke, my phone didn't stop ringing: "Are women comfortable on the Net?" "Should women use gender-neutral names on the Net?" "Are women harassed on the Net?" Reporters called from all over the country with basically the same question. I told them all: your question is ill-formed. "The Net" is not one thing. It's like asking: "Are women comfortable in bars?" That's a silly question. Which woman? Which bar?

The summer I was 18, I was the computer counselor at a summer camp. After the campers were asleep, the counselors were allowed out, and would go bar hopping. First everyone would go to Maria's, an Italian restaurant with red-and-white-checked table cloths. Maria welcomed everyone from behind the bar, greeting regular customers by name. She always brought us free garlic bread. Next we'd go to the Sandpiper, a disco with good dance music. The Sandpiper seemed excitingly adult—it was a little scary at first, but then I loved it. Next, we went to the Sportsman, a leather motorcycle bar that I found absolutely terrifying. Huge, bearded men bulging out of their leather vests and pants leered at me. I hid in the corner and tried not to make eye contact with anyone, hoping my friends would get tired soon and give me a ride back to camp.

Each of these bars was a community, and some were more comfortable for me than others. The Net is made up of hundreds of thousands of separate communities, each with its own special character. Not only is the Net a diverse place, but "women" are diverse as well—there were leather-clad women who loved the Sportsman, and plenty of women revel in the fiery rhetoric of Usenet's alt.flame. When people complain about being harassed on the Net, they've usually stumbled into the wrong online community. The question is not whether "women" are comfortable on "the Net," but rather, what types of communities are possible? How can we create a range of communities so that everyone—men and women—can find a place that is comfortable for them?

If you're looking for a restaurant or bar, you can often tell without even going in: Is the sign flashing neon or engraved wood? Are there lots of cars parked out front? What sort of cars? (You can see all the Harleys in front of the Sportsman from a block away.) Look in the window: How are people dressed? We are accustomed to diversity in restaurants. People know that not all restaurants will please them, and employ a variety of techniques to choose the right one.

It's a lot harder to find a good virtual community than it is to find a good bar. The visual cues that let you spot the difference between Maria's and the Sportsman from across the street are largely missing. Instead, you have to "lurk"—enter the community and quietly explore for a while, getting the feel of whether it's the kind of place you're looking for. Although published guides exist, they're not always very useful—most contain encyclopedic lists with little commentary or critical evaluation, and by the time they're published they're already out of date. Magazines like *NetGuide* and *Wired* are more current and more selective, and therefore more useful, but their editorial bias may not fit with your personal tastes.

> *As people gather online, they need to be able to distinguish between the electronic equivalent of a biker's hangout and a cozy restaurant.*

Commonly available network-searching tools are also useful. The World Wide Web is filled with searching programs, indexes, and even indexes of indexes ("metaindexes"). Although browsing with these tools can be a pleasant diversion, it is not very efficient, and searches for particular pieces of information often end in frustration. If you keep an open mind, however, you may come across something good.

Shaping an Online Society

But what happens if, after exploring and asking around, you still can't find an online environment that suits you? Don't give up: start your own! This doesn't have to be a difficult task. Anyone can create a new newsgroup in Usenet's "alt" hierarchy or open a new chat room on America Online. Users of Unix systems can easily start a mailing list. If you have a good idea but not enough technical skill or the right type of Net access, there are people around eager to help. The more interesting question is: How do you help a community to become what you hope for? Here, I can offer some hard-won advice.

In my research at the MIT Media Lab (working with Professor Mitchel Resnick), I design virtual communities. In October of 1992, I founded a professional community for media researchers on the Internet called MediaMOO. Over the past three years, as MediaMOO has grown to 1,000 members from 33 countries, I have grappled with many of the issues that face anyone attempting to establish a virtual community. MediaMOO is a "multi-user dungeon" or MUD—a virtual world on the Internet with rooms, objects, and people from all around the world. Messages typed in by a user instantly appear on the screens of all other users who are currently in the same virtual "room." This real-time interaction distinguishes MUDs from Usenet newsgroups, where users can browse through messages created many hours or days before.

The MUD's virtual world is built in text descriptions. MOO stands for MUD object-oriented, a kind of MUD software (created by Pavel Curtis of the Xerox Palo Alto Research Center and Stephen White, now at InContext Systems) that allows each user to write programs to define spaces and objects.

The first MUDs, developed in the late 1970s, were multiplayer fantasy games of the dungeons-and-dragons variety. In 1989, a graduate student at Carnegie Mellon University named James Aspnes decided to see what would happen if you took away the monsters and the magic swords but instead let people extend the virtual world. People's main activity went from trying to conquer the virtual world to trying to build it, collaboratively.

Most MUDs are populated by undergraduates who should be doing their homework. I thought it would be interesting instead to bring together a group of people with a shared intellectual interest: the study of media. Ideally, MediaMOO should be like an endless reception for a conference on media studies. But given the origin of MUDs as violent games, giving one an intellectual and professional atmosphere was a tall order. How do you guide the evolution of who uses the space and what they do there?

A founder/designer can't control what the community ultimately becomes—much of that is up to the users—but can help shape it. The personality of the community's founder can have a great influence on what sort of place it becomes. Part of what made Maria's so comfortable for me was Maria herself. She radiated a warmth that made me feel at home.

Similarly, one of the most female-friendly electronic communities I've visited is New York City's ECHO (East Coast Hang Out) bulletin board, run by Stacy Horn. Smart, stylish, and deliberately outrageous, Horn is role model and patron saint for the ECHOites. Her outspoken but sensitive personality infuses the community, and sends a message to women that it's all right to speak up. She added a conference to ECHO called "WIT" (women in telecommunications), which one user describes as "a warm, supportive, women-only, private conference where women's thoughts, experiences, wisdom, joys, and despairs are shared." But Horn also added a conference called "BITCH," which the ECHO-ite calls "WIT in black leather jackets. All-women, riotous and raunchy."

Horn's high-energy, very New York brand of intelligence establishes the kind of place ECHO is and influences how everyone there behaves. When ECHO was first established, Horn and a small group of her close friends were the most active people on the system. "That set the emotional tone, the traditional style of posting, the unwritten rules about what it's OK to say," says Marisa Bowe, an ECHO administrator for many years. "Even though Stacy is too busy these days to post very much, the tone established in the early days continues," says Bowe, who is now editor of an online magazine called *Word*.

Beyond the sheer force of a founder's personality, a community establishes a particular character with a variety of choices on how to operate. One example is to set a policy on whether to allow participants to remain anonymous. Initially, I decided that members of MediaMOO should be allowed to choose: they could identify themselves with their real names and e-mail addresses, or remain anonymous. Others questioned whether there was a role for anonymity in a professional community.

As time went on, I realized they were right. People on MediaMOO are supposed to be networking, hoping someone will look up who they really are and where they work. Members who are not willing to share their personal and professional identities are less likely to engage in serious discussion about their work and consequently about media in general. Furthermore, comments from an anonymous entity are less valuable because they are unsituated—"I believe X" is less meaningful to a listener than "I am a librarian with eight years of experience who lives in a small town in Georgia, and I believe X." In theory, anonymous participants could describe their professional experiences and place their comments in that context; in practice it tends not to happen that way. After six months, I proposed that we change the policy to require that all new members be identified. Despite the protests of a few vocal opponents, most people thought that this was a good idea, and the change was made.

Each community needs to have its own policy on anonymity. There's room for diversity here too: some communities can be all-anonymous, some all-identified, and some can leave that decision up to each individual. An aside: right now on the Net no one is either really anonymous or really identified. It is easy to fake an identity; it is also possible to use either technical or legal tools to peer behind someone else's veil of anonymity. This ambiguous state of affairs is not necessarily unfortunate: it's nice to know that a fake identity that provides a modicum of privacy is easy to construct, but that in extreme cases such people can be tracked down.

Finding Birds of a Feather

Another important design decision is admissions policy. Most places on the Net have a strong pluralistic flavor, and the idea that some people might be excluded from a community ruffles a lot of feathers. But exclusivity is a fact of life. MIT wouldn't be MIT if everyone who wanted to come was admitted. Imagine

if companies had to give jobs to everyone who applied! Virtual communities, social clubs, universities, and corporations are all groups of people brought together for a purpose. Achieving that purpose often requires that there be some way to determine who can join the community.

A key decision I made for MediaMOO was to allow entry only to people doing some sort of "media research." I try to be loose on the definition of "media"—writing teachers, computer network administrators, and librarians are all working with forms of media—but strict on the definition of "research." At first, this policy made me uncomfortable. I would nervously tell people, "It's mostly a self-selection process. We hardly reject anyone at all!" Over time, I've become more comfortable with this restriction, and have enforced the requirements more stringently. I now believe my initial unease was naive.

Even if an online community decides to admit all comers, it does not have to let all contributors say anything they want. The existence of a moderator to filter postings often makes for more focused and civil discussion. Consider Usenet's two principal newsgroups dealing with feminism—alt.feminism and soc.feminism. In alt.feminism, anyone can post whatever they want. Messages in this group are filled with the angry words of angry people; more insults than ideas are exchanged. (Titles of messages found there on a randomly selected day included "Women & the workplace (it doesn't work)" and "What is a feminazi?") The topic may nominally be feminism, but the discussion itself is not feminist in nature.

The huge volume of postings (more than 200 per day, on average) shows that many people enjoy writing such tirades. But if I wanted to discuss some aspect of feminism, alt.feminism would be the last place I'd go. Its sister group, soc.feminism, is moderated—volunteers read messages submitted to the group and post only those that pass muster. Moderators adhere to soc.feminism's lengthy charter, which explains the criteria for acceptable postings—forbidding ad hominem attacks, for instance.

Moderation of a newsgroup, like restricting admission to a MUD, grants certain individuals within a community power over others. If only one group could exist, I'd have to choose the uncensored alt.feminism to the moderated soc.feminism. Similarly, if MediaMOO were the only virtual community or MIT the only university, I'd argue that they should be open to all. However, there are thousands of universities and the Net contains hundreds of thousands of virtual communities, with varying criteria for acceptable conduct. That leaves room for diversity: some communities can be moderated, others unmoderated. Some can be open to all, some can restrict admissions.

The way a community is publicized—or not publicized—also influences its character. Selective advertising can help a community achieve a desired ambiance. In starting up MediaMOO, for example, we posted the original announcement to mailing lists for different aspects of media studies—not to the general-purpose groups for discussing MUDs on Usenet. MediaMOO is now rarely if ever deliberately advertised. The group has opted not to be listed in the public, published list of MUDs on the Internet. Members are asked to mention MediaMOO to other groups only if the majority of members of that group would probably be eligible to join MediaMOO.

New members are attracted by word of mouth among media researchers. To bring in an influx of new members, MediaMOO typically "advertises" by organizing an online discussion or symposium on some aspect of media studies. Announcing a discussion group on such topics as the techniques for studying behavior in a virtual community or strategies for using computers to teach writing attracts the right sort of people to the community and sets a tone for the kinds of discussion that take place there. That's much more effective than a more general announcement of MediaMOO and its purpose.

In an ideal world, virtual communities would acquire new members entirely by self-selection: people would enter an electronic neighborhood only if it focused on something they cared about. In most cases, this process works well. For example, one Usenet group that I sometimes read—sci.aquaria—attracts people who are really interested in discussing tropical fishkeeping. But self-selection is not always sufficient. For example, the challenge of making MediaMOO's culture different from prevailing MUD culture made self-selection inadequate. Lots of undergraduates with no particular focus to their interests want to join MediaMOO. To preserve MediaMOO's character as a place for serious scholarly discussions, I usually reject these applications. Besides, almost all of the hundreds of other MUDs out there place no restrictions on who can join. MediaMOO is one of the few that is different.

Emotionally and politically charged subject matter, such as feminism, makes it essential for members of a community to have a shared understanding of the community's purpose. People who are interested in freshwater and saltwater tanks can coexist peacefully in parallel conversations on sci.aquaria. However, on alt.feminism, people who want to explore the implications of feminist theory and those who want to question its basic premises don't get along quite so well. Self-selection alone is not adequate for bringing together a group to discuss a hot topic. People with radically differing views may wander in innocently, or barge in deliberately—disrupting the conversation through ignorance or malice.

Such gate crashing tends to occur more frequently as the community grows in size. For example, some participants in the Usenet group alt.tasteless decided to post a series of grotesque messages to the thriving group rec.pets.cats, including recipes for how to cook cat. A small, low-profile group may be randomly harassed, but that's less likely to happen.

Random and pointless postings can dilute the value of virtual communities that are open to everyone. Collecting even a token fee for participation can elevate the level of discussion.

In the offline world, membership in many social organizations is open only to those who are willing and able to pay the dues. While it may rankle an American pluralistic sensibility, the use of wealth as a social filter has the advantages of simplicity and objectivity: no one's personal judgment plays a role in deciding who is to be admitted. And imposing a small financial hurdle to online participation may do more good than harm. Token fees discourage the random and pointless postings that dilute the value of many newsgroups. One of the first community networks, Community Memory in Berkeley, Calif., found that charging a mere 25 cents to post a message significantly raised the level of discourse, eliminating many trivial or rude messages.

Still, as the fee for participation rises above a token level, this method has obvious moral problems for a society committed to equal opportunity. In instituting any kind of exclusionary policy, the founder of a virtual community should first test the key assumption that alternative, nonexclusionary communities really do exist. If they do not, then less restrictive admissions policies may be warranted.

Building on Diversity

Anonymity policy, admissions requirements, and advertising strategy all contribute to a virtual community's character. Without such methods of distinguishing one online hangout from another, all would tend to sink to the least common denominator of discourse—the equivalent of every restaurant in a town degenerating into a dive. We need better techniques to help members of communities develop shared expectations about the nature of the community, and to communicate those expectations to potential new members. This will make it easier for people to find their own right communities.

> *The decision on whether to allow anonymous participation helps determine the quality of online discourse.*

Just as the surest way to find a good restaurant is to exchange tips with friends, word of mouth is usually the best way to find out about virtual communities that might suit your tastes and interests. The best published guides for restaurants compile comments and ratings from a large group of patrons, rather than relying on the judgment of any one expert. Approaches like this are being explored on the Net. Yezdi Lashkari, cofounder of Agents Inc., designed a system called "Webhound" that recommends items of interest on the World Wide Web. To use Webhound, you enter into the system a list of Web sites you like. It matches you with people of similar interests, and then recommends other sites that they like. Not only do these ratings come from an aggregate of many opinions, but they also are matched to your personal preferences.

Webhound recommends just World Wide Web pages, but the same basic approach could help people find a variety of communities, products, and services that are likely to match their tastes. For example, Webhound grew out of the Helpful Online Music Recommendation Service (HOMR), which recommends musical artists. A subscriber to this service—recently renamed Firefly—first rates a few dozen musical groups on a scale from "the best" to "pass the earplugs"; Firefly searches its database for people who have similar tastes, and uses their list of favorites to recommend other artists that might appeal to you. The same technique could recommend Usenet newsgroups, mailing lists, or other information sources. Tell it that you like to read the Usenet group "rec.arts.startrek.info," and it might recommend "alt.tv.babylon-5"—people who like one tend to like the other. While no such tool yet exists for Usenet, the concept would be straightforward to implement.

Written statements of purpose and codes of conduct can help communities stay focused and appropriate. MediaMOO's stated purpose, for example, helps

set its character as an arena for scholarly discussion. But explicit rules and mission statements can go only so far. Elegant restaurants don't put signs on the door saying "no feet on tables" and fast food restaurants don't post signs saying "feet on tables allowed." Subtle cues within the environment indicate how one is expected to behave. Similarly, we should design regions in cyberspace so that people implicitly sense what is expected and what is appropriate. In this respect, designers of virtual communities can learn a great deal from architects.

Vitruvius, a Roman architect from the first century B.C., established the basic principle of architecture as commodity (appropriate function), firmness (structural stability), and delight. These principles translate into the online world, as William Mitchell, dean of MIT's School of Architecture and Planning, points out in his book *City of Bits: Space, Place, and the Infobahn:*

> Architects of the twenty-first century will still shape, arrange and connect spaces (both real and virtual) to satisfy human needs. They will still care about the qualities of visual and ambient environments. They will still seek commodity, firmness, and delight. But commodity will be as much a matter of software functions and interface design as it is of floor plans and construction materials. Firmness will entail not only the physical integrity of structural systems, but also the logical integrity of computer systems. And delight? Delight will have unimagined new dimensions.

Marcos Novak of the University of Texas at Austin is exploring some of those "unimagined dimensions" with his notion of a "liquid architecture" for cyberspace, free from the constraints of physical space and building materials. But work of this kind on the merging of architecture and software design is regrettably rare; if virtual communities are buildings, then right now we are living in the equivalent of thatched huts. If the structure keeps out the rain—that is, if the software works at all—people are happy.

More important than the use of any of these particular techniques, however, is applying an architect's design sensibility to this new medium. Many of the traditional tools and techniques of architects, such as lighting and texture, will translate into the design of virtual environments. Depending on choice of background color and texture, type styles, and special fade-in effects, for instance, a Web page can feel playful or gloomy, futuristic or old-fashioned, serious or fun, grown-up or child-centered. The language of the welcoming screen, too, conveys a sense of the community's purpose and character. An opening screen thick with the jargon of specialists in, say, genetic engineering, might alert dilettantes that the community is for serious biologists.

As the Net expands, its ranks will fill with novices—some of whom, inevitably, will wander into less desirable parts of cybertown. It is important for such explorers to appreciate the Net's diversity—to realize, for example, that the newsgroup alt.feminism does not constitute the Internet's sole contribution to feminist debate. Alternatives exist.

I'm glad there are places on the Net where I'm not comfortable. The world would be a boring place if it invariably suited any one person's taste. The great promise of the Net is diversity. That's something we need to cultivate and cherish. Unfortunately, there aren't yet enough good alternatives—too much of the Net is like the Sportsman and too little of it is like Maria's. Furthermore, not enough people are aware that communities can have such different characters.

People who accidentally find themselves in the Sportsman, alt.feminism, or alt.flame, and don't find the black leather or fiery insults to their liking, should neither complain about it nor waste their time there—

they should search for a more suitable community. If you've stumbled into the wrong town, get back on the bus. But if you've been a long-time resident and find the community changing for the worse—that's different. Don't shy away from taking political action within that community to protect your investment of time: speak up, propose solutions, and build a coalition of others who feel the same way you do.

With the explosion of interest in networking, people are moving from being recipients of information to creators, from passive subscribers to active participants and leaders. Newcomers to the Net who are put off by harassment, pornography, and just plain bad manners should stop whining about the places they find unsuitable and turn their energies in a more constructive direction: help make people aware of the variety of alternatives that exist, and work to build communities that suit their interests and values.

SESSION WITH THE CYBERSHRINK

An Interview with Sherry Turkle

While the online experience can enrich and expand people's lives, it can also seduce the vulnerable into ignoring the real world.

ATTEMPTING TO UNLOCK HER OFFICE door, Sherry Turkle fumbles with her keys. She tries one way, then another. After good-naturedly grousing about the recalcitrant lock—so much more troublesome than opening a fresh window on a computer screen—Turkle finally succeeds, and the door swings open to a most uncybernetic office: wicker furniture, riverside view of the Boston skyline, photo of her four-year-old daughter. Surely a computer lurks somewhere in this den of reigning psycho-guru of cyberspace, but it is tastefully unobtrusive.

Turkel has established herself as the Margaret Mead of the computer culture. Her 1984 book *The Second Self: Computers and the Human Spirit* examined the way people interacted with personal computers, just then becoming a common appliance. The book catapulted her into the pantheon of academic superstars: *Ms.* magazine named her its woman of the year, and *Esquire* entered her in its "registry of America's new leadership class."

The Brooklyn-born Turkle, with a joint doctorate in sociology and psychology from Harvard university, is a professor in MIT's Program in Science, Technology, and Society. Her interests in concepts of identity predates her fascination with computers; she has written extensively about psychoanalysis, and rarely does she give an interview or lecture without referring in some way to Freud, whose division of human identity into id, ego, and superego presaged the infinitely more diverse personas that people voluntarily assume in their travels through cyberspace.

Her latest book—*Life on the Screen: Identity in the Age of the Internet*, published in November by Simon and Schuster—assesses the impact of computer networks on the way people think about themselves and their role in society. Turkle, who is a licensed clinical psychologist, lived among the Net natives in order to learn their ways. In the spirit of the new medium, she sometimes donned a disguise—such as a thin veil in the persona of "Doctor Sherry," or even assumed a male persona to experience for herself the Net's fabled gender-bending abilities.

Turkle spoke with senior editor Herb Brody not only about the potential of the Net to enhance human experience but about elements of the online phenomenon that disturb her—in particular the fear that young people will succumb to the temptation to leave "real life" behind for the ever-so-much more controllable realm of cyberspace.

TR: When people in real life exhibit multiple distinct personalities, we call them psychotic, or at least sinister: In Robert Louis Stevenson's story, Dr. Jekyll shed his "gentle doctor" identity to liberate the "beast" within him as Mr. Hyde. Why are multiple personas not only accepted on the Net but considered cool?

TURKLE: People who suffer from multiple personality disorder have fragmented selves where different pieces are walled off from the others—often in the service of protection from

From MIT's *Technology Review* magazine, February/March 1996, pp. 41-47. © 1996 by Sherry Turkle. Reprinted by permission of the author.

F or some Net enthusiasts, "real life" is just another window, equivalent to the ones that represent their invented personas in virtual communities.

traumatic memories. People who suffer in this way can have the experience of opening their closet in the morning and not knowing who bought some of the suits inside it. By contrast, people who assume online personas are aware of the lives they have created on the screen. They are playing different aspects of themselves and move fluidly and knowledgeably among them. They are having an experience that encourages them to challenge traditional ways of thinking about healthy selves as single and unitary.

TR: How so?

TURKLE: We live an increasingly multi-roled existence. A woman may wake up as a lover, have breakfast as a mother, and drive to work as a lawyer. A man might be a manager at the office and a nurturer at home. So even without computer networks, people are cycling through different roles and are challenged to think about their identities in terms of multiplicity. The Internet makes this multiplicity more concrete and more urgent.

TR: But the multiple personas people assume online are of a different sort from the roles you've described. In cyberspace a person may be a man sometimes and a woman another, for example.

TURKLE: Yes, cyberspace takes the fluidity of identity that is called for in everyday life and raises it to a higher power: people come to see themselves as the sum of their distributed presence on all the windows they open on the screen. The technical metaphor of cycling through computer windows has become a metaphor for thinking about the relationship among aspects of the self.

TR: So cyberspace is kind of a fun house mirror of our society—essentially reflecting what goes on off-line, but with some exaggeration?

TURKLE: Yes. And in a way, because it does allow for an extravagance of experimentation —with gender switching, age-flexibility, and all the rest made so easy—experiences in cyberspace are challenging us to revisit the question of what we mean by identity.

TR: But in the frenzy of attaining multiple identities, some people seem to be losing the sense that their "real world" self is any more important than their menagerie of online personas.

In your book you describe one young man who tells you that for him, real life—RL, as he calls it—doesn't have any special status. It's just another window, along with the ones where he plays roles in a number of virtual communities.

TURKLE: Right. And he said RL is usually not even his best window.

TR: That sounds obsessive. Do you encounter that attitude a lot?

TURKLE: It's not uncommon. But for me, his case is important because it demonstrates how a bright young man who is doing well in school and who has real-life friends can easily go through a period when things are more interesting on the Net than off. This is what leads him to see his online experiences as a "genuine" part of his life. He still had a life offline, but at the time of our conversation, events there were not going so well. From this perspective, the comment about RL not being his best window seems a bit less sinister.

TR: So retreat into online community is just a phase?

TURKLE: It can be. And in some cases it is not so much a retreat as a first step in developing strengths that can be brought into "real" life. I met a student who had a very bad time in his freshman year in college. His father was an alcoholic, and he was dealing with his own sense of his vulnerability to alcoholism. He coped by taking a job of great responsibility in a virtual community. When I met him the following summer, he was interested in going back to try things out in RL. In the best of cases, positive online experiences leave their mark on both the virtual and the real. And they can change the way people see their possibilities; it can affect self-esteem.

TR: Are social skills acquired online applicable in RL?

TURKLE: They can be. Much of what it takes to get along socially are things like having enough self-esteem to be willing to take risks, to have somebody not like you and yet be able to move on, to be able to take no for an answer, to not see things in black and white. An absence of these skills can make life on the Net seem attractive as a place of escape. But they can be learned by interacting with people within virtual communities. That's why I don't get upset that people, even children, are spending a lot of time online. They may be working through important personal issues in the safety of life on the screen. They may come out the other side having had some experience they're able to use to make their lives more fulfilling.

TR: Can casual relationships formed online survive the transition to the real world, where it's not so easy to hide behind an invented identity?

TURKLE: Sometimes, online relationships do not survive the voyage to the real. But in other cases, they survive very well. I know of real-life marriages between people who met each other in cyberspace. The way such intimacies develop usually follows a rather unsurprising pattern. You're in an online discussion group and you "hear" one of the contributors to the group sound interesting and appealing over a three-month period. You're finally going to want to talk to him or her in person. People want that flesh-and-blood connection. Of course, this can lead to problems too. Someone may begin an online extramarital affair thinking of it as a form of interactive erotic literature, typing provocative sentences back and forth, and then discover that the involvement has become a lot more complicated—something that they want to bring into their real life.

TR: Parents I know are ambivalent about their kids' use of computers. It's wonderful that children have this other world that they can inhabit and master. On the other hand, there seems to be an element of compulsion that's not particularly attractive. There are only so many hours in the day, and time spent on a computer is time not spent with friends, family, playing sports, or just reading.

TURKLE: If the computer is replacing time with peers and parents, that's not good. But if the computer is replacing television, then that may well be an upgrade.

TR: Do you worry that some people—children in particular—might be becoming addicted to computers?

TURKLE: It's not an addiction like with cocaine, where everyone on it develops a physical dependency, which is never good. When people respond to the holding power of computers, the situation is far more complex. A person can use computers in different ways at different times, and for different developmental tasks. A six-year-old who uses a computer, for example, may be working on an issue of mastery. A year later he may have shifted his attention to baseball cards. Both are developmentally appropriate, and there's little reason to think that mastery of the online world is much different from mastery of box scores in baseball. This is especially true now that kids can share their experiences online in much the same way that they can share their interest in baseball cards. In the same sense, computer programming is not that much different from, say, chess.

Palliative for a Vulnerable Time

TR: Many of the people you study are students attending college—traditionally a time when people leap into political activity. Are these young adults using the Net to try to change the world?

TURKLE: As someone whose political sensibilities were developed in the 1960s, I'm sorry to say that I see some evidence that things are not going in that direction. I talked with one young man of 22 or 23, who told me how involved he is in political activity within one of the Internet's virtual worlds—a multi-user domain (or MUD) where people create characters and build their own virtual living and working spaces as a backdrop for their online social lives. He just loved the grassroots feel of the involvement. Since this was right before the last congressional elections, and some key seats in his home state were up for grabs, I said, well—what about real-life politics? He said no, that was of no interest to him: politicians were all cynics and liars. Part of me wanted to cry.

TR: Why do you find that so disturbing?

TURKLE: I hear many of the people I interview expressing a genuine confusion, a sense of impotence, about how to connect to the political system. In cyberspace, they feel they know how to connect, how to make things happen. This is disturbing because as of now, most of the community life in MUDs and other virtual places has little effect in the real world—these online societies essentially disappear when you turn off your computer. It would be exciting to see online communities used more to address real-world social crises such as those around the environment, health, drugs, and education. This is starting to happen; I would like to see more of it. Online activists are learning a great deal as they build virtual worlds —it's like thousands of social experiments being conducted simultaneously, all over the world. I would like to see some of the knowledge gained from these efforts used to improve our off-line communities.

TR: Why do you think some young people are withdrawing from real political involvement and jumping instead into cyberspace?

TURKLE: For some people I interviewed who are in their twenties, cyberspace offers them a status that RL does not. These people grew up in middle class families, went to college, and many feel that they are slipping out of the middle class. They work jobs in fast food or sales, most share apartments, some have moved back to live with parents. They're not living in the way they were brought up to think somebody with a college education would live.

TR: But in cyberspace, they have higher status?

TURKLE: Right. In cyberspace they feel that they have rejoined the middle class. They are spending time with people whose interests and cultural background they recognize. They feel at home and in a political environment where they can make a difference. As one person put it, "I have more stuff on the MUD than off it," meaning that in her virtual community, she was able to build and furnish her own "room." Meanwhile, the real-world culture is supporting this notion with the hype that computers are sexy, that cyberspace is where it's happening. But I think that some of this hype can encourage a notion that what we do to the physical environment, say, doesn't count because we're creating a new environment in cyberspace. You don't want to lose a sense of urgency about the state of your city because you feel you have this other ready alternative. Yet, this is what I pick up in the attitudes of many cyber-enthusiasts I speak to.

TR: That would seem to be a self-fulfilling prophecy—as people withdraw from the real world, their talents are not available to solve our real problems. But they are available in cyberspace, which then becomes a more and more attractive option.

TURKLE: Yes. As a society, we are at a particu-

larly vulnerable point. There is a tremendous amount of insecurity about what kinds of jobs we are going to have and where they will be. How are we going to address the serious problems facing our children: drugs, violence, deteriorating education? How are we going to address problems of the environment and of cities and of health care? Do we have the political will to attempt to do all of these things? The challenges seem overwhelming. So people are very susceptible now to the notion that there's a better place—somewhere over the rainbow, way up high, where there isn't any trouble. Of course, that place is the online world. In other words, our confusion and insecurity make us want to believe that there is a technological alternative.

Having It All

TR: Why do you think there's been a recent backlash against the Internet, with the publication of critical books and articles?

TURKLE: There are several reasons. Partly it is opportunistic—after a lot of hype, people sense that it's the right time in the news cycle to present a contrary point of view. Also, the same frustrations and the same desire for an easy fix that leads people to the safety of the Internet leads people to complain about it rather than other things. We don't know what to do about violence or about the poor quality of education in many schools. We don't know how to bring families back together. It's easy to blame technology for our ills. So you see the widespread fantasy that what's causing moral decay in America is online pornography. People are spending a lot of political capital making waves about the urgency of cleaning up the Internet. I think that energy might be better spent elsewhere.

TR: Pornography on the Net doesn't overly concern you?

TURKLE: Do I want my four year old sitting there scrolling through filthy pictures? Of course not. But I would rather not interfere with free speech and I prefer to keep the monitoring of children as something that gets done by parents in the home rather than have government agencies policing cyberspace. Yes, there is pornography online. But we should be able to recognize that it is a displacement of our social anxieties to be focusing disproportionately on cyberporn as a pressing problem.

Many young people are tempted to apply their energies only in cyberspace, where they know how to make things happen.

TR: Many critics seem turned off by how shallow the Internet is, both in its informational content and in the kind of relationships it fosters.

TURKLE: When a new technology is introduced, people respond by complaining that it's not as good as what we have had before. But it is hard to argue that online information doesn't compete favorably with what television offers. And online communication is in many ways a return to print—to reading and writing. In any case, it has usually worked out that the introduction of a new medium does not displace the old in any simple sense. Television didn't kill movies, and neither did video games.

TR: So instead we end up with everything.

TURKLE: Yes—that seems to be a general pattern. I do not believe that people are going to choose between relationships in cyberspace and face-to-face relationships. I think that people are going to have all kinds. It's not going to be one or the other. What I'm interested in—psychologically, socially, and politically—is making real life more permeable to cyberspace and cyberspace more permeable to real life. We need to think of ways to make the resources that are online have a positive impact on real life.

TR: But such "permeability" could come at a cost. For instance, if kids pursue more education through the Net and less through schools with other kids, won't they miss much of the socialization that schools have traditionally provided?

TURKLE: Well, in that sense the advent of a new technology leads us to ask what it is we most value in our way of life. Do we care, for example, about public schools? Because if the schools continue to deteriorate, and pose physical dangers, and an online alternative arises, then who could blame parents for keeping their kids home and having them just log on instead? It's a rational choice. Now if you don't like that, if you think that kids ought to be getting an education with other children, then you have to be willing to pay for it. And that will mean investing public money to make the schools better and safer. Online possibilities are forcing us to examine what we really care about. They are serving as a kind of a wake-up call.

Not All Boys and Their Toys

TR: Has the rise of the Internet made the computer culture more female-friendly?

TURKLE: Definitely. Computer technology is moving in a direction that makes it easier for women to see it as something that is culturally theirs. We're hearing a lot less of that stuff about girls having "computer phobia," which I never thought was a good way to explain what was going on.

TR: You don't think girls have tended to be more apprehensive than boys about using computers?

TURKLE: Maybe they were at one time, but the label "phobia" does not correctly describe the phenomenon and does not help girls get over what some of them feel, which is much more like computer *reticence*. Girls weren't afraid of computers, but many felt that dealing with a computer was just not very girl-like. The computer was culturally constructed as male, just as much of technology was. When I was a girl, I once wanted to build a crystal radio. My mother, usually very encouraging, said no, don't touch it, you'll get a shock. It wasn't that I didn't want to build it—I wasn't phobic. But somehow, this just wasn't what girls did. I became reticent about such things.

Traditionally, the computer culture has carried many associations that tended to alienate girls—I mean, if you made a mistake, the computer asked you if you wanted to "abort" or "execute" or "kill." Those words convey images that just didn't appeal to a girl. Also, computers took you away from people.

TR: But the Internet is making the computer more of a social tool?

TURKLE: Yes—using computers today tends not to involve conquest metaphors or isolation from other human beings. Interfaces encourage you to manipulate them, to play with objects on the screen as though they were tangible entities, like elements of a collage. And the Net is all about chatting with people, being with people. Women who get onto the Net are often turned off by the flaming and the ad hominem rudeness they see. But they find places on the Net where this is not the case, and when they don't find them, they can create

Online activists are learning a great deal as they build virtual worlds. I would like to see some of this knowledge used to improve our off-line communitites.

them. The Net desperately needs more of the characteristics that in our culture have been associated with women—skills such as collaboration and diplomacy. And many online communities are not only civil but actively encourage friendships and networking—it's not all boys and their toys.

TR: Still, the Net remains mostly male, doesn't it?

TURKLE: Women are present on the Net in greater and greater numbers. But I am often struck by the preponderance of messages that seem to come from men, even in places where there are many women around. Women tend to be less visible than men because when confronted with a rowdy group-flame session, women will move their conversations to private e-mail.

TR: Is there some way that women are using the Net more than men are?

TURKLE: Many women are getting access to the Internet in order to keep in touch with their families. For example, a parent with kids at college can use the Net to communicate with them. Parents know that their kids are logging on every day to get their e-mail. They're not going to resent an e-mail message from mom the way they might resent a badly timed phone call. A channel of communication that wasn't there before is opening.

TR: Does this new channel lead to new kinds of interactions?

TURKLE: Yes. A parent can send e-mail to a child away at college, saying, you know, it's 3 o'clock in the morning, I couldn't sleep, I was watching an old movie, I just thought I'd send you a note. In one case when this happened, the child, a freshman at college, responded immediately to a note from his mother and told her that he was up too—studying for a chemistry exam. The mother wrote right back, I wish you luck. The son appreciated the nurturance, something that he would not have permitted himself if he had had to call home. So all of a sudden you have an interaction that gratifies both people that never would have happened.

TR: So for many women, the Internet is a way to strengthen family ties?

TURKLE: Yes. Of course, the appeal of

cyberspace for communication with family also draws in many men as well. And once they're in touch with their kids, why shouldn't they join a newsgroup about investments?

The Peril of the Black Box

TR: Time was, effective use of a computer required at least a basic understanding of how the machine worked. One benefit of more advanced computers is that this is no longer the case—people can now control a powerful technology without knowing much of anything about how it operates. What are the consequences of relying on a technology that is so opaque?

TURKLE: I'm very concerned that technology may be fostering a kind of intellectual passivity, feeding into a cultural acceptance of a lack of understanding of how a lot of things work. I'm troubled by people's sense that this is all basically magic. I don't think people should have no idea how computer technology works. And increasingly, people have no idea. I interviewed one man who said that when BMW started using microchips in its cars, he lost interest in them although he had been an avid enthusiast. For him, the cars had become opaque. He enjoyed transparent technology because it made him feel more empowered to understand other things in his world. I have a lot of sympathy for his perspective.

TR: Cars that use computer chips need less maintenance and run better. A Macintosh is usable by millions more people than a DOS or Unix computer. Aren't such benefits worth the loss of "transparency"?

TURKLE: But some undesirable things may go along with this movement. When people deal every day with objects that are powerful but impenetrably complex, it can lead to feelings of impotence. Or, alternatively, to feelings of unreasonable power and retreat to radical oversimplifications. We need to be attentive to the social and psychological impact of a technology that encourages you to think that all you need to do is click, click. Double click and make public education go away. Double click and make taxes go away. Double click—three strikes and you're out and solve the crime problem. As a society, we're doing a lot of double clicking. And I think it is not a bad thing for us to get a better understanding of how this mentality might be flowing out of the habits of thought encouraged by our technology.

TR: All in all, are you an optimist or pessimist about the effects of the computer on the human psyche?

TURKLE: I think that computers offer dramatic new possibilities for personal growth—for developing personal senses of mastery, for forming new kinds of relationships, and for communicating with friends and family all over the world in immediate, even intimate ways. But I don't like thinking of things in terms of optimism or pessimism because it makes it sound as though one gets to take bets on whether the technology is going to have one kind of effect or another. I think that a lot of the effect of computers and the Internet is going to depend on what people do with it. We have to see ourselves as in a position to profoundly affect the outcome of how things are going to go. Hyping or bashing technology puts the emphasis on the power of the technology. I'm trying to put the spotlight on people, and the many human choices we face as we try to assimilate this technology.

Ultimately, there is a limit to the sorts of satisfactions that people can have online. We live in our bodies. We are terrestrial. We are physical as well as mental beings—we are cerebral, cognitive, and emotional. My optimism comes from believing that people are going to find ways to use life on the screen to express all these sides of themselves.

The Computer
D E L U S I O N

*There is no good evidence that most uses of computers significantly improve
teaching and learning, yet school districts are cutting programs—music,
art, physical education—that enrich children's lives to make room for this dubious
nostrum, and the Clinton Administration has embraced the goal of "computers
in every classroom" with credulous and costly enthusiasm*

TODD OPPENHEIMER

Todd Oppenheimer is the associate editor of Newsweek
Interactive. He has won numerous awards for his writing
and investigative reporting.

I N 1922 Thomas Edison predicted that "the motion
picture is destined to revolutionize our educational
system and . . . in a few years it will supplant largely,
if not entirely, the use of textbooks." Twenty-three
years later, in 1945, William Levenson, the director of the
Cleveland public schools' radio station, claimed that "the
time may come when a portable radio receiver will be as
common in the classroom as is the blackboard." Forty years
after that the noted psychologist B. F. Skinner, referring to
the first days of his "teaching machines," in the late 1950s
and early 1960s, wrote, "I was soon saying that, with the
help of teaching machines and programmed instruction, students could learn twice as much in the same time and with
the same effort as in a standard classroom." Ten years after
Skinner's recollections were published, President Bill Clinton campaigned for "a bridge to the twenty-first century . . .
where computers are as much a part of the classroom as
blackboards." Clinton was not alone in his enthusiasm for a
program estimated to cost somewhere between $40 billion
and $100 billion over the next five years. Speaker of the
House Newt Gingrich, talking about computers to the Republican National Committee early this year, said, "We
could do so much to make education available twenty-four
hours a day, seven days a week, that people could literally
have a whole different attitude toward learning."

If history really is repeating itself, the schools are in serious trouble. In *Teachers and Machines: The Classroom Use
of Technology Since 1920* (1986), Larry Cuban, a professor
of education at Stanford University and a former school superintendent, observed that as successive rounds of new
technology failed their promoters' expectations, a pattern
emerged. The cycle began with big promises backed by the
technology developers' research. In the classroom, however,
teachers never really embraced the new tools, and no significant academic improvement occurred. This provoked consistent responses: the problem was money, spokespeople
argued, or teacher resistance, or the paralyzing school bureaucracy. Meanwhile, few people questioned the technology advocates' claims. As results continued to lag, the blame
was finally laid on the machines. Soon schools were sold on
the next generation of technology, and the lucrative cycle
started all over again.

Today's technology evangels argue that we've learned our
lesson from past mistakes. As in each previous round, they
say that when our new hot technology—the computer—is
compared with yesterday's, today's is better. "It can do the
same things, plus," Richard Riley, the U.S. Secretary of Education, told me this spring.

How much better is it, really?

The promoters of computers in schools again offer prodi-
gious research showing improved academic achievement after using their technology. The research has again come under occasional attack, but this time quite a number of
teachers seem to be backing classroom technology. In a poll
taken early last year U.S. teachers ranked computer skills
and media technology as more "essential" than the study of

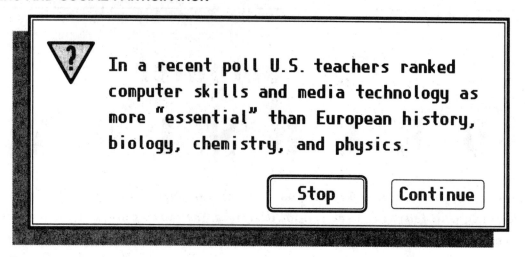

In a recent poll U.S. teachers ranked computer skills and media technology as more "essential" than European history, biology, chemistry, and physics.

Stop   Continue

European history, biology, chemistry, and physics; than dealing with social problems such as drugs and family breakdown; than learning practical job skills; and than reading modern American writers such as Steinbeck and Hemingway or classic ones such as Plato and Shakespeare.

In keeping with these views New Jersey cut state aid to a number of school districts this past year and then spent $10 million on classroom computers. In Union City, California, a single school district is spending $27 million to buy new gear for a mere eleven schools. The Kittridge Street Elementary School, in Los Angeles, killed its music program last year to hire a technology coordinator; in Mansfield, Massachusetts, administrators dropped proposed teaching positions in art, music, and physical education, and then spent $333,000 on computers; in one Virginia school the art room was turned into a computer laboratory. (Ironically, a half dozen preliminary studies recently suggested that music and art classes may build the physical size of a child's brain, and its powers for subjects such as language, math, science, and engineering—in one case far more than computer work did.) Meanwhile, months after a New Technology High School opened in Napa, California, where computers sit on every student's desk and all academic classes use computers, some students were complaining of headaches, sore eyes, and wrist pain.

Throughout the country, as spending on technology increases, school book purchases are stagnant. Shop classes, with their tradition of teaching children building skills with wood and metal, have been almost entirely replaced by new "technology education programs." In San Francisco only one public school still offers a full shop program—the lone vocational high school. "We get kids who don't know the difference between a screwdriver and a ball peen hammer," James Dahlman, the school's vocational-department chair, told me recently. "How are they going to make a career choice? Administrators are stuck in this mindset that all kids will go to a four-year college and become a doctor or a lawyer, and that's not true. I know some who went to col-

lege, graduated, and then had to go back to technical school to get a job." Last year the school superintendent in Great Neck, Long Island, proposed replacing elementary school shop classes with computer classes and training the shop teachers as computer coaches. Rather than being greeted with enthusiasm, the proposal provoked a backlash.

Interestingly, shop classes and field trips are two programs that the National Information Infrastructure Advisory Council, the Clinton Administration's technology task force, suggests reducing in order to shift resources into computers. But are these results what technology promoters really intend? "You need to apply common sense," Esther Dyson, the president of EDventure Holdings and one of the task force's leading school advocates, told me recently. "Shop with a good teacher probably is worth more than computers with a lousy teacher. But if it's a poor program, this may provide a good excuse for cutting it. There will be a lot of trials and errors with this. And I don't know how to prevent those errors."

The issue, perhaps, is the magnitude of the errors. Alan Lesgold, a professor of psychology and the associate director of the Learning Research and Development Center at the University of Pittsburgh, calls the computer an "amplifier," because it encourages both enlightened study practices and thoughtless ones. There's a real risk, though, that the thoughtless practices will dominate, slowly dumbing down huge numbers of tomorrow's adults. As Sherry Turkle, a professor of the sociology of science at the Massachusetts Institute of Technology and a longtime observer of children's use of computers, told me, "The possibilities of using this thing poorly so outweigh the chance of using it well, it makes people like us, who are fundamentally optimistic about computers, very reticent."

Perhaps the best way to separate fact from fantasy is to take supporters' claims about computerized learning one by one and compare them with the evidence in the academic literature and in the everyday experiences I have observed or heard about in a variety of classrooms.

Five main arguments underlie the campaign to computerize our nation's schools.

• Computers improve both teaching practices and student achievement.

• Computer literacy should be taught as early as possible; otherwise students will be left behind.

• To make tomorrow's work force competitive in an increasingly high-tech world, learning computer skills must be a priority.

• Technology programs leverage support from the business community—badly needed today because schools are increasingly starved for funds.

• Work with computers—particularly using the Internet—brings students valuable connections with teachers, other schools and students, and a wide network of professionals around the globe. These connections spice the school day with a sense of real-world relevance, and broaden the educational community.

"The Filmstrips of the 1990s"

CLINTON'S vision of computerized classrooms arose partly out of the findings of the presidential task force—thirty-six leaders from industry, education, and several interest groups who have guided the Administration's push to get computers into the schools. The report of the task force, "Connecting K–12 Schools to the Information Superhighway" (produced by the consulting firm McKinsey & Co.), begins by citing numerous studies that have apparently proved that computers enhance student achievement significantly. One "meta-analysis" (a study that reviews other studies—in this case 130 of them) reported that computers had improved performance in "a wide range of subjects, including language arts, math, social studies and science." Another found improved organization and focus in students' writing. A third cited twice the normal gains in math skills. Several schools boasted of greatly improved attendance.

Unfortunately, many of these studies are more anecdotal than conclusive. Some, including a giant, oft-cited meta-analysis of 254 studies, lack the necessary scientific controls to make solid conclusions possible. The circumstances are artificial and not easily repeated, results aren't statistically reliable, or, most frequently, the studies did not control for other influences, such as differences between teaching methods. This last factor is critical, because computerized learning inevitably forces teachers to adjust their style—only sometimes for the better. Some studies were industry-funded, and thus tended to publicize mostly positive findings. "The research is set up in a way to find benefits that aren't really there," Edward Miller, a former editor of the *Harvard Education Letter*, says. "Most knowledgeable people agree that most of the research isn't valid. It's so flawed it shouldn't even be called

research. Essentially, it's just worthless." Once the faulty studies are weeded out, Miller says, the ones that remain "are inconclusive"—that is, they show no significant change in either direction. Even Esther Dyson admits the studies are undependable. "I don't think those studies amount to much either way," she says. "In this area there is little proof."

Why are solid conclusions so elusive? Look at Apple Computer's "Classrooms of Tomorrow," perhaps the most widely studied effort to teach using computer technology. In the early 1980s Apple shrewdly realized that donating computers to schools might help not only students but also company sales, as Apple's ubiquity in classrooms turned legions of families into Apple loyalists. Last year, after the *San Jose Mercury News* (published in Apple's Silicon Valley home) ran a series questioning the effectiveness of computers in schools, the paper printed an opinion-page response from Terry Crane, an Apple vice-president. "Instead of isolating students," Crane wrote, "technology actually encouraged them to collaborate more than in traditional classrooms. Students also learned to explore and represent information dynamically and creatively, communicate effectively about complex processes, become independent learners and self-starters and become more socially aware and confident."

Crane didn't mention that after a decade of effort and the donation of equipment worth more than $25 million to thirteen schools, there is scant evidence of greater student achievement. To be fair, educators on both sides of the computer debate acknowledge that today's tests of student achievement are shockingly crude. They're especially weak in measuring intangibles such as enthusiasm and self-motivation, which do seem evident in Apple's classrooms and other computer-rich schools. In any event, what is fun and what is educational may frequently be at odds. "Computers in classrooms are the filmstrips of the 1990s," Clifford Stoll, the author of *Silicon Snake Oil: Second Thoughts on the Information Highway* (1995), told *The New York Times* last year, recalling his own school days in the 1960s. "We loved them because we didn't have to think for an hour, teachers loved them because they didn't have to teach, and parents loved them because it showed their schools were high-tech. But no learning happened."

Stoll somewhat overstates the case—obviously, benefits can come from strengthening a student's motivation. Still, Apple's computers may bear less responsibility for that change than Crane suggests. In the beginning, when Apple did little more than dump computers in classrooms and homes, this produced no real results, according to Jane David, a consultant Apple hired to study its classroom initiative. Apple quickly learned that teachers needed to change their classroom approach to what is commonly called "project-oriented learning." This is an increasingly popular teaching method, in which students learn through doing and teachers act as facilitators or partners rather than as didacts. (Teachers sometimes

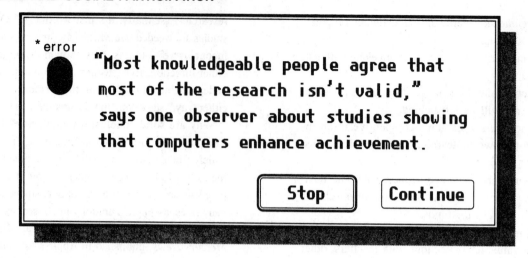

*error

"Most knowledgeable people agree that most of the research isn't valid," says one observer about studies showing that computers enhance achievement.

Stop   Continue

refer to this approach, which arrived in classrooms before computers did, as being "the guide on the side instead of the sage on the stage.") But what the students learned "had less to do with the computer and more to do with the teaching," David concluded. "If you took the computers out, there would still be good teaching there." This story is heard in school after school, including two impoverished schools—Clear View Elementary School, in southern California, and the Christopher Columbus middle school, in New Jersey—that the Clinton Administration has loudly celebrated for turning themselves around with computers. At Christopher Columbus, in fact, students' test scores rose before computers arrived, not afterward, because of relatively basic changes: longer class periods, new books, after-school programs, and greater emphasis on student projects and collaboration.

During recent visits to some San Francisco–area schools I could see what it takes for students to use computers properly, and why most don't.

On a bluff south of downtown San Francisco, in the middle of one of the city's lower-income neighborhoods, Claudia Schaffner, a tenth-grader, tapped away at a multimedia machine in a computer lab at Thurgood Marshall Academic High School, one of half a dozen special technology schools in the city. Schaffner was using a physics program to simulate the trajectory of a marble on a small roller coaster. "It helps to visualize it first, like 'A is for Apple' with kindergartners," Schaffner told me, while mousing up and down the virtual roller coaster. "I can see how the numbers go into action." This was lunch hour, and the students' excitement about what they can do in this lab was palpable. Schaffner could barely tear herself away. "I need to go eat some food," she finally said, returning within minutes to eat a rice dish at the keyboard.

Schaffner's teacher is Dennis Frezzo, an electrical-engineering graduate from the University of California at Berkeley. Despite his considerable knowledge of computer programming, Frezzo tries to keep classwork focused on physical projects. For a mere $8,000, for example, several

teachers put together a multifaceted robotics lab, consisting of an advanced Lego engineering kit and twenty-four old 386-generation computers. Frezzo's students used these materials to build a tiny electric car, whose motion was to be triggered by a light sensor. When the light sensor didn't work, the students figured out why. "That's a real problem—what you'd encounter in the real world," Frezzo told me. "I prefer they get stuck on small real-world problems instead of big fake problems"—like the simulated natural disasters that fill one popular educational game. "It's sort of the Zen approach to education," Frezzo said. "It's not the big problems. Isaac Newton already solved those. What come up in life are the little ones."

It's one thing to confront technology's complexity at a high school—especially one that's blessed with four different computer labs and some highly skilled teachers like Frezzo, who know enough, as he put it, "to keep computers in their place." It's quite another to grapple with a high-tech future in the lower grades, especially at everyday schools that lack special funding or technical support. As evidence, when *U.S. News & World Report* published a cover story last fall on schools that make computers work, five of the six were high schools—among them Thurgood Marshall. Although the sixth was an elementary school, the featured program involved children with disabilities—the one group that does show consistent benefits from computerized instruction.

Artificial Experience

CONSIDER the scene at one elementary school, Sanchez, which sits on the edge of San Francisco's Latino community. For several years Sanchez, like many other schools, has made do with a roomful of basic Apple IIes. Last year, curious about what computers could do for youngsters, a local entrepreneur donated twenty costly Power Macintoshes—three for each of five classrooms, and one for each of the five lucky teachers to take home. The teachers who got the new machines were delighted. "It's the best thing we've ever done," Adela Najarro, a third-grade bilingual teacher, told me. She mentioned one boy, perhaps with a learning disability, who had started to hate school. Once he had a computer to play with, she said, "his whole attitude changed." Najarro is now a true believer, even when it comes to children without disabilities. "Every single child," she said, "will do more work for you and do better work with a computer. Just because it's on a monitor, kids pay more attention. There's this magic to the screen."

Down the hall from Najarro's classroom her colleague Rose Marie Ortiz had a more troubled relationship with computers. On the morning I visited, Ortiz took her bilingual special-education class of second-, third-, and fourth-graders into the lab filled with the old Apple IIes. The students look forward to this weekly expedition so much that Ortiz gets exceptional behavior from them all morning. Out of date though these machines are, they do offer a range of exercises, in subjects such as science, math, reading, social studies, and problem solving. But owing to this group's learning problems and limited English skills, math drills were all that Ortiz could give them. Nonetheless, within minutes the kids were excitedly navigating their way around screens depicting floating airplanes and trucks carrying varying numbers of eggs. As the children struggled, many resorted to counting in whatever way they knew how. Some squinted at the screen, painstakingly moving their fingers from one tiny egg symbol to the next. *Tres, cuatro, cinco, seis . . . ,* one little girl said loudly, trying to hear herself above her counting neighbors. Another girl kept a piece of paper handy, on which she marked a line for each egg. Several others resorted to the slow but tried and true—their fingers. Some just guessed. Once the children arrived at answers, they frantically typed them onto the screen, hoping it would advance to something fun, the way Nintendos, Game Boys, and video-arcade games do. Sometimes their answers were right, and the screen did advance; sometimes they weren't; but the children were rarely discouraged. As schoolwork goes, this was a blast.

"It's highly motivating for them," Ortiz said as she rushed from machine to machine, attending not to math questions but to computer glitches. Those she couldn't fix she simply abandoned. "I don't know how practical it is. You see," she said, pointing to a girl counting on her fingers, "these kids still need the hands-on"—meaning the opportunity to manipulate physical objects such as beans or colored blocks. The value of hands-on learning, child-development experts believe, is that it deeply imprints knowledge into a young child's brain, by transmitting the lessons of experience through a variety of sensory pathways. "Curiously enough," the educational psychologist Jane Healy wrote in *Endangered Minds:*

Why Children Don't Think and What We Can Do About It (1990), "visual stimulation is probably not the main access route to nonverbal reasoning. Body movements, the ability to touch, feel, manipulate, and build sensory awareness of relationships in the physical world, are its main foundations." The problem, Healy wrote, is that "in schools, traditionally, the senses have had little status after kindergarten."

Ortiz believes that the computer-lab time, brief as it is, dilutes her students' attention to language. "These kids are all language-delayed," she said. Though only modest sums had so far been spent at her school, Ortiz and other local teachers felt that the push was on for technology over other scholastic priorities. The year before, Sanchez had let its librarian go, to be replaced by a part-timer.

When Ortiz finally got the students rounded up and out the door, the kids were still worked up. "They're never this wired after reading group," she said. "They're usually just exhausted, because I've been reading with them, making them write and talk." Back in homeroom Ortiz showed off the students' monthly handwritten writing samples. "Now, could you do that on the computer?" she asked. "No, because we'd be hung up on finding the keys." So why does Ortiz bother taking her students to the computer lab at all? "I guess I come in here for the computer literacy. If everyone else is getting it, I feel these kids should get it too."

Some computerized elementary school programs have avoided these pitfalls, but the record subject by subject is mixed at best. Take writing, where by all accounts and by my own observations the computer does encourage practice—changes are easier to make on a keyboard than with an eraser, and the lettering looks better. Diligent students use these conveniences to improve their writing, but the less committed frequently get seduced by electronic opportunities to make a school paper look snazzy. (The easy "cut and paste" function in today's word-processing programs, for example, is apparently encouraging many students to cobble together research materials without thinking them through.) Reading programs get particularly bad reviews. One small but carefully controlled study went so far as to claim that Reader Rabbit, a reading program now used in more than 100,000 schools, caused students to suffer a 50 percent drop in creativity. (Apparently, after forty-nine students used the program for seven months, they were no longer able to answer open-ended questions and showed a markedly diminished ability to brainstorm with fluency and originality.) What about hard sciences, which seem so well suited to computer study? Logo, the high-profile programming language refined by Seymour Papert and widely used in middle and high schools, fostered huge hopes of expanding children's cognitive skills. As students directed the computer to build things, such as geometric shapes, Papert believed, they would learn "procedural thinking," similar to the way a computer processes information. According to a number of studies, however, Logo has generally failed to deliver on its promises. Judah Schwartz, a professor of education at Harvard and a co-director of the school's Educational Technology Center, told me that a few newer applications, when used properly, can dramatically expand children's math and science thinking by giving them new tools to "make and explore conjectures." Still, Schwartz acknowledges that perhaps "ninety-nine percent" of the educational programs are "terrible, really terrible."

Even in success stories important caveats continually pop up. The best educational software is usually complex—most suited to older students and sophisticated teachers. In other cases the schools have been blessed with abundance—fancy equipment, generous financial support, or extra teachers— that is difficult if not impossible to duplicate in the average school. Even if it could be duplicated, the literature suggests, many teachers would still struggle with technology. Computers suffer frequent breakdowns; when they do work, their seductive images often distract students from the lessons at hand—which many teachers say makes it difficult to build meaningful rapport with their students.

With such a discouraging record of student and teacher performance with computers, why has the Clinton Administration focused so narrowly on the hopeful side of the story? Part of the answer may lie in the makeup of the Administration's technology task force. Judging from accounts of the task force's deliberations, all thirty-six members are unequivocal technology advocates. Two thirds of them work in the high-tech and entertainment industries. The effect of the group's tilt can be seen in its report. Its introduction adopts the authoritative posture of impartial fact-finder, stating that "this report does not attempt to lay out a national blueprint, nor does it recommend specific public policy goals." But it comes pretty close. Each chapter describes various strategies for getting computers into classrooms, and the introduction acknowledges that "this report does not evaluate the relative merits of competing demands on educational funding (e.g., more computers versus smaller class sizes)."

When I spoke with Esther Dyson and other task-force members about what discussion the group had had about the potential downside of computerized education, they said there hadn't been any. And when I asked Linda Roberts, Clinton's lead technology adviser in the Department of Education, whether the task force was influenced by any self-interest, she said no, quite the opposite: the group's charter actually gave its members license to help the technology industry directly, but they concentrated on schools because that's where they saw the greatest need.

That sense of need seems to have been spreading outside Washington. Last summer a California task force urged the state to spend $11 billion on computers in California schools,

which have struggled for years under funding cuts that have driven academic achievement down to among the lowest levels in the nation. This task force, composed of forty-six teachers, parents, technology experts, and business executives, concluded, "More than any other single measure, computers and network technologies, properly implemented, offer the greatest potential to right what's wrong with our public schools." Other options mentioned in the group's report—reducing class size, improving teachers' salaries and facilities, expanding hours of instruction—were considered less important than putting kids in front of computers.

"Hypertext Minds"

TODAY'S parents, knowing firsthand how families were burned by television's false promises, may want some objective advice about the age at which their children should become computer literate. Although there are no real guidelines, computer boosters send continual messages that if children don't begin early, they'll be left behind. Linda Roberts thinks that there's no particular minimum age—and no maximum number of hours that children should spend at a terminal. Are there examples of excess? "I haven't seen it yet," Roberts told me with a laugh. In schools throughout the country administrators and teachers demonstrate the same excitement, boasting about the wondrous things that children of five or six can do on computers: drawing, typing, playing with elementary science simulations and other programs called "educational games."

The schools' enthusiasm for these activities is not universally shared by specialists in childhood development. The doubters' greatest concern is for the very young—preschool through third grade, when a child is most impressionable. Their apprehension involves two main issues.

First, they consider it important to give children a broad base—emotionally, intellectually, and in the five senses— before introducing something as technical and one-dimensional as a computer. Second, they believe that the human and physical world holds greater learning potential.

The importance of a broad base for a child may be most apparent when it's missing. In *Endangered Minds*, Jane Healy wrote of an English teacher who could readily tell which of her students' essays were conceived on a computer. "They don't link ideas," the teacher says. "They just write one thing, and then they write another one, and they don't seem to see or develop the relationships between them." The problem, Healy argued, is that the pizzazz of computerized schoolwork may hide these analytical gaps, which "won't become apparent until [the student] can't organize herself around a homework assignment or a job that requires initiative. More commonplace activities, such as figuring out how to nail two boards together, organizing a game . . . may actually form a better basis for real-world intelligence."

Others believe they have seen computer games expand children's imaginations. High-tech children "think differently from the rest of us," William D. Winn, the director of the Learning Center at the University of Washington's Human Interface Technology Laboratory, told *Business Week* in a recent cover story on the benefits of computer games. "They develop hypertext minds. They leap around. It's as though their cognitive strategies were parallel, not sequential." Healy argues the opposite. She and other psychologists think that the computer screen flattens information into narrow, sequential data. This kind of material, they believe, exercises mostly one half of the brain—the left hemisphere, where primarily sequential thinking occurs. The "right brain" meanwhile gets short shrift—yet this is the hemisphere that works on different kinds of information simultaneously. It shapes our multi-faceted impressions, and serves as the engine of creative analysis.

Opinions diverge in part because research on the brain is still so sketchy, and computers are so new, that the effect of computers on the brain remains a great mystery. "I don't think we know anything about it," Harry Chugani, a pediatric neurobiologist at Wayne State University, told me. This very ignorance makes skeptics wary. "Nobody knows how kids' internal wiring works," Clifford Stoll wrote in *Silicon Snake Oil*, "but anyone who's directed away from social interactions has a head start on turning out weird. . . . No computer can teach what a walk through a pine forest feels like. Sensation has no substitute."

This points to the conservative developmentalists' second concern: the danger that even if hours in front of the screen are limited, unabashed enthusiasm for the computer sends the wrong message: that the mediated world is more significant than the real one. "It's like TV commercials," Barbara Scales, the head teacher at the Child Study Center at the University of California at Berkeley, told me. "Kids get so hyped up, it can change their expectations about stimulation, versus what they generate themselves." In *Silicon Snake Oil*, Michael Fellows, a computer scientist at the University of Victoria, in British Columbia, was even blunter. "Most schools would probably be better off if they threw their computers into the Dumpster."

Faced with such sharply contrasting viewpoints, which are based on such uncertain ground, how is a responsible policymaker to proceed? "A prudent society controls its own infatuation with 'progress' when planning for its young," Healy argued in *Endangered Minds*.

Unproven technologies . . . may offer lively visions, but they can also be detrimental to the development of the young plastic brain. The cerebral cortex is a wondrously well-buffered mechanism that can withstand a good bit of well-intentioned bungling. Yet there is a point at which fundamental neural substrates for reasoning may be jeopardized for children who lack proper physical, intellectual, or emotional nurturance. Childhood—and the brain—

have their own imperatives. In development, missed opportunities may be difficult to recapture.

The problem is that technology leaders rarely include these or other warnings in their recommendations. When I asked Dyson why the Clinton task force proceeded with such fervor, despite the classroom computer's shortcomings, she said, "It's so clear the world is changing."

Real Job Training

IN the past decade, according to the presidential task force's report, the number of jobs requiring computer skills has increased from 25 percent of all jobs in 1983 to 47 percent in 1993. By 2000, the report estimates, 60 percent of the nation's jobs will demand these skills—and pay an average of 10 to 15 percent more than jobs involving no computer work. Although projections of this sort are far from reliable, it's a safe bet that computer skills will be needed for a growing proportion of tomorrow's work force. But what priority should these skills be given among other studies?

Listen to Tom Henning, a physics teacher at Thurgood Marshall, the San Francisco technology high school. Henning has a graduate degree in engineering, and helped to found a Silicon Valley company that manufactures electronic navigation equipment. "My bias is the physical reality," Henning told me, as we sat outside a shop where he was helping students to rebuild an old motorcycle. "I'm no technophobe. I can program computers." What worries Henning is that computers at best engage only two senses, hearing and sight—and only two-dimensional sight at that. "Even if they're doing three-dimensional computer modeling, that's still a two-D replica of a three-D world. If you took a kid who grew up on Nintendo, he's not going to have the necessary skills. He needs to have done it first with Tinkertoys or clay, or carved it out of balsa wood." As David Elkind, a professor of child development at Tufts University, puts it, "A dean of the University of Iowa's school of engineering used to say the best engineers were the farm boys," because they knew how machinery really worked.

Surely many employers will disagree, and welcome the commercially applicable computer skills that today's high-tech training can bring them. What's striking is how easy it is to find other employers who share Henning's and Elkind's concerns.

Kris Meisling, a senior geological-research adviser for Mobil Oil, told me that "people who use computers a lot slowly grow rusty in their ability to think." Meisling's group creates charts and maps—some computerized, some not—to plot where to drill for oil. In large one-dimensional analyses, such as sorting volumes of seismic data, the computer saves vast amounts of time, sometimes making previously impossible tasks easy. This lures people in his field, Meisling believes, into using computers as much as possible. But

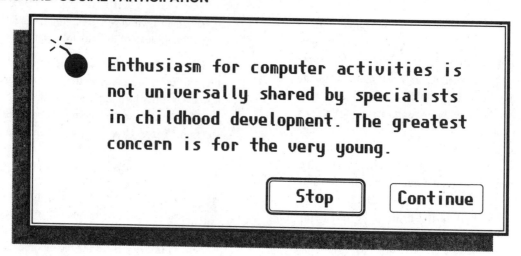

Enthusiasm for computer activities is not universally shared by specialists in childhood development. The greatest concern is for the very young.

Stop   Continue

when geologists turn to computers for "interpretive" projects, he finds, they often miss information, and their oversights are further obscured by the computer's captivating automatic design functions. This is why Meisling still works regularly with a pencil and paper—tools that, ironically, he considers more interactive than the computer, because they force him to think implications through.

"You can't simultaneously get an overview and detail with a computer," he says. "It's linear. It gives you tunnel vision. What computers can do well is what can be calculated over and over. What they can't do is innovation. If you think of some new way to do or look at things and the software can't do it, you're stuck. So a lot of people think, 'Well, I guess it's a dumb idea, or it's unnecessary.'"

I have heard similar warnings from people in other businesses, including high-tech enterprises. A spokeswoman for Hewlett-Packard, the giant California computer-products company, told me the company rarely hires people who are predominantly computer experts, favoring instead those who have a talent for teamwork and are flexible and innovative. Hewlett-Packard is such a believer in hands-on experience that since 1992 it has spent $2.6 million helping forty-five school districts build math and science skills the old-fashioned way—using real materials, such as dirt, seeds, water, glass vials, and magnets. Much the same perspective came from several recruiters in film and computer-game animation. In work by artists who have spent a lot of time on computers "you'll see a stiffness or a flatness, a lack of richness and depth," Karen Chelini, the director of human resources for LucasArts Entertainment, George Lucas's interactive-games maker, told me recently. "With traditional art training, you train the eye to pay attention to body movement. You learn attitude, feeling, expression. The ones who are good are those who as kids couldn't be without their sketchbook."

Many jobs obviously will demand basic computer skills if not sophisticated knowledge. But that doesn't mean that the parents or the teachers of young students need to panic. Joseph Weizenbaum, a professor emeritus of computer sci-

ence at MIT, told the *San Jose Mercury News* that even at his technology-heavy institution new students can learn all the computer skills they need "in a summer." This seems to hold in the business world, too. Patrick MacLeamy, an executive vice-president of Hellmuth Obata & Kassabaum, the country's largest architecture firm, recently gave me numerous examples to illustrate that computers pose no threat to his company's creative work. Although architecture professors are divided on the value of computerized design tools, in MacLeamy's opinion they generally enhance the process. But he still considers "knowledge of the hands" to be valuable— today's architects just have to develop it in other ways. (His firm's answer is through building models.) Nonetheless, as positive as MacLeamy is about computers, he has found the company's two-week computer training to be sufficient. In fact, when he's hiring, computer skills don't enter into his list of priorities. He looks for a strong character; an ability to speak, write, and comprehend; and a rich education in the history of architecture.

The Schools That Business Built

NEWSPAPER financial sections carry almost daily pronouncements from the computer industry and other businesses about their high-tech hopes for America's schoolchildren. Many of these are joined to philanthropic commitments to helping schools make curriculum changes. This sometimes gets businesspeople involved in schools, where they've begun to understand and work with the many daunting problems that are unrelated to technology. But if business gains too much influence over the curriculum, the schools can become a kind of corporate training center—largely at taxpayer expense.

For more than a decade scholars and government commissions have criticized the increasing professionalization of the college years—frowning at the way traditional liberal arts are being edged out by hot topics of the moment or strictly business-oriented studies. The schools' real job, the technology critic Neil Postman argued in his book *The End of Education* (1995), is to focus on "how to make a life, which is quite different from how to make a living." Some see the arrival of boxes of computer hardware and software in the schools as taking the commercial trend one step further, down into high school and elementary grades. "Should you be choosing a career in kindergarten?" asks Helen Sloss Luey, a social worker and a former president of San Francisco's Parent Teacher Association. "People need to be trained to learn and change, while education seems to be getting more specific."

Indeed it does. The New Technology High School in Napa (the school where a computer sits on every student's desk) was started by the school district and a consortium of more than forty businesses. "We want to be the school that business built," Robert Nolan, a founder of the school, told me last fall. "We wanted to create an environment that mimicked what exists in the high-tech business world." Increasingly, Nolan explained, business leaders want to hire people specifically trained in the skill they need. One of Nolan's partners, Ted Fujimoto, of the Landmark Consulting Group, told me that instead of just asking the business community for financial support, the school will now undertake a trade: in return for donating funds, businesses can specify what kinds of employees they want—"a two-way street." Sometimes the traffic is a bit heavy in one direction. In January, *The New York Times* published a lengthy education supplement describing numerous examples of how business is increasingly dominating school software and other curriculum materials, and not always toward purely educational goals.

People who like the idea that their taxes go to computer training might be surprised at what a poor investment it can be. Larry Cuban, the Stanford education professor, writes that changes in the classroom for which business lobbies rarely hold long-term value. Rather, they're often guided by labor-market needs that turn out to be transitory; when the economy shifts, workers are left unprepared for new jobs. In the economy as a whole, according to a recent story in *The New York Times*, performance trends in our schools have shown virtually no link to the rises and falls in the nation's measures of productivity and growth. This is one reason that school traditionalists push for broad liberal-arts curricula, which they feel develop students' values and intellect, instead of focusing on today's idea about what tomorrow's jobs will be.

High-tech proponents argue that the best education software does develop flexible business intellects. In the *Business Week* story on computer games, for example, academics and professionals expressed amazement at the speed, savvy, and facility that young computer jocks sometimes demonstrate. Several pointed in particular to computer simulations, which some business leaders believe are becoming increasingly important in fields ranging from engineering, manufacturing, and troubleshooting to the tracking of economic activity and geopolitical risk. The best of these simulations may be valuable, albeit for strengthening one form of thinking. But the average simulation program may be of questionable relevance.

Sherry Turkle, the sociology professor at MIT, has studied youngsters using computers for more than twenty years. In her book *Life on the Screen: Identity in the Age of the Internet* (1995) she described a disturbing experience with a simulation game called SimLife. After she sat down with a thirteen-year-old named Tim, she was stunned at the way

Tim can keep playing even when he has no idea what is driving events. For example, when his sea urchins become extinct, I ask him why.

Tim: "I don't know, it's just something that happens."

ST: "Do you know how to find out why it happened?"

Tim: "No."

ST: "Do you mind that you can't tell why?"

Tim: "No. I don't let things like that bother me. It's not what's important."

Anecdotes like this lead some educators to worry that as children concentrate on how to manipulate software instead of on the subject at hand, learning can diminish rather than grow. Simulations, for example, are built on hidden assumptions, many of which are oversimplified if not highly questionable. All too often, Turkle wrote recently in *The American Prospect*, "experiences with simulations do not open up questions but close them down." Turkle's concern is that software of this sort fosters passivity, ultimately dulling people's sense of what they can change in the world. There's a tendency, Turkle told me, "to take things at 'interface' value." Indeed, after mastering SimCity, a popular game about urban planning, a tenth-grade girl boasted to Turkle that she'd learned the following rule: "Raising taxes always leads to riots."

The business community also offers tangible financial support, usually by donating equipment. Welcome as this is, it can foster a high-tech habit. Once a school's computer system is set up, the companies often drop their support. This saddles the school with heavy long-term responsibilities: maintenance of the computer network and the need for constant software upgrades and constant teacher training—the full burden of which can cost far more than the initial hardware and software combined. Schools must then look for handouts from other companies, enter the grant-seeking game, or delicately go begging in their own communities. "We can go to the well only so often," Toni-Sue Passantino, the principal of the Bayside Middle School, in San Mateo, California, told me recently. Last year Bayside let a group of seventh- and eighth-graders spend eighteen months and countless hours creating a rudimentary virtual-reality program, with the support of several high-tech firms. The companies' support ended after

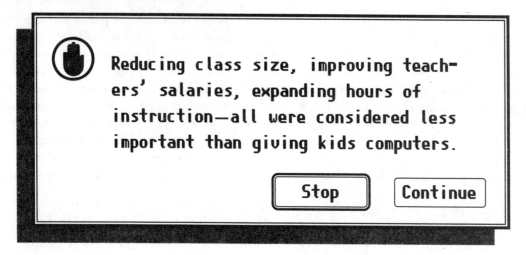

Reducing class size, improving teachers' salaries, expanding hours of instruction—all were considered less important than giving kids computers.

Stop   **Continue**

that period, however—creating a financial speed bump of a kind that the Rand Corporation noted in a report to the Clinton Administration as a common obstacle.

School administrators may be outwardly excited about computerized instruction, but they're also shrewdly aware of these financial challenges. In March of last year, for instance, when California launched its highly promoted "Net-Day '96" (a campaign to wire 12,000 California schools to the Internet in one day), school participation was far below expectations, even in technology-conscious San Francisco. In the city papers school officials wondered how they were supposed to support an Internet program when they didn't even have the money to repair crumbling buildings, install electrical outlets, and hire the dozens of new teachers recently required so as to reduce class size.

One way around the donation maze is to simplify: use inexpensive, basic software and hardware, much of which is available through recycling programs. Such frugality can offer real value in the elementary grades, especially since basic word-processing tools are most helpful to children just learning to write. Yet schools, like the rest of us, can't resist the latest toys. "A lot of people will spend all their money on fancy new equipment that can do great things, and sometimes it just gets used for typing classes," Ray Porter, a computer resource teacher for the San Francisco schools, told me recently. "Parents, school boards, and the reporters want to see only razzle-dazzle state-of-the-art."

Internet Isolation

IT is hard to visit a high-tech school without being led by a teacher into a room where students are communicating with people hundreds or thousands of miles away—over the Internet or sometimes through video-conferencing systems (two-way TV sets that broadcast live from each room). Video conferences, although fun, are an expensive way to create classroom thrills. But the Internet, when used carefully,

offers exciting academic prospects—most dependably, once again, for older students. In one case schools in different states have tracked bird migrations and then posted their findings on the World Wide Web, using it as their own national notebook. In San Francisco eighth-grade economics students have E-mailed Chinese and Japanese businessmen to fulfill an assignment on what it would take to build an industrial plant overseas. Schools frequently use the Web to publish student writing. While thousands of self-published materials like these have turned the Web into a worldwide vanity press, the network sometimes gives young writers their first real audience.

The free nature of Internet information also means that students are confronted with chaos, and real dangers. "The Net's beauty is that it's uncontrolled," Stephen Kerr, a professor at the College of Education at the University of Washington and the editor of *Technology in the Future of Schooling* (1996), told me. "It's information by anyone, for anyone. There's racist stuff, bigoted, hate-group stuff, filled with paranoia; bomb recipes; how to engage in various kinds of crimes, electronic and otherwise; scams and swindles. It's all there. It's all available." Older students may be sophisticated enough to separate the Net's good food from its poisons, but even the savvy can be misled. On almost any subject the Net offers a plethora of seemingly sound "research." But under close inspection much of it proves to be ill informed, or just superficial. "That's the antithesis of what classroom kids should be exposed to," Kerr said.

This makes traditionalists emphasize the enduring value of printed books, vetted as most are by editing. In many schools, however, libraries are fairly limited. I now volunteer at a San Francisco high school where the library shelves are so bare that I can see how the Internet's ever-growing number of research documents, with all their shortcomings, can sometimes be a blessing.

Even computer enthusiasts give the Net tepid reviews.

"Most of the content on the Net is total garbage," Esther Dyson acknowledges. "But if you find one good thing you can use it a million times." Kerr believes that Dyson is being unrealistic. "If you find a useful site one day, it may not be there the next day, or the information is different. Teachers are being asked to jump in and figure out if what they find on the Net is worthwhile. They don't have the skill or time to do that." Especially when students rely on the Internet's much-vaunted search software. Although these tools deliver hundreds or thousands of sources within seconds, students may not realize that search engines, and the Net itself, miss important information all the time.

"We need *less* surfing in the schools, not more," David Gelernter, a professor of computer science at Yale, wrote last year in *The Weekly Standard.* "Couldn't we teach them to use what they've got before favoring them with three orders of magnitude *more*?" In my conversations with Larry Cuban, of Stanford, he argued, "Schooling is not about information. It's getting kids to think about information. It's about understanding and knowledge and wisdom."

It may be that youngsters' growing fascination with the Internet and other ways to use computers will distract from yet another of Clinton's education priorities: to build up the reading skills of American children. Sherry Dingman, an assistant professor of psychology at Marist College, in Poughkeepsie, New York, who is optimistic about many computer applications, believes that if children start using computers before they have a broad foundation in reading from books, they will be cheated out of opportunities to develop imagination. "If we think we're going to take kids who haven't been read to, and fix it by sitting them in front of a computer, we're fooling ourselves," Dingman told me not long ago. This doesn't mean that teachers or parents should resort to books on CD-ROM, which Dingman considers "a great waste of time," stuffing children's minds with "canned" images instead of stimulating youngsters to create their own. "Computers are lollipops that rot your teeth" is how Marilyn Darch, an English teacher at Poly High School, in Long Beach, California, put it in *Silicon Snake Oil.* "The kids love them. But once they get hooked. . . . It makes reading a book seem tedious. Books don't have sound effects, and their brains have to do all the work."

Computer advocates like to point out that the Internet allows for all kinds of intellectual challenges—especially when students use E-mail, or post notes in "newsgroup" discussions, to correspond with accomplished experts. Such experts, however, aren't consistently available. When they are, online "conversations" generally take place when correspondents are sitting alone, and the dialogue lacks the unpredictability and richness that occur in face-to-face discussions. In fact, when youngsters are put into groups for the "collaborative" learning that computer defenders celebrate, realistically only one child sits at the keyboard at a time. (During my school visits children tended to get quite possessive about the mouse and the keyboard, resulting in frustration and noisy disputes more often than collaboration.) In combination these constraints lead to yet another of the childhood developmentalists' concerns—that computers encourage social isolation.

Just a Glamorous Tool

IT would be easy to characterize the battle over computers as merely another chapter in the world's oldest story: humanity's natural resistance to change. But that does an injustice to the forces at work in this transformation. This is not just the future versus the past, uncertainty versus nostalgia; it is about encouraging a fundamental shift in personal priorities—a minimizing of the real, physical world in favor of an unreal "virtual" world. It is about teaching youngsters that exploring what's on a two-dimensional screen is more important than playing with real objects, or sitting down to an attentive conversation with a friend, a parent, or a teacher. By extension, it means downplaying the importance of conversation, of careful listening, and of expressing oneself in person with acuity and individuality. In the process, it may also limit the development of children's imaginations.

Perhaps this is why Steven Jobs, one of the founders of Apple Computer and a man who claims to have "spearheaded giving away more computer equipment to schools than anybody else on the planet," has come to a grim conclusion: "What's wrong with education cannot be fixed with technology," he told *Wired* magazine last year. "No amount of technology will make a dent. . . . You're not going to solve the problems by putting all knowledge onto CD-ROMs. We can put a Web site in every school—none of this is bad. It's bad only if it lulls us into thinking we're doing something to solve the problem with education." Jane David, the consultant to Apple, concurs, with a commonly heard caveat. "There are real dangers," she told me, "in looking to technology to be the savior of education. But it won't survive without the technology."

Arguments like David's remind Clifford Stoll of yesteryear's promises about television. He wrote in *Silicon Snake Oil,*

"Sesame Street" . . . has been around for twenty years. Indeed, its idea of making learning relevant to all was as widely promoted in the seventies as the Internet is today.

So where's that demographic wave of creative and brilliant students now entering college? Did kids really need to learn how to watch television? Did we inflate their expectations that learning would always be colorful and fun?

Computer enthusiasts insist that the computer's "interactivity" and multimedia features make this machine far superior to television. Nonetheless, Stoll wrote,

I see a parallel between the goals of "Sesame Street" and those of children's computing. Both are pervasive, expensive and encourage children to sit still. Both display ani-

3. COMPUTERS AND SOCIAL PARTICIPATION

mated cartoons, gaudy numbers and weird, random noises. . . . Both give the sensation that by merely watching a screen, you can acquire information without work and without discipline.

As the technology critic Neil Postman put it to a Harvard electronic-media conference, "I thought that television would be the last great technology that people would go into with their eyes closed. Now you have the computer."

The solution is not to ban computers from classrooms altogether. But it may be to ban federal spending on what is fast becoming an overheated campaign. After all, the private sector, with its constant supply of used computers and the computer industry's vigorous competition for new customers, seems well equipped to handle the situation. In fact, if schools can impose some limits—on technology donors and on themselves—rather than indulging in a consumer frenzy, most will probably find themselves with more electronic gear than they need. That could free the billions that

Clinton wants to devote to technology and make it available for impoverished fundamentals: teaching solid skills in reading, thinking, listening, and talking; organizing inventive field trips and other rich hands-on experiences; and, of course, building up the nation's core of knowledgeable, inspiring teachers. These notions are considerably less glamorous than computers are, but their worth is firmly proved through a long history.

Last fall, after the school administrators in Mansfield, Massachusetts, had eliminated proposed art, music, and physical-education positions in favor of buying computers, Michael Bellino, an electrical engineer at Boston University's Center for Space Physics, appeared before the Massachusetts Board of Education to protest. "The purpose of the schools [is] to, as one teacher argues, 'Teach carpentry, not hammer,'" he testified. "We need to teach the whys and ways of the world. Tools come and tools go. Teaching our children tools limits their knowledge to these tools and hence limits their futures."

A CAMPUS OF OUR OWN

Thoughts of a Reluctant Conservative

BY SUSAN SALTRICK

Having attained my 39th birthday, I've been observing more frequently the signs of impending middle age. Besides the usual cosmetic distress, I realize I'm now being labeled as one of the conservatives of the new media scene. I find myself agreeing a lot with the Neil Postmans and the Sven Birkertses of the world who urge us all, when asked about technology, to just say no. If I don't watch myself, I'll soon be voting Republican....

All this is a somewhat disconcerting state to find myself in—after spending 12 years as a new media director for a major book publisher where I was, by executive fiat, the brave scout out on the wild frontier, clearing the trail so the rest of the folks back East could settle down and homestead.

Susan Saltrick's independent consulting practice, Proteus Consulting, based in New York City, specializes in educational technology, business development, and market research. The author retains the copyright for this article.

I used to be a real new media cheerleader. My talks of only a few years ago were upbeat panegyrics to the scintillating adventures that awaited us all in the digital future, if we could only navigate the tricky water that surrounded us today. Given that I was in higher education publishing, I used to talk a lot about technology's potential for transforming the educational process—for exploiting new modes of learning, for expanding to new types of students.

And, you know, I pretty much believed it. And, you know, I pretty much still do. But what I find myself thinking about these days is a question Steve Gilbert poses when considering any technological change: "What is it," he asks, "that we cherish and don't want to lose?" In other words, what are the things we need to watch out for—the things we risk sacrificing if we are too readily seduced by technology's siren song?

Two recent works have provoked some thoughts in this area. The first of these, *The City of Bits*, by William Mitchell, the dean of architecture at MIT, is an exploration of how our notion of space—and the structures we humans have created to order that space—are being transformed by our increasing involvement with, or better put, our envelopment in, cyberspace.

The second is Eli Noam's recent article in *Science* magazine, "Electronics and the Future of the University." Noam notes that universities flourished because they were the centralized repositories for information—and that scholars and students gathered there because that was where they found the raw materials they needed to do their work. But now that information is distributed and available all over the Net, he asks, what becomes of the physical university?

Both Mitchell and Noam are concerned with how the Infobahn is changing our notion of community from a spatially defined entity to a virtually connected body—and both address the notion of the virtual communities that are developing out on the Web. But, for me, at least, the Net is so damned evanescent. We may bookmark our favorite sites, but we never really retrace our steps. With each Web journey, we inscribe a new path, spinning a digital lace as unique and convoluted as our genetic code. Click by click, we spiral down, seeking those elusive gems of content, while all around us the landscape is in constant flux—links forming and dissolving like a seething primordial soup. We never quite know where we're going, and God only knows where we'll end up—Accidental Tourists all in this floating world, this web.

So let's be careful when we use that term: community. Doesn't it imply some sort of common code of behavior or attitude or association? Can something so mutable, so ephemeral, count? If we gain admittance to it through a mere mouse click, can something so easily won, so temporary, truly impart a sense of belonging? If we can belong to as many communities as time and carpal tunnel strength permit, what then of loyalty? Can it be so diffuse? Is community then a less binding concept in this less bounded world?

How we define community is critical, because the notion of community is at the heart of any speculation about the university in the 21st century. Of course, the university is not one community, but many. But for simplicity's sake, let's focus on two groups within academe—the faculty and the students—and see how their roles, their be-

haviors, and their sense of belonging have been and will be affected by technology's advance.

I need first to acknowledge that my thinking is, not surprisingly, the result of my experience. I was fortunate to have an exceptional undergraduate experience at a beautiful residential college with a very low student-to-teacher ratio, with world-class faculty, and a diverse and stimulating student body. I would wish that educational setting for everyone, but with tuition at my college now exceeding $18,000, that's clearly not going to happen. As a student, I received financial aid, but the national grants that made it possible for me to attend aren't around anymore. But this is an old, sad story for another time and another forum.

So keep my bias in mind; perhaps it will explain some of my nostalgia. Or perhaps it will just make it easier for you to call me a snob. But let's look now at the faculty and their use of technology.

College faculty make up one of the most plugged-in professions in their use of technology for research—and one of the most retrograde in their use of technology for teaching. This seeming paradox has a lot to do with simple human behavior. If a tool makes it easier to perform a frequent task, it will be adopted. If, however, the tool requires a new type of behavior, or doesn't conform well with the existing modus operandi, then you can build it, but they probably won't come. For many faculty, the Internet has become a basic way of life because it meshes well with their work patterns. It mirrors nicely their image of themselves.

Communication with one's peers is integral to any line of work. And for many workers outside academia, their office location and the colleagues housed therein define their professional communities. Academics, though, have always embraced the idea of a geographically dispersed community of scholars. In the Middle Ages, universities—and the Church— functioned as true multinational institutions, at a time when most people never traveled more than 20 miles from the hovel in which they were born. Today, though, academics are likely to affiliate along disciplinary lines. A chemistry professor in Ann Arbor is likely to have more interaction with a chemistry professor in Palo Alto than with her counterpart in Germanic Languages in the building 50 yards away.

When the Net functions as a scholarly connectivity tool, it is just continuing the tradition of information-sharing that has always linked faculty who share a common disciplinary focus. So as a means of facilitating academic collaboration and resource sharing, the Net's a no-brainer.

But what of the professor's other hat—the teaching enterprise? There the Net offers no neat analogue to the usual work patterns because classroom instruction, unlike scholarly research, has traditionally been a highly autonomous, largely decentralized activity. No wonder, then, that until very recently the percentage of courses utilizing the Internet—or any new media at all—hovered in the single digits.

Finally, though, the winds of change appear to be blowing. On quite a few campuses today, computer access is a given, and the network is almost ubiquitous. But we're still just at the beginning. The epistemological transformations, the ones that change not just the way one teaches but *what* one teaches, are still few and far between. The big changes are still going to take a long time—and a fair amount of pain—to achieve.

My conservatism is founded on some very practical—and one could say short-sighted—concerns. Number one, who's going to pay for all this stuff? In *The City of Bits*, Mitchell tells of sitting in his Cambridge office instructing students from six different universities across the globe via two-way teleconferencing. With all due respect to him and the great institution he represents, we don't all have the same craft to navigate the information ocean. It's one thing to sit at MIT in front of one's high-end workstation complete with video camera, hooked to a super-high-speed network with monster bandwidth—but that's not quite the reality for the rest of us. At a community college I visited last spring, the faculty were no longer able to make long-distance calls because the school couldn't afford it. While enrollments keep going up at this school, the state and local governments keep decreasing the funding. How long will it be before they have what MIT has today?

I'm sure we'd all love to sit in on that MIT teleconferenced course, sharing ideas with Mitchell's great

mind and with students all across the world: it sounds extraordinary. And I'm afraid it's just that—anything but ordinary. The notion of increased access to higher education is an unarguably worthwhile societal goal. Unfortunately, in marked contrast with Mitchell's class, a lot of what passes for distance education today seems a pretty poor substitute for an admittedly less-than-ideal large classroom lecture delivered live. That's because a lot of distance education is just asynchronous transposition of that same ol' large-classroom lecture—but now you get to watch it on TV. And as we all know from watching our home videos, video tends to flatten reality. Any mediated experience has to be at one remove from the real thing. And a flattened version of the average large-audience lecture is a rather dismal thing to contemplate.

But despite all this gloom, there's some cause for optimism. E-mail might just be the flying wedge. It could ultimately have the biggest impact on instruction of all the new technologies. It may not be as sexy as a two-way teleconference with Hong Kong, but e-mail changes behavior. With e-mail, students who didn't talk before, now do—and faculty find they're working longer hours to keep up with them. Steve Gilbert tells me of numerous conversations in which his correspondents say they started with e-mail and ended up rethinking what teaching is and how they could do it better.

On the train from Washington, DC, to New York this fall, I had the opportunity to overhear the conversation of two students—the woman a college sophomore and the young man a high school senior. Their conversation centered on how she had chosen her school and on the criteria he was using to determine his college next year. She's studying international relations and had chosen her school because of its proximity to the nation's capital. Her major gripe was that she was a residential student on a largely commuter campus, and that made for some pretty lonely weekends.

He had just returned from a visit to Georgetown—which was high on his list because of the beauty of the campus. And as a kid from Queens who had spent the last four years in a very small town in Delaware, he was eager to return to an urban location. As a prospective business major, he felt a city location would provide him more internship opportunities.

What's so unusual about this conversation? Absolutely nothing, and that's the whole point. Every one of their stated pros or cons was based on a reaction to the physical environment, be it access to certain urban resources or the attributes of a particular style of architecture—their criteria were all material. Where the students were, or wanted to be, mattered. It was all about place. Their conversation just demonstrated what we all know—that college is more than academics (a topic notably absent from the students' discussion).

College for many of us is a process of socialization, a rite of passage, which requires its own material culture—its real things— whether this means football games, fraternity row, the quad in front of Old Main, or any of the myriad other places on campus where students connect with one another, including those places their parents don't want to think about. In the *Science* article, Noam states, "The strength of the future physical university lies less in pure information and more in college as community."

The student body is, of course, a community, one largely defined today by a connection with a physical place—a campus. I think many students will still want to experience this kind of community. What's less clear is how the colleges of today are going to be able to offer that kind of experience. Soaring costs coupled with drastic budget reductions don't offer a lot of hope. Undoubtedly, other kinds of educational experiences are going to be available—and other kinds of educational institutions will arise to deliver them.

Perhaps higher education in the future will resemble the proverbial onion: at the core, the traditional type of real-time, face-to-face instruction, surrounded by rings of other educational experiences. Some instruction will be imported onto the campus from long-distance professors, while other types of instruction will be exported from the campus to long-distance students. I'd hope that college life in the future will be more like our work life right now—a rich mixture of real-time and asynchronous interaction with peers, advisors, and external information sources.

When we think about the future, the trap we keep falling into is to see technology as a replacement for experience rather than an enhancement of capability. The old ways don't always get supplanted, they just get crowded as more and newer options come into play. Technology permits more, makes more possible, but it doesn't obliterate what went before.

There's a lot of black or white thinking out there. Computer logic may be binary, but our rational processes don't have to be. We're not hurtling towards a digital apocalypse (at least not faster than towards any other), but that doesn't mean we should unquestioningly adopt any technology, heedless of the consequences, simply because everyone seems to be doing it. Technology will change us—it will change us fundamentally—but that doesn't mean we can't influence its course. And let's remember, we can always just turn the damned things off.

> *Technology will change us—it will change us fundamentally—but that doesn't mean we can't influence its course. And let's remember, we can always just turn the damned things off.*

We hear a lot these days about the social implications of technology—ironically much of it is going on between the covers of the good old-fashioned book. The argument seems to have polarized many commentators. On the one hand, we have the high priests of the digital culture, who see all things as reducible to data. In their eyes, the human enterprise is just another bunch of bits in the cosmic data stream. On the other side, the neo-Luddites practice their own form of reductionism, fearing that silicon will eradicate all that is carbon. Can't we instead pursue some middle course? I don't accept the notion that the only difference between a computer-mediated exchange and a lover's kiss is bandwidth—nor do I fear that I will become a mere appendage on the ubiquitous Web.

Technology enables us to do more work. We can connect with more people; we can learn from more sources; we can cast our nets farther. The irony is that—thanks to my computer, thanks to the Net—I now have more face-to-face encounters, more meetings, more travel, more experiences in the real world. I still have to, want to, and need to get out there and talk to people. Between my three e-mail accounts, my two voice mailboxes, and the fax machine—not to mention the plain old phone and mail—I spend most of my day dealing with representations of reality (isn't that what text and images are?). Because of this, and because I no longer work in an office, I find I need to get out for a walk once a day just to connect with tangible things, with flesh-and-blood humans, even if my primary contact with them occurs across the counter of the nearest coffee bar.

Just look at the crowded airways, the boom in business travel, the explosion of conferences. We all still board those planes and drive those cars to travel hours in order to meet with our colleagues. Theoretically, at least, we could do it all by phone. We could receive print-outs of the talks and just read them. We could watch it on TV. But we don't. We like it live.

Why? Because we all know the good stuff at a conference happens during the coffee breaks. Because we all know we don't really know someone until we've eaten with them. Because we all know the camera doesn't always follow the ball carrier. Because we know that even the world's best programmer can't anticipate all the possibilities that real life throws at us every second of the day.

We used to say computers would be pretty good if only they could talk—then they did. Then we said, well, if only they had pictures—and now they've got those in spades. Touch may be more difficult—but there's a pretty good simulacrum of that already in the labs. But something will always be missing, because while they are wonderful amplifiers of the human potential, computers can never be replacements for the human experience. Someone else said it, but my yoga classes confirm it: "There's no prahna in a computer," no *qi*, no life-force. And all the bandwidth in the world won't ever change that.

In our rush to embrace the wonders that technology can provide, let's never confuse its images, its sounds, its symbols, with what's real. Perhaps all this talk of reality seems patently obvious, yet with the new media hype we are sometimes unable to distinguish the real from the *trompe l'oeil* of the screen. We need to be aware of the danger of complacency, and be ever alert for opportunities to celebrate the real. Our lives are ever more built upon mediated experience, but in our increasing immersion in the digital sea, let's not forget that at bottom, it's just zeroes and ones.

And just in case we do forget, there's Virginia Woolf to remind us in *A Room of One's Own*:

> What is meant by "reality"? It would seem to be something very erratic, very undependable—now to be found in a dusty road, now in a scrap of newspaper in the street, now in a daffodil in the sun. It lights up a group in a room and stamps some casual saying. It overwhelms one walking home beneath the stars and makes the silent world more real than the world of speech—and then there it is again in an omnibus in the uproar of Picadilly. Sometimes, too, it seems to dwell in shapes too far away for us to discern what their nature is. But whatever it touches, it fixes and makes permanent. That is what remains over when the skin of the day has been cast into the hedge; that is what is left of past time and of our loves and hates.

The happiest day of my life was April 14, 1995. My husband and our two preschoolers were in Rome. I was watching, awestruck, as the kids used the Forum as a sort of archeological playground—clambering about the columns that Julius Caesar and Pompey and Claudius and Titus and all the rest had walked through conducting the affairs of the world a couple millennia ago. What made that day so extraordinary? I can't quite put it into words, but it was all about history, it was all about place, it was all about being there. It could not have happened in a Virtual Reality park in Las Vegas. It was real.

I recognize that that's a privileged story, the personal equivalent of teleteaching at MIT, but the second happiest time of my life is just about every day—when the kids come home and they run into my office. I turn from the computer and see them there, beaming and bright, and wondrously, miraculously, real.

And I'm reminded once again that what really counts is the ineluctable—the mystery, the reality of life. It's what remains over from the skin of the day—it's what we cherish and don't want to lose. It's what belongs to the realm of the sensuous—it's walking home beneath the stars—it's those things we can't program or code. These are the things that will save us.

Social Values: Ethics, Law, and Privacy

Given the diversity and complexity of a modern society, clashes over social and political values or economic interests are inevitable. Most social conflict is of the kind found in the debate of the political forum, the competition of the marketplace, and at the labor-management negotiation table. These types of conflict provide appropriate opportunities for the expression of dissent and exercise of choice—vital elements of the democratic process.

Unfortunately, conflict does not always lead to a beneficial resolution. As he witnessed the decline of a shared value system in nineteenth-century Europe, French sociologist Émile Durkheim hoped that a new form of social order would emerge, one based on the rule of law and contracts. However, the articles in this unit point to the difficulty in formulating computer-related laws and norms in the absence of consensus over basic values.

Edwin Diamond and Stephen Bates look at a range of value and legal conflicts surrounding the Internet in "Law and Order Comes to Cyberspace." In particular, the authors outline problems related to the protection of free speech, whose rules should apply when laws and mores differ among geographic regions, accountability for offensive expression, shielding children from harmful material, and protecting digital works from theft.

The next two articles look at different sides of computers and crime. Richard Behar describes the mischief and criminal activities of spies, thieves, rogue employees, and bored teens, as well as ways of improving security in "Who's Reading Your E-Mail?" Then, Arielle Emmett looks at how computers are being used to present information in civil and criminal court cases in her report "Simulations on Trial." While computer simulations can provide valuable insights, they also offer the potential to present speculation and outright falsehood as "fact." The challenge, argues Emmett, is to use "the tool's power wisely, to ensure that animations tell the truth, the whole truth, and nothing but the truth."

The final two articles consider the impact of computing on privacy—one of the most cherished values in Western culture. Government agencies, businesses, and even charities are amassing ever greater quantities of computerized data about individuals and their habits, whereabouts, and attitudes. Even where electronic files serve legitimate purposes, civil libertarians worry that too much information is collected and that a good deal of it is incomplete, irrelevant, and inaccurate. And in an era when many data banks can be accessed via far-flung networks, there are mounting concerns about information falling into the hands of those who do not have a legitimate "need to know." As Reed Karaim relates in "The Invasion of Privacy," the boundary between the private and public spheres is shifting in ways "that challenge our fundamental notion of what part of one's life belongs to oneself." Moving to another level of privacy concerns, Mary Graham reveals that the latest generation of spy satellites and geographical information systems can make a lot of things difficult to hide—including crops, environmental hazards, or a car in the driveway—in "High Resolution Unresolved."

Looking Ahead: Challenge Questions

Are you a "consequentialist"—one who believes that whether actions are ethically justifiable depends on whether or not they lead to a desired outcome (the ends justify the means); or a "deontologist"—one who believes that certain actions are intrinsically right or wrong regardless of their consequences? Explain how your answer clarifies your views on computer hacking or software piracy.

Several years ago, Yoneji Masuda of Japan argued that privacy is an outmoded social value and that the "human right to protect secrets . . . [should] change into a human duty or ethic to share information." What are the pros and cons of Masuda's position? Must we give up our right to privacy for the sake of the "Information Society"?

References

Yoneji Masuda, *The Information Society as Post-Industrial Society* (Washington, DC: The World Future Society, 1981).

UNIT 4

Law and Order Comes to Cyberspace

At the electronic frontier of computer networks, rules and regulations have been few. But as millions of settlers move into cyberspace, the new medium must accommodate the sometimes ill-suited legal restraints of civilization.

Edwin Diamond and Stephen Bates

Edwin Diamond is a journalist and director of the News Study Group at New York University. Stephen Bates, a writer and lawyer, is a senior fellow at the Annenberg Washington Program in Communications Policy Studies, a nonpartisan think tank. They are the authors of, among other books, The Spot: The Rise of Political Advertising on Television *(MIT Press, 3d ed., 1992). Individually or jointly, they have written about the Internet for* American Heritage, *the* New York Times, *the* Wall Street Journal, The Hill, *and other publications. Peter Hyman and Julie Ziegler, members of the News Study Group, provided research help for this article.*

CYBERENTHUSIASTS sing the praises of the body electric, a global realm of freewheeling computer networks where speech is open and no restrictive rules apply. But because the Internet ("the Net") exists within societies that have long-standing traditions and laws, its rapid assimilation into the "real world" is provoking tensions and confrontations that are now being played out in the legal domain.

This spring, for example, the U.S. Senate passed the Communications Decency Act, authored by Sen. James Exon (D-Nebr.), a bill that would give the Federal Communications Commission the power to regulate "indecency" on the Internet. A number of state legislatures are considering similar legislation. Net enthusiasts and systems operators argue that the Exon bill and proposals like it are unconstitutional as well as unworkable: if a literary magazine put its contents on-

line, for example, and included a short story with a four-letter word, the law could leave the editor liable for a $50,000 fine and six months in jail. Speaker Newt Gingrich, professed cyberspace-enthusiast, also opposes Exon; the bill is now awaiting action in the House of Representatives. Following the Oklahoma City explosion, Sen. Diane Feinstein (D-Calif.) introduced a bill to crack down on bomb-making guides on the Internet, an understandable, if somewhat emotional, reaction to domestic terror acts. The Feinstein bill passed the Senate and is awaiting House consideration. Meanwhile, several states are considering bills to criminalize "online stalking"—repeatedly making cybercontact with an unwilling subject. Connecticut has enacted one into law.

Whatever the fate of these regulations, in the legislatures and in the courts, the concerns they reflect won't go away. Battles over the boundaries of online free speech have erupted with increasing frequency over the past year or so, as the Internet has grown in population and in public awareness. The Net is a breeding ground for all kinds of expression, some of it lyrical and wise, but some of it vile and hateful, all of it easily accessible to anyone who logs on. Because freedom of expression is generally contested only when the speech is repugnant, the cases that have arisen tend to focus on the seamier side of the Net.

Indeed, a major factor driving such legislation is the prevalence of pornography in cyberspace. A Carnegie Mellon study found 68 commercial "adult" computer bulletin board systems (BBSs) located in 32 states with a repertory of, in the researchers' dry words, "450,620 pornographic images, animations, and text files which had been downloaded by consumers 6,432,297 times." Concerned by these findings and attempting to comply with Pennsylvania's obscenity laws, the university banished many Internet "newsgroups" that offered sexually explicit photographic images, movie clips, sounds, stories, and discussions, noting that Pittsburgh-area high schools had access to these newsgroups through the Carnegie Mellon system. Under fire for censorship, the university restored the text-only sex newsgroups, but not the ones carrying photographic images.

FIVE DIFFICULT ISSUES

The Net has thus become a First Amendment battleground. The resolution of the ensuing legal battles—some of which are likely to reach the Supreme Court—will help shape the conduct and culture of computer communications in the decades ahead. These conflicts revolve around a few fundamental questions.

1. How far does the Constitution go in protecting repugnant or defamatory speech on the Net?

Earlier this year, University of Michigan undergraduate Jake Baker was arrested by FBI agents for posting to the alt.sex.stories newsgroup a violent narrative of rape and torture that used the real name of a female classmate for the victim. Baker subsequently e-mailed a friend that "just thinking about it [his fantasies] doesn't do the trick anymore. I need to do it." The university suspended him and a federal judge ordered him held without bail, charged with the federal crime of "transporting threatening material" across state lines.

Some civil liberties groups rushed to the student's defense, arguing that the Constitution guarantees freedom even for repugnant fantasies broadcast worldwide. In June, a federal judge in Detroit implicitly agreed, throwing out the case. While the university acted properly in disciplining the student for his behavior, the judge ruled, there was no cause for a criminal indictment.

The press critic A. J. Liebling once observed, "Freedom of the press is guaranteed only to those who own one." On the Internet, for better or worse, everybody "owns" a press. Baker did not have to send his grotesque tale to a series of kinky magazines until one finally accepted it for publication; he, like any other Internet user, could simply upload his word-processed file to alt.sex.stories, where no editor checks for spelling or grammar, let alone merit.

The young woman could still bring civil action against Baker for libel. When *Penthouse* published a piece of short fiction about the sexual adventures of a "Miss Wyoming" a few years ago, the real Miss Wyoming sued. Her case was thrown out because the piece was unambiguously fictional, but a Baker-like case, where the writer knows the subject, might reach a jury.

The Jake Bakers of the world, and their supporters, could also be stopped by gatekeepers, aka censors. Although Net boosters extol the new medium for providing the freest speech the world has ever known, more and more monitors have been showing up, like hall patrols in a rowdy high school. For example, some online services screen messages sent to public chat areas, often using software that scans for comedian George Carlin's seven dirty words. The moderators of some mailing lists and Usenet groups exclude materials that they deem inappropriate. And some exclusions can be downright aggressive: renegade users have created software agents—"cancelbots"—that delete other users' public Usenet messages by forging a cancel command that seems to originate with the author of the original message.

But when public officials try to restrict information, such as in public schools, state universities, or government offices, they are potentially infringing on the First Amendment. We therefore foresee the day when a court might well order a state university to restore students' access to the alt.sex hierarchy. Restrictions of online speech, including hate speech, would also be subject to protection under the Constitution. In the past, the courts have established a "public forum doctrine" guaranteeing the right to speak in public parks and streets; some states have extended the doctrine to cover large private gathering places, such as shopping malls. Some courts will no doubt rule that the idea of a public forum applies to privately owned computer bulletin boards as well.

Litigation isn't the only way to resolve conflicts over free speech on computer networks. America Online general counsel Ellen Kirsch recently lit a small candle of good sense in the gathering cyber gloom. A lawyer from a major midwestern firm complained to America Online about postings that, he wrote, "defamed" the product of one of his clients. Kirsch responded by sending the lawyer an AOL starter kit with three hours of free time and urged him to put up his own postings defending the product. Her move was in the tradition of Supreme Court Justice Louis Brandeis, who believed that the solution to "bad speech" was not censorship but more speech.

Yet system operators may still be caught in the middle. If the sysop allows a user to post defamatory statements, for instance, the victim may sue for libel;

if the operator deletes the posting, the author may sue for abridgment of free speech. Network operators, along with their attorneys and, ultimately, judges, will have to decide such issues case by case; the process of demarcating the boundaries of free speech online will therefore undoubtedly take years.

2. Laws and mores differ among towns, states, and countries. Whose rules apply in cyberspace?

Say that a New York City user downloads a favorite Sherlock Holmes story from a London computer. The works of Arthur Conan Doyle are in the public domain in the United Kingdom but some are still under copyright in the United States. Which country's law prevails? Or what happens if a member of the California bar offers to answer legal questions on a Usenet newsgroup? Is the attorney guilty of practicing law without a license outside California? *Penthouse* has created a World Wide Web edition whose first page instructs: "If you are accessing Penthouse Internet from any country or locale where adult material is specifically prohibited by law, go no further." Is that disclaimer enough? Or would Penthouse executives be wise to avoid any travel to a puritanical country where they might face prosecution? Such questions will pop up with increasing frequency as the Internet becomes more popular.

Because it spans the globe, the Net can subvert attempts by governments to restrict the flow of information. Ontario officials, for example, forbade publication of information about a particularly sensational murder case in an attempt to avoid an O.J. Simpson-like circus of publicity. The gag order did restrain mainstream media outlets but was swept away on the Internet when someone created a Usenet group called alt.fan.karla.homolka (the name of one of the defendants). After users began posting news and rumors concerning the case, officials ordered Canadian systems operators to delete the group from their storage disks. The operators complied—but some Canadians found they could easily use the Internet to reach the newsgroup from servers in the United States, Japan, or elsewhere.

The Homolka newsgroup isn't alone in evading national laws. According to reports in Ontario newspapers, the leader of a Canadian group that claims the Holocaust never happened plans to promote his views on the Net. The Canadian, Ernst Zundel, supposedly will use an Internet access provider based in the United States in hopes of avoiding prosecution under Canadian laws against hate mongering (on the Net, he'll find others of his ilk on the thriving newsgroup called alt.revisionism).

One need not even leave the United States to encounter a broad range of standards on acceptable forms of expression. Consider the saga of Robert and Carleen Thomas, a married couple in their late 30s living in California's Silicon Valley. Until four years ago, Robert had churned through a series of white-collar sales jobs on the fringes of the valley's booming, high-tech industries. Then he and Carleen found their own entrepreneurial niche. Working out of their tract home in Milpitas, they started the Amateur Action Bulletin Board System (AABBS), which enabled subscribers to download sexually explicit images and join in chat groups to discuss the materials.

The Thomases' digitized collection reached 20,000 images, largely gleaned from a photographer friend who once worked for *Playboy* and from magazines published abroad. The most frequently downloaded images depicted partially clad children, bestiality, and bondage. The Thomases promoted their service as "the nastiest place on earth" and advertised on the Net that they accepted Visa and MasterCard. By 1994, AABBS had more than 3,600 subscribers, each paying $99 per year for the privilege of accessing the collection.

Unhappily for the Thomases, they received too much publicity. In mid-1993, a Tennessee man surfing the Net came across an AABBS publicity post in the form of suggestive picture captions. The surfer, upset by what seemed to him to be child pornography, notified U.S. Postal Service authorities in Memphis. These officials activated Operation Longarm, a government anti-obscenity drive that focuses on child porn and, most recently, computer networks. As Longarm officials see it, the anonymous nature of the Internet makes it the perfect place for pedophiles to lurk.

The Memphis authorities assigned the complaint to postal investigator David Dirmeyer, who joined AABBS (under the alias "Lance White") and began downloading its images and tapping into its chat groups. Based on Dirmeyer's findings, postal investigators raided the Thomases' home in January 1994, armed with a 32-page search warrant, and seized computers, videotape-dubbing machines, and the AABBS database of photographs and videotapes. The couple was indicted, tried in federal district court in Memphis, and convicted of distributing obscene materials in interstate commerce. Last December, Robert Thomas was sentenced to 37 months; Carleen to 30 months.

The Thomas case reveals the difficulty of interpreting, in a world of computer networks, the meaning of "community standards"—the test by which a piece of work is to be judged obscene, according to the legal doctrine that the Supreme Court established in its 1973 decision in *Miller v. California*. In *Miller*, the Supreme Court ruled in effect that residents of Bible Belt towns need not put up with Times Square raunch. But in cyberspace, where physical proximity to an information source is unimportant, *Miller*-style community standards are essentially unenforceable.

Civil libertarians worry that if the Thomases' convictions hold, the Net will be governed by the standards of the most restrictive communities in the nation. In appealing their conviction, the Thomases argue that the materials they offered were not obscene by the standards of their Bay Area community. In fact, in 1992 the San Jose high-tech crime unit—essentially the Thomases' hometown police—seized the AABBS computers, scrutinized the collection of images, and found them insufficiently offensive to justify prosecution.

In the United States, individuals have the constitutional right to own obscenity in the privacy of their home, so long as the owner doesn't sell it, publicly display it, or show it to children; a Memphis citizen could therefore fly to San Francisco, purchase a book of AABBS-style photos, and bring it home without breaking any law. Many Net users and civil libertarians would like the courts to treat travel on the information superhighway in the same way—as if Lance White had motored to Milpitas. Indeed, some Thomas supporters argue that the international network of computers constitutes a "community" unto itself for *Miller* purposes, a frontier that cannot be subjected to offline restrictions. If the Net can't make its own law, then the natives at least want it insulated from the Memphises of the world.

But judges have rejected similar virtual-travel arguments concerning mail-order pornography and phone sex. In the 1989 phone sex case *Sable Communications v. FCC*, Sable argued that the government was creating "an impermissible national standard of obscenity" that forced providers "to tailor all their messages to the least tolerant community." The Supreme Court was unpersuaded, holding that "if Sable's audience is comprised of different communities with different local standards, Sable ultimately bears the burden of complying."

Courts are likely to treat online services the same way. An information provider may be expected to comply with the law's geographic limitations whenever access to its material is contingent on a transaction—such as the payment of money—that allows the purveyor to check the user's locale. Operators of computer bulletin board services, for example, would be made to ask for, and check on, users' locations. They may be required to use an 800 or 900 number that is programmed to block certain area codes, thus ensuring that people from conservative communities don't log on. The Thomases knew enough law to understand the hazards of letting underage users subscribe (they spot-checked names on credit card orders, calling the listed cardholder to be sure that he or she was the actual subscriber), but neither they nor their lawyer recognized the perils of community standards.

In this respect, members-only bulletin boards like the Thomases' hold less potential for charting new legal ground than cases where material is broadly available on the Internet. In fact, the Net offers many megabytes of raw and unsettling information, almost all of which can be obtained anonymously and for free; there is no way for a supplier of, say, pornographic pictures to know whether those images are being downloaded in a Bible Belt town.

3. When offensive expression is distributed on a computer network, who is accountable?

Are people who post pornographic pictures to a Usenet newsgroup liable for obscenity in, say, Memphis, given that they had no way of knowing where images might be downloaded ? Would they be liable if children downloaded the images? For that matter, would the operators of an Internet access service in Memphis be liable for importing obscene material into town, or for making pornographic material (which adults can legally view) unlawfully accessible to children, merely for providing the conduit over which users reached such postings? The law is still murky on these questions of accountability.

As more and more people gain Net access through their schools and employers, such institutions are facing an uncertain future. At Santa Rosa Junior College in California, two female students were the subjects of sexually derogatory comments on a chat group restricted to male students. The women filed a civil rights claim against the college, arguing that the group violated federal law by excluding women and that the messages—discussing the two women in graphic "bathroom wall" language, according to one description—constituted sexual harassment. The students demanded that the journalism instructor who ran the online system be fired for aiding and abetting the harassment. The school hastily settled the suit, awarding the women cash compensation for both complaints and putting the instructor on indefinite administrative leave—and, in the process, exerting a considerable chilling effect on the people who run online services at other universities.

Academia isn't the only place where online sexual (or sexist) chatter will collide with freedom of speech. For example, if employers provide desktop access to Usenet discussion groups, including the gamy alt.sex hierarchy, could they be sued by women workers for creating a "hostile workplace"? In the past, courts have ruled that tacking up *Playboy*-style centerfolds on office bulletin boards can constitute sexual harassment of female workers—is the display of such images on computer screens any different?

The question of responsibility is also pivotal in a suit that Stratton Oakmont, a brokerage firm based in Lake Success, N.Y., brought against the Prodigy online service. Individuals sent a series of postings accusing Stratton Oakmont of criminal behavior and violations of Securities and Exchange Commission rules to Prodigy's "Money Talk" forum. Last year, Stratton Oakmont sued Prodigy for $200 million in libel damages. Prodigy lawyers argued that the service is a passive carrier of information, like the telephone company. Stratton Oakmont, however, countered that Prodigy is in the publishing business and is therefore responsible for all communication on its service.

A New York state judge ruled that Prodigy, which routinely screens postings for obscene or potentially libelous content, does in fact exert a form of editorial control over content on its system and could be sued as a publisher. Prodigy is appealing the state court's decision. (The man accused of writing the messages, a former Prodigy employee, says someone forged his ID. Such impersonation is relatively easy for even a journeyman hacker, and is bound to become more common—further muddying the waters of responsibility.)

In deciding whether Prodigy is liable for libelous material posted by its users, the appeals court will have to rely on few—and ambiguous—legal precedents. One court ruled that CompuServe was not responsible for material placed on its system by a subcontractor. Another court, however, held that a bulletin board operator was liable for copyright infringements perpetrated by its users. One certainty: if systems operators are deemed responsible, they will monitor users much more closely—and pass on the cost of new staff to their customers. User fees will increase as Net access providers spend money on legal fees fighting off lawsuits.

4. How can children be insulated from the Net's raunchier material?

A few years ago, protesters in Fresno, Calif., used a magnifying glass to find offensive textbook illustrations, including what they termed "phallic bicycle seats." A group in suburban New York City recently claimed that it had spotted a drawing of a topless bather in a beach scene in one of the *Where's Waldo?* children's books. After the threat of legal action, the book was removed from the school library shelves. It doesn't take a magnifying glass to find hard-core pornography on the Internet—and since many youngsters can navigate circles around their elders on the Net, some adults are in a near panic.

Not without reason. In one afternoon of online prospecting, we unearthed instructions for making bombs,

an electronic pamphlet called "Suicide Methods," and a guide for growing marijuana at home. Besides NASA photos of Jupiter, worldwide weather reports, and the Library of Congress catalog, kids can access *Penthouse, The Anarchist's Cookbook,* and the poisonously anti-Semitic tract, *Protocols of the Elders of Zion.* It is as if every modem owner in the world—including porn fans, skinheads, bazooka lovers, anarchists, bigots, harassers, and Holocaust deniers—selects the books for everyone else's school library. As President Clinton told a meeting of the American Society of Newspaper Editors this spring, "It is folly to think that we should sit idly by when a child who is a computer whiz may be exposed to things on that computer which in some ways are more powerful, more raw, and more inappropriate than those from which we protect them when they walk in a 7-11."

Any user of the Internet can post pornography or sexual invitations to any unmoderated Usenet group: according to the Toronto arts paper *Eye Weekly,* a Canadian recently sent a detailed post on oral sex to newsgroups populated by children. Moreover, the facelessness of the Net makes it impossible to determine who is accessing information. The manager of an adult bookstore can recognize and eject a 12-year-old; the operator of an Internet file archive cannot.

Several companies are now developing "lock-out" Internet accounts that block access to certain regions of the Net known to contain material inappropriate for children. Many online services, public schools, and universities block out particular Usenet groups—often all of the alt.sex groups; sometimes only the most repugnant, such as alt.sex.pedophilia. Some sites have modified the Internet search tool Veronica to reject requests that include, for example, the word erotica. The American Library Association and other anticensorship organizations are keeping a watchful eye on these efforts to guard children—ready to oppose measures that tip the scales too far away from protection of free speech.

In any case, Net-savvy kids can breach such safeguards. If a school's Usenet system blocks the alt.sex groups, for example, a sufficiently motivated young hacker can use a common Internet tool called telnet to gain access to a system that does offer them. Such surfing gets even easier with the online menu system called gopher; the user can start at a "clean" site and, sooner or later, reach a "dirty" one. We started from the U.S. Department of Education's gopher server, for instance, and in seven gopher hops reached "The School Stopper's Textbook," which instructs students on how to blow up toilets, short-circuit electrical wiring, and "break into your school at night and burn it down." On the World Wide Web, with its tens of thousands of hyperlinks, similar short hops can whisk a student from a stuffy government site to an X-rated one. Even without access to gopher, telnet, or the

Web, students can find plenty of inappropriate material; automated servers in Japan and elsewhere send out individual postings, including those from the alt.sex hierarchy, to anyone who sends the proper command through e-mail.

Most states have laws against giving children pornography, and some also prohibit providing minors with "dangerous information" (for example, guides to building explosives). Thus, in hopes of limiting their liability, many school districts are requiring parents to sign forms before their children can have Internet accounts—in effect, permission slips for virtual field trips. The lawyers drafting the documents are treading a fine line. A form vaguely referring to the possibility of "offensive material" may not hold up in court as proof that consent was adequately informed. On the other hand, a parental form that is too specific, spelling out the multifold possibilities of pornography, racism, sexism, munitions manuals, and all the rest, may frighten mom and dad into keeping the kids offline altogether—or into shopping for another school district.

Schools will do the best they can to corral children in safe cyberspaces. But will that be enough? Many on-liners worry that Congress will in effect mandate that the entire Internet become a child-safe "Happynet." The political pressures may indeed prove irresistible, especially now that the Christian Coalition is lobbying for laws against online pornography. A Happynet Act would violate the First Amendment, but litigating the case up to the Supreme Court could take several years and hundreds of thousands of dollars.

5. How can creative artists protect their online work from digital theft?

A different kind of "free speech" issue involves the possible use of proprietary material. Writers have belatedly discovered that full texts of their copyrighted works are being marketed—without their permission and without compensation—by for-profit data-retrieval companies. Firms such as CARL Corp. and Information Access have in the past typed or electronically scanned in a published piece or writing, uploaded it to a database, and then charged customers for each online retrieval, or "hit."

Earlier this year, both the publishers of *Modern Maturity* magazine and the owners of the K-III group (which includes *New York* magazine, among others) ended agreements with Information Access; *Reader's Digest* has already severed its connections with CARL's UnCover service. In each case, executives not only wanted to retain potentially lucrative rights but were also responding to the threat of legal action from freelance writers for a share of online royalties.

In a similar conflict, litigation has gone beyond the threat stage. The National Writers Union (NWU), a spirited group representing freelance authors, has filed a federal suit against six large communications companies, including the *New York Times*, seeking damages for "electronic piracy." The suit alleges that the companies have been selling what they don't own, the electronic republication rights to freelancers' contributions—rights that standard freelance contracts didn't cover. The case is slowly proceeding toward trial.

Writers' union representatives have been negotiating with several such services to work out an arrangement for assuring that electronic duplication of magazine articles and books will be accompanied by royalty payments. The precedent is the ASCAP system set up decades ago by the American Society of Composers, Authors, and Publishers, which provides that every time radio stations play a recording the creator gets a few pennies. As a result of these negotiations, some database services have promised to make reprint payments directly to authors who retain copyright.

One knotty issue is whether a "hit" on an electronic article more closely resembles republication in an anthology or sale of a back issue. This is an important distinction. Freelance writers ordinarily sell one-time publication rights for their magazine articles. If the magazine wants to reprint the article, in an anthology or elsewhere, it must pay the writer something extra. But if the magazine sells additional copies of a back issue, it doesn't owe the writer anything more.

To defend their territory, magazines and newspapers are redrafting their standard contracts to stipulate that writers are selling unlimited electronic rights along with one-time print rights. This development doesn't please writers' organizations, who worry that hungry freelancers will heedlessly sign away rights that may eventually prove valuable. In 1993, the National Writers Union urged the intellectual property working group of the Clinton administration's National Information Infrastructure initiative to prohibit publishers from contractually claiming "those rights (usually electronic-based rights) that do not yet exist, and/or those rights that, at the time of negotiation, lack a measurable economic value." Not surprisingly, publishers opposed the proposal; the administration, faced with more pressing business, did not push the issue. Established writers, meanwhile, have instructed their agents to shop new book projects around rather than sign over electronic rights—in some cases severing long-standing relationships with publishers as a result. Here, as elsewhere, the online technologies are reopening struggles that offline society thought it had settled decades ago.

BRAVE NEW NETWORKS

These and other situations reflect the growing conflict between the law and computer-network technology. The legal mind constructs a time and computer-network space-bound world; cybernauts inhabit a world where physical location is immaterial. "Our laws didn't envision the Internet," says Larry Kramer, professor of constitutional law at New York University. In a notable effort to bridge the gap, a new Center for Informatics Law has been established at the John Marshall Law School in Chicago. The center promotes the need to create a separate set of principles just for cyberspace that may depart from the old common-law system.

Rhetorically, at least, the conflict between the old spatial laws and the new Net technology has been one-sided. The technologists are better poets, and they have appropriated the most vibrant images to advance their cause. Indeed, the Progress and Freedom Foundation, a conservative Washington think tank, produced a document earlier this year with the less-than-modest title "Magna Carta for the Knowledge Age." The document talks grandly, if somewhat vaguely, of "liberation in cyberspace" from "rules, regulations, taxes and laws"—calling for, among other things, the abolition of the Federal Communications Commission.

In this way, the eager explorers of cyberspace like to draw a parallel between the emergence of the new world information order and the development of the frontier in the American West. This is the conceit promoted by the Electronic Frontier Foundation, which has been working since 1990 to promote online civil liberties. But we find two metaphorically opposed images of "the frontier." One is the heroic, colorized frontier of romantic fiction and television and movies, populated by manly sheriffs and spunky womenfolk. The other is the actual frontier, where life was often nasty, brutish, and short.

Eventually, in both fiction and fact, civilization arrived, bringing with it rules, social order, and taxes. To all but die-hard survivalists, this was regarded as progress. The Internet is now undergoing a similar transition, as the new, inchoate medium of unfettered individual freedom begins to evolve. The Wild West of the cyberfrontier is already morphing before our eyes—on the screen and in the courts.

Who's reading your
e-mail?
by Richard Behar

As the world gets networked, spies, rogue employees, and bored teens are invading companies' computers to make mischief, steal trade secrets—even sabotage careers.

This is it. We're in.
There are things here I can now destroy.
This is a good thing. The geek in me is happy.
—*Three hackers in San Antonio, 11:10 P.M.*

T was the week before Christmas, and the employees of XYZ Corp. were logging off a successful year with holiday parties at company headquarters in New York City. Meanwhile, inside their locked, darkened offices, not a creature was stirring, not even a computer mouse—or so they thought. Unbeknownst to the merrymakers, a team of professional hackers in Texas was preparing to invade XYZ's system from 1,600 miles away.

Operation Nutcracker, as we'll call it, spanned two nights. By the time the sun started to scroll over San Antonio on the

REPORTER ASSOCIATES *Amy Kover and Melanie Warner*

second day, the hackers had penetrated seven of XYZ's computers. They'd invaded a subsidiary near Washington, D.C., and the corporate tax division in Manhattan. They'd gained "root access" on five systems, meaning that they'd seized the full powers enjoyed by XYZ's systems administrators. Most alarmingly, they'd invaded XYZ's electronic heart—sophisticated computers used exclusively by its technology department. (For a detailed account of the hack, see box.)

The operation was never detected; fortunately for XYZ, the hackers had no malicious intent. They were experts at WheelGroup Corp., a San Antonio security firm that conducts "external assessments" as a diagnostic service for clients. Two months before, a WheelGroup executive

had boasted to FORTUNE that the firm had yet to find a network it couldn't pierce electronically. "It's really very easy to do," he'd said. "If it's a big network, it may take us an evening. Otherwise, it may take two hours."

That was Texas optimism; all computer systems are different, and making Nutcracker succeed took longer. But WheelGroup has the requisite hacker talents—technical ingenuity and stare-at-the-screen obsessiveness—in abundance. Most of its founders are ex-military men who served in the Air Force Information Warfare Center; in 1994, four of them teamed up to capture one of the military's most notorious hackers.

FORTUNE saw the boast as a challenge. It took some time, but we found a well-

> *"The only secure computer is one that's turned off, locked in a safe, and buried 20 feet down in a secret location—and I'm not completely confident of that one either."*

regarded FORTUNE 500 company that was willing to serve as a guinea pig, provided its name wasn't disclosed. To make the exercise realistic, XYZ agreed that its chief of information systems would be kept on the sidelines; a team of computer experts from the Coopers & Lybrand accounting firm was retained to monitor the break-in and safeguard XYZ's computers and data.

Nutcracker's success attests to what every technology manager knows: The more the computers of the business world become interconnected—via the Internet and private networks—the more exposed they are to break-ins. Says Bruce Schneier, author of the book *E-mail Security*: "The only secure computer is one that is turned off, locked in a safe, and buried 20 feet down in a secret location—and I'm not completely confident of that one either."

On a planet where at least 200 million E-mail messages traverse cyberspace each day, and where companies depend increasingly on networks to speed communications with customers and suppliers, enemies and mischief-makers no longer need to trespass physically on corporate turf. Computers offer ready points of en-

How we invaded a Fortune 500 company

The operations room at WheelGroup is crammed with computers, modems, phone lines, and a handful of Texans whom any CEO would like to have on his side. "This is where we bring the world to us," says Toney Jennings, a former Air Force captain who runs the San Antonio security company. To his left sits Jerry Lathem, who won't talk about the computer work he did for ten years at the National Security Agency. Nearby are Scott Waddell and Kevin Ziese, who slept under their desks for three weeks at the Air Force Information Warfare Center in 1994, "hacking backwards" until they caught a 16-year-old Briton who had broken into military computers 150 times.

WheelGroup's task tonight, Operation Nutcracker, is to penetrate computers at "XYZ Corp.," a FORTUNE 500 company in New York. It will begin with a procedure called network mapping. Conveniently for hackers, a snapshot of every company's Internet links is available on the Network Information Center (NIC), a public registry of all computer domain names. What's a domain? Think of the Internet as a country and of corporations as individual states. The domains are like cities, and each corporation owns at least one. Why register the name? If you don't, legitimate visitors would have no way of reaching you electronically.

A second public registry, Domain Name Service (DNS), goes deeper. It lists subnets—streets and buildings—within each domain, as well as E-mail gateways for a company's messages. We find two gateways listed for XYZ Corp. DNS data also reveal the numerical addresses of computers within the gateways. "We now have individual targets," says Waddell, "but first we want to know how many computers or networks are sitting between WheelGroup and XYZ's employees."

1:10 A.M. (day one)

WheelGroup has found its answer by "bouncing" some E-mail. When the U.S. Postal Service returns a letter as undeliverable, the envelope carries postmarks indicating its journey. So, too, with E-mail. "A simple typo can give you valuable information about a network," says Doug Webster, WheelGroup's marketing director. The team sends E-mail to an XYZ employee in New York, but purposely misspells the person's name so the message bounces back—with data about the path it has traveled. In this case, good news: There's only one hop between the employee's computer and one of XYZ's gateways. Crack the gateway and the employee's confidential files will be just a few keystrokes away.

2:02 A.M.

The next step is called pinging. "With a software program, we're sending an electronic beam to every [XYZ] address, asking the machine if it's alive," says Waddell. Eight computers respond. Since each can have as many as 65,000 ports, or communications windows, the next stage is a so-called port scan to find the active ones.

Companies with tight computer security can usually determine if a hacker is pinging or conducting a port scan. But XYZ detects none of our activities. Even so, the port scan, which takes about five minutes, elicits automatic warnings from XYZ's computers about how we might be prosecuted if we trespass. The warnings satisfy legal requirements—a hacker can't argue, for instance, that he broke in accidentally.

We also discover that XYZ has done something that is potentially risky: It lists its brand of firewall—the software it uses to ward off hackers. This is like posting a sign on your backyard fence that reads PROTECTED BY ACE SECURITY, but it gives would-be invaders a useful clue. Hacker bulletin boards on the Internet regularly post weaknesses in firewall products.

try for spies, thieves, disgruntled employees, sociopaths, and bored teens. They're all hackers, a term that once meant hobbyist but now denotes someone who barges into a system uninvited. Once they're in your company's network, they can steal trade secrets, destroy data, sabotage operations, even subvert a particular deal or career.

Computer vulnerability is becoming a giant, expensive headache. Corporate America spent $6 billion on network security last year, according to Dataquest. Nevertheless, when the FBI and a respected think tank surveyed some 400 companies and institutions last March, more than 40% reported recent break-ins. Some 30% of all break-ins involving the

Internet took place despite the presence of a firewall, a computer equipped with costly software that is supposed to let only legitimate traffic pass. The going estimates for financial losses from computer crime reach as high as $10 billion a year.

But the truth is that nobody really knows. Almost all attacks go undetected—as many as 95%, says the FBI, like our invasion of XYZ Corp. What's more, of the attacks that are detected, few—perhaps 15%—are reported to law-enforcement agencies. Even at that level, the good guys can't cope. Speaking before hundreds of computer experts from IBM, Fidelity Investments, Mobil, the Secret Service, U.S. Customs, and other institutions last

fall, Dennis Hughes of the FBI declared flatly: "The hackers are driving us nuts. Everyone is getting hacked into. It's out of control." Hughes should know: He is the FBI's senior expert on computer crime.

The companies Hughes was addressing did recently get a break: In October, President Clinton signed into law a new bill that should make it easier to prosecute hackers. The bill allows for criminal forfeiture, fines of $10 million, and sentences of 15 years in computer cases involving economic espionage—broadly defined as stealing trade secrets from U.S. companies. The law permits corporate victims to use court orders to safeguard secrets in the courtroom. There's just one caveat: The corporation is re-

2:17 A.M.

XYZ, it turns out, has reason to brag. Its firewall—a $25,000 Raptor Eagle—is one of the most powerful, and it thwarts WheelGroup utterly. The team spends nearly three hours unsuccessfully trying to peer into XYZ's computer ports. (They identify a tempting-looking MCI computer router on XYZ's premises, but, unlike real hackers, refrain from tampering with it because they don't have the owner's permission.)

Bottom line: Without inside information or the luxury of more time, the Internet gateways of XYZ are virtually impregnable. But so was the Maginot Line the French built to keep out the Germans after World War I. The Nazis simply went around the fortification, invading France by way of Belgium. "Firewalls are the biggest form of false security," says David Rivera, a computer expert at Coopers & Lybrand who has been hired to protect XYZ throughout the experiment. "A corporation can't just lock its front door and expect to be safe."

5:00 A.M.

WheelGroup will now try to gain access by avoiding the Internet and attacking XYZ's individual computers. It will use a method called war-dialing. Consulting the phone number on the business card of an XYZ employee, the hackers assume (correctly) that computer modems at the company will use the same area code and three-digit prefix. Waddell downloads a free program from the Internet called ToneLoc, written by hackers named Minor Threat and Mucho Maas. It comes with a manual that explains how to automatically call thousands of phone numbers within a specific range.

To thwart war-dialers, many phone companies have equipment that detects sequential dialing and shuts it down. ToneLoc randomizes the numbers it calls to elude such gear. It then compiles a list of numbers that connect to modems. Using just one computer and one phone line, WheelGroup war-dials 1,500 numbers at XYZ in the space of 16 hours.

9:13 P.M.

We return to the operations room to find that ToneLoc has identified more than 55 modems at XYZ. Two dozen have responded to ToneLoc's call in ways that look especially promising. In just under two hours, the WheelGroupers hit pay dirt.

Hey, we're in. I got a prompt.
Uw, that's a big leap. This is a hot one.
Bingo! bingo!
That's a big fish. Hope it's not a stand-alone machine. Oh, man.
I wanna see network and haven't been able to locate it. Security is not strong on this box.

The machine, a fax server at one of XYZ's subsidiaries, has presented a "log in" prompt. The hackers enter a common account name for that particular kind of computer; they then guess that the password might be the same name. They are correct. Security on the computer is abysmal. Within minutes, they are able to access a dial-out line that lets them place long-distance calls anywhere in the country—at XYZ's expense. "This is a hacker's dream," says Rivera. "Free long-distance service!"

The hackers use the long distance line to hack into one of WheelGroup's own computers. "You can now hack into any company from XYZ's modem," explains Ziese. "We could even use XYZ to war-dial someone else. If it's traced, XYZ could be blamed. We'd be long gone by tomorrow morning."

Ziese is able to play chess and hangman on the fax server (the server wins). Then he leaps electronically to an XYZ office near Washington, D.C., where he gains the ability to issue purchase orders, review lists of vendors and products, and even set currency exchange rates for international sales. "They probably think they're safe because they're not on the Internet," he says. "Surprise! If I was [XYZ's] competitor, I'd spend a lot of time here." Ziese and Waddell never obtain system-administrator privileges on the machines, but they've gained enough power to alter data and inflate XYZ's phone bill by tens of thousands of dollars. Eventually, they move on to another modem and hit pay dirt again.

(continued)

quired to have taken "reasonable measures" (like installing firewalls) to keep its data secret.

Companies that fail to take reasonable measures may lose more than just secrets. A new concept—"downstream liability"—is emerging in computer law. Say a hacker exploiting XYZ's lax security invades its network and uses it as a springboard to disrupt computer operations at other companies. If the other companies' damages are substantial, they might seek to hold XYZ liable—especially since hackers rarely have deep pockets. While there hasn't been such a case to date, computer experts say it's only a matter of time.

A terrifying variant of downstream lia-

bility arose in the case WheelGroup's experts solved in the Air Force. During three weeks in 1994, more than 150 Internet intrusions came through Rome Laboratory, the Air Force's top command-and-control R&D facility. The perpetrators—a 16-year-old British hacker and an associate who was never identified—used the Air Force computers as a hopping-off point to invade computers of several defense contractors and the South Korean Atomic Research Institute. (For a time, investigators feared that the atomic-research computers belonged to North Korea, whose leaders could have taken the intrusion as an act of war by the United States.)

Another victim of the British hacker was Xilinx, a $600-million-a-year computer-

chip maker in San Jose. Recalls Eric Schemmerling, Xilinx's technical manager: "Our people were tricked into giving password information about our system. The passwords wound up on computer bulletin boards all over Europe. We eventually had a ring of people using our site to hop into government facilities. We became a public hack express."

Despite these and other horror stories, thousands of companies have yet to install even the most rudimentary defenses—such as insisting that employees use hard-to-guess passwords. A 1995 survey by the American Society for Industrial

12:01 A.M. (day two)

We're into one. We're at a C prompt.

Oh, good. Bet the farm. Go ahead and run WIN. It may crash the box.

WELCOME TO THE [XYZ] CORPORATE TAX DEPT. LOCAL AREA NETWORK.

We're trying to be careful not to hose the connection.

He could trash the system. There's data that he can destroy at this point. What are your intentions, Kevin?

I'm an honorable girl.

The hackers have gotten into a Windows PC that belongs to a woman in the tax department at XYZ's headquarters. It is running a popular program called pcAnywhere, and the owner has neglected to set up the machine to require password authentication. After determining this, WheelGroup simply loads its own copy of pcAnywhere software into its Texas computer and uses it to connect into hers.

The team now has full "root" power on the tax-department PC. In other words, says Waddell, "a command, a couple of keystrokes, and I could destroy everything." It is a chilling thought, particularly since the data they've accessed seems sensitive. It includes information on XYZ's investments and interest expenses, as well as amortization rates for its trademarks. Starting with this PC, a hacker could plant a destructive virus that would proliferate across the company as the woman used her machine to exchange data with others in her department and elsewhere. "We can put child pornography on there and tip off the feds!" exclaims Ziese, before settling down to try another modem.

2:02 A.M.

GUEST lets me in. I got in.

I feel root coming on. Let's own the box.

My mouth is watering here. Everybody has stopped breathing.

Root. Now we're really root. No kidding around. I could shut this box down so that not only couldn't you reboot it, but you'd have to send it back to the manufacturer. One command could do that.

Look, people were logged into this box after midnight tonight.

WheelGroup has scored its biggest coup: Root access on a sophisticated workstation used by employees in XYZ's technology department. Ironically, the same department has issued a memo urging all XYZ employees to switch to hard-to-guess passwords. Yet WheelGroup has invaded the workstation using a common account name called "Guest," which requires no password.

The hackers now have the ability to read, modify, or destroy files. With one command, they claim, they can shut down the machine in such a way as to make it impossible to restart without removing and reprogramming one of its chips.

Within one hour, WheelGroup is able to leverage its power, gaining root access to three more systems in the technology department that are linked to the workstation. A real intruder would install sniffer software, a type of traffic analyzer, to capture account names and passwords as they traverse the network during business hours. (We do not install a sniffer because it could crash the computer.) These compromised accounts would then lead to access to other systems. Before long, the hackers would have the information they needed to make their way from one department to another. All this from a single dial-in connection that has an account with no password.

Nutcracker ends with one final trick on XYZ: E-mail spoofing. Using the Internet, Waddell sends a bogus electronic message to a busy division executive—the same executive who approved FORTUNE's experiment—proposing a $5,000 Christmas bonus for an employee who helped plan the project. Waddell disguises the message so that when it shows up in the executive's electronic mailbox, it appears to have come not from WheelGroup in Texas, but from his own deputy in New York. The spoof works. Upon reading the message, the boss fires back an E-mail reply to his puzzled subordinate: "Okay, fine."

Had Waddell wanted to go undetected, he could have devised a mechanism to intercept the response, keeping the deputy out of the loop. But the point is already clear: An electronic Machiavelli could wreak havoc inside a corporation today.

Security found that 24% of corporations have no procedures for safeguarding proprietary data. Another industry survey revealed that nearly half of U.S. companies don't even have a basic security policy for their computer systems. Warns WheelGroup's Lee Sutterfield: "If CEOs don't believe that this is a problem, at some point they're gonna get whacked."

David Rivera, one of the Coopers & Lybrand experts who monitored Nutcracker, has helped test-hack two dozen corporate clients. The latest: a pharmaceuticals giant whose systems he invaded in December. "We were led to a computer in a conference room that was accessible to every employee," he says. "In less than an hour, we got so far into the payroll system that we could have given anyone a bonus. Within two hours, we cracked 30% of their passwords. They were shocked."

Wind River Systems learned its lesson the hard way. A publicly traded, $44-million-a-year software company in Alameda, California, Wind River had set up an Internet site to exchange E-mail with customers. The system was protected by just a rudimentary firewall. By guessing some passwords, hackers in Germany were able to sneak through the firewall and gain access to Wind River computers in France and California.

An inflated bill for Internet access tipped off systems administrators that something was wrong; they checked the computer logs and found hacker footprints. Says Steve Sekiguchi, the company's top technology manager: "You could see them logging into various machines in our network and wandering around in the middle of the night. The legitimate users were home asleep."

Like many computer-crime victims, Wind River cannot determine whether anything was stolen; at worst, the hackers made off with programming code whose circulation could hurt future sales. "Our family jewels are software, and once it's out, it can be duplicated forever," says Sekiguchi, who is now outsourcing computer security to a firm called Pilot Network Services. "We're like a lot of companies. Once a hacker gets in the front door, he's in the house. Nobody locks the doors between the bedrooms, the kitchen, and the dining room. So once a hacker is inside, you don't know which rooms he's been in."

Wind River's problem is common; its willingness to discuss it is not. Most companies that have been electronically molested won't talk to the press—or even the police. "Nobody wants to be on the front page of a newspaper because they were broken into," says Lloyd Hession, a key architect of Internet security for IBM. "A big concern is loss of public trust and public image." Not to mention making your company a target for shareholder suits or copycat hackers. Moreover, many executives fear that calling the cops will hinder their operations. "There's a common misconception that if you call the FBI, we'll haul your entire computer system away in a 40-foot trailer," says an FBI agent in San Francisco. "The level of ignorance out there is just amazing."

When Citibank discovered in 1994 that a group of Russian hackers had made $10 million in illegal transfers, the bank had a private security firm quietly crack the case. All but $400,000 was recovered. Citibank eventually spoke to the FBI and the media. It was apparently an outside job, the first such grand larceny in cyberspace—or at least the first a major bank has admitted to. Citibank's reward for being forthright? It saw its top 20 customers wooed by rival banks, all claiming their computer systems were more secure.

If money in the bank is vulnerable, how safe are the secrets you put in your E-mail? When sent via the Internet, E-mail is like a postcard that can be read by hackers or copied in every "post office," or Internet computer, it passes through. E-mail confined to a private network isn't necessarily more secure: Tools for getting to it are readily available to hackers. "Just assume that anything you can do, someone else can do, like accessing E-mail from a remote location," says security expert Schneier.

Computer attacks can originate anywhere. Even in the age of the globe-girdling Internet, the perp frequently is no farther away than the office next door. At Intel, a technical contractor named Randal Schwartz used his access to company premises to steal a password file from a network server. The file was encrypted, or scrambled, for safety, but Schwartz simply ran a program designed to break the codes. Intel had him arrested before he did any damage.

Chemical Bank suffered a security breach several years ago involving one of the top technology administrators at headquarters in New York. The administrator, who went by the office nickname Mad Dog, was caught erasing E-mail that was unfavorable to him from colleagues' computers. Subsequent investigation revealed that Mad Dog had also been using his computer to do consulting work for a rival bank. His career was over.

At the same time, security breaches from outside are on the upswing. Last February, FBI director Louis Freeh told a Senate panel that 23 countries are engaged in economic spying against American business, succeeding in some cases "with a few keystrokes." Major culprits: China, Canada, France, India, and Japan. The FBI's Hughes says that at least seven nations are training intelligence agents to hack U.S. computers for commercial data.

More and more freelancers are getting into the act. Hackers thrive in the Internet's anarchic subculture, which glamorizes their skills. For some, sneaking into computers is an adolescent phase they outgrow; others never do. Consider Brooklyn's Morty Rosenfeld, 25, who was convicted in 1992 after a Secret Service raid on his house netted 176 credit reports he had hacked from TRW, the giant credit-information provider. Rosenfeld's grand plan was to build and sell PCs using parts bought with stolen credit card numbers.

Having paid his debt to society with eight months in prison, Rosenfeld is back in Brooklyn. He feels he is reformed, but he's still hacking. "I'm invading systems on a regular basis," he says. "You have to learn new techniques to stay current." One recent target: a McDonald's office in Manhattan. "Security was lax, and they were running some software I wanted to test," Rosenfeld says. "McDonald's is a training hack, a baby hack."

There's demand for a man of his skills. Rosenfeld has been in talks with Panasonic Interactive Media to sign a juicy six-figure deal to develop a computer handball game. "So he was arrested for hacking—that's no big deal," says Panasonic manager Jim Jennings. "I've done stuff like that too. I'm 40 years old, and most guys in my generation did. That's how you learn. You break into programs, commit piracy, all kinds of wild and crazy things."

Another admirer is Rosenfeld's local Internet service provider, Escape Internet Access Services. It gives him free Internet service in exchange for security advice and the latest gossip about hackers. "Trust me, it's better to have them on your side than against you," says a manager at Escape. Of course, Rosenfeld did use Escape's service to hack McDonald's.

Rosenfeld is also a master at "social engineering," hacker-speak for tricking workers into offering information that will help during break-ins. That appeals to Al

117

Zaretz, a private eye who has worked with Rosenfeld in the past. Zaretz runs A-Z Investigative Services in New York City and is in the business of corporate espionage. He knows not to ask too many questions about the source of valuable data. "Corporations don't hire me to infiltrate computers," he says. "They hire me to get the information. I've paid as much as $100,000 for a file. I don't always know the method we use because I subcontract it, but the information generally is taken out of a computer."

Whatever a hacker's motive, in the frontier world of the Internet, virtually every weapon he needs is just a keystroke away. The renegade Intel contractor got convicted, but the software he used to decode stolen passwords, a program called Crack, is still available free on the Internet. (In a recent test, WheelGroup used Crack to break 42% of a client's passwords.) Rootkit is another Internet freebie; it helps hackers gain root access to computers they invade. "War-dialing" programs, like the one WheelGroup used to penetrate XYZ, are also freely available on the Net. They let hackers scan thousands of phone numbers in search of those connected to modems.

Periodicals like *Phrack* and *2600: The Hacker Quarterly* provide step-by-step tips for hackers. They claim they're performing a public service by helping people exploit gaps in computer security. *Secrets of a Super Hacker*, available in paperback at bookstores everywhere, offers many ideas for committing computer crime at corporations, including posing as a journalist to get a company tour. Once you're in the door, writes the author, who calls himself Knightmare, "if you're suave enough, you can talk a proud computer owner into showing off the power of his machine ... This can only help you when you go home that night and hack the place." Theft is another option. Knightmare writes coyly: "I am not going to suggest that you actively steal [computer] disks that you find in an office or wherever, but if you can manage to sneak one away for a few days ..."

Among the most potent intelligence-gathering tools are "sniffers." These are programs that, planted in a computer that is connected to a network, work like hidden recorders, capturing E-mail messages and passwords as they flow by. "You can get inside information on everything flowing through a company," says Daniel Kozin, a Boston computer-networking expert. Dan Webb, a Seattle security consultant, once helped a major real estate developer nab an employee who was sniffing a colleague's E-mail. He'd been selling the information to a Japanese rival, which had used it to win bidding contests.

Hacker technology gets more exotic still. The FBI won't comment, but security experts believe it used a so-called Van Eck device to capture CIA double-agent Aldrich Ames. The gizmo is named after a Dutch scientist who in 1985 published a paper explaining how an ordinary TV set can be modified to pick up emissions from any particular computer screen at a distance of up to two kilometers. The National Security Agency routinely classifies information on the subject, but today you can buy a high-quality Van Eck unit for $4,000 out of a catalogue. It will let you see everything your victim sees on-screen, and even watch him type—keystroke by keystroke.

In 1992, Chemical Bank discovered a

The myth of **E-mail privacy**

by Eryn Brown

In October 1994, Michael Smyth, a regional manager at Pillsbury in Pennsylvania, fired an E-mail to his supervisor blasting company managers and threatening to "kill the backstabbing bastards." Backstabbing may have been the right word. Though Pillsbury had assured employees that E-mail was private, it intercepted the message and fired Smyth. When he sued for wrongful discharge, the court threw out the case. He learned the hard way: Never expect privacy for E-mail sent through a company system.

Assumptions about privacy haven't been so sorely tested since the invention of windows—the glass kind, not the software. When you belly up to your keyboard to trade notes with a colleague, you may feel you're in cozy conversation. Legally and technologically, however, you are as exposed as dummies in a department store window. Note well: If your computer belongs to the company, so does its content. The law lets bosses read what you put there, and because of the herd-of-elephants memory capacity of modern systems, there's rarely a keystroke a suspicious or vengeful boss can't dredge up.

As Oliver North discovered when investigators confronted him with his Iran-Contra memoranda, you shouldn't be fooled by the cute little trash can in the corner of your screen. "Deleted" E-mail keeps going and going and going. Many networks routinely store backups of all mail that passes through them.

The issue of E-mail privacy is confusing for companies too. Estimates indicate that only about one-third of U.S. businesses with E-mail systems have policies. Typically they assert ownership of E-mail messages. To boost morale and encourage communication among employees, they may also promise a degree of privacy. But as the Pillsbury episode shows, such promises aren't binding. It will take time for practices to become more coherent.

Employees who are adept with computers occasionally take privacy into their own hands. Using software they buy or download from the Internet, they encrypt, or scramble, mail they don't want the boss to see. Before you try this, beware. Encryption is still somewhat cumbersome—penpals must have the same software, for one thing. And if you're working for a paranoid boss, scrambling may afford less protection than you think. Says a computer designer in an office where the boss's E-mail snooping preceded a savage firing spree: "I was afraid that if I merely sent an encrypted letter, they'd think I was up to something bad."

Bottom line: If you write love notes on a company PC, you're wearing your heart on your screen. The only truly safe ways to send? Be subtle when you flirt or lampoon the boss. Or pay for your own America Online account and use it at night on your home machine.

Van Eck aimed at its credit-card-processing facility in Manhattan. The police offered to help, but the bank turned them down. More recently, a unit of a major chemical company spotted a Toyota van with a suspicious antenna in its parking lot. "It was clearly a remote Van Eck interception program," says Winn Schwartau, a Florida consultant who describes the devices in his book, *Information Warfare: Cyberterrorism*. "We brought jamming equipment and within three days the van was gone. The company didn't confront the spies. It was conducting a lot of corporate and government business and just wanted the problem to go away."

One of the smartest things a company can do to ward off hackers is to scramble the traffic that flows through its networks. Encryption software, which jumbles messages so they are virtually impossible to decipher without the requisite keys, is becoming easier to use and will eventually be common in corporations.

Companies also need to teach employees to be security-conscious. Passwords are a notorious weak link. Operation Nutcracker succeeded largely because some passwords were lacking and others easily guessable. Technology managers are forever urging users to create codes that are hard for even a computer to guess, but people prefer passwords they can relate to—favorite sports teams, astrological signs, children's names. Police last year raided a Mob-linked gambling house in New York where bookies were using IBM computers to handle $65 million of bets per year. Police cracked the system's security after discovering that one of the gangsters was using his mother's name as a password. Writes Knightmare: "The dumb password will be a good guess for a long time to come."

Using the Internet tends to compound security problems. Companies love the Internet for the ease with which it lets them unite disparate networks and form links with customers and suppliers. Yet the risks can be daunting. At Pinkerton, the world's oldest security firm, executives debated for years whether to start using the Internet for business. The company was growing fast in part by scooping up smaller firms, and was having difficulty unifying the E-mail systems of the new units any other way. But technology managers like Ed Lien were cautious. "Can you imagine what would happen to the Pinkerton name if we had an infraction through the Internet?" he says. The decision to move forward went all the way up to the CEO.

"We're like a lot of companies. Once a hacker gets in the front door, he's in the house. You don't know which rooms he's been in."

The challenge of invading companies like Pinkerton is what truly inspires amateur hackers. One underground group, the Internet Liberation Front, claims it can penetrate virtually any firewall. "Just a friendly warning to Corporate America," reads its manifesto. "We have already pillaged your million-dollar research data … So you'd better take an axe to your petty f---ing firewall machine before we do." Hacker braggadocio? Perhaps. *LAN Times*, a trade magazine, tested seven leading firewalls last June and found all lacking.

Some innovative defense systems have begun to emerge. Today Pilot Network Services in Alameda, California, is widely considered the state of the art. Rather than connect directly to the Internet, Pilot's corporate clients hook their networks to one of the company's service centers around the country. There, for about $5,000 per client per month, Pilot provides supervised Internet access. This involves a "dynamic" five-layered firewall with data pathways it routinely alters to fool hackers. The system is monitored around the clock by a team of electronic cops (human ones). Explains founder and CEO Marketta Silvera, a 28-year computer industry veteran: "You're dealing with a challenge that moves. If you buy a static, shrink-wrapped firewall in a box, so can a hacker."

Complex as it seems, Pilot's system works. Seeing it in action is what persuaded Pinkerton to venture onto the Net. Last year Trident Data Systems, a well-known security consultant for the Pentagon, conducted an independent review of Pilot's system. Its report concluded that "of all the various audits Trident has performed, Pilot was by far the most secure network we have encountered." Clients like the Gap, Hitachi America, PeopleSoft, Playboy Enterprises, and Twentieth Century Fox echo that kind of praise. Each still attracts anywhere from one to 30 intrusion attempts per day, most of which are considered minor. Serious attacks often originate over-

seas, particularly in Germany, Japan, and Eastern Europe.

A typical one occurred at sunup on October 3. An alarm buzzer sounded in Pilot's operations room in Alameda. As the engineers watched, an outside computer made nearly 1,000 unsuccessful attempts, at a rate of 20 per second, to invade a customer's network. The pattern suggested that the hacker was using scanning software in search of a vulnerable computer port. Quickly the engineers identified the intruder's host computer and blocked its access to Pilot's customers. But Pilot doesn't always cut off an invader right away. Sometimes the engineers will let a hacker penetrate one or two layers of the system's defenses, the better to study his methods. "We can watch a hacker's keystrokes like we're sitting behind one-way glass," says Silvera. "They don't even get close to my clients."

WheelGroup, meanwhile, has developed an innovative solution aimed at thwarting hacker attacks within corporate networks. It is a hardware and software package called NetRanger that lets a customer monitor and alter computer traffic in real time—like a flight controller guiding planes. The $25,000 device can also be programmed to work automatically, squelching suspicious internal activity and sounding an alarm when it detects any. Says Allen Forbes, a top computer-security expert with AT&T Wireless Services: "This is definitely the cutting edge."

Last summer, after the National Security Agency tested and verified the NetRanger's traffic-filtering component, the Pentagon bought 32 of the devices. One application: to help prevent what a Defense Department panel, warning darkly of national-security threats posed by hackers, has called an "electronic Pearl Harbor." Unlike missile systems, H-bombs, and other old-fashioned defenses, computer-security devices are practical in peace as well as war. In the coming century, they may prove just as essential in the affairs of commerce as those of state.

Simulations on Trial

Computer-generated animations are helping judges and juries visualize the final moments of an air crash, the ballistics of an unsolved murder, even botched medical care. But should viewers believe what they see?

Arielle Emmett

ARIELLE EMMETT *is a freelance writer based in Wallingford, Pa.*

During the last few seconds of an otherwise routine descent into Dallas/Fort Worth airport one sultry August night in 1985, Delta Flight 191 flew suddenly into a killer thunderstorm. Wind-shear forces quickly dashed the craft to the ground, where it rolled violently across the airfield into some reservoir tanks, killing all 137 people on board. Two years later, Delta sued both the Federal Aviation Administration and the National Weather Service for failing to warn the pilots that a storm of such severity had developed.

Preparing to do battle with Delta's lawyers before a lone federal judge, Kathlynn Fadely, a young attorney with the U.S. Department of Justice, commissioned a series of computer-generated animations to simulate the Lockheed Tristar's performance and explain critical instrument readings in the last moments of flight. It soon became clear from the aircraft's maneuvers that the pilots knew at least as much about the weather as ground control did. "They were playing Russian roulette by flying into that storm," she says. "The judge said the animations were both helpful and powerful," Fadely recalls. By translating digital data from the aircraft's "black box" into striking images of the pilots' actions, and superimposing the cockpit soundtrack, she was able to weave a convincing narrative of pilot overconfidence and horrifying errors. She won the case, exonerating the federal government.

The animations in the Delta case are not unique. According to estimates by Forensic Technologies International (FTI), a San Francisco-based animation firm, computer animations are becoming powerful evidentiary tools in 10 percent of all U.S. trials. These animations translate data into intelligible images, illustrate expert testimony, and teach courtroom juries complex facts in record time. Though embryonic just a few years ago, the courtroom-animation industry, ranging from tiny startups to sophisticated engineering firms, exceeds $30 million in annual billings.

In a sense, forensic animations are a natural evolution of the video technology now used to capture scenes of violent crime, such as in the recent Rodney King and Reginald Denny cases in Los Angeles. A chief difference between live video and computer animation, however, is that animations create sequences of images based on information available only after the fact. Unfortunately, such information is frequently incomplete or colored by human bias. Thus, while the precise renderings of computer animations may lend an air of scientific authenticity to courtroom proceedings, they often reconstruct versions of reality that may not represent the truth.

Where Animations Shine

If a single picture is worth a thousand words, a convincing series of computer-generated moving pictures may be worth millions—in both words and dollars—in today's high-stakes courtroom trials. Indeed, forensic animations have gained a strong foothold in technically oriented cases where the dollar figures are high—such as in medical malpractice law, environmental and patent litigation, arson, and crash incidents of all kinds.

"Technical cases are where computer animations really shine," declares Alan Treibitz, president of Z-Axis, a forensic animation firm based in Englewood, Colo. For example, technical animations have illustrated dynamic forces acting on an aircraft, the human brain, or a building set on fire. Others have plotted the probable trajectory of cars involved in a crash or bullets used in a murder. "Jurors say they understand technical concepts much better with such animations than they could have with verbal testimony alone," says Treibitz.

Although the impact of animations varies considerably—depending on the case, the quality of the animation, and, in some instances, the willingness of the judge to accept the animation as evidence—attorneys may spend tens, if not hundreds, of thousands of dollars on

From *Technology Review,* May/June 1994, pp. 30-36. © 1994 by Arielle S. Emmett. Reprinted by permission of the author.

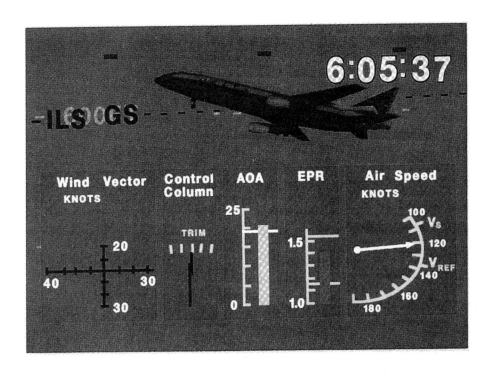

Digital flight-recorder data taken from Delta Flight 191's "black box," which are updated along with the aircraft's roll, pitch, and yaw every quarter second, were translated into a simulation showing how the pilots lost control of the aircraft as it was tossed and turned by the storm's wind-shear forces. The gauge readings show (left to right) wind speed and direction, the position of the pilot's steering-wheel-like pitch controller, the aircraft's actual pitch angle, engine throttle position, and the aircraft's air speed.

them to support technical arguments and settle questions of time, place, and human activity. For example:

❑ In March 1991, Edward Walsh, a personal injury attorney in Wheaton, Ill., spent $24,000 on computer animations to support a malpractice claim involving a baby girl whose congenital brain-stem defect prevented her from breathing normally at night. After being placed on a home-ventilator system, the girl suffered a stroke at the age of 15 months that debilitated her for the rest of her life. The computer-drawn images helped Walsh's medical experts explain how the human respiratory system normally works and how a slowdown in bloodflow from improper ventilation, not her abnormal physiology, was responsible for the damage. Walsh believes the animation was one of the most important pieces of evidence in educating the jury during the trial. He won the case and $10 million for his client.

❑ In a contentious four-month trial that ended in January 1992, Honeywell paid computer animators at FTI $150,000 to help prove that Minolta infringed on Honeywell's patented autofocus camera technology. Minolta in turn hired FTI's rival, Z-Axis, to create similarly sophisticated animations for its defense.

Jurors viewed dozens of competing tutorial animations featuring material on optics, camera focusing, and patent-protection regulations. Honeywell used one video to carefully disassemble Minolta's focusing apparatus and expose it as virtually identical to Honeywell's

autofocus technology. That approach paid off. Honeywell won the case and received $127 million in damages from Minolta.

❑ In 1993, Alexander Jason, a San Francisco-based ballistics consultant, made history when his computer-generated animation of a murder became the first one admitted into a criminal trial. Using physical evidence such as bullet casings, autopsy reports, 911 recordings, and the angles of bullet holes in the doors and walls, Jason reconstructed the shooting of San Francisco businessman Artie Mitchell by his older brother, Jim. The four-minute simulation showed that the murder was not, as the defendant claimed, the result of a panic shooting committed in self-defense. Instead, by illustrating the sequence of shots, where they were fired from, and the location of the victim throughout the incident, the animation showed that the bullets were fired at regular intervals and therefore that the shooting was a deliberate murder.

Jim Mitchell was found guilty of voluntary manslaughter, though some jurors thought the verdict should have been first-degree murder. He was sentenced to seven years in prison.

Potential for Distortion

Despite these successes, the use of computer animation in the courtroom has come under intense scrutiny.

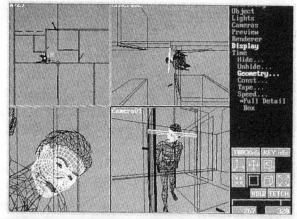

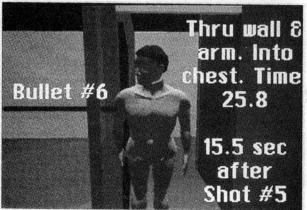

Computer animator Alexander Jason used physical evidence—911 (police emergency) recordings, the angles of bullet holes in the walls—to create a three-dimensional reconstruction of the murder of San Francisco businessman Artie Mitchell. By showing that the victim's brother Jim fired the bullets carefully and at regular intervals, the animation helped prove that the shooting was premeditated and not committed hurriedly in self-defense.

Although most participants in the legal system believe that it is fully prepared to handle the visual complexity of such animations, many judges, attorneys, and even some forensic animators wonder whether the industry is adequately monitored.

"The potential for distortion of computer animations is enormous," notes Terry Day, president of Engineering Dynamics Corp., makers of "Edcrash," a program for reconstructing car accidents. "Software can be manipulated and images digitally enhanced or doctored so that something that isn't true can appear to be true," he says.

For example, in a recent Louisiana football-injury case, the defendant, a helmet manufacturer, wanted to prove that a player, the plaintiff in the case, broke his neck and was rendered quadriplegic not because of a faulty helmet but because he had lowered his head into a vulnerable position before making the injury-inducing tackle. Defense attorneys asked Litigation Sciences, a Los Angeles-based forensic-animation firm, to digitally enhance a video taken of the critical impact to determine the position of the tackler's head.

"The video was taken at a wide angle, and the players were hard to see," says Robert Seltzer, executive director of graphic evidence at Litigation Sciences. "But after we sharpened the video picture to get a better understanding of the motion and zoomed in on the tackler in slow motion, it was clear that he had put his head down."

The plaintiff's "enhanced" version of the video, however, was entirely different, showing that the tackler kept his head up. Ten days before the trial, defense attorneys who had received the plaintiff's video for review asked Litigation Sciences to account for the discrepancy. To create the false image, Seltzer explains, the plaintiff's animation company isolated six critical frames from the video and used a computer painting system to create a digital copy of another player's helmet and paste it on the tackler's shoulders in the head-up position. The player suddenly had two heads, but the head that was up appeared more prominently.

"When it was the defendant's turn to testify, we rolled the original video in slow motion to show the head-down position," says Seltzer. "We then showed the doctored video and how two heads were painted onto one." In effect, the tampering was perjury, and the defense won the case.

Matters of Opinion

A more subtle problem arises when animations present an expert's theories about what may have happened rather than the pure facts of the case. Although federal regulations mandate that a judge must carefully weigh the factual value and relevance of any piece of evidence before allowing it in the courtroom, many judges acknowledge that animations of what-if scenarios can be difficult to evaluate.

One example is the series of animations used in the

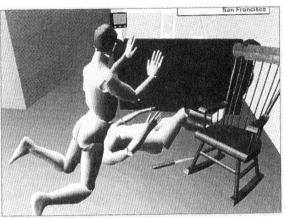

Animators often contend that too much detail can be distracting. For example, Alexander Jason once painstakingly constructed human models that resembled individuals involved in violent crimes. But when he found that viewers tended to focus on facial expressions— whether the models looked pleasant or mean or afraid—instead of the actual events, he switched to featureless mannequin-like figures.

1989 trial to decide whether Northwest Airlines or McDonnell-Douglas was responsible for the crash of Northwest Flight 255, which killed 156 people on take-off in Detroit in August 1987. During the 18-month legal slugfest, the longest aviation trial in history, the adversaries presented dueling reconstructions of the accident.

McDonnell-Douglas, maker of the MD-80 aircraft in question, decided to present a literal reconstruction. Jeffrey Morof, an attorney with Bryan Cave, a Los Angeles law firm representing McDonnell-Douglas, showed animations based on the aircraft's black-box data, as well as on cockpit voice-recorder data and eyewitness reports, arguing that pilot error was responsible for the fatal crash. In particular, he demonstrated that the crew ignored a stall warning and improperly set the aircraft's flaps and slats.

Northwest, by contrast, presented a series of videos that reconstructed hypothetical situations for which there was no hard evidence—for instance, that the crash was caused by the failure of a critical circuit-breaker warning system, not the incompetence of the pilots. The video showed what the crew would have done if the warning system had worked properly during the flight.

Northwest's approach proved unsuccessful. Chief Judge Julian Cook of the Third District Court in Detroit accepted most of McDonnell-Douglas's animations into evidence but dismissed Northwest's "what-if" approach as "speculative and argumentative." McDonnell-Douglas won the case, expected to exceed $10 million in liability damages. (Northwest was granted an appeal, now pending, after its attorneys claimed they had inadequate time to determine the accuracy of the McDonnell-Douglas animations.)

Still, judges often waver when walking the astonishingly fine line between computer animations purporting to tell the facts and those that make speculative claims. For example, judges may allow animations that go beyond simply illustrating what is or what was, according to the Department of Justice's Kathlynn Fadely, because they may want to understand "not only why an accident happened but alternate scenarios of how the accident could have been avoided in an attempt to answer who or what was responsible."

When judges are besieged by thousands of conflicting pieces of evidence, bias is almost impossible to weed out, argues Michael Selter of Graham & James, attorneys for Northwest. In fact, Judge Cook himself admitted a McDonnell-Douglas video that may have made equally speculative arguments about the infamous circuit-breaker warning system, according to Northwest attorneys. The video attempted to show that, contrary to Northwest's claims, particle contaminants could not have blocked current to the circuit breaker.

"That video was clearly misleading," says Selter. "The video purported to be general and tutorial in nature, yet it clearly implied that particle contamination could not possibly have affected the circuit breaker on that flight. It left the jury with the impression that the video was an accurate and specific representation of what happened."

Judges and juries should be crystal clear about the subjective nature of what they are seeing. But even animators wonder whether this is the case. "Juries tend to think, this is computer-generated, so it must be objective; it must be reality," says Z-Axis's Treibitz. But computer animations combine artistry and facts to make clear one side's position, he says. "It's telling a story, but it's a story from an advocate's point of view."

Questionable Programs

Perhaps even more worrisome is the question of whether software programs designed to analyze data are adequately peer reviewed and tested. In the growing field of car-accident reconstruction, for example, they aren't. At least that's the conclusion of some forensic experts regarding a crop of untested personal-computer analysis tools routinely used by local police departments and engineering organizations reporting on collisions.

The programs typically ask users to provide information about which vehicles were hit, their position at impact and at rest, their probable trajectories, and the amount of damage. Often using algorithms constructed from staged collisions, the programs create animated versions of the speeds and crash trajectories of the vehicles that indicate which party is responsible.

"These programs, where you put crash data in and the computer does an analysis and draws a nice picture, are far more dangerous than a graphic that simply illustrates one person's conclusion," notes Thomas Bohan, an attorney and technical consultant from Portland, Maine. The problem is that "the authors say the programs are proprietary, and they're not going to tell you how they work."

Bohan's colleague, Arthur Damask, a physicist who in 1984 made the first computer animation of a fatal car accident, has similar reservations. "None of these PC-based crash-reconstruction programs have won widespread acceptance in the scientific community," he says. Although presumably based on crash-analysis algorithms developed several years ago for mainframes at Calspan, a highway safety research institute at Cornell University, "not a single one of the newer programs has undergone the kind of peer testing and review that has become the sine qua non for scientific acceptance."

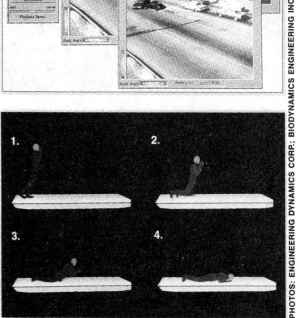

Car-crash reconstruction programs (top) first ask users to provide crash data, including the position of the vehicles and the amount of damage. The programs then create animations that indicate which party is responsible. Dynamic modeling software, designed to show what happens to car-crash victims, was used in the Rodney King trial (above) to demonstrate how much force King's face sustained when he fell to the ground in a struggle with Los Angeles police.

"You don't know whether the program is being accurate or just playing with numbers," notes David Muir, senior vice president of FTI. "There are a lot of ways of analyzing the physics of a car crash."

Terry Day of Engineering Dynamics argues that the leading collision-reconstruction programs, some of them developed for the more powerful engineering workstations, are in fact rigorously tested by comparing calculated results with actual test crashes. "But there's a fly in the ointment," he admits. "It must still use data gathered by people watching the crash or measuring it many minutes or hours later. If the input is incomplete, the accuracy of the program's result is anyone's guess."

Despite these caveats, some judges seem to be snowed by any kind of computer-analysis program. "It's frustrating when somebody on the other side has a program that has not been peer reviewed," says Muir, "and you get a judge who lets it in, despite the fact that you make arguments against it."

To Use the Power Wisely

The legal and engineering communities are actively seeking ways to resolve these issues. In fact, a growing number of forensic animators and attorneys with experience in the area have been writing articles and putting on seminars that explain how to evaluate computer animations in court.

For example, to address some of the potential abuses, the Detroit-based Society of Automotive Engineers is drawing up guidelines to help attorneys, judges, juries, and engineers decide when animations contain misleading or inaccurate elements. Wesley Grimes, chair of the task force, wants attorneys and judges to ask more probing questions about the pictures jurists are about to see, including where the information comes from and the basis for the "environment" of the video.

For example, says Grimes, if forensic animators are depicting a visibility problem during an aircraft accident, attorneys should ask how they determined the visibility shown in the simulation and what the visibility should have been. In many cases, elements are put into videos that can be purposefully distracting. "We are trying to classify every pictorial element in an animation as primary or secondary," he says. "Primary elements are critical; secondary elements can be removed completely with no adverse effect on the presentation."

Grimes also worries that in many states, attorneys have inadequate time at depositions to question the opposing side or to consult with experts regarding the reliability of the underlying data and assumptions. "Some states require advanced notification that one side or the other will be presenting an animation, but others don't," he says. And while federal law requires notification, many attorneys complain that the time allotted for analyzing computer animations and, if necessary, for preparing "defensive" videos is insufficient. Northwest's attorneys used this argument to appeal their case against McDonnell-Douglas.

The most important caveat for judges and juries is to treat skeptically the arguments that the flat lighting, smooth surfaces, and cartoonish unreality of computer animations provide a "cooler," more detached environment in which to review crimes of passion, accidents, and other upsetting events. "Computer animations are powerful emotional instruments because they appeal to all the senses, including sight and hearing," notes Judge Julian Cook.

Simply watching a computer-generated video of an air accident coupled with a soundtrack of dying pilots is enough to prove that animations can be as painful as they are persuasive: the so-called "sanitized medium" never obviates the horror of reliving the moment. Indeed, it may amplify it. No matter how much denial is in the air, attorneys and forensic animators are banking on the emotional impact of animations to keep juries believing in their case. The challenge now is to use that tool's power wisely, to ensure that animations tell the truth, the whole truth, and nothing but the truth—just like any good witness.

The Invasion of
Privacy

In the information age, we are surrendering the most intimate details of our lives to government agencies and big business

REED KARAIM

MET THE DIGITAL VERSION OF MY LIFE IN A SMALL, CLUT-tered office in downtown Washington. A woman I had just been introduced to clicked a few keys on her computer and a remarkable summary of my existence flickered across the screen.

In short order, she found the places I had lived for the last 10 years, the names of my neighbors, an accurate estimate of my household income, my age, height, weight, eye color, Social Security number, my wife's name, evidence of my past divorce. Confidential (I thought) information about my mortgage appeared in minutes, as did a detailed description of my home, right down to the number of bathrooms and fireplaces and the type of siding. The bankruptcy of a relative surfaced, but so did a reassuring indication that my electronic self has not acquired a criminal record, at least in my home state, Virginia.

Everything that Betsy Wiramidjaja, a researcher for the Investigative Group, Inc., found about me was in databases that can be accessed for as little as $1.50 a minute or $30 a month. The information is available to businesses and the general public through several different providers. Had I turned to a slightly less ethical company willing to probe credit and marketing data, much more—from my bank balances to my personal interests—could have appeared on the screen.

I'd come to the offices of IGI, a heavyweight investigative firm, for a firsthand look at the data that floats in the virtual ether about almost every one of us. In a time of talk shows, minicams and thousand-gigabit databases, my concern was an old-fashioned, faintly Victorian notion: the question of privacy.

The information age has brought us many wonders, but it has also made possible an unprecedented level of recordkeeping and high-tech snooping into the lives of others. While we dazzle ourselves in virtual worlds and strange new digital communities that stretch around the globe, it's easy to forget that the same technology that connects us can keep track of us as never before.

"Privacy is to the information economy what environmental protection was to the industrial economy," says Marc Rotenberg, director of the Electronic Privacy Information Center, a Washington-based advocacy group. "This new economy is incredibly productive and important, but there are costs. We are now confronting these costs."

The price is more than just the unease of realizing that your mortgage or the number of bathrooms in your home has become a matter of public record. Both government and corporate America have found the new technology irresistible. In their embrace of the latest high-tech tools, they are shifting the boundary between the private and the public spheres in ways that challenge our fundamental notion of what part of one's life belongs to oneself.

EAR THE END OF THE 18TH CENTURY, ENGLISH philosopher Jeremy Bentham promoted the idea of a prison built with a ring of cellblocks around a central tower. From this tower—which would be kept shadowed from the inmates' sight—a few watchmen could monitor the prisoners' every move while keeping themselves completely invisible. Bentham called his prison the "Panopticon."

"In a Panopticon prison," he wrote, "there ought not anywhere be a single foot square on which man or boy shall be able to plant himself … under any assurance of not being observed." The truly ingenious part, Bentham felt, was that with the idea of surveillance firmly planted in the prisoners' minds, it wouldn't even be necessary to watch them. The *possibility* of constant surveillance would give them no choice but to behave as if they were always being watched.

We have no such prisons these days, but the Panopticon workplace is another matter.

Let's imagine it's Friday, nearly quitting time and you've been at your desk all week. Winding down, you send a few e-mail messages to friends asking what they've got planned for the weekend, exchanging a little company gossip. Bored, you dial into the Internet, maybe even briefly scanning a little of that cyberporn your elected officials are always bringing to your attention. The day almost done, you stroll over to the water cooler and kill the last half-hour chatting with Bob from accounting, long known as the office malcontent.

With today's technology your every move and communication could have been monitored by a supervisor and downloaded into a continuing record of your work habits. Indeed, high-tech monitoring of employees is a fast-growing part of the security and surveillance business. A recent convention in Las Vegas of the American Society for Industrial Security, which drew more than 13,000 registrants, according to *Wired* magazine, featured hundreds of security firms touting the newest technology for keeping an eye on employees.

One of the latest innovations is the "Active Badge," a device that allows workers to be tracked as they move around company grounds. The badges emit an infrared signal to a network of ceiling-mounted sensors. A central computer keeps track of employees' locations, which can all be displayed on a screen. The amount of time workers spend at the water cooler, in the bathroom, even whom they hang around with at work, can be recorded and analyzed. Those few minutes with the office malcontent? In your file.

Software that monitors the number of keystrokes an employee makes on his computer has been around for years. Newer programs allow managers to keep track of what's on an employee's screen, even of where a worker wanders in the Internet. Surveillance capability is now routinely built into managerial software for office networks.

It's apparently being used. In a 1993 survey, *Macworld* magazine found that 22 percent of companies searched their employees' voice mail, e-mail or computer files. Almost a third of companies that had 1,000 or more employees engaged in

such snooping. On the basis of its survey, the magazine estimated that 20 million working Americans may be subject to computer monitoring.

Employers have more freedom to infringe on the privacy of employees than do the police, who still need court approval to tap most telephone or data lines, notes André Bacard, author of *The Computer Privacy Handbook*. Supervisors, he says, "can tap an employee's phones, monitor her e-mail, watch her on closed-circuit TV, and search her computer files, without giving her notice." The courts, moving in a stately manner resolutely disconnected from the pace of the information age, have been slow to grapple with the privacy issues arising out of the latest technology. But so far, judges have generally taken the position that what happens on company time or on company equipment is the company's business. Responding to the most notable legal challenge to employer snooping, a California court held that a manager at Epson America, Inc. had the right to print out and read employee e-mail, even though employees were not aware that their electronic correspondence could be intercepted.

Whatever ends up in your company file is unlikely to remain confidential. A recent survey of 84 Fortune 500 companies commissioned by the Institute of Government and Public Affairs at the University of Illinois found that 70 percent disclosed personal information to creditors and almost half gave information to landlords, often without telling employees. Almost 40 percent of the companies did not even inform workers what kind of records were being maintained on them, says survey director David Linowes.

Corporate surveillance, its proponents claim, is a necessary response to feckless workers who steal from the company or abuse drugs. But much of the technology also monitors employees in the routine completion of their work. The goal,

Even a democracy can be Orwellian. Our government uses surveillance methods that would be the envy of Big Brother

whether anyone wants to admit it or not, clearly is to create the feeling that the boss is always looking over your shoulder.

Humanity has been plagued by overly zealous overseers since the days of the galley slaves, of course. The struggle between workers and their bosses over mutual rights and responsibilities is timeless. But today's information-age technology dramatically shifts the balance of power. Even Ebenezer Scrooge could not have imagined keeping track of every letter transcribed or word uttered by poor Bob Cratchit, but today's plugged-in manager can. Indeed, there is even technology out there allowing managers to tie in to their office security systems while in their cars.

4. SOCIAL VALUES: ETHICS, LAW, AND PRIVACY

It's hard to be certain how Jeremy Bentham would feel about this, but his brother Samuel no doubt would be pleased. Although Jeremy gets credit for popularizing the Panopticon design for constant surveillance, Samuel actually first came up with the idea while working as a military engineer for Catherine the Great of Russia, commanding a battalion of shipbuilders.

Samuel's use for the Panopticon? The constant supervision of his workers.

THE ARCHETYPAL VISION OF A WORLD WITH-out privacy is that of George Orwell's *1984:* a grim totalitarian state where an omnipresent Big Brother peers into every corner of existence. That vision hardly resembles America's unfettered society. But even a democracy, it turns out, can be Orwellian. In its increasingly desperate battle against crime and illegal drugs, our government has turned to high-tech methods of supervision that would be the envy of Big Brother.

These range from improving on old favorites such as wiretapping to sophisticated use of computers to track the financial transactions of thousands of Americans. The IRS, FBI and the Drug Enforcement Agency have even obtained marketing lists that provide consumer profiles of most American families. The IRS planned to use the information to spot candidates for audits, but found too many errors for it to be useful. The FBI and DEA, however, are using the profiles for investigations— although they won't discuss how, says David Burnham, an investigative journalist whose book *Above the Law* is a harsh critique of the Justice Department's record of protecting citizens' rights.

"Twenty-five years ago, if someone had said the Drug Enforcement Agency and the FBI had a national database on all citizens, Congress would have gone bananas," Burnham says. "But people have been so conditioned by the propaganda about crime, they're willing to accept these things without thinking about the consequences."

Burnham reports that a little-known special team of FBI agents now conducts, on average, six break-ins a week to implant surveillance equipment, tiny bugs and cameras, in people's homes and businesses. The effort seems largely tied to the battle against the drug trade and international terrorism.

A steady growth in wiretapping has occurred with little public debate. Roughly 2.4 million conversations were overheard by law-enforcement officers in 1994 alone, according to an annual government assessment of wiretap activity. (Since all calls on a tapped line are monitored, many if not most of these conversations likely involved no criminal wrongdoing.) The number of federal wiretap orders has lately been increasing by 30 to 40 percent each year, officials estimate, and the government is expanding its surveillance efforts into new areas. Last summer, as part of its settlement of a price-fixing investigation, the Justice Department forced Wall Street securities firms to begin taping a random sample of their traders' conversations. The government also obtains "millions and millions" of records detailing calls made to and from certain phones, "on a very casual basis," according to Burnham, who says federal investigators can often obtain the information without the formal court proceedings required for wiretaps.

The government wants to make sure it will always be able to listen in. Law-enforcement officials insisted on provisions in 1994's Digital Telephony Act requiring phone companies to ensure the phone system remains wiretap-friendly. Privacy advocates so far have succeeded in blocking spending to implement the provisions. Still, the law requires that satellite uplinks, ground switches and other parts of future communication networks be designed to make sure tapping is simple. A preliminary government estimate indicated that the FBI was seeking the technological capability to listen to one out of every 100 calls being made at any time in places such as Manhattan.

A related battle, the "Clipper Chip" controversy, is now being fought. The Clipper Chip is an encryption system capable of scrambling telephone conversations, supposedly providing secure communications. (A similar device, the Capstone Chip, would scramble computer messages.) The Clinton administration has proposed that the chip—which would allow federal agents, using a special access code, to decipher all encrypted computer and telephone communications—become the industry standard. Once again, law-enforcement officials say the requirement is necessary to battle crime and terrorism. They say coded messages would only be broken with a court order. Privacy advocates say that if government had the keys to the code, there would be no such thing as a private computer message.

Computers are essential to one of the government's little-publicized surveillance efforts, an operation within the Treasury Department that comes as close as any to the traditional notion of Big Brother. The Financial Crimes Enforcement Network, FinCEN, as it is known, tracks suspected criminals through the database labyrinth. FinCEN's analysts use databases created by the IRS, intelligence agencies, law enforcement and a host of other organizations in pursuit of dirty money, whether it be money in the drug trade or the savings and loan scandal.

FinCEN relies heavily on the Currency and Banking Database, which contains roughly 50 million reports of financial transactions of more than $10,000. The system contains an amazing amount of information, but it's not enough for some in government. For several years there has been a proposal for a new system that would be able to track almost all U.S. banking transactions. Put a thousand dollars into your checking account, take out $500 the next day, and the government would know.

Defenders of the effort to expand government surveillance say the innocent should have nothing to hide. But critics such as André Bacard scoff at that notion. "Show me any person who had no secrets from her family, her neighbors, or her colleagues," he says, "and I will show you someone who is an extraordinary exhibitionist or an incredible dullard."

Still, even if more people knew about the level of government oversight, many of them might not object. "Everyone claims to want privacy," says Burnham. "But in fact, there's a strong belief that we need more social control these days." Indeed, we have quietly acquiesced to changes of all kinds that erode privacy to increase security. Michael Brill, an architect and teacher at the University of Buffalo, notes that our parks and other public spaces, once designed with nooks and crannies so people could steal away for a moment of solitude or shared intimacy, now are designed so every corner is laid bare for the alert eyes of the police.

It's a new way of thinking about the world: For a long time, people thought it was the *lack* of privacy that they had to fear. That is why Orwell's vision of the future was so chilling. And if some of us have changed our minds about Big Brother, it may be because we've forgotten how much we have at stake.

THE HISTORY OF PRIVACY IS A HISTORY OF THE modern West. The notion hardly exists in many tribal cultures and has little significance in the heavily populated nations of the Far East. Even in Western societies, the notion of an inviolable space into which others should not intrude is a recent phenomenon: Diaries from the 17th century and earlier recount the commonplace of sharing beds with strangers while traveling, bodily functions casually displayed, and a ribald lewdness that would be right at home on MTV.

John Kasson, a historian of social customs, says our traditional notions of privacy largely developed in reaction to the crush of cities in the industrial age. The crowded, fluid nature of places like London and New York pushed people of all classes together and began to dissolve the social order. In defense, the Victorians established an elaborate perimeter of ritual courtesies, codes of behaviors and social taboos to guard personal space. They tried to build a temple of the self too sacred for others to violate.

So also came a world constructed around ever-deepening layers of intimacy. There were streets and squares and other public spaces, in which one was expected to appear neat and clean and act with decorum. There was the neighborhood, in which a more casual, less affected appearance was acceptable, but emotion often remained hidden under a veil of sociability. There was the home, in which certain courtesies, such as offering food and drink, became paramount. There was the family gathered around the dinner table. There was the husband and wife in bed at day's end. There was, finally, the private echo chamber of the mind with its Freudian cellar full of Gothic desires and fantasies.

Kenneth Gergen, a professor of psychology at Swarthmore College, describes the notion that the "self" was found in the last, inmost place as the "romantic idea of the deep interior." In his book *The Saturated Self*, Gergen notes that this idea still holds great sway. "The notion is related to a sense of deep privacy," he says, "of having a place within one's self which is not open to the public."

But if we long for privacy in an increasingly complex and hectic world, the irony is that the nature of that world makes it ever-more necessary for strangers to keep track of us. In a society where the family doctor has been replaced by the multistate health-care corporation, for example, detailed medical records are a necessity. Accurate credit and bank information have become essential to a highly mobile population. We claim to hate "junk mail," but the catalogs and subscription notices targeted to our lifestyle result in convenient purchases more often than we admit, or they wouldn't be sent.

The fax machine, call waiting, e-mail and cellular phones have all brought, along with their obvious benefits, further encroachments into that small part of the universe into which we can retreat in solitude. But these intrusions pale when compared to the redefinition of public and private space wrought by the computer. It's not simply that computers make it easier to compile vast amounts of information on all of us, but that through the creation of virtual, on-line worlds, they create another reality in fundamental opposition to the idea of privacy. The World Wide Web and other networks exist to *share*. That is their reason for being. It's hardly surprising that the electronic trail that Betsy Wiramidjaja found so easily for me is out there somewhere for almost every one of us.

"When we first started, I remember being staggered by the amount of information that we were able to obtain on people in a matter of seconds. We probably have 50 or 60 databases we can access," says Terry Lenzner, who heads the Investigative Group, Inc. "There's a huge amount of information now in the public record." Most of us probably are dimly aware that our names and spending habits are sold on computerized marketing lists. (How else to explain the flood of junk mail that follows every significant event in our lives, from buying a house to having a child?) Most of us also recognize that personal material is alive in government and medical computers. We reassure ourselves with the belief that the most sensitive information—our tax records, for example—is securely held.

Our faith may be naive. In his book *Privacy for Sale*, Jeffrey Rothfeder, a former *Business Week* editor, interviewed "information brokers" who would provide a person's tax record for the last three years for a modest $550. The brokers could

Computers have brought about a redefinition of public and private space, creating an electronic trail for almost all of us

obtain almost anything stored in a computer somewhere: bank balances, credit-card information, even a record of all telephone calls made from a number for the last 60 days. The cost for the last service was only $200.

Even the IRS, it turns out, is hardly the secure vault we would like to believe it to be. In 1993, nearly 470 IRS employees were investigated or disciplined for browsing through the tax records of neighbors, acquaintances and celebrities, or for creating fraudulent tax refunds. A congressional investigation four years earlier found similar problems. Last year two IRS employees were charged with using their access to the service's computer system to obtain tax records for political reasons. One examiner was collecting information on the primary opponent of a U.S. House member. The other, Richard W. Czubinski, was indicted for illegally investigating several political aides in the Boston area. Czubinski was involved in the white-supremacist movement, and investigators believe he also was seeking tax information on right-wing associates he suspected of being government informers.

4. SOCIAL VALUES: ETHICS, LAW, AND PRIVACY

Our medical histories may be the most intimate information contained about us in computer memory. But in 1995, state clerks in Maryland's Medicaid office were charged with illegally selling those records to HMO sales representatives for as little as 50 cents per file. The *Privacy Journal*, a newsletter that tracks privacy issues, reports that the clerks downloaded and sold thousands of records to the sales reps, who used them to help find new clients. According to the *Journal*, 24 people were indicted in the scheme. In another case, a banker serving on a state health commission reportedly used his access to medical records to discover which of his customers were battling cancer. According to a health-care newsletter, he then called in their loans.

Under the current health-care system, even authorized uses of medical records often violate our privacy. *The New York Times* recently described the case of a Boston woman who visited a new doctor at her HMO for routine treatment of a urinary-tract infection: The physician "glanced over her medical file and then said flippantly, 'I can certainly help you with your medical problems, but I can't help you with your mental problems.'" The patient was being treated for a stress disorder by one of the HMO's psychiatrists and had thought the treatment was confidential. Instead, she discovered, detailed notes on every session had been stored in the central database, where any employee of the huge HMO could read them. Companies are already testing medical cards that contain a person's health records on a computer chip. The cards would allow medical staff quickly to download information in an emergency, but they also present an additional privacy risk: Lose your wallet and a record of your medical disabilities or diseases could fall into the hands of anyone.

The question of medical privacy becomes even more disturbing when genetic data is considered. This spring two Marines made headlines when they were court-martialed for refusing to provide genetic samples for a "DNA registry" intended to help identify the bodies of soldiers killed in battle. The Marine corporals, Joseph Vlacovsky and John Mayfield, feared that the information could be used by the government for other purposes.

They had reason to worry, according to a study by the Council for Responsible Genetics. The study documented more than 200 cases of what Wendy McGoodwin, the committee's executive director, described as "genetic discrimination." These included several cases where people were denied health insurance because genetic information indicated they had a greater likelihood of developing a particular condition such as Huntington's disease. Some were denied coverage even though they were currently healthy. As scientists further map the genetic code of the human species, the possibility of discrimination based on genetics increases. Researchers are already able to run genetic tests that indicate a person's likely susceptibility to Alzheimer's disease. What if we someday isolate the genes that relate to agility, intelligence or sexual orientation?

Such issues could grow even more acute as medical records and other sensitive data are stored on the World Wide Web. Because of the pressure for companies and organizations to keep up with the latest on-line technology, they sometimes hurry to put information on the Web without paying much attention to security precautions. And even sites that use passwords and other protection can fall prey to hackers, including "cyberspace vandals" who open Web sites and alter the information inside for the same reason regular vandals spray-paint buildings.

The last great repositories of information about us, of course, are the marketing databases used by companies to track what we like to buy, eat, read, watch and do in our spare time. These databases cover even the very young. Metromail, for example, maintains basic information such as ages and addresses on 32 million children nationwide. Reportedly, a subcontractor for the company once employed prison inmates to work on its databases.

How hard is the information to obtain? Earlier this year, a Los Angeles television reporter put Metromail to the test when she sent them a money order for $277, using the name Richard Allen Davis. Davis is the man who was recently convicted in the 1993 kidnapping and murder of 12-year-old Polly Klaas. Nonetheless, Metromail sent the reporter a list of 5,000 children's names, ages, phone numbers and addresses—no questions asked.

Before long, it may become even easier to get your hands on such sensitive data. In 1990 a major software firm and Equifax, one of the nation's credit-report firms, hatched a joint venture that would have put personal information about more than 100 million citizens on a set of CD-ROM discs for sale. (Want a list of wealthy women living alone in a neighborhood? You would have been able to run a search.) The companies abandoned the idea in the face of intense criticism. But does anyone familiar with the history of commerce doubt it will return?

The idea of companies making money by selling information about us without our knowledge or consent is strange, when you think about it. Ram Avrahami of Arlington, Virginia, has thought about it a lot, and, in a lawsuit that could dramatically affect the direct-marketing industry, he is suing *U.S. News & World Report* for selling his name as part of a marketing list. (Many magazines—including CIVILIZATION—rent subscriber lists to other magazines and marketing firms, as well as obtain such lists to identify prospective subscribers.)

Avrahami's suit is based on a Virginia law that says others cannot use a person's "name, portrait or picture" in trade without obtaining permission. Avrahami took action after getting fed up with junk mail and telephone solicitations. "It was intrusive enough, repetitive enough, annoying enough that it caused me to think," he says. The more Avrahami pondered what was happening, the more it bothered him. Somewhere out there, information about him, including his name, was being traded like a pork-belly future. The key to Avrahami's suit is the principle that he is entitled to share any financial rewards that come from selling his name. Although a Virginia circuit court ruled against him in June, he has decided to appeal his case to the state supreme court. Avrahami knows any payment would be minuscule but says his goal is to remove the financial incentive for companies to sell names back and forth without permission. "As long as they have the commercial incentive," he says, "some of my privacy will be stolen."

Direct marketing is only one example of the relentless creep of consumer culture into every corner of our lives, an invasion of privacy greatly aided by information technology. The onslaught of advertising and sales pitches has already overrun the Internet. Junk e-mail could be the next great marketing tool: There are proposals to allow advertisers to clog your home computer's memory with the same stuff that clogs your mailbox.

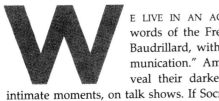E LIVE IN AN AGE CONSUMED, IN THE words of the French philosopher Jean Baudrillard, with "the ecstacy of communication." Americans line up to reveal their darkest secrets, their most intimate moments, on talk shows. If Socrates were alive today, he'd have to change his famous aphorism: The unexposed life, he would conclude, is not worth living. So it may seem absurd to worry that privacy is endangered because somebody has our Social Security number and our purchases from Lands' End on file.

But the battle is not about how much privacy some of us choose to do without. It's about the freedom to choose. "It's really about people's ability to move back and forth between a public world and a private world," says Marc Rotenberg.

There are those enamored with the onrush of technology, who believe that the best of all worlds is one in which everyone can peer into everyone else's life. Science writer Charles Platt concluded an article on electronic surveillance in *Wired* with this observation: "Personally, I look forward to a time when no one will be exempt from surveillance. So long as corporations, governments, and citizens are equally vulnerable, lack of privacy will be the ultimate equalizer."

Prophets of every revolution have always believed in remaking humankind, and the idea of complete openness has a kind of idealistic appeal. But it flies in the face of history. There is no indication that the powerful would be any more willing to disrobe and accept equality with the powerless than they have ever been. There is no indication that a world without privacy would protect the unpopular, dissenters, those in the minority.

Privacy advocates point out that there is no inherent reason some of the technology of the information age cannot be used actually to *enhance* privacy. Encryption programs, for example, can make computer and telephone communications as secure as whispering in someone's ear—more secure, in fact, since the best bugs these days pick up even whispers. "Technology can be used both to promote privacy and invade privacy," says Rotenberg. "The old equation—the more technology, the less privacy—is breaking down. We're heading toward a real choice between technologies of privacy and technologies of surveillance."

As we debate the choices we will make about privacy in the digital age, the final question we should ask has nothing to do with technology. The question is what value privacy still has in our lives. Supreme Court Justice Louis Brandeis famously described privacy as "the right to be let alone." But the notion is also interwoven with something more profound. Privacy, finally, comes down to the right to keep secrets, and it can be argued that in our secrets we define our truest sense of self.

This sense is also the basis for our most intimate relationships. "Part of a relationship is the unfolding of the other, with a sense of mystery, fascination, awe and excitement," says Kenneth Gergen. "The reason why people are not simply a piece of talking meat is that sense that ... deep down in there is something valuable, something that can create poetry, inspiration."

Robert Ellis Smith, author of *Our Vanishing Privacy*, says we are in danger of losing the power secrets have to form bonds between people. "One privacy expert wrote about 'the right to huddle.' Maybe privacy isn't just the right to keep a secret," he says, "but to have something to share with a small circle of intimate friends." In the end, a world without privacy is a world spread as thin as the electrons dancing on a television screen, a world without hollows, ghosts, nightmares or the quiet voice in the back of the mind that briefly fills you with sadness, shame or confidential delight. It is, as Baudrillard observes, a world of the endlessly commonplace. When everything is shared, everything becomes common.

Through much of this century we have been haunted by totalitarian fantasies in which our lives are stolen from us by all-powerful forces. The assault on privacy, however, ends up being more a matter of convenience, inattention and the thoughtless embrace of technology than a conspiracy by unseen overlords. There is no Big Brother. But in our childlike craving for security, we are creating a world in which Big Brother—like Sartre's idea of hell—is other people.

The change is no less profound or troubling because it comes half-willingly and in dribs and drabs. It is now taken for granted that our finances, political predisposition, consumer preferences, even our sexual habits are a legitimate matter of public record—ideas that would have been considered a vision straight out of *1984* not that long ago.

We also have come to accept the idea that our desires and identity are just more commodities to be sold on the infobahn. It's hard not to cheer for Ram Avrahami as he tries to regain control of how his name is used by others. His battle is, in one sense, the battle all of us face as technology nibbles away at the private space in our lives.

The era of the million-gigabyte memory, the microchip and the minicam has given us a world turned inside out, but this could be its ultimate paradox: In the information age, the information that truly matters is still the information you can keep to yourself.

High Resolution, Unresolved

*Private companies will soon
launch satellites powerful enough to spot
environmental hazards—or a car
in your driveway. Should we worry about
snooping from space?*

Mary Graham

Mary Graham is a lawyer and writer who lives in Washington, D.C.

FOR more than thirty years spy satellites launched by the United States have been gathering a "virtual time-machine record of the earth," as Vice President Al Gore has described it. The public has paid close to $100 billion for that record. But national-security and personal-privacy concerns have blocked the use of the world's most powerful sensors to make current information about natural resources, environmental hazards, and private property in the United States available to environmental scientists, government agencies, and businesses. Because the Central Intelligence Agency is barred by federal law from spying on Americans, it shares current environmental information about the United States only in rare instances—for example, in response to natural disasters.

Now, though, spy-satellite technology that has been used for a single purpose—espionage—with extraordinary government controls can suddenly be used for any purpose with few controls. In 1994, concerned about the post–Cold War health of the U.S. aerospace industry and fearful that foreign competition might challenge U.S. leadership in satellite technology, the Clinton Administration decided that private companies could launch satellites with high-resolution sensors previously available only to the intelligence community, and could provide information to anyone willing to pay for it. As government officials take cautious steps to share information gathered by military satellites, four U.S. companies are racing to launch satellites of their own equipped with similar technology. The first launch is scheduled for later this summer.

At a recent conference in Washington, D.C., Mark Brender, ABC's Pentagon producer, predicted that precise pictures from space will revolutionize television news, both by freeing reporters from relying on government-provided information during international crises and by freeing viewers from relying solely on what reporters tell them. David Bohrman, an executive producer at NBC, demonstrated how networks could use satellite pictures to simulate flyovers of troop encampments in Bosnia. At his command a technician in New York using prerecorded images zoomed in on villages, scanned rivers, and hovered over military bases, producing a moving picture that resembled a helicopter ride around the countryside.

WHAT is really at stake is the ground rules for the next phase of mapping the earth. By next year three of the four companies plan to produce images of one-meter resolution—100 times as precise as those of current civilian satellites. The ability to see hazy outlines of large buildings will be replaced with the ability to see the clear shapes of small cars. The ability to observe the same farm or city block every sixteen days will be replaced with the ability to observe the same point every two or three days; three to six images a day of most places in the United States are promised within four years.

Fundamental issues are being decided now. When should the government be allowed to censor images to protect national security? Should fears of military snooping from space be replaced with fears of snooping by corporations or domestic agencies? Will access to satellites' most detailed pictures pass from a small cadre of military clients with top-secret clearance to a small cadre of corporate clients with the means to pay for them?

Since commercial use of this technology is new, no one has a ready framework for resolving questions about national security, the protection of privacy, and public access to information. Time-tested principles that allow the government to block information in emergencies, keep homes and their surroundings free from intrusion, and treat geographic information as a national resource can provide guidance—if they are heeded. The breadth of the government's power to censor images may be decided this fall, when the Commerce Department is expected to issue final policies setting the conditions for commercial licenses to operate satellites. Privacy questions may be decided in an international context: strict privacy rules adopted by the European Union last July require consent for the use of information that identifies an individual. They may keep companies in the United States from selling images abroad unless similar rules are approved in this country. Access questions—whether images can be copied and distributed to the public, for example—will probably be negotiated between satellite companies and their customers, including government agencies.

No longer simply the source of spectacular views of the earth, satellite images have a new capacity to influence what people do and how they think. Using sophisticated software and powerful, inexpensive computers, businesses, government agencies, citizens' groups, and individuals can now produce layered maps (called Geographic Information Systems, or GIS) that combine new environmental findings with information already available to the public, such as property ownership and census data. New satellites will make such maps more useful by providing high-resolution images with digital precision and offering predictable repeat visits. Neither aerial photography nor current civilian satellites like Landsat or the French SPOT can produce this combination.

The investigative powers of satellites derive not just from photography but from sensors measuring visible and invisible wavelengths of the sun's energy. These can reveal more about an object's character than can be discovered standing next to it: each species of plant, type of soil, and kind of rock or building material, for example, uniquely reflects and absorbs wavelengths. Experts add a few caveats: measures of reliability are critical; interpretation is complicated; and much of this science is still in its infancy. And like all maps, these reflect the quality of underlying information.

Information from sensors can give early warning of environmental hazards. Kass Green, the president of Pacific Meridian Resources, a mapping firm, expects that new images will help minimize the damage done by wildfires like those that sweep through urban areas such as Los Angeles and Oakland, California. For the first time, she says, it will be possible to easily distinguish asphalt, wood-shake, and synthetic-shake roofs and to assess from week to week the dryness of vegetation around homes. Planning firebreaks and other preventive measures depends on accurately predicting a fire's path.

Satellite maps can help to settle political controversies—or create them. When, for example, environmental groups and the Bush Administration clashed over how much old-growth forest in the Pacific Northwest should be protected as habitat for the spotted owl, competing layered maps produced by the Wilderness Society and the federal Forest Service provided a basis for negotiation, by clarifying different ways of defining old growth. New maps of Latin America that were completed last fall by the World Wildlife Fund have led to a debate about how to use limited conservation funds: the maps make clear that tropical dry forests and grasslands are as important to biodiversity as rain forests, and are more severely threatened.

Satellite images can make things harder to hide. The Environmental Protection Agency has used such images to help identify hazardous-waste sites and sources of water pollution. European farmers, who receive crop subsidies of $50 billion a year, have new reasons to submit accurate information: their planting patterns are monitored from space by the European Commission. When farm boundaries are layered over images of the countryside, infrared color codes reveal whether a field is growing barley, wheat, corn, or something else.

OF course, newly explicit images can also be used to make mischief. Foreign intelligence agencies are expected to be among the largest buyers of high-resolution images. "International security issues are serious," says Ray Williamson, a senior research scientist at the George Washington University Space Policy Institute. "Iraq would be interested in information about Saudi Arabia. Iran would like to see data about Israel. India and Pakistan would like to have information about each other. If you were concerned about troop buildup on your border, you could put in a standing order for the satellite to take a picture every time it passed over." During international conflicts this greater access could lessen the information advantage the United States has over other countries.

Some experts argue that expanded access could be beneficial. Neighboring countries might be less quick to threaten each other when troop movements were visible to all. When U.S. troops are involved in international conflicts, though, the U.S. government has a strong interest in controlling the flow of information. "One reason we were able to best the Iraqis," Williamson says, "was that we had very good information about them and they didn't know what we were doing."

To minimize security risks, the U.S. government is working to keep "shutter control"—broad latitude to turn off sensors when images might compromise "national security, international obligations and/or foreign policies." Representatives of television networks and other news media argue that the government's authority to stop the use of satellite images should be no broader than its authority to stop the publication or airing of other sensitive information, and that exercising it should require the same judicial process.

Whatever the outcome of that debate, growing international competition means that customers who want high-resolution images will probably be able to buy them. The CIA has been cautious about declassifying spy-satellite pictures: so far only archives from 1960 to 1972 have been released to the public, and the results of a joint U.S.-Russian effort to study environmentally important sites around the world using spy satellites will be kept secret for the foreseeable future. But Russia is already selling some current two-meter images from military satellites, and France, Israel, and Japan plan to market high-resolution imagery.

WHERE to draw the line between personal privacy and the public and commercial need for information will become urgent when high-resolution surveillance is routine. For the first time, detailed pictures of every piece of private property in the United States will be routinely compiled and marketed. Commercial satellites cannot yet produce images of people, but they can show vehicles parked in driveways and structural changes to homes. They can provide images within a few hours and exact comparisons of the same property at precise intervals without giving clues about their presence—things that aerial photography cannot do.

For the police, precise images mean a new investigative tool, says James Frelk, the vice-president of EarthWatch, the company that plans the first new satellite launch. Officers monitoring a suspected crack house, for example, will be able to see the pattern of vehicles arriving and leaving. "They can see the difference between a van, a truck, and a car," Frelk says, "and make a good guess about whether the same car was there yesterday." He expects local governments to be regular customers for other uses, such as updating tax assessments and spotting

additions to homes and outbuildings that are in violation of building codes.

The Fourth Amendment to the Constitution has traditionally been understood to protect homes and the areas immediately surrounding them from unreasonable government intrusion; laws of trespass have protected against snooping by businesses or individuals. In the days before electronic wizardry, that meant freedom from physical entry. When wiretapping and hidden microphones made intrusion possible without breaking down doors or climbing fences, the idea of privacy became more subjective. The Constitution was then taken to mean that areas where individuals have "a reasonable expectation of privacy," including homes and yards, must remain free of government intrusion—physical or electronic.

But in the past ten years judicial support for the use of aerial photography to spot marijuana crops in the war against drugs has left doubt about whether any outdoor space can be considered private. The last time the Supreme Court ruled on the question, in 1986, it upheld the legality of an aerial backyard search that produced pictures of a stand of marijuana plants, hidden from view on the ground by a ten-foot-high fence. In the war against drugs "one of the casualties has been the Fourth Amendment," says Yale Kamisar, a professor of constitutional law at the University of Michigan and a leading authority on privacy issues. Most constitutional scholars agree that increasingly sophisticated technology is no justification for lessening the protection of privacy in one's home and yard. Yet courts continue to uphold warrantless searches of yards by means of aerial surveillance, even though the searches would be illegal if the police jumped a fence. "We have much less privacy than we think," Kamisar says. "If the Fourth Amendment doesn't adapt to new technology, it's going to wither and die."

Corporate privacy, too, is shrinking. On the same day that it upheld the aerial search for marijuana plants, the Supreme Court ruled on a case in which inspectors from the Environmental Protection Agency sought entry without a warrant to the 2,000-acre Dow Chemical plant in Midland, Michigan, in order to check

emissions from power plants and take photographs, and were denied it. The inspectors then rented a plane and took seventy-five color photos using an aerial mapping camera; the Court found that inspection using aerial photography did not violate the Constitution.

Confusing matters further, the Court left clues that government satellite surveillance might be an invasion of privacy even when aerial photography is not. The majority said that "surveillance of private property by using highly sophisticated surveillance equipment not generally available to the public, such as satellite technology, might be constitutionally proscribed absent a warrant." In each of the two cases four dissenting justices thought that there should be more protection of privacy than the Court provided.

Other threats to privacy arise when scattered public information is combined with precise images of homes or farms. A new wing on a house, a trip to the Caribbean, and a few major purchases could together signal a change in lifestyle of interest to tax collectors, business partners, or ex-spouses. Farmers competing for high yields could profit from a week-by-week record of a neighbor's success in using irrigation, fertilizers, and pesticides. New satellites will make information accessible on personal computers within hours.

Congress and state legislatures have in some instances restricted the free flow of information among companies and between government agencies and companies. Self-restraint by businesses and government agencies, too, can go a long way toward avoiding consumers' worst nightmares. But advances in technology are running far ahead of efforts to limit their use. Any further privacy protection will have to be legislated. "Whenever privacy questions occur in the context of new technology, it takes a long time for the courts to respond," says Gilbert S. Merritt, the chief judge of the U.S. Court of Appeals for the Sixth Circuit, who wrote the appellate opinion upholding the EPA's aerial surveillance of the Dow Chemical plant. "The last issues arose with wiretapping. It's taken forty years to reach some kind of stability in that law."

OST new information, of course, will not raise privacy questions. But on what terms will it be shared? Until now geographic data have been treated as a national resource. Only a few governments have been capable of launching earth-observing satellites. The last generation of U.S. civilian satellites, the Landsat series, was financed by taxpayers, and most of its images are available to the public for the cost of duplicating the information. (Landsat images have been distributed commercially since 1985.) But the next group of earth-observing satellites is being financed and launched by private companies. Their images will be produced under contract, customized for clients, and made available at market prices. EarthWatch will retain the ownership of all its images, licensing their use by individual customers and restricting their reproduction,

just as computer companies now limit the copying of software. Foreign governments, large corporations, and other paying clients will get exclusive rights to information they pay for—a big change. "Up to now, when we have acquired mapping information by contract, it has been in the public domain," says Gale TeSelle, who coordinates geographic data at the Department of Agriculture. "We give it away or we sell it as inexpensively as possible." TeSelle believes that by using such information to encourage farmers to fight erosion, for example, or to use a minimum of chemicals against pests, the government can "increase the conservation ethic."

None of these concerns should slow the next steps in mapping the earth. It is cause for celebration that we are entering a time of competitive, unpredictable

exploration just when description of the seven continents seemed virtually complete. Amid budget pressures and privatization efforts, however, there is real danger that simple and familiar protections will be compromised. Whatever the public and commercial value of creating precise maps linking physical characteristics of residences with other publicly available information, the making of those maps should be limited by the traditional notion that a person's home and surrounding areas are private. And commercial satellite ventures should be limited by the idea that geographic information remains a national resource, to be shared at minimal cost. Dangers lie not in what satellite sensors can record but in how the political system allows that information to be used. The clearer the protections now, the greater the likely benefits later.

Politics and the State

UNIT 5

This is the first time that a unit devoted to politics and government has been included in *Computer Studies: Computers in Society.* Many of the issues addressed here are, or could have been, included in other units as well. However, governments have features that distinguish them from other social institutions. To cite just one obvious example, the state has special powers, such as the right to enact laws and obtain compliance through the use of coercion—including (in some cases) the right to use deadly force. Because of such unique features and concerns, it was felt that it is appropriate to have a separate politics and government section in the anthology. Fortunately, there was an excellent selection of articles available.

The first of four articles presented here is concerned with the democratic political process in general and the 1996 U.S. presidential election in particular. In "Digital Politics," Hal Berghel discusses the potential for the Web and other Internet resources to enhance political communication, inform the electorate, and foster participatory democracy. He also identifies potential problems, however, and warns that networks should not become simply a cheaper and more efficient means of spreading propaganda.

The next article sheds some new light on the state's above-mentioned powers. It concerns the right and ability of local governments to impose and collect sales taxes. These governments depend heavily on sales tax revenues in order to provide a wide range of public goods and services. Now, the growth of online commerce (along with mail order sales) is slamming the door on the sales tax collector and threatening the financial stability of states and cities that have a major stake in retail development. Nathan Newman explains the dilemma and proposes remedies in "The Great Internet Tax Drain."

One topic that has received a great deal of attention is the potential for totalitarian governments to use computing and other technologies to increase their power over the people. Information technologies (IT) may enhance government power in some respects and undermine it in other ways. L. T. Greenberg and S. E. Goodman discuss issues related to both beneficial and abusive government uses of IT as well as threats to legitimate information practices in "Is Big Brother Hanging by His Bootstraps?"

In the last unit selection, Bruce Berkowitz considers the ultimate role of the nation-state—that of protecting and defending its borders and citizens. Writing from a U.S. perspective, Berkowitz relates that technology has always played a crucial yet two-sided role in military strategy. In "Warfare in the Information Age," he outlines new threats and opportunities in the areas of waging war, deterrence, civil defense, and the democratic control of information warfare policy.

Looking Ahead: Challenge Questions

Should governments have a right ultimately to intercept and decipher any information? Why or why not? How might this ability undermine or protect citizens' interests?

According to Bryan Kocher, a former president of the Association for Computing Machinery, some computer expertise is necessary to make good computer laws. He observes that legislatures tend to have "many lawyers, morticians, and tavern keepers, but few computer professionals." This lack of computer experts could lead to some very bad laws, argues Kocher. Do you think government would formulate better technology-related laws and policies if more computer professionals were elected? Why or why not?

References

Bryan Kocher, "President's Letter," *Communications of the ACM*, June 1989: 660, 662.

Digital Politics

Hal Berghel

Hal Berghel *(http://www.acm.org/~hlb/) is a professor of Computer Science at the University of Arkansas.*

With the U.S. presidential election upon us, it may be useful to reflect on the political future of cyberspace. An exciting new technology like the World-Wide Web is simply too much for a politician to overlook. Attracted to the hype like moths to flame, politicians throughout the computerized world seek to establish a presence on the Web—in many cases before they connect their offices to the Internet.

There is nothing inherently wrong with politics on the Web. The Web, and other Internet resources, are tools that may be used to better connect the voter, the politician, and the issues. Nothing wrong there.

In fact, digital networks could actually help enlarge the informed electorate. While most of the requisite technologies have been around for some time, they have been largely ignored by politicians. Email—a technological staple of the federal (and most progressive states') governments for years—has heretofore been used primarily as an internal communication medium by politicians and their staffs. Now that the citizenry is going digital, the constituent email will begin to flow (and quickly produce an un-expected new source of information overload for the unwary politicians).

In any event, the Internet revolution has the ability to change the nature of political communication from internal, organizational, and private—as it is now—to external, constituent-based and public. One-way political pronouncements might evolve into two-way political dialogs. Democracy may never be the same again. Perhaps.

Digital Propaganda

As happens with any emerging technology, the technological imperative is rearing its ugly head. This imperative compels us to use technologies for their own sake—for no other reason than we know how. The lure of the exciting and new seems somehow more gratifying than the time-honored, enduring rewards of old.

So it is with politics on the Web. After visiting a few hundred political Web sites, the adjective "uninspired" comes to mind. Political Web sites seem to fall in the middle of the Web content/quality continuum; securely nested in what Howard Rheingold calls the "document phase" of the Web experience, where the focus is primarily on multimedia display to the exclusion of interactivity. And even at that, current political multimedia leaves something to be desired.

But the growth of generic multimedia is really not the problem with the political part of cyberspace. There is a real possibility that the ever-pragmatic politicians will follow the lead of the direct marketers to use the digital networks primarily for electronic junk mail and digital billboards. Political staffers may soon narrowcast and broadcast their political messages to the farthest reaches of cyberspace. Of course, the use of the networks as a mass-marketing tool is not only an under-utilization of the technology, but also a tremendous abuse of the electorate.

I see at least three potential problems with the use of the Web and the Internet as propaganda vehicles, all of which could have potentially serious social consequences.

The least harmful of these is the additional proliferation, far beyond the mandate of need and good taste, of cyber junkmail. If future political junkmail further de-sensitizes us to the enormous collective time hit that such media take on us, society will only be worse for the experience.

A far more onerous problem is that over time politicking on the net may actually further rectify the information flow between politician and the body politic. That is, future cybernation could easily evolve to the point where canned, tailored responses can be crafted for individuals and groups of all stripes and sizes—with less human intervention than common sense and good government

From *Communications of the ACM*, October 1996, pp. 19-25. © 1996 by the Association for Computing Machinery, Inc. Reprinted by permission.

Figure 1. The White House Homepage at http://www.whitehouse.gov/. Respectable but generic.

dictates. Such automation could ultimately elevate spin-doctoring to an art form as each ethnic and socio-economic group hears their customized, spun-doctored version of the party line.

Third, there is the "noise factor." Unlike Gallo wine, political discourse, especially in the form of speech and press release, tends to get released before its time. Try to recall memorable political speeches. Stripped of the audible and visual components, the actual content of political speeches tend not to, and for good reason, reside long in the public mind. I suspect that, for most of us, the more memorable speeches were committed to memory in grammar school (except, perhaps, for a few that might have been especially humorous or embarrassing to the speaker). Any technology that encourages more political rhetoric for its own sake is likely to work against the common good. The health and well-being of our political future lies with dialog and not declamation.

Political rhetoric also doesn't seem to scale well. Unlike the finely crafted poem or novel that withstands analysis, and indeed reveals insights and understandings at a number of different levels, political discourse tends to degrade as it grows. The clever, cogent sound bite more commonly begets confusion than argumentative depth as it expands. That may account for much of the negativity in political campaigns—it's easier to produce in quantity than compelling argumentation. In any case, when it comes to political talk, the incontrovertible sentence tends to grow into the dubious and inconclusive paragraph.

In addition to propagandizing on the Web, a second potential abuse is the invasion of privacy. As anyone familiar with Web technology may attest, the use of Common Gateway Interface (CGI) and Server-Side Include (SSI) environment variables to determine and catalog the user's name, IP address, email address, operating

system type, name and version of browser, local time, and the URL of the previously visited Web site that links to the present site, is easily accomplished. This information may be effortlessly collected, and shared between, a multitude of databases and electronic mailing lists. While it certainly seems within the sphere of the Web's de facto standards of fair use to keep track of this information to help improve Web services, I'm not sure that many Web users would agree fair use entails using this information for political purposes. But it can be done easily, and probably will be.

So it is far from obvious this increased political connectivity will necessarily be in the public interest. The price society will have to exert to avoid intrusive abuses such as those mentioned will be perpetual vigilance.

Electioneering on the Web

At this writing, politicians and political organizations have yet to take advantage of the interactive and participatory capabilities of the Web. Most political sites are passive repositories of staid media with an occasional interactive form. The Clinton/Gore White House and Dole for President Web pages are illustrative of the more polished political cyberspheres.

Befitting a sitting president, the White House cybersphere is fairly rich in content. In addition to the traditional political fare of white papers, speeches, policy statements, lists of accomplishments categorized by affected state, and so forth, there are useful public-domain resources: portrait galleries of former presidents with attached biographies, guides to federal services and resources, an annotated Declaration of Independence, and a collection of White House documents, to name a few. Sitting presidents can console the nation in times of grief, open olympic games, keynote meetings, and fill cyberspheres with government resources. The advantages of incumbency will apply to cyberspace as they do in other aspects of political life.

OFFICIAL WORLD WIDE WEB INTERNET SITE

Breaking News:
Dole Statement on Flight 800 Crash

Guest Book | Volunteers | Mailing List

Why Bob Dole should be President.
CLICK HERE

About Bob Dole
Learn more about one of America's great leaders through a personal look at his life: from his childhood in the fields of Kansas through his heroism on the field of battle to his ongoing leadership in Congress. Also includes a personal message from Senator Dole.

Dole Coast to Coast
Through an interactive map of the U.S., learn about the Dole campaign's progress in your state. Find out which local political leaders have joined the Dole team, when your state's primary or caucus takes place, and how to take a more active role in the campaign locally.

Dole Interactive
Test your knowledge of trivia about Senator Dole! Design your own campaign poster! Download exciting screen savers and desktop images! Send a friend a personalized Dole postcard! This is the place to have fun and interact with the campaign.

Electronic Mailing List
Subscribe to our official email subscription list. You'll automatically receive email updates about the campaign's status, news, and messages from Senator Dole about renewing America's spirit and strengthening our future.

The Dole Library
A broad range of past and current press releases, fact sheets, speeches, photos, sounds, video, and weekly updates. Using our interactive search form, you can also explore Senator Dole's voting record and speeches in Congress. If you want to learn more about the Dole For President campaign or how Senator Dole stands on the issues, this is the place to look.

Figure 2. The Dole for President Homepage at http://www.dole96.com. Equally respectable, equally generic. Content would improve immensely if Dole had the same range of government media resources to work with as the president.

From a technical point of view, the White House homepage appears respectable, though generic. The splash page has the pro forma gratuitous Java applet to which so many of us succumb nowadays. In this case the applet presents dual, unfurled American flags undulating in the virtual digital breeze alongside a tasteful color photo of the White House, set in relief (see Figure 1). In addition, CGI scripting changes the welcome from "good morning" to "good afternoon" to "good evening" (unfortunately, only at the correct time of day for those in EST) and updates the White House photo with appropriate shadowing and light. Like the Dole cybersphere, however, there is no advantage taken of the later Netscape extensions, frames and plug-ins.

To illustrate there are still many slips twixt cup and lip in the Web development game, until very recently the White House homepage restricted audio offerings to Sun AU files used primarily on Unix workstations. According to the Fourth Web Survey, this amounted to only 6.8% of Web audience. WAV would seem to be the more reasonable format given that 61.5% of the Web clients seem to be running Windows. A recent expansion of offerings includes Real Audio, but still no WAV. The administration doesn't seem to understand that most of the hoi polloi won't go to the trouble to install a new audio player in their Web browser's launchpad just to hear the president reflect on Bosnia.

ACM STUDENT WEBBIE PRIZE BALLOT

A special thanks to all of the nominators and candidates who participated in this project. The thirteen finalists appear below.

VOTING RULES: (1) Voters must be either ACM student members or members of ACM student chapters
(2) Voters may vote only once. Subsequent ballots will disqualify all of the voter's ballots
(3) Voters may vote for as many or as few nominees as they wish

Your email address: _____

Your ACM membership number: _____
and/or
Name of ACM Student Chapter to which you belong: _____

- ☐ Lake Superior State University (http://www.lssu.edu/) [Educational Homepage]
- ☐ LandUser and PondLady (http://acm.msu.edu/~groomden/) [Personal Homepage]
- ☐ Submit It! (http://www.submit-it.com/) [Support Tools]
- ☐ Ryan Alva Stuart (http://www.affect.org/~stuart/) [Personal Homepage]
- ☐ Lenny's Wonder Land (http://www.seas.upenn.edu/~lzeltser/) [Personal Homepage]
- ☐ Cary's Home Page (http://osiris.csufresno.edu/~cary/) [Personal Homepage]
- ☐ The Sensus Site (http://www.ccrc.wustl.edu/~lorracks/sensus/) [Support Tools]
- ☐ The DUKE! (http://www.acm.usl.edu/~dxh0844/) [Personal Homepage]
- ☐ San Diego State Student Chapter (http://rohan.sdsu.edu/acm/) [ACM Chapter Homepage]
- ☐ Shodouka (http://csclub.uwaterloo.ca/u/kryee/shodouka/) [Support Tools]

Figure 3. The ACM Student Webbie Prize Digital Ballot Box. Votes cast here are authenticated and tallied on the server. When the election is over, the outcome is automatically posted and available for public view.

The Dole for President cybersphere attempts to achieve much the same effect as the White House, but through a linear interface (see Figure 2). Sensitized icons along the left side of the homepage offer the same range of information as the White House. However, where the White House can offer indexes to White House and federal documents, candidate Dole is limited to offering Dole trivia quizzes and a potpourri of Dole for '96 screen savers. The campaign advantages for presidents with easy access to government resources are made especially obvious in cyberspace.

Technically, the Dole homepage is about as mainstream as that of the White House. The differences are that Java script (Dole) substitutes for Java applets (WH) and lip service is paid to HTML 2.0 compliance as different cyberspheres are offered according to whether the user hosts a Netscape 2.x-compatible Web browser (not in WH). Our inspection didn't reveal any support of frames, applets, plug-ins, or any of the recent technological extensions supported by Netscape.

The Case for Optimism
The central concern I have for future use of the digital networks for political end is that it will become a cheaper and more efficient means of propagandizing via direct email supplemented with occasional dynamic Web documents and interactive forms.

However, there is the possibility that politicians will eventually come to understand that the potential of the Web resides in interactivity and in the possibility of greater individual participation in the political process. There are several opportunities in this regard which shouldn't be overlooked.

Digitizing the Political Memory
Digital connectivity, through Web-like protocols, may provide the electorate with unparalleled political accountability. Modern network databases, indexing tools, and search engines could penetrate politics and government to the point where every congres-

sional vote can be cross-indexed by topic, theme, political party, outcome and elected official. Just imagine—voting records on demand, in real time and cross-indexed. Patterns of poor or self-serving judgment might actually be discernible before crises develop. The public might have the opportunity to react to the pork barrel, the log roll, paired voting, and patronage appointments before they became fait accompli. Political malingering and double speak could be identified as such. It would become almost impossible for politicians to enjoy the anonymity that a forgetful electorate permits.

There would emerge a political memory that will be unfailing over time, unforgiving of concealment, and intolerant of deception. Politicians might become more circumspect when they realize each one of their constituents could have perfect digital recall through the Web.

While it would be naive to assume that many citizens would actively use the digital network resources to monitor political performance, that wouldn't be necessary. The accountability would be achieved through the increased scope and depth of reporting by the fourth estate. As the Watergate experience revealed, the difficulty in exposing abuses of government are not due so much to the absence of information, but rather to the difficulty journalists have in collecting, integrating and assessing diffuse information from variegated sources in a timely fashion. It has taken 20 years for journalists to assemble a relatively complete story of Watergate on which the surviving principals seem in agreement. Political accountability and journalistic efficiency are wed in this regard.

Animating Political Communication
Modern network technology allows us to have group conversations where political ideas and notions can be exposed, rebutted, revised, refuted and rejoined to any desired degree. An enormous opportunity for high-fidelity decision making awaits the politicians

and political organizations who can figure out how to harness this interactivity without drowning in it. However, this won't just happen automatically because there is precious little wheat amidst the group-speak chaff. Success in this area will require both considerable technical skill and a significant investment of time and money, but the rewards could be revolutionizing.

Lacking the technical sophistication to take advantage of the technology, we predict most politicians will only pay lip service to this level of interactivity.

Participatory Democracy
The weakness of modern participatory democracy is that it isn't very participatory. Active participation requires time, energy, commitment and, most of all, the belief that the participation is likely to have some beneficial outcome. This last point must not be overlooked as now nearly half of U.S. citizens fail to vote in national elections for they believe they have little to gain or lose in the outcome. Over time participatory democracy has degenerated into rule-by-influential-minority. But it doesn't have to be that way, and the Web can help reverse the trend because it can eliminate many of the obstacles between the citizen and participation in the political process. The social costs of participating in digital democracy are low.

Digitizing the Electoral Process
Not to be overlooked is the extreme ease with which digital balloting may be implemented on the Web. Santayana's dictum about learning from past mistakes is relevant here, lest the phrase "digital election fraud" enter our vocabulary. Western democracies have begun, just in the latter part of this century, to achieve a high degree of integrity in the voting process. Our challenge will be to see if we can port this over to the networks without problem through programs and procedures that will ensure voting remains untraceable under authentication.

5. POLITICS AND THE STATE

Accomplished from home or office, such "no pain" voting is certain to have a major impact on both the political and electoral processes.

Incidentally, the ACM actually uses a primitive form of a digital ballot box (see Figure 3) in conducting the nomination and voting for the annual Student Webbie Prize for student achievement in cyberspace (http://www.acm.org/webbie/).

Not a Panacea

Of course the digitization of politics will not be a panacea. It will not just reduce or eliminate current political problems, it will also spawn new ones. This is the inevitable price we pay for technological advance. As the automobile contributed to the homogeneity of nations, it also facilitated the growth of the suburbs and the eventual decay of the inner cities. The great challenge before society is to ensure new problems are easier to deal with than the old.

Digital politics may also contribute to the balkanization of the electorate. The ease by means of which electronic communities may form would actually tend to encourage this since geographical constraints are absent in cyberspace. As these "digital enclaves" spawn, new strategies will have to be developed to nurture consensus.

It also remains to be seen whether, or to what extent, virtual communities will figure into digital politics. Our observations are neutral in this regard. We are looking at the digital politics through the lens of technological capability as it augments a traditional political process. There is another perspective that derives from the study of society and online social movements. Studies into the nature of online interpersonal and group relationships, and the degree to which these relationships are sustainable in cyberspace, are also relevant but beyond our ability to assess. For answers to these and other pressing problems we must ultimately turn to sociology and psychology.

The Great Internet Tax Drain

As commerce migrates onto the Net, the door is slamming shut on the sales-tax collector—potentially shredding the financial stability of states and cities that have pinned their economic future on retail development.

Nathan Newman

As Orange County goes bankrupt and cities and towns from Los Angeles to New York teeter on the edge of financial chaos, local governments crave some good financial news. This article can't deliver it. This is the story of how the Internet may deal the final body blow to the financial security of local governments. Governments could once count on local economic development to produce local jobs where local employees would spend money in local stores, thereby generating local tax revenue for further development. This virtuous cycle has been fatally undermined by the new technology of cyberspace.

One great promise of the Internet is that it will not only supply amusement and information but also serve as a marketplace. Advocates paint happy pictures of consumers shopping through the ultimate collection of catalogs—giving them access to a nationwide and worldwide marketplace—and ordering and paying for goods from their computers. Often overlooked is the fact that little of this buying and selling will be subject to state and local sales taxes. That's good news for the consumer—but a potential catastrophe for the state and local governments that have come to rely on sales-tax revenues.

States already lose at least $3.3 billion each year because of retail sales that have migrated to mail-order businesses, estimates the U.S. Advisory Commission on Intergovernmental Relations (an agency that brings together representatives of state governments to improve the effect of federal policy on states). That is, roughly $3.3 billion worth of tax revenue would have flowed to state governments if goods had been pur-

chased in stores rather than through mail order. In 1994, California alone lost $483 million, according to the commission, and eight other states lost more than $100 million each.

The Internet's impact has yet to be fully felt. Total retail sales transacted on the Net added up to only about $200 million in 1994, according to CommerceNet, a consortium of businesses exploring use of the Internet—less than one-tenth of 1 percent of what was spent on mail-order shopping. But corporate America is turning to the Internet at a dizzying pace. Companies are establishing sites on the Net at the rate of about 120 per day, according to Anthony Rutkowski, vice-president of the Internet Society, an organization that oversees standards-setting on the Net. The number of World Wide Web pages advertising businesses and products is growing at about 12 percent a month, say industry analysts. Many of these pages make it easy for Net surfers to purchase goods by typing in a credit-card number and mailing address. Businesses offering products online can "provide information 24 hours a day and not have to have people on the phone all the time to service an international market," observes CommerceNet program manager Mark Masotto.

This trend is likely to accelerate as one of the key barriers to Net commerce—lack of security—starts to fall. Fears that hackers could intercept messages and steal passwords or credit-card numbers are becoming more and more unfounded. Last summer, Netscape Communications, which created the most popular program for browsing the World Wide Web, released software and public standards for a "secure digital envelope" that can ensure the privacy of financial data transported over the Internet. Intuit, which makes popular personal finance software, and MasterCard International are among companies announcing support for the new protocol.

NATHAN NEWMAN, *a sociologist studying the impact of information technology on regional economies, is codirector of the Center for Community Economic Research at the University of California at Berkeley. His e-mail address is newman@garnet.berkeley.edu.*

In an ominous collision of trends, the growth of retail activity online coincides with municipalities' increasing dependence upon sales taxes as a source of revenue.

The floodgates of Internet commerce, it appears, are about to open.

In an ominous collision of trends, this growth coincides with the emergence of sales taxes as a major revenue source for state governments. Beginning in the early 1980s, broad cutbacks in federal funding forced states to pay for more and more services out of their own budgets. With voters typically unwilling to approve higher income taxes, sales taxes often became the only politically feasible way to make up for lost federal revenues. Only Delaware, Montana, New Hampshire, and Oregon now collect no state or local sales taxes; altogether, one-quarter of all tax revenues that states collect stems from sales tax.

In many states, local governments tack on their own sales tax as well. In all, 6,000 counties, cities, and school districts collect sales tax. Ironically, the state most severely hit by the move to catalog and online shopping is California—home to many of the companies and universities that invented the technology that makes the Internet possible. Because of Proposition 13, which limits California's ability to raise money through property taxes, towns and cities are extremely dependent on sales taxes. Cupertino, for example, where Apple Computer has its headquarters, depends on sales taxes for 45 percent of all city revenues, prompting mayor Wally Dean to call the sales-tax dependence "a house of cards for government finances."

DISTORTED DEVELOPMENT

Right now, local governments that rely heavily on sales tax naturally have an incentive to encourage large retailers to move within their borders by granting them large subsidies—typically in the form of property-

tax exemptions. But the competition for retail has distorted economic development. The retail establishments that a city or town recruits have tended to succumb to competition from the next wave. First, shopping in urban centers gave way to retail in the suburban towns. Then, those suburban concentrations of stores began to weaken in the face of competition from malls. Now, general purpose department stores in malls are losing out to discount "big box" retailers such as Home Depot and Toys R Us. Cities are vying against one another to attract discount giants that suck in business from a whole region, often devastating the more dispersed retail establishments that local governments, especially in the West, depend on for financing their budgets.

Direct marketing through telephone or the Internet takes this economic cannibalism to a new level. Cities and states are competing with a vengeance to attract order-processing "call centers" to service direct marketing companies. Oklahoma, for example, has worked hard to replace disappearing oil-patch jobs with the data entry, computer programming, and accounting employment that these call centers provide. The state excuses direct marketing companies from having to pay sales tax on 800 numbers, WATS, and private-line service—the essential tools of the mail-order trade—and grants data-processing firms that move to the state a five-year exemption from property taxes. In the end, however, such policies merely reward the flight of local retail to tax-exempt mail order.

Each individual state or municipality is betting that jobs from such call centers will endure and that the gain in long-term jobs will offset the cost of the subsidies. But as the Internet blossoms, even that hope may wither. People will be able to "window shop" the Web the way they do in malls and downtowns—comparing product features and prices, seeing demonstrations, and making purchases. As such online activity becomes more common, the whole job classification of entry-level data clerks at call centers may melt away, leaving only a much smaller set of more specialized, and skilled, troubleshooters. "You'll still need some people to deal with hysterical customers, but that's about it," says Bruce Lowenthal, Tandem Corporation's program manager for electronic commerce over the Internet.

A CONSTITUTIONAL BARRIER

There is one obvious response to this problem: allow states to tax mail-order and Internet sales. But the courts have said no. The U.S. Supreme Court, in its 1967 *National Bell Hess, Inc. v. Department of Revenue* decision, prohibited states from taxing out-of-state sales. The court based its ruling on the Constitution's so-called "commerce clause," which restricts the federal government's power over commerce between states and that prevents states from imposing tariffs on one another. In *National Bell Hess*, the court ruled that allowing a state to tax a company located in another state would violate the principle that there should be uniformity in the rules of commerce for companies crossing state lines.

The court reaffirmed this principle in its 1992 *Quill Corp. v. North Dakota* decision, in this case defining "in-state" sales extremely narrowly. The court held that for a state to collect taxes on sales, the vendor must have significant sales operations—such as personnel, inventory, or showrooms—within the state. If no such "nexus" exists between the seller and the state in which the purchase originates, then the transaction must be regarded as interstate commerce and is thus constitutionally out of reach of a state sales tax. Already, direct marketing companies have used toll-free numbers, computers, and faxes to dispense with the need to place operations within a sales-tax-collecting state. As World Wide Web pages begin to eclipse printed catalogs, the physical connection between mail-order retailers and states trying to tax them will recede even farther.

The company at the center of the 1992 decision exemplifies the problem for states. Quill sells more than 9,500 different office products ranging from paper clips to computers; annual sales in excess of $340 million in 1992 make it the nation's third largest mail-order company, trailing only L.L. Bean and Land's End. About half of the more than 200,000 orders that Quill receives monthly come in by telephone. The other half, however, arrive by mail, fax, telex, or computer network. To expand its business, Quill leased computer software that gives customers direct access to Quill's computer for direct orders. The Internet will make these kinds of transactions far easier.

CUTTING LOSSES

In the *Quill* case, the Supreme Court did leave one option. While no individual state is allowed to unilaterally impose an out-of-state sales tax, the federal government may establish what would amount to a national sales tax—and remit the proceeds to the states in which the purchaser resides. In 1994, Sen. Dale Bumpers (D-Ark.) introduced legislation—the Tax Fairness for Main Street Business Act—that would have established such a tax, but the bill foundered on opposition from the Direct Marketing Association and allied business and consumer groups. These organizations contended that forcing mail-order companies to collect sales taxes would create an unbearable administrative burden; the complexity of tracking tax rates in all the states and local municipalities around the country that charge sales tax would overwhelm most businesses.

Another way that states might tap into the mail-order and online-sales revenue stream would be to levy a fee directly on consumers for the use of any retail channel that bypassed the sales tax. Present court rulings make this constitutional; while states cannot tax companies

The federal government could establish a national sales tax and remit the proceeds to states and localities to compensate them for lost revenues.

located in other states, they have full power to tax people located in their own states, regardless of where they buy their goods.

Such a "use tax" would be difficult to collect, however. If compliance were made voluntary, individuals would have to account for their purchases much as they now account for their income in filing their income tax returns—requiring a horrendous amount of bookkeeping that few people would be likely to perform with any degree of accuracy. Alternatively, states could audit individual citizens' purchasing activities by collecting information directly from individual credit-card and checking account records. So far no state has dared to enact such a tax, but legislators may move in this direction if their sales-tax revenues continue to fall. Some states, like California, have in their constitutions strong privacy guarantees that prohibit such actions. But in other places, we may have the specter of Big Brother looking over our shoulders to collect on mail-order purchases.

The Republican majority in Congress is seeking to shift responsibilities from the federal government to state and local levels. They liken the huge federal government to yesterday's mainframe computers—awkward and obsolete. State and local governments, by extension, are analogous to the nimble microchips and personal computers that have achieved supremacy in the information age.

But this metaphor misrepresents the situation. In reality, new information technologies call for more centralized revenue collection, not less. Since so much commerce is national and even international in scope, state taxes should be preferred to local taxes, and federal taxes to state taxes. Otherwise, state and local governments engage in a "race to the bottom" as they cut back on services for their citizens to pay for wasteful tax subsidies. Centralized revenue collection—while admittedly running counter to the political winds favoring "devolution"—also can help erase disparities in services between poor and rich communities, especially in the area of public education. This was the goal that led Michigan's voters in 1994 to approve a new system of school financing that replaced local property taxes with statewide taxes. Likewise, centralization at the national level can help eliminate disparities among states and thus reduce states' incentives to lower taxes as an inducement to business relocation.

Ultimately, states should scale back and even eliminate sales taxes as a revenue source. Continued reliance on a sales tax leaves a government's finances vulnerable to the powerful trend in retail toward mail order and, in the coming decade, Internet-based shopping that crosses state lines. In this environment, a sales tax is the worst economic policy possible for a state, as it gives an economic edge to out-of-state businesses.

Indeed, in the game of mail order, a state's population works against it. Since companies are required to collect sales tax from in-state customers, mail-order companies are drawn to locate in states with small populations. That way, these companies can maximize the number of people that it can market to on a sales-tax-free basis. As retail establishments go online, therefore, they will tend to flee large states such as California.

The best way to make up for the revenue lost by lowered sales taxes would be through a state income tax. One benefit would be progressivity: the average state income tax rate for a family of four is only 0.7 percent of income for the poorest 20 percent of residents and 4.6 percent of the income of the richest 1 percent. (Property taxes are usually little more progressive than sales taxes.) Moreover, income taxes apply no matter how the money is spent, and so are not undermined by increases in online and mail-order shopping. An even better option is to use federal income taxes to substitute for lost revenue at both the local and state level. Although not politically likely right now, this option seems only fair—it was federal cutbacks in aid to states that led states to rely so heavily on sales taxes to begin with.

Fortunately, eliminating state sales taxes would not necessarily require much of any new revenue—if governments would stop squandering money to lure companies to relocate within their borders. Officials all over the country are in a cutthroat scramble to attract high-tech businesses to their locales, hoping to replace tax bases decimated by the decline of manufacturing employment. While some new jobs may appear, state and local governments may see little gain in revenue if trends continue toward untaxable out-of-state and on-line sales. "Even though it is rational for individual states to compete for specific businesses, the overall economy is worse off for their efforts," wrote Arthur Rolnick and Melvin Burstein last March in *The Region*, a magazine published by the Federal Reserve Bank of Minneapolis. (Rolnick is senior vice-president and director of research at the Fed in Minneapolis; Burstein is that bank's executive vice-president and general counsel.) At least six states, two cities, and Puerto Rico, they note, have begun to prohibit the use of tax subsidies to recruit retailers.

The federal government has contributed to wasteful relocation subsidies. Its biggest job-subsidies programs—including industrial revenue bonds, the Department of Housing and Urban Development's community development block grants, and most Department of Commerce programs—not only permit but encourage local governments to apply the federal money they receive toward incentives to draw companies from elsewhere. The federal government could end such job piracy quickly if it mandated that any state that engages in interstate job-raiding would lose its federal funding.

The loss of local sales taxes owing to mail-order and online commerce should be treated as an opportunity to look more closely at how technology is changing the burdens we put on local and state governments. We should question whether such burdens make sense in a world where multinational corporations often outpower whole states in total assets and can pit such local governments against each other in competition for jobs and local revenue. While much information-age rhetoric harkens to images of small firms and decentralization, the reality is of soon-to-be trillion-dollar corporations straddling the globe. Even modest-sized enterprises operate more and more on a global basis. Faced with such a disparity in power, local governments can hardly be expected to devise fair and efficient systems of taxation or make informed economic development decisions. The rise of national and global commerce calls for national and even global solutions, regulations, and revenue sources.

We must recognize that while the microchip may be getting smaller, the plane of economic activity encouraged by this technology is national and global. The growing fragility of the basis for state and local sales taxes should make us aware of the need for government to operate more strongly on the national and global level.

Is Big Brother Hanging by His Bootstraps?

L. T. Greenberg and S. E. Goodman

Since the early days of the industrial revolution, national governments have been closely tied to information technologies (IT), driving technological development and using them to pursue the business of governing. For example, revolutionary France funded the construction of an optical "télégraphe" network in 1793, to speed up military communications and permit Paris to exert greater control over what was then a huge country. Similarly, the roles of the U.S., British, and Soviet governments in the early development of electronic digital computers are well known. Conversely, the pioneering work of Charles Babbage in the 19th Century languished after the British government failed to fund construction of his machines. But just as governments affect the development of IT, so too does IT influence the development of governments.

Until fairly recently, commentators on technology and society argued that IT would enable the development of omniscient, omnipotent central authorities that would control every aspect of civil life. The best illustration of this view may be George Orwell's classic novel *1984*, in which two-way television monitors the protagonist's daily exercise, and the state, symbolized by "Big Brother,"

uses its control of IT to rewrite history to support the rulers' goals [11]. Orwell's real-world prototype, the Soviet Union, pursued visions of large-scale cybernetic control and centralized economic planning into the 1980s. Even today, polls indicate the U.S. public fears the government's accumulation of personal information, and some observers see Singapore as an emerging model for strong forms of IT-based control over populations.

More recently, observers have argued that rather than empowering national governments, IT may weaken or even contribute to the ultimate demise of the nation-

state. These observers, including Walter Wriston, the former chairman of Citibank, and Jean Marie Guéhenno, former French Ambassador to the European Union, have argued that the diffusion of IT has given people the ability to obtain information, communicate, organize, and conduct economic and political transactions without regard for borders and beyond the control of national governments [6, 14]. At the recent World Economic Forum in Davos, Switzerland, John Perry Barlow, vice-chair of the Electronic Frontier Foundation (EFF), prophesied that as more of business and daily life takes place in cyberspace, national governments will find themselves unable to govern, and "The nation-state is doomed . . . and ought to be."[4] Or as Bill Frezza, founder of the libertarian DigitaLiberty organization, has written: "When the combined might of nations tries to chase society's producers of goods and services down the information superhighway, making claims on the fruits of their labor, they will simply disappear into the ether."[2]

These polar images illustrate the tension that arises from the development and diffusion of IT, as it empowers both state and nonstate actors. Like other revolu-

Russ Willms

tions, the "information revolution" will have winners and losers. Some institutions will prosper, others will vanish, but few will be unaffected. In this changing environment IT weakens national governments in some ways, but they are not vanishing. IT increases some governmental capabilities, and a government may leverage its jurisdiction over the physical world into influence over the cyberworld.

The Roles of the Nation-State and Challenges of IT

The nation-state has been the fundamental unit of organization in the international system since before the industrial revolution. Nation-states are characterized by a central authority with political power over a discrete geographical territory, a claim to the allegiance of that territory's

ernment to manage widely scattered troops or bureaucrats, helps health officials to track the spread of disease, allows law enforcement to search vast libraries of fingerprints and other data to solve crimes, and supports a state's attempts to monitor a national economy or take a census. Nevertheless, the diffusion of IT may undermine a state's ability to control events within its borders.

In Orwell's Oceana, the archetypal totalitarian state, IT was critically important to the state's efforts to control information. It was used to indoctrinate citizens, restrict the information available to them and outsiders, and monitor behavior. Such control objectives are not unique to authoritarian or totalitarian regimes, although they are the most dedicated practitioners. Rather, all states, from the most

national boundaries, and gives individuals access to tremendous amounts of information, including information formerly available only to a few governments, such as satellite imagery. As this volume rises, and as technologies such as encryption spread, data and transactions could evade government monitors, defeating, or at least subverting, efforts to enforce government policies and laws. Space constraints permit us to consider briefly only two of the subject areas in which IT affects governments' abilities: taxation and money laundering, and the flow and control of ideas.

Taxation and Money Laundering

Without the ability to tax, the modern state cannot support its personnel and activities. IT chal-

Money laundering, a $300 billion annual global industry, may be aided where funds can travel around the world instantly and anonymously, so that they cannot be traced.

population, and the sole capacity to represent the territory in relations with the similar entities that control other territories. Not all states govern themselves identically, of course, and some, such as Somalia, are states in name only. But states' governments share a core set of functions, including defending their territory and citizens against foreign threats; maintaining domestic order; playing some role in the domestic economy, particularly in creating national economic and physical infrastructures; and extracting wealth (through taxes) to support their activities.

On first glance, IT would appear to reinforce state power as it helps states work more efficiently and perform new tasks. For example, IT enables a central gov-

liberal to the most authoritarian, try to regulate communications of some kind or another, for purposes ranging from the prevention of child pornography or political or religious dissidence to the protection of their citizens from crime, fraud, or invasion of privacy. Because money has become notional, rather than physical, these communications also include financial transactions, which may occur so quickly, on such a geographical scale, and in such volume as to shock currency or stock markets.

The Orwellian view underemphasizes the effects of the broad diffusion of IT, particularly into the private sector. Where it is available, modern IT permits rapid, inexpensive, widespread communication even across

lenges that ability, as it permits international, instantaneous fund transfers, potentially cloaked by anonymity and encryption, that could hinder governments' efforts to discover what people are doing with their money, or to reach the assets and transactions that they need to tax. Barlow has proclaimed that digital cash will rearrange the financial world and "taxes will become voluntary."[8] Money laundering, a $300 billion annual global industry, may also be aided where funds can travel around the world instantly and anonymously, so that they cannot be traced. This mobility diminishes governments' abilities to interfere with money flows to adversaries such as rogue states or international organized crime [12, 13].

IT may enhance countries' abilities to establish themselves as havens for tax avoidance, money laundering, or similar activities. Anonymous, untraceable "E-cash" may exacerbate the difficulties that tax collectors and law enforcement authorities already face in the bank confidentiality of nations such as the Cayman Islands, Lebanon, Morocco, or Thailand. For example, in December 1995 the Seychelles enacted an Economic Development Act that grants citizenship, including absolute immunity from extradition or asset forfeiture, to anyone investing $10 million there. As it establishes a banking system with secret numbered accounts and wired into the world financial system, that nation might expect an influx of electronic money and new citizens [2, 13].

The Flow of Ideas

For some states, the most challenging aspect of the diffusion of IT is the flow of ideas it promotes. Television, broadcast by satellite, can disseminate news and culture viscerally and instantly. Computer networks, especially the Internet, permit anyone to broadcast political or religious messages widely at little marginal cost, and may help individuals to form groups or to act in concert.

The unfettered ability to communicate may particularly threaten authoritarian or totalitarian regimes, such as the Soviet Union, Iraq, or North Korea, whose survival depends upon their ability to control the information their citizens and others receive. The mere fact that dictatorships strive to control their nations' means of communications indicates the significance of these means, and they probably contributed to the Soviet Union's ultimate collapse. The survival of the Soviet state depended in part upon its ability to control what its people knew about their country and the outside world and what outsiders knew about the USSR. Developments in IT undermined

both aspects of that control [14].

IT also aids dissidents' efforts to organize, communicate, or proselytize, even from beyond a nation's borders. While Ayatollah Khomeini was in exile in France during the 1970s, he preached to the Iranian faithful through audiotaped sermons smuggled into Iran. During the 1989 antigovernment demonstrations in Beijing's Tiananmen Square, demonstrators communicated with each other and outside supporters via fax. Leaders of the Zapatista rebels in Chiapas issue orders and agitate against the Mexican government both within Mexico and before the world media through email. The Internet has enabled the establishment of virtual communities for citizens and expatriates of nondemocratic Middle Eastern and Asian countries.

The explosive diffusion of IT makes this flow of information difficult for governments to control. As John Gilmore, founder of Cygnus Support and the EFF, has noted, "The Internet interprets censorship as damage and routes around it."[9] Information can be stored at multiple "mirror" sites, beyond the reach of an individual national government; its source may be disguised; and it may be encrypted beyond a government's practical ability to decode. Anonymous remailers can strip the return addresses from email messages, making it difficult, if not impossible, for authorities to determine their sources. Furthermore, where a government blocks one route of access to forbidden information, computer users may easily find another. A German, for example, could use the "Great Web Canadianizer" to circumvent his government's blocking of a Californian Holocaust-denial World-Wide Web site by having the Canadian site copy information from California to a server in Canada and only then send it into Germany [5, 7]. Similarly, when the French government blocked the sale of a

book detailing its late President Francois Mitterand's misrepresentations about his health, the book's contents soon appeared on Web sites outside France.

The Resilience of the Nation-State

Despite some prognostications, the state is not sublimating quietly, if at all. Consciously or unconsciously, motivated by stubbornness, institutional inertia, or real desires to serve and protect their businesses and citizenry, governments are maintaining or expanding their roles.

Traditional Roles

The information revolution has not fundamentally changed most of the objectives that the nation-state serves, as they occur mainly in the physical world, rather than in the cyberworld. Sovereign governments are still the primary actors in international affairs, and they interact to address problems relating to trade, pollution, the allocation of the electromagnetic spectrum, and other issues. National armed forces still defend borders, or project force beyond them. States set health and safety standards, build and repair transportation systems and regulate traffic, enforce civil order, provide welfare services, and provide courts for the settlement of disputes. Few of these missions appear likely to disappear or to be taken up by any other entity soon.

While people live in the physical world, demands for national government will probably persist. To the extent IT adds to or improves functional capabilities, extending the reach of official agencies or improving their efficiency, these technologies may strengthen governments in traditional areas.

Expanded Roles

Ironically, the growing IT-enabled power of nongovernmental entities, such as multinational corporations or the news media, has put additional demands on national governments, most notably that of protecting their citizens' privacy. For example, after a newspaper published a video store's records of Judge Robert Bork's movie rentals while the Senate was considering his nomination to the U.S. Supreme Court, public outcry prompted Congress to enact the Video Privacy Act to prohibit such disclosure. Other laws regulate business practices and disclosures by credit bureaus, cable companies, and hospitals. More ambitiously, many European countries, including Spain, France, Denmark, and the U.K., have omnibus privacy or data protection acts, and the European Union has enacted an omnibus data protection directive [1].

Although IT can make organizations leaner and more efficient, it can also drive governmental efforts to create new bureaucracies, or expand old ones, to address new challenges. Already the U.S. and dozens of European and Asian countries have created their own committees examining policies relating to national and global information infrastructures. The government of the People's Republic of China (PRC) seems to be establishing a new group of bureaucrats to monitor the Internet, and Singapore may expand its Broadcasting Authority to implement an Internet service and content provider registration scheme [3, 10]. Indeed, as governments perceive that diffusion of IT threatens their authority, they may expand the corps of officials who address the threat, just as the drug scourge has driven expansion of U.S. law enforcement agencies.

States are not passively letting their powers ebb in cyberspace; rather, many governments are trying to use the new technologies to maintain their positions. Although the fate of such efforts is uncertain, some governments are creating controlled information environments. The PRC, hoping to take advantage of network connectivity while minimizing the risks, is attempting to build a national "intranet" that it will protect from dangerous outside influences by limiting access to forbidden communications [3]. Similarly, the Organization of the Islamic Conference wants to create OICIS-NET, a protected network to connect 51 countries that will carry material deemed suitable for Muslim sensibilities.

Additionally, where they might once have tried (or continue to try) to suppress opposing points of view, some states are using the Internet to participate in the marketplace of ideas. Officials in Indonesia and Singapore, for example, respond to Internet criticism of their respective governments, and several nations, including the U.S. and South Africa, operate Web sites for government information.

Leverage

Despite the difficulty in controlling the flow of bits through and around nations, governments may be able to "bootstrap" their control of the physical world into some control over the electronic one. This may take several forms. First, governments control the land over or under which the information conduits must pass, and they may set conditions for network construction or operation.

The government of Pakistan, for example, will require operators of cellular telephone systems to install monitoring devices in their systems as a condition of licensing. Even wireless satellite communication is subject to control; a government may ban or regulate the equipment necessary for its citizens to receive broadcasts, as Iran, China, and others have attempted. Particularly where little electronic infrastructure exists, an aggressive central government may regulate what is built, and it is relatively easy to monitor a handful of Internet gateways. The PRC or Vietnam may thus have a better chance of controlling what enters or leaves their countries than would the U.S. Extreme isolationists like North Korea and Myanmar, or a country like Guyana, which has announced plans to monitor the Internet before it has any full gateway and to prohibit unauthorized installation of Internet service, have at least temporarily succeeded in their own draconian ways.

Second, governments may control information through their ability to permit or forbid companies to do business within their borders. The PRC forced Rupert Murdoch to remove the BBC from his Star TV satellite broadcasts into its country, as well as Taiwan and Hong Kong, before it would permit him to operate in China. Similarly, European prohibitions against the transfer of personal data to sites without adequate safeguards are given teeth by the respective governments' ability to prevent violators from doing business within their jurisdictions [1]. Governments could thus also require that financial institutions keep records or structure transactions to improve their visibility to tax collectors.

Third, a government's ability to assert jurisdiction over people and corporate assets may give it influence over what individuals and companies do even beyond its borders. Bavarian prosecutors' concern about child pornography, for example, prompted Compuserve to cut off access to 200 Usenet newsgroups for all of its subscribers, not just those in Germany. Similarly, the Singaporean government's threats of libel suits in its own courts have reportedly inhibited the *New York Times* and the *Washington Post* from running critical articles in their globally distributed *International Herald Tribune* [1].

Fourth, communications are subject to the danger of the "unreliable ear," (a U.S. legal doctrine whereby one party to a conversation bears the risk that another party has consented to governmental monitoring) as they all have at least two parties. As Benjamin Franklin observed, "Three may keep a secret, if two of them are dead." Senders cannot be certain that a government will not read even their invincibly encrypted communications, either because the recipients are government agents or because a government can make those recipients' lives miserable. Similarly, those seeking to hide income or other transactions need the cooperation of banks and business partners, but governments can reduce these entities' incentives or abilities to cooperate.

Finally, although states may provide sanctuaries for those whose activities might threaten other states, that ability is not unchallengeable. Other states can apply pressure to those who shelter threats, through means ranging from economic sanctions to military force. As soon as the Seychelles enacted its Economic Development Act, developed nations began to lobby for the Act's amendment or repeal, threatening to withhold foreign aid [13].

This year, too, Great Britain tried to appease Saudi Arabia, a major trade partner, by ordering the deportation of a Saudi dissident who was using the Internet and other media to agitate against the Saudi royal family. (British courts subsequently blocked deportation.) More drastically, when the Mexican government was unwilling or unable to try or extradite a Mexican citizen who had participated in the murder of a U.S. drug enforcement agent, the U.S. government abducted him and tried him in the U.S.

Little Brothers?

For now, at least, IT is causing neither a sweeping aggrandizement nor a precipitous decline of the nation-state. IT supercharges people's abilities to communicate and gain access to information, perhaps beyond government control. Yet it gives governments new capabilities and does not replace their traditional functions in the tangible world, as people still expect and demand functions that only states are equipped to provide. These expectations and demands give national governments some opportunity to bootstrap control over atoms into control over bits.

But expectations can change, and IT may help to change them. As IT promotes communication among people, without regard for national boundaries, and as governments must address the resulting transnational challenges, perhaps people will transfer allegiances and expectations to something other than the nation-state, or perhaps IT, coupled with the continuing integration of the world economy, will enable a decentralization of governmental power. Conversely, a small world may not be a friendly one; cyberspace could be a place where people meet, get to know, and hate each other, or where ethnic or other subnational or transnational groups organize themselves.

Global networking may thus facilitate political and other forms of fragmentation, perhaps making it harder to maintain any form of diverse, geographically bounded, civil society. Neo-Nazi and other hate groups in the U.S. and Germany, for example, organize and communicate across the Internet, and ethnic hate radio encouraged or perhaps even triggered the recent genocides in Rwanda and Bosnia. It would be unfortunate if IT contributed to the demise of Big Brother, only to help nasty Little Brothers take his place.

Acknowledgments
We would like to thank Stewart Baker, Michael Barletta, Avron Barr, Marjory Blumenthal, Ann Danowitz, Melanie Greenberg, Edward Roche, Kevin Soo Hoo, Ross Stapleton-Gray, Shirley Tessler, and Peter Wolcott for their constructive reviews.

Readers are encouraged to send comments, suggestions, anecdotes, insightful speculation, raw data, and articles on subjects relating to international aspects of IT. Correspondence should be addressed to:

Sy Goodman
CISAC
320 Galvez St., Stanford University
Stanford, CA 94305-6165
Fax: 415-723-0089.

References
1. Baker, S.A. The spider in the web: Censorship. *L.A. Times* (Mar. 5, 1995), M5.
2. Chapman, G. Battles over on-line disguises rage in courts and cyberspace. *San Jose Mercury News* (Apr. 8, 1996), 5E.
3. Chinese firewall. *Wall St. J.* (Jan. 31, 1996), A1, A4.
4. Drohan, M. Internet could pose threat to nations' sovereignty. *Dallas Morning News* (Feb. 11, 1996), 20A.
5. Electronic Frontier Canada. Net censorship backfires. Press Release, Feb. 1, 1996.
6. Guèhenno, J.M. *The End of the Nation-State.* University of Minnesota Press, Minneapolis, 1995.
7. Http://www.io.org/~themaxx/canada/can.html.
8. Leo, J. Life among the cyberfolk. *US News & World Rep.* (Mar. 20, 1995) 26.
9. Lewis, P. Limiting a medium without boundaries. *N.Y. Times* (Jan. 15, 1996), D1.
10. McDermott, D. Singapore unveils sweeping measures to control words, images on internet. *Wall St. J.* (March 6, 1996), B6.
11. Orwell, G. *1984.* New American Library, New York, 1981.
12. U.S. Dept. Of State, Bureau for International Narcotics and Law Enforcement Affairs. *Office of International Criminal Justice,* Winter 1996, 4–5.
13. U.S. Dept. Of State, Bureau for International Narcotics and Law Enforcement Affairs, International Narcotics Control Strategy Report, Mar. 1996 496–503, 581–582.
14. Wriston, W.B. *The Twilight of Sovereignty.* Macmillan Publishing Company, New York, 1992.

Lawrence Greenberg (ltgreen@leland.stanford.edu), a political scientist and attorney, is with the Center for International Security and Arms Control at Stanford University.
Seymour Goodman (sgoodman@leland.stanford.edu) is Carnegie Science Fellow at CISAC and Professor of MIS at the University of Arizona.

Warfare in the Information Age

BRUCE D. BERKOWITZ

New threats and new opportunities will require the Pentagon to develop a fundamentally new approach to planning and operations.

Pentagon officials and defense analysts have a new topic to add to their list of post-Cold War concerns: information warfare, or IW, in the usual manner of military-speak. The term refers to the use of information systems—computers, communications networks, databases—for military advantage, either by the United States or by a variety of unfriendly parties.

IW is drawing increasing attention for at least two reasons. First, the United States is potentially vulnerable to IW attack. The United States, in civilian as well as military matters, is more dependent on electronic information systems than is anyone else in the world. In addition to the possibility that computer and communications systems might prove to be a vulnerable weak link for military forces, there is also a danger that hostile parties—countries, terrorist groups, religious sects, multinational corporations, and so on—could attack civilian information systems directly. Attacking these systems could be easier, less

expensive, and certainly less risky than, say, sabotage, assassination, hijacking, or hostage-taking, and a quick cost-effectiveness calculation may make IW an aggressor's strategy of choice.

The second reason why the defense community is so intrigued with IW is that it may be as much an opportunity as it is a threat. The United States may be able to develop new military strategies using IW that are perfectly tailored to world conditions following the Cold War. Information technology is a U.S. strong suit, and military forces could use this know-how to improve our defense capabilities, perhaps dramatically, against hostile attack and to defeat any aggressors—and to accomplish both missions at the lowest possible cost. Indeed, U.S. military planners are already taking the first steps in this direction.

Yet, despite all of the attention that IW is receiving, several basic questions about information warfare remain to be resolved. These include:

• What is the actual IW threat, and how much should the United States worry about it? IW aficionados have suggested a number of scenarios in which IW might be used against us, but other observers think at least some of them are far-fetched.

Bruce D. Berkowitz is an adjunct professor at Carnegie Mellon University. Based in Alexandria, Virginia, he consults frequently on national security issues.

From *Issues in Science and Technology*, Fall 1995, pp. 59-66. © 1995 by the University of Texas at Dallas. Reprinted by permission.

• If the IW threat is real, what does the United States need to do in order to protect itself? Conversely, what must we do in order to make the most of the IW opportunity?

• As a practical matter, how should information warfare be integrated into overall U.S. defense planning? Will IW replace some military capabilities or merely supplement them? Should IW be considered "special," like atomic weapons or chemical weapons, and kept separate from other military forces, or should IW be part of the military's overall organization and planning process?

• What are the implications of IW for current concepts of offense, defense, coercion, and deterrence? For example, is it more difficult to deter an IW attack? Does information warfare automatically escalate to conventional warfare, or vice versa?

• What is the relationship between the military and civilian society in preparing for information warfare? Also, how can the nation protect democratic values—namely, freedom of expression and personal privacy—while taking the measures necessary to defend against an IW threat?

These are very basic issues. We have experience in dealing with similar questions in other areas of defense policy, but information warfare is in many ways quite different. So, if the world is indeed entering an Information Age and IW has the potential to improve, undermine, or just generally complicate U.S. military planning, we need to address such issues now.

Origins of the threat

Military weapons and military strategy usually reflect the politics, economy, and—most especially—the technology of any given society. Even the writers of scripture understood the technological relationship between plowshares and swords, and we take for granted the two-sided nature of nuclear power, long-range jet aircraft, and rockets. Thus, today's improvements in computers, communications, and other electronic data-processing systems that are driving economic growth and changing society are also changing military thinking and planning.

Armies have always used information technology—smoke signals in ancient days, telegraphs at the turn of the century, precision-guided munitions today—but until recently information systems were second in importance to "real" weapons, such as tanks, aircraft, and missiles. Today, information systems are so critical to military operations that it is often more effective to attack an opponent's information systems than to concentrate on destroying its military forces directly.

Also, because modern societies are themselves so dependent on information systems, often the most effective way to attack an opponent is to attack its civilian information infrastructure—commercial communications and broadcasting networks, financial data systems, transportation control systems, and so on. Not only is this strategy more effective in crippling or hurting an opponent, but it often has some special advantages of its own, as will be seen.

Some recent books and films have raised the issue of information mayhem, although they may have exaggerated the dangers. High school students cannot phone into the U.S. military command-and-control system and launch a global thermonuclear strike (à la the 1984 movie *War Games*), and it would be hard for a band of international cyber-terrorists to totally eradicate a woman's identity in the nation's computer systems (as in this year's screen thriller *The Net*).

But consider some of the scenarios that the Department of Defense has studied:

• Approximately 95 percent of all military communications are routed through commercial lines. U.S. troops depend on these communications; in some cases, even highly sensitive intelligence data is transmitted in encrypted form through commercial systems. Although hostile countries may not be able to intercept and decipher the signals, they might be able to jam the civilian links, cutting off U.S. forces or rendering useless numerous intelligence systems costing hundreds of millions of dollars.

• The United States buys most of the microchips used in military systems from commercial vendors, many of which are located in foreign countries. The chips are dispersed throughout a variety of weapons and perform a range of functions. Some experts are concerned that someone might tamper with these chips, causing the weapons to fail to perform when needed.

• One lesson of Operation Desert Storm is that it is unwise to provoke a full-scale conventional military conflict with the United States and its allies. A more subtle alternative might be to send several hundred promising students to school to become computer experts and covert hackers. Such a cadre could develop the training and tactics to systematically tamper with U.S. government and civilian computer systems. But unlike pranksters, they would play for keeps, maximizing the damage they cause and maintaining a low profile so that the damage is hard to detect.

• Some strategic thinkers believe that "economic warfare" between countries is the next area of international competition. This may or may not be so, but it is possible for government experts, skilled in covert action, to assist their countries' industries by well-designed dirty tricks. For example, a bogus "beta tester" could sabotage the market for a new software product by alleging on an Internet bulletin board that the prerelease version of the program has major problems.

• Modern military aircraft, such as the B-2 bomber and F-22 fighter, are designed without a single blueprint or drawing. Rather, they use computer-assisted design/computer-assisted manufacturing (CAD/CAM), in which all records and manufacturing instructions are maintained on electronic media and shared on a closed network. This makes it possible for plants across the country to share databases and to manufacture components that fit together with incredible precision. But it also makes these programs dependent on the reliability and security of the network, which might be compromised by an insider with access.

• Like many large-scale industrial operations today, the military uses "just-in-time" methods for mobilization. That is, to cut costs and improve efficiency, the military services trim stockpiles of spare parts and reserve equipment to the minimum, and they use computers to make sure that the right part or equipment is delivered precisely when needed to the specific user. If the computers go down, everything freezes.

• There is a hidden "data component" in virtually every U.S. weapon system deployed today; this component may be in the form of targeting information that must be uploaded into a munitions guidance system or a "signature" description that tells the guidance sensor what to look for on the battlefield (for example, the distinctive infrared emission that a particular type of tank produces from its exhaust). If this information is unavailable or corrupted, even the smartest bomb regresses into stupidity.

DOD and think tanks have in recent years been actively studying the national security threats that these and other IW scenarios present to U.S. security. But it is also important to remember that, in addition to the threat to military forces, many of these same vulnerabilities apply to commercial industry and the civilian infrastructure. Virtually all communications systems are computer-controlled. Virtually all aircraft and land vehicles have computer-based components. Most transportation systems—aircraft, railroads, urban transit—are directed by remote communications and computers. Thus, virtually all of these civilian systems are also vulnerable to IW attack and could become targets to unfriendly parties.

The changing face of war

One way to understand the impact of IW on military thinking is to recall the evolution of mechanized warfare. Beginning in the mid-1800s, the Industrial Revolution made it possible to develop new weapons that were much more capable than anything produced before: mass-produced machine guns, steam-powered armored warships, long-range artillery capable of hitting targets from several miles away, and so on. The military also benefited from technology that had been developed mainly for civilian purposes, such as railroads and telegraphs, which vastly improved the ability of military forces to mobilize and to maneuver once they arrived at the battlefield. War became faster, longer-ranged, and more deadly. Just as important, new technology also created new targets. Military forces became critically dependent on their nation's industrial base—no factories, no mass-produced weapons, and no mass-produced weapons meant no victory. So, destroying a nation's industrial base became as important as destroying its army, if not more so.

Planning for IW requires cooperation between the defense sector and the commercial sector.

The result was not just an adjustment in military thinking but a complete rethinking of how to wage war. Military planners began to understand that the faster, longer-range weapons offered the opportunity of leapfrogging the front lines on a battlefield in order to destroy an enemy's factories, railroads, and telegraph lines directly. A classic case in point is the progression from the invention of the airplane to the development of the entirely new doctrine of strategic bombing. Moreover, these military planners realized that such an expanded warfare plan was not only a possibility; in many cases, it was likely to be the dominant strategy.

Today's information revolution presents a similar situation. And just as new theories and doctrines were developed for industrial-age warfare, so have thinkers begun to develop a theory and doctrine for IW. As with mechanized warfare and strategic bombing, where it took awhile for military thinking to catch up with the technology, IW concepts have required a few years to mature. In fact, just as aircraft had been in use for almost three decades before the doctrine of strategic bombing was invented, the roots of IW also go back many years. For example, most of the tactics envisioned for attacking an opponent through its information systems—destruction, denial, exploitation, and deception—can be traced to classical military and intelligence fields, such as signals intelligence and cryptography, electronic countermeasures and jamming, "black" propaganda and disinformation, and measures for concealment and camouflage.

What stands clear today is that information technology has reached critical mass. Information systems are so vital to the military and civilian society that they can be the main targets in war, and they can also serve as the main means for conducting offensive operations. In effect, IW is really the dark side of the Information Age. The vulnerability of the military and society to IW attack is a direct result of the spread of information technology. Conversely, IW's potential as a weapon is a direct result of U.S. prowess in information technology.

Indeed, many of the problems of dealing with IW are linked to the nature of information technology itself. The most important feature may simply be the falling cost of information processing; since the 1950s, costs have declined at a rate of about 90 percent every five years, and most experts expect this trend to con-

tinue for the foreseeable future. One result is that information technology—and, with it, the ability to play in the IW game—is constantly becoming more available, and quite rapidly. Unlike nuclear weapons technology or aerospace weapons technology, which have been spreading steadily but slowly, the diffusion of IW technology is likely to accelerate. If a party cannot afford some form of information technology and IW capability today, it probably will be able to afford the technology tomorrow. This is evidenced in the spread of dedicated military electronic systems, but even more in the availability of commercial information technology such as computer networks, satellite and fiber-optic communications, cellular telephone systems, and so on. All of these can be used for hostile purposes, and all can be attacked by a hostile power.

A second feature of information technology that affects IW is that as the technology becomes cheaper and cheaper, it becomes less and less efficient to control information from a central authority. Indeed, one reason for the current increasing pressure in society to decentralize government, corporations, and other organizations is that low-cost information technology makes it affordable and feasible to decentralize. The demand and incentives for decentralization are following the technological opportunity.

This trend runs counter to several centuries of military tradition and experience, which are based on hierarchical command structures, rank, and centralized control. The new technology does not support the traditional military model. Also, the trend toward decentralized information systems changes the government's ability to interact with the commercial sector. As a result, national security officials and military planners must find new ways of issuing instructions and implementing policies.

Dealing with infowar

With these characteristics in mind, it is possible to discuss some specific issues and problems that the United States will face in dealing with information warfare.

The IW threat will grow because entry costs are low. As the cost of information technology falls, a greater number of foreign governments and nongovernment organizations will present a potential IW threat to the United States. Countries that could not match the United States and its Western allies in expensive modern weapons systems, such as tanks, aircraft, and warships, will be able to buy the computers and communications systems necessary to carry out IW.

One defining feature of the post-Cold War era has been that the single, large threat of the Soviet Union has been replaced by a greater number of lesser threats. The declining cost of information technology has facilitated this trend, and many of the new threats will take the form of IW. As a result, the U.S. military will need to think about IW threats coming from a number of different directions.

To complicate matters further, each threat will probably be somewhat different. One terrorist group might like to fiddle with transportation control systems; another might be dedicated to compromising DOD databases. In the past, the United States has tailored its forces and plans to deal with the single Soviet threat, and has assumed that, if it could defeat the Soviet Union militarily, it could also deal with what the Pentagon calls "lesser included threats." In the IW world, threats are likely to be as varied as tailored software, and U.S. military forces will need to deal with each on its own terms.

There will be an international learning curve. Not only will more players engage in IW, they will steadily get better at it. Because information is so easily transferred, everyone can quickly learn from the IW mistakes that others make. For example, Desert Storm was essentially a situation in which one side fought a classical 20th-century conventional war while the other side fought a classical 21st-century IW war. The Iraqi army was not outgunned; indeed, it had a numerical edge, as well as the advantages of fighting from prepared defensive positions and its experience in battle gained during Iraq's decade-long war with Iran. The U.S. advantage was in information technology—intelligence, communications, precision-guided munitions, night vision equipment, stealth technology, and electronic countermeasures. As a result, the United States and its coalition partners were well-coordinated and could adjust their operations in real time, whereas Iraqi forces were isolated, disorganized, and blind.

It's unlikely future foes will repeat Iraq's mistakes and permit opponents such a free hand in the contest for what DOD has taken to calling "information superiority" on the battlefield. Indeed, a country or organization with even a rudimentary knowledge of IW could take countermeasures that can greatly reduce the U.S. advantage. The upshot is that the United States will have to work hard and persistently in order to maintain its present IW advantage. Also, because the U.S. advantage could potentially be tenuous and fleeting, it will be necessary to monitor the changing IW threat and develop the systems and expertise necessary to deal with it.

The changing face of deterrence

During the past 50 years, a well-developed body of theory about conventional and nuclear deterrence has accumulated. Although Star Wars advocates may quibble, most strategic thinkers would agree with U.S. military analyst Bernard Brodie, who noted in 1947 that it is hard to mount a foolproof defense against nuclear attack, so the more plausible strategy is to deter a nuclear attack through the threat of retaliation. Alas, the problem seems doubled for IW. So far, evidence suggests that not only will defense against IW be difficult; even an effective plan for deterrence will be hard to pull off.

One of the greatest difficulties in deterring a would-be IW threat is that an attacker may be anonymous. A country or nongovernmental group could tamper with U.S. communications and computer systems just enough to cause damage, but not enough so the perpetrator can be identified. To paraphrase a metaphor offered by Thomas Rona, a long-time IW thinker, we will be unlikely to find a smoking gun because our opponents will likely use smokeless powder. With no "attacker ID," it would be hard to determine who deserves retaliation, and without the threat of retaliation, deterrence usually fails. Indeed, a truly diabolical enemy would most likely adopt the strategy of an unseen parasite, quietly causing problems that would be attributed to normal glitches we routinely accept with software and information systems. (Have you tried installing OS-2 Warp or Windows 95 on your computer? Many people simply expect electronics to be difficult.)

Another problem for deterrence is that, even if an IW attack is identified, it may be difficult to develop an effective option for retaliation. As one DOD official has said, "What are we going to do, nuke them for turning off our TVs?" An IW attack may be just crippling and expensive, rather than lethal, so conventional retaliation (say, an airstrike) may be unpopular. On the other hand, because the United States is so dependent on information technology, we would likely come out on the losing end of a game of IW tit for tat. And mere diplomatic responses are likely to be ineffective.

Who will be responsible for IW? In the past, the usual response of the military to a new technology has been to assign responsibility for it to a new organization; for example, the Strategic Air Command (now simply Strategic Command) was created to assume responsibility for long-range bombers and missiles. Indeed, within DOD responsibility for information technologies has historically been assigned to specific organizations— the National Security Agency (NSA) in the case of signals intelligence and information systems security, the Central Intelligence Agency (CIA) in the case of covert operations such as black propaganda and covert political action, the National Reconnaissance Office (NRO) in the case of surveillance satellites, and so on.

Currently, each of the military services is developing an IW strategy to assist it in developing new weapons and doctrine, and commanders of U.S. military units deployed in the field are developing plans for IW in their theater of operation. DOD officials have mused—briefly—whether to consolidate responsibilities for IW in a single organization. Most have quickly concluded that this would not make sense. Not only would there be turf battles among existing organizations; such an organization would be inconsistent with the trend in which information systems are, in fact, becoming more decentralized.

Indeed, the more appropriate question may be why we need large operating organizations such as NSA and NRO when information systems are becoming cheaper, networked, and decentralized. It may soon be more efficient for military units to operate their own signals intelligence and even re-

Unless U.S. leaders deal with the problem of reconciling secrecy and democracy, IW will likely remain a marginal asset.

connaissance systems. There already is some movement in that direction; for example, Army and Navy units operate their own reconnaissance drone aircraft.

The objective should be to permit IW technology to spread throughout the DOD organization while ensuring that IW operations are coordinated so that they are consistent with national policy and the strategy of military commanders. At the same time, DOD needs to ensure that IW systems in the military can operate with each other and with those in the civilian world, without creating an unwieldy bureaucracy or body of specifications.

Planning for IW "civil defense"

Planning for IW requires cooperation between the defense sector and the commercial sector. Civilian information systems are prime candidates for attack. So just as cities are targeted in strategic bombing, in future wars we can expect civilian information systems to be hacked, tapped, penetrated, bugged, and infected with computer viruses.

Another reason for cooperation is that DOD itself depends heavily on the civilian information infrastructure. As noted earlier, not only does the military use civilian information systems for "routine" activities such as mobilization; sometimes even the transmission of sensitive intelligence data is routed through commercial links. Obviously, it would be impossibly expensive for DOD to make the entire civilian information infrastructure secure to military standards. And even if it were affordable, the passwords, encryption systems, and other security measures would make it incredibly inconvenient for public use.

Moreover, the government's ability to control or influence the civilian information industry is limited. DOD lacks the leverage it has enjoyed in other situations. For example, the Air Force can influence the design of spacecraft because it is the largest operator of space systems, but DOD's share of the total computing and communications market is quite small compared with commercial users. Also, today's commercial information industry is often ahead of the defense industry in developing new technology. So, whereas DOD once could effectively create industry standards in order to enhance security though its leading-edge role in research and development and its buying power, standards are now being set by companies in the market. Add to this the burgeoning information industry worldwide and DOD's influence is diminished further.

The upshot is that DOD cannot use traditional-style directives or specifications to improve the ability to defend the nation against the IW threat. If it tries, no matter how well-intentioned, it will likely fail. As evidence, consider the recent Clipper Chip episode, in which the federal government tried to cajole and coerce the information industry to adopt a NSA-developed encryption system. The Clipper Chip was supposedly indecipherable, but critics claimed that any system designed by the government would permit the government to read messages using the code (in cryptography parlance, this is called "back door access"). According to the critics, the government's objective was to preserve the ability of NSA and law enforcement agencies to read encrypted communications that they intercepted.

Not only did the industry reject the Clipper Chip, but the government was unable to prevent private computer programmers from developing and illegally distributing their own encryption systems that the government supposedly could not crack or systems (such as SATAN) that can detect "back doors." The lesson of the Clipper Chip is that DOD must use a more sophisticated, less heavy-handed approach to get the civilian sector to take measures to protect itself against the IW threat. Because directives and standards usually will not work, DOD officials need to learn how to use incentive systems instead.

For example, simply informing industry and individuals that they could be IW targets will often lead them to adopt "street smart" information behavior to protect themselves from both foreign and domestic attack. DOD officials themselves have suggested that the government could encourage insurance companies to charge appropriately higher rates to corporations that did not take reasonable steps to protect their data or information systems (again, on the assumption that making the insurance companies aware of the damage an IW attack could cause will generally suffice). In cases in which DOD is critically dependent on a civilian information link, it may even make sense for the government to subsidize the civilian operators so that they adopt protective measures.

In other cases, the government may need to face the fact that some of its traditional activities will simply no longer be possible—for example, easily reading most transmissions that it intercepts. Instead, the government could concentrate on providing industry with the means to protect its information system. Indeed, in at least some cases it would seem that using the government's technical expertise to give U.S. industry an edge in the IW wars may do more for national security than collecting and decoding signals.

Ensuring democratic control of IW policy

Reconciling information security obviously collides with allowing easy access to information systems and freedom of expression. However, IW presents another problem for American democracy.

It is possible to imagine ways in which offensive IW tactics might cost less or be more effective than conventional military options; suffice it to say that almost all the tactics ascribed to our opponents could, at least potentially, be considered for adoption by the United States. Yet the defense community rarely discusses the offensive use of information warfare. The reason for this reticence is that, like intelligence plans and systems, IW options are easily compromised once the opponent learns about them. Even in the case of defensive IW, some government officials are reluctant to discuss the threat, thinking that raising attention to U.S vulnerabilities will encourage new groups to target the United States.

The problem is that it will be hard to integrate IW into U.S. defense planning without building public support. Citizens will need to understand why the government is undertaking IW programs and how the programs may permit other military programs to be phased out. Without public discussion and understanding of how IW capabilities might replace some conventional military systems, the nation may needlessly spend money for both conventional and IW programs. Secrecy also tends to increase costs by limiting competition and reducing the ability of DOD to draw on unclassified and commercial programs. One reason why commercial information technology is usually equal or superior to its military counterparts, and almost always less expensive, is that greater competition in the private sector forces innovation and pushes down prices.

Unless U.S. leaders deal with the problem of reconciling secrecy and democracy, IW will likely remain a marginal asset. In fact, the political system has considerable experience in dealing with such issues; nuclear weapons, intelligence operations, and covert action are all routinely reviewed by Congress and, at a more general level, are discussed in the public media. It seems reasonable that the nation can also have a public debate over the place of IW in U.S. defense policy without compromising the policy itself.

Prescriptions for preparedness

Dealing with the IW threat and especially with aggressive attackers who use IW as their main weapon against the United States will require new approaches. In most cases, it will probably be impossible to build a foolproof defense for the civilian information infrastructure. But it should be possible to prevent "cheap kills" by informing the general public and industry of the threat though formal and informal networks for government-civilian cooperation.

In the case of vital military communications links and computer systems, it may be possible to build hardened "point defenses," taking extra steps to thwart attackers. These could include, for example, building dedicated transmission lines for communications, isolating critical computers from all outside networks, and using hardware and software security systems that might be excessively expensive or inconvenient for commercial use but which are necessary for vital DOD systems. These measures would also need to be repeated in the production of hardware and software, and in some cases dedicated production lines might be necessary for the most sensitive systems.

Yet, because defense and deterrence are both so difficult to achieve in IW, the best strategy to protect the most vital information systems may be stealth—keeping the very existence of such an information system a secret so that it does not become a target. Of course, "secret information system" is the ultimate oxymoron, which is another way of saying that such systems will also likely be among the most expensive, inefficient, and difficult to use.

The most challenging measures, though, are likely to be political, economic, and cultural. IW requires new concepts within DOD because traditional approaches to military planning and military command and control will not work for it. And the same is true across society, where the measures for countering the IW threat will often collide with the essential features of the democratic, free-market system that an IW policy is intended to protect.

Recommended reading

Office of the Secretary of Defense, Assistant Secretary for Command, Control, Communications, and Intelligence, "Information Warfare," Washington, D.C.: Department of Defense, 1995.

Department of Defense, "Defensive Information Warfare Strategy," Washington, D.C.: Department of Defense, Feb. 22, 1995.

Department of the Army, Information Operations, FM 100-6, Washington, D.C.: July 22, 1994.

Technological Risks

Any new and powerful technology poses unforeseen hazards. In conducting research for a magazine article on the history of American technological achievements, engineer/writer Samuel Florman found that nearly every new technological triumph was initially accompanied by disastrous effects. He learned, for example, that during the early days of steamboat transport, 42 explosions killed 270 persons between 1825 and 1830. These events, and public outrage, led to government-funded research that ultimately led to legislation on safety standards. Florman tells a similar story of the early days of railroading, and in particular, of railroad bridges:

> In the late 1860s more than 25 American bridges were collapsing each year, with appalling loss of life. In 1873 the American Society of Civil Engineers set up a special commission to address the problem, and eventually the safety of our bridges came to be taken for granted.

As these examples illustrate, the solution to these terrible problems was not to abandon but to improve technology. Florman summarizes the pattern of technological advance as "progress/setback/renewed-creative-effort."

Computers have been relatively common for a few decades now and, compared with the steamboat and railroad examples above, they have caused few physical injuries to humans. Yet, as the articles in this section show, we cannot take it for granted that computers will operate flawlessly. When failures occur, the consequences can be serious indeed.

The lead article in this unit highlights one problem that has gone largely unrecognized. Because computers are famous for their ability to keep track of huge amounts of data, many people may be surprised to learn that it is actually hard to preserve and control computerized data. In "It's 10 O'Clock: Do You Know Where Your Data Are?" Terry Cook explains that electronic records are vulnerable to loss and distortion. Cook relates some of the problems that can arise from losses in organizational memory, and he outlines measures to minimize the risks.

While computer-related errors that have resulted in physical harm to humans are extremely rare, many vital operations, from air traffic control systems to nuclear power plants, are controlled by computers. Sociologist Charles Perrow has argued that the risk of malfunction is greatly increased when complex technical systems arise from and operate within complex social systems. In "Software's Chronic Crisis," W. Wayt Gibbs illustrates this point with several nightmarish examples of what can go wrong when developing large-scale software systems. Gibbs also highlights why it is so hard to detect and fix errors. Barbara Wade Rose then reports in her essay "Fatal Dose" on several tragedies that occurred because of a malfunctioning computer-controlled radiation therapy machine.

The unit next focuses on liability for faulty electronic information. Legal scholar Pamela Samuelson argues that issues surrounding liability are unclear because software is more like a book than a machine. Traditionally, courts have been reluctant to impose liability on authors, publishers, and booksellers for defective information because of constitutional protection of the free exchange of ideas and information. However, Samuelson concludes that providers of electronic information should think not only about their rights but also about their responsibilities, and start addressing liability problems.

Looking Ahead: Challenge Questions

Should the principle of "caveat emptor," or "let the buyer beware," apply to software? Why or why not?

As complex computer systems become more widespread, do you think that they will become more reliable and thus safer, or will the risks increase? Why?

What political, social, economic, and technical factors should be taken into account when assessing computer risks?

It's 10 O'Clock: Do You Know Where Your Data Are?

Terry Cook

TERRY COOK is the director of the Records Disposition Division at the National Archives of Canada. A former editor of three national journals on archives and history, he has written and lectured widely on archival issues.

Ontario Hydro's nuclear power plant near Toronto was losing its memory. The condition—a breakdown of its electronic record-keeping faculties—first appeared when the utility could find no record of a crucial reactor sealing ring that had suddenly begun wearing out several years earlier than expected. To obtain some replacement rings fast, the plant's managers and scientists had to know immediately who sold them the parts, when they had been ordered, and whether the contractor provided guarantees against defects.

The records manager of the huge provincial utility blamed the lost records on the recently installed computer network and worker unfamiliarity with the company's new practices for storing documents. But as she and the staff searched frantically for the stray document, she discovered that the problem was now a chronic one. Despite management directives that all employees print out paper versions of electronic documents and place them on file, the volume of paper records arriving at the central storage office had dropped by 50 percent within six months of the network's installation. The actual work was still being done, but workers were now deciding that they were their own best records managers and archivists.

In the company's former paper-only system, information about a defective part could easily have been found by retrieving a carbon copy of the purchase order, which a secretary would have typed and given to a clerk for filing in the records office. But in the electronic world Ontario Hydro had adopted, few secretaries and records clerks remained. The only "filed" copy of a purchase order, if it existed, would reside on an individual's hard disk drive, but then only if the employee remembered to save it in the first place, and if he or she had not deleted the years-old document while freeing up disk space. Moreover, given that employees were allowed to name files according to personal whimsy, and that files were password-protected, access to the electronic version of the purchase order would be possible only if the employee had not left the company and was available when needed.

Ontario Hydro is not alone. Reports of lost or scrambled electronic data are coming in from a variety of sources, including major governmental organizations. For example, the United Nations recently discovered that methods for identifying, storing, and retrieving vital electronic data, such as field reports on social and economic issues in developing countries, had been completely ignored since the widespread introduction of office-automation technology. Similarly, the National Archives of Canada recently investigated the electronic files of one of the country's cabinet ministers and found not only that 30 of 100 randomly chosen policy documents could not be found in the government's paper records, but also that no system was in place to safeguard the contents of the electronic system. The National Archives and Records Administration in Washington, D.C., a repository for all government records, reports that older magnetic tapes containing data received from various government departments were suddenly unreadable after just 15 years. Because the temperature and humidity of storage areas in several

Computers can generate megabytes of data at near light speeds but can delete essential records just as quickly. Archivists are working to adapt traditional methods for managing paper, and devise new ones, for the brave new world of electronic virtual documents.

departments were uncontrolled and the tapes were not rewound regularly or copied every few years, as recommended by archival conservation standards, the tapes became so brittle that they melted or caught fire when run on new drives that spun the tape some 10 times faster than earlier models.

Perhaps the most spectacular example of a government agency losing its electronic memory recently occurred at the National Aeronautics and Space Administration when space scientists were eager to access some 1.2 million magnetic tapes of observations that NASA created during three decades of space flight. The researchers were hoping to reveal "long-term trends like global climate change, tropical deforestation, and the thinning of the atmospheric ozone layer," according to NASA, as well as new nuggets of information about the moon and planets. But the information could not be read or sometimes even found. Tapes were uncataloged. Some had been damaged by heat or floods. Many were unlabeled as to which mission or spacecraft or computer system created them. Because no proper archival controls for these records were in place, NASA officials estimate that it will take millions of dollars and years of detective work to link each of the files to their spacecraft or mission and then decode the information so that it can be read by hardware and software now in use.

Underlying each case of lost data is a fundamental change in the way institutions now store information. For the first time in 3,500 years of archival activity we produce records that do not exist to the human eye—unlike Babylonian clay tablets, Egyptian papyrus, Roman and medieval parchment, modern paper, even microfilm. For the first time, business and professional people with no training and usually no aptitude for managing records are responsible for creating and storing them. Perhaps most significant, for the first time, we are not producing, managing, and saving physical artifacts, but rather trying to understand and preserve virtual patterns that give the electronic information its content, structure, context, and thus its meaning. Yet these patterns are completely controlled by software, which over the years will be modified, updated, and

replaced countless times. Unless organizations adopt a means to control key records and continually migrate them to current software and new storage media, the long-term memory of our modern institutions will be in jeopardy, as will their ethical, legal, and economic health.

Unchained Memories

Disaster can occur not only because electronic information is hard to preserve but also because it is hard to control. Imagine that a chief executive officer sends a crucial policy-related e-mail message to her corporate administrators on November 23, 1994, and attaches a report containing graphs generated from spreadsheets linked to a database whose values change daily. The message and attachments detail investment strategies for the company and key clients.

Imagine also that one of the managers is later fired for failing to carry out the CEO's directives, thus having cost the company several important clients, and that he sues the company for wrongful dismissal, claiming he never received the CEO's e-mail message. If that same message had been sent in 1984 or 1974, or even 1904, it would have been a typed paper memorandum, addressed to the group, copied to others, and signed by the CEO, with a hand-drawn chart in the body of the text and figures and statistical tables in an appendix that would be physically stapled or paper-clipped to the CEO's memo. Any legal dispute could thus be settled by recourse to the paper file where the whole package sent by the CEO would reside, with evidence of signatures, routing-slip initials, or acknowledgment-of-receipt stamps.

Not so with the electronic version. Even if the computer system's backup tapes survive, which is no guarantee in many workplaces, could the corporation retrieve and, more important, reconstruct the CEO's compound electronic document two years, or maybe even ten years, after the fact? Could it prove that the offending administrator had actually been on the original e-mail distribution list and had been sent the document? Could it prove that he had received the document and either filed or deleted it? Could it recreate the attachment as it actually existed on November 23, 1994, from the ever-changing spreadsheet tables? Could it prove that no subsequent alteration or unauthorized access to the data or system had occurred?

The key to maintaining critical electronic information lies in being able to determine, sometimes long after the fact, not only the content but also the context of a record in question. Such a contextual view of information is the purview of archivists, who, unlike librarians, want to know not just what was communicated but when, by whom, to whom, where, how, why, using what media, and connected to what broader programs and activities, both now and over time. Using skills

Oganizations need techniques for controlling key records and continually migrating them to contemporary software and storage media.

honed in managing the voluminous paper records of the modern state, archivists are now obviously obliged to develop similar approaches to stop the memory loss of the electronic age.

At the center of all archival thinking is the "record." Whether a parchment court roll, a frontier-land patent, a business report on a paper file, or an electronic message, all records have three properties: content, structure, and context.

For paper records, all three elements are represented on the same physical medium. Content is most obvious: it is the words, phrases, numbers, and symbols composing the actual text. The structure of paper documents is also readily evident from the form used for special kinds of transactions: a business tax return is different from a land-grant certificate. The context for paper records is derived from the signature lines, the signature itself, the address and salutation, the letterhead, the date, the carbon copies or "cc" line on the bottom of the page, perhaps the surviving envelope, various stamp impressions or annotations of date of receipt or filing, the position of the document within a larger paper file of related documents, the file heading or title, the file's own place within a larger records classification system, charge-out cards recording who has read the file on what date, and cross references to related documents in other media, including photographs, maps, and so forth.

Archivists consider this contextual information essential to the comprehension of any "record" as a reflection of acts and transactions, and thus of institutional accountability. Without context, one is left with information but not a record, and no memory on which to base future decisions or defend earlier ones.

For electronic media, the content, structure, and context of the record change significantly from that of the traditional paper world. The only approximate match with paper is the content element, where the letters and numbers look much the same on the computer screen as on paper. But the structure and especially the context of electronic records are not apparent when retrieved from the text only.

Think of the CEO who sent out her message on investment strategies electronically. The interconnections of her compound document are not part of what the user sees on the screen, as they would be in a paper world, but rather are links in software or in the operating system. These instruct the computer to query the database, drop the relevant values found there into the spreadsheet, build a graph using spreadsheet formulas, and place the resulting graph in the appropriate spot in the word-processed report that is attached to the e-mail.

No such product is actually stored anywhere in the computer. Rather, at a particular moment in time, the software and operating system must stitch together information that is scattered in many places to form that virtual document. Upgrade or change that software and system, alter any of the data values, and those relationships among the e-mail, report, graphic, spreadsheet, and database are lost, as they are in the vast majority of systems operating in businesses and governments today. The virtual document vanishes. Corporate memory is wiped clean.

Preserving Electronic Records

What can be done to stop the erosion of institutional memory in an electronic world? How do we protect the content, structure, and context of electronic records over time? Before addressing what will work, it may be useful to look at three options that have been proposed or tried, each of which has serious flaws.

The first option proposed and rejected by numerous corporations and government agencies is to impose a single hardware and software standard on all records creators—everyone within the organization must use WordPerfect 6.0 with Windows, for example. Such policy fiats would be virtually impossible to implement and enforce outside rigidly hierarchical organizations like the military and the police. Nor are they desirable, for they undermine end-user creativity, lead to unhealthy monopoly situations for the makers of the hardware or software of choice, and curtail levels of comfort with preferred technology. A related approach would be to preserve only generic data, such as ASCII text, which is not hardware or software dependent and thus could be read using "off-the-shelf" standard software. This in fact was the archival preservation option used in the 1970s and 1980. But it is no longer feasible for today's software-dependent records, which are too complex to translate into ASCII format.

A second option proposed by several entrepreneurs in the past few years is to create a cybernetic museum with working models of every known piece of obsolete computer hardware and software, so that institutions and archives may gain access to old files and convert them to whatever may be the present-day standard. Unfortunately, the likelihood of keeping any piece of machinery running for many decades is simply not very high, since replacement parts, chips, and software could not be easily reproduced. A computer system is far more complex than a steam locomotive or shuttle loom.

A third option increasingly favored by information technology professionals is to dump all electronic information in no particular order on CD-ROMs or high-density diskettes, and then to search them for the required subjects using ever more powerful artificial-intelligence text-retrieval programs. But while related material can be retrieved in this approach, so would be a great mass of extraneous information containing the same search strings.

For example, one researcher at the National Archives of Canada recently used such a strategy to try to find information from the defunct Trade Negotiations Office concerning plans to expand sales of Canadian freshwater to the United States. He searched the agency's electronic files for references containing the word "water." Even though the trade office was in operation for only a couple of years and employed only a few people, the researcher found more than 600 items containing the word "water." Yet while some related to the subject, many did not, especially since archivists, faced with a save-all or delete-all situation, chose to preserve all the backup tapes of the system. Thus the researcher found many items like "Meet me at the water cooler," and "My report was sure watered down by the boss."

Moreover, references that might have detailed crucial policy decisions but did not contain the word "water" were missed entirely: "About that matter we discussed this morning, the Prime Minister instructs me to tell you that under no circumstances shall we bargain it away unless the United States makes major concessions in agricultural products." Free-text searching, while better than nothing, does not uncover all the relevant records related to a particular function, activity, or transaction, nor does it preserve the context of or reason why a record was created.

A fourth option, now being explored by a team of archivists led by Richard Cox and David Bearman in a project at the University of Pittsburgh, and by John McDonald at the National Archives of Canada, is to determine the functional requirements of defining and safeguarding a record in a world of virtual rather than physical documents. The Pittsburgh project team has thus far determined the following set of needs for capturing, maintaining, and using electronic records:

■ Records must be comprehensive: a record reflecting who, what, when, where, why, with whom, and so on, must be created for every business transaction. Courts accept records as evidence when they are produced under identifiable controls and standards. Thus records cannot be created for some transactions and not for others, or else the trustworthiness of the institution's record-keeping system would be thrown into doubt and its value as evidence considerably weakened.

■ Records must be authentic: authorizations for access to the data, or parts of it, must be recorded, and traceable to each record and transaction. Verifying what was sent, seen, received, and deleted by whom requires capturing the kind of security controls that exist in the paper documents in the electronic records as well, or the overall context of the communication is lost.

Software should enable users to store electronic documents in a way that preserves both their content and their context.

■ Records must be tamper-proof: no deletion or alteration to a record should occur once the transaction to which it relates has taken place. If a record is changed or corrected, a second record must be created and linked to the first. Moreover, each use, viewing, indexing, classifying, filing, or copying of a record is also a transaction and thus must generate its own record. To determine in a lawsuit whether the parties to a business decision were negligent, lawyers have to know on which computer records the responsible officers based their decisions. That is impossible unless the indexing and searching patterns used by the system are captured for the time each decision was made.

The Pittsburgh team believes that each organization should assign to a chief information officer or other senior staff formal responsibility for implementing these and other guidelines for generating and protecting records in new system designs and system reengineering plans. In fact, the next steps of the Pittsburgh project, which is funded by the U.S. National Historical Publications and Records Commission and scheduled to be completed in 1995, will help information officers meet these goals.

The team plans to translate the guidelines into technical specifications that programmers can use to instruct computers to automatically create appropriate records. In the terminology of the field, programmers would be creating metadata, which are additional data that encapsulate or surround the original data and tell them how to act, place them in the context of the business transactions to which they relate, and maintain their integrity and authenticity.

Software companies would design these record-keeping capabilities into their new products, especially integrated business applications such as word processing, spreadsheet, graphics, and database programs. End users will create the markets for such new software products either by recognizing their intrinsic value for safeguarding corporate memory or by responding to the growing number of data disasters and lost records.

As society shifted a millennium ago from the oral to the written record, the focus of archivists changed from remembering an action to caring for the written artifacts that gave evidence of the action. As society now moves from written records to virtual documents, archivists are offering their traditional understanding of the structure and context of recorded evidence as protection against the widespread amnesia now threatening our electronic world.

Software's Chronic Crisis

Despite 50 years of progress, the software industry remains years—perhaps decades—short of the mature engineering discipline needed to meet the demands of an information-age society

W. Wayt Gibbs

Denver's new international airport was to be the pride of the Rockies, a wonder of modern engineering. Twice the size of Manhattan, 10 times the breadth of Heathrow, the airport is big enough to land three jets simultaneously—in bad weather. Even more impressive than its girth is the airport's subterranean baggage-handling system. Tearing like intelligent coal-mine cars along 21 miles of steel track, 4,000 independent "telecars" route and deliver luggage between the counters, gates and claim areas of 20 different airlines. A central nervous system of some 100 computers networked to one another and to 5,000 electric eyes, 400 radio receivers and 56 bar-code scanners orchestrates the safe and timely arrival of every valise and ski bag.

At least that is the plan. For nine months, this Gulliver has been held captive by Lilliputians—errors in the software that controls its automated baggage system. Scheduled for takeoff by last Halloween, the airport's grand opening was postponed until December to allow BAE Automated Systems time to flush the gremlins out of its $193-million system. December yielded to March. March slipped to May. In June the airport's planners, their bond rating demoted to junk and their budget hemorrhaging red ink at the rate of $1.1 million a day in interest and operating costs, conceded that they could not predict when the baggage system would stabilize enough for the airport to open.

To veteran software developers, the Denver debacle is notable only for its visibility. Studies have shown that for every six new large-scale software systems that are put into operation, two others are canceled. The average software development project overshoots its schedule by half; larger projects generally do worse. And some three quarters of all large systems are "operating failures" that either do not function as intended or are not used at all.

The art of programming has taken 50 years of continual refinement to reach this stage. By the time it reached 25, the difficulties of building big software loomed so large that in the autumn of 1968 the NATO Science Committee convened some 50 top programmers, computer scientists and captains of industry to plot a course out of what had come to be known as the software crisis. Although the experts could not contrive a road map to guide the industry toward firmer ground, they did coin a name for that distant goal: software engineering, now defined formally as "the application of a systematic, disciplined, quantifiable approach to the development, operation and maintenance of software."

A quarter of a century later software engineering remains a term of aspiration. The vast majority of computer code is still handcrafted from raw programming languages by artisans using techniques they neither measure nor are able to repeat consistently. "It's like musket making was before Eli Whitney," says Brad J. Cox, a professor at George Mason University. "Before the industrial revolution, there was a nonspecialized approach to manufacturing goods that involved very little interchangeability and a maximum of craftsmanship. If we are ever going to lick this software crisis, we're going to have to stop this hand-to-mouth, every-programmer-builds-everything-from-the-ground-up, preindustrial approach."

The picture is not entirely bleak. Intuition is slowly yielding to analysis as programmers begin using quantitative measurements of the quality of the software they produce to improve the way they produce it. The mathematical foundations of programming are solidifying as researchers work on ways of expressing program designs in algebraic forms that make it easier to avoid serious mistakes. Academic computer scientists are starting to address their failure to produce a solid corps of software professionals. Perhaps most important, many in the industry are turning their attention toward inventing the technology and market structures needed to support interchangeable, reusable software parts.

"Unfortunately, the industry does not uniformly apply that which is well-known best practice," laments Larry E. Druffel, director of Carnegie Mellon University's Software Engineering Institute. In fact, a research innovation typically requires 18 years to wend its way into the repertoire of standard programming techniques. By combining their efforts, academia, industry and government may be able to hoist software development to the level of an industrial-age engineering discipline within the decade. If they come up short, society's headlong rush into the information age will be halting and unpredictable at best.

Shifting Sands

"We will see massive changes [in computer use] over the next few years, causing the initial personal computer revolution to pale into comparative insignificance," concluded 22 leaders in software development from academia, industry and research laboratories this past April. The experts gathered at Hedsor Park, a corporate retreat near London, to commemorate the NATO conference and to analyze the future directions of software. "In 1968 we knew what we wanted to build but couldn't," reflected Cliff Jones, a professor at the University of Manchester. "Today we are standing on shifting sands."

The foundations of traditional programming practices are eroding swiftly, as hardware engineers churn out ever faster, cheaper and smaller machines. Many fundamental assumptions that programmers make—for instance, their acceptance that everything they produce will have defects—must change in response. "When computers are embedded in light switches, you've got to get the software right the first time because you're not going to have a chance to update it," says Mary M. Shaw, a professor at Carnegie Mellon.

"The amount of code in most consumer products is doubling every two years," notes Remi H. Bourgonjon, director of software technology at Philips Research Laboratory in Eindhoven. Already, he reports, televisions may contain up to 500 kilobytes of software; an electric shaver, two kilobytes. The power trains in new General Motors cars run 30,000 lines of computer code.

Getting software right the first time is hard even for those who care to try. The Department of Defense applies rigorous—and expensive—testing standards to ensure that software on which a mission depends is reliable. Those standards were used to certify *Clementine*, a satellite that the DOD and the National Aeronautics and Space Administration directed into lunar orbit this past spring. A major part of the Clementine mission was to test targeting software that could one day be used in a space-based missile defense system. But when the satellite was spun around and instructed to fix the moon in its sights, a bug in its program caused the spacecraft instead to fire its maneuvering thrusters continuously for 11 minutes. Out of fuel and spinning wildly, the satellite could not make its rendezvous with the asteroid Geographos.

SOFTWARE IS EXPLODING in size as society comes to rely on more powerful computer systems (*top*). That faith is often rewarded by disappointment as most large software projects overrun their schedules (*middle*) and many fail outright (*bottom*)—usually after most of the development money has been spent.

Errors in real-time systems such as *Clementine* are devilishly difficult to spot because, like that suspicious sound in your car engine, they often occur only when conditions are just so [see "The Risks of Software," by Bev Littlewood and Lorenzo Strigini; SCIENTIFIC AMERICAN, November 1992]. "It is not clear that the methods that are currently used for producing safety-critical software, such as that in nuclear reactors or in cars, will evolve and scale up adequately to match our future expectations," warned Gilles Kahn, the scien-

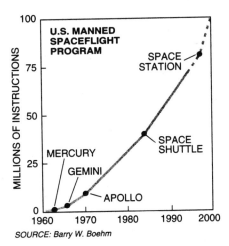

SOURCE: Barry W. Boehm

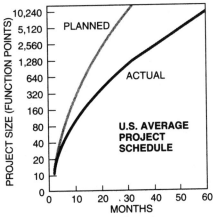

SOURCE: Software Productivity Research

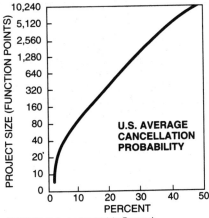

SOURCE: Software Productivity Research

tific director of France's INRIA research laboratory, at the Hedsor Park meeting. "On the contrary, for real-time systems I think we are at a fracture point."

Software is buckling as well under tectonic stresses imposed by the inexorably growing demand for "distributed systems": programs that run cooperatively on many networked computers. Businesses are pouring capital into distributed information systems that they hope to wield as strategic weapons. The inconstancy of software development can turn such projects into Russian roulette.

Many companies are lured by goals that seem simple enough. Some try to reincarnate obsolete mainframe-based software in distributed form. Others want to plug their existing systems into one another or into new systems with which they can share data and a friendlier user interface. In the technical lingo, connecting programs in this way is often called systems integration. But Brian Randell, a computer scientist at the University of Newcastle upon Tyne, suggests that "there is a better word than integration, from old R.A.F. slang: namely, 'to graunch,' which means 'to make to fit by the use of excessive force.'"

It is a risky business, for although software seems like malleable stuff, most programs are actually intricate plexuses of brittle logic through which data of only the right kind may pass. Like handmade muskets, several programs may perform similar functions and yet still be unique in design. That makes software difficult to modify and repair. It also means that attempts to graunch systems together often end badly.

In 1987, for example, California's Department of Motor Vehicles decided to make its customers' lives easier by merging the state's driver and vehicle registration systems—a seemingly straightforward task. It had hoped to unveil convenient one-stop renewal kiosks last year. Instead the DMV saw the projected cost explode to 6.5 times the expected price and the delivery date recede to 1998. In December the agency pulled the plug and walked away from the seven-year, $44.3-million investment.

Sometimes nothing fails like success. In the 1970s American Airlines constructed SABRE, a virtuosic, $2-billion flight reservation system that became part of the travel industry's infrastructure. "SABRE was the shining example of a strategic information system because it drove American to being the world's largest airline," recalls Bill

Curtis, a consultant to the Software Engineering Institute.

Intent on brandishing software as effectively in this decade, American tried to graunch its flight-booking technology with the hotel and car reservation systems of Marriott, Hilton and Budget. In 1992 the project collapsed into a heap of litigation. "It was a smashing failure," Curtis says. "American wrote off $165 million against that system."

The airline is hardly suffering alone. In June IBM's Consulting Group released the results of a survey of 24 leading companies that had developed large distributed systems. The numbers were unsettling: 55 percent of the projects cost more than expected, 68 percent overran their schedules and 88 percent had to be substantially redesigned.

The survey did not report one critical statistic: how reliably the completed programs ran. Often systems crash because they fail to expect the unexpected. Networks amplify this problem. "Distributed systems can consist of a great set of interconnected single points of failure, many of which you have not identified beforehand," Randell explains. "The complexity and fragility of these systems pose a major challenge."

The challenge of complexity is not only large but also growing. The bang that computers deliver per buck is doubling every 18 months or so. One result is "an order of magnitude growth in system size every decade—for some industries, every half decade," Curtis says. To keep up with such demand, programmers will have to change the way that they work. "You can't build skyscrapers using carpenters," Curtis quips.

Mayday, Mayday

When a system becomes so complex that no one manager can comprehend the entirety, traditional development processes break down. The Federal Aviation Administration (FAA) has faced this problem throughout its decade-old attempt to replace the nation's increasingly obsolete air-traffic control system [see "Aging Airways," by Gary Stix; SCIENTIFIC AMERICAN, May].

The replacement, called the Advanced Automation System (AAS), combines all the challenges of computing in the 1990s. A program that is more than a million lines in size is distributed across hundreds of computers and embedded into new and sophisticated hardware, all of which must respond around the clock to unpredictable real-time events. Even a small glitch potentially threatens public safety.

To realize its technological dream, the FAA chose IBM's Federal Systems Company, a well-respected leader in software development that has since been purchased by Loral. FAA managers expected (but did not demand) that IBM would use state-of-the-art techniques to estimate the cost and length of the project. They assumed that IBM would screen the requirements and design drawn up for the system in order to catch mistakes early, when they can be fixed in hours rather than days. And the FAA conservatively expected to pay about $500 per line of computer code, five times the industry average for well-managed development processes.

According to a report on the AAS project released in May by the Center for Naval Analysis, IBM's "cost estimation and development process tracking used inappropriate data, were performed inconsistently and were routinely ignored" by project managers. As a result, the FAA has been paying $700 to $900 per line for the AAS software. One reason for the exorbitant price is that "on average every line of code developed needs to be rewritten once," bemoaned an internal FAA report.

Alarmed by skyrocketing costs and tests that showed the half-completed system to be unreliable, FAA administrator David R. Hinson decided in June to cancel two of the four major parts of the AAS and to scale back a third. The $144 million spent on these failed programs is but a drop next to the $1.4 billion invested in the fourth and central piece: new workstation software for air-traffic controllers.

That project is also spiraling down the drain. Now running about five years late and more than $1 billion over budget, the bug-infested program is being scoured by software experts at Carnegie Mellon and the Massachusetts Institute of Technology to determine whether it can be salvaged or must be canceled outright. The reviewers are scheduled to make their report in September.

Disaster will become an increasingly common and disruptive part of software development unless programming takes on more of the characteristics of an engineering discipline rooted firmly in science and mathematics [see box on page 171]. Fortunately that trend has already begun. Over the past decade industry leaders have made significant progress toward understanding how to measure, consistently and quantitatively, the chaos of their development processes, the density of errors in their

products and the stagnation of their programmers' productivity. Researchers are already taking the next step: finding practical, repeatable solutions to these problems.

Proceeds of Process

In 1991, for example, the Software Engineering Institute, a software think tank funded by the military, unveiled its Capability Maturity Model (CMM). "It provides a vision of software engineering and management excellence," beams David Zubrow, who leads a project on empirical methods at the institute. The CMM has at last persuaded many programmers to concentrate on measuring the process by which they produce software, a prerequisite for any industrial engineering discipline.

Using interviews, questionnaires and the CMM as a benchmark, evaluators can grade the ability of a programming team to create predictably software that meets its customers' needs. The CMM uses a five-level scale, ranging from chaos at level 1 to the paragon of good management at level 5. To date, 261 organizations have been rated.

"The vast majority—about 75 percent—are still stuck in level 1," Curtis reports. "They have no formal process, no measurements of what they do and no way of knowing when they are on the wrong track or off the track altogether." (The Center for Naval Analysis concluded that the AAS project at IBM Federal Systems "appears to be at a low 1 rating.") The remaining 24 percent of projects are at levels 2 or 3.

Only two elite groups have earned the highest CMM rating, a level 5. Motorola's Indian programming team in Bangalore holds one title. Loral's (formerly IBM's) on-board space shuttle software project claims the other. The Loral team has learned to control bugs so well that it can reliably predict how many will be found in each new version of the software. That is a remarkable feat, considering that 90 percent of American programmers do not even keep count of the mistakes they find, according to Capers Jones, chairman of Software Productivity Research. Of those who do, he says, few catch more than a third of the defects that are there.

Tom Peterson, head of Loral's shuttle software project, attributes its success to "a culture that tries to fix not just the bug but also the flaw in the testing process that allowed it to slip through." Yet some bugs inevitably escape detection. The first launch of the space shuttle in 1981 was aborted and delayed for two days because a glitch prevented the five on-board computers from synchronizing properly. Another flaw, this one in the shuttle's rendezvous program, jeopardized the *Intelsat-6* satellite rescue mission in 1992.

Although the CMM is no panacea, its promotion by the Software Engineering Institute has persuaded a number of leading software companies that quantitative quality control can pay off in the long run. Raytheon's equipment division, for example, formed a "software engineering initiative" in 1988 after flunking the CMM test. The division began pouring $1 million per year into refining rigorous inspection and testing guidelines and training its 400 programmers to follow them.

Within three years the division had jumped two levels. By this past June, most projects—including complex radar and air-traffic control systems—were finishing ahead of schedule and under budget. Productivity has more than doubled. An analysis of avoided rework costs revealed a savings of $7.80 for every dollar invested in the initiative. Impressed by such successes, the U.S. Air Force has mandated that all its software developers must reach level 3 of the CMM by 1998. NASA is reportedly considering a similar policy.

Mathematical Re-creations

Even the best-laid designs can go awry, and errors will creep in so long as humans create programs. Bugs squashed early rarely threaten a project's deadline and budget, however. Devastating mistakes are nearly always those in the initial design that slip undetected into the final product.

Mass-market software producers, because they have no single customer to please, can take a belated and brute-force approach to bug removal: they release the faulty product as a "beta" version and let hordes of users dig up the glitches. According to Charles Simonyi, a chief architect at Microsoft, the new version of the Windows operating system will be beta-tested by 20,000 volunteers. That is remarkably effective, but also expensive, inefficient and—since mass-produced PC products make up less than 10 percent of the $92.8-billion software market in the U.S.—usually impractical.

Researchers are thus formulating several strategies to attack bugs early or to avoid introducing them at all. One idea is to recognize that the problem a system is supposed to solve always changes as the system is being built. Denver's airport planners saddled BAE with $20 million worth of changes

to the design of its baggage system long after construction had begun. IBM has been similarly bedeviled by the indecision of FAA managers. Both companies naively assumed that once their design was approved, they would be left in peace to build it.

Some developers are at last shedding that illusion and rethinking software as something to be grown rather than built. As a first step, programmers are increasingly stitching together quick prototypes out of standard graphic interface components. Like an architect's scale model, a system prototype can help clear up misunderstandings between customer and developer before a logical foundation is poured.

Because they mimic only the outward behavior of systems, prototypes are of little help in spotting logical inconsistencies in a system's design. "The vast majority of errors in large-scale software are errors of omission," notes Laszlo A. Belady, director of Mitsubishi Electric Research Laboratory. And models do not make it any easier to detect bugs once a design is committed to code.

When it absolutely, positively has to be right, says Martyn Thomas, chairman of Praxis, a British software company, engineers rely on mathematical analysis to predict how their designs will behave in the real world. Unfortunately, the mathematics that describes physical systems does not apply within the synthetic binary universe of a computer program; discrete mathematics, a far less mature field, governs here. But using the still limited tools of set theory and predicate calculus, computer scientists have contrived ways to translate specifications and programs into the language of mathematics, where they can be analyzed with theoretical tools called formal methods.

Praxis recently used formal methods on an air-traffic control project for Britain's Civil Aviation Authority. Although Praxis's program was much smaller than the FAA's, the two shared a similar design problem: the need to keep redundant systems synchronized so that if one fails, another can instantly take over. "The difficult part was guaranteeing that messages are delivered in the proper order over twin networks," recalls Anthony Hall, a principal consultant to Praxis. "So here we tried to carry out proofs of our design, and they failed, because the design was wrong. The benefit of finding errors at that early stage is enormous," he adds. The system was finished on time and put into operation last October.

Praxis used formal notations on only

the most critical parts of its software, but other software firms have employed mathematical rigor throughout the entire development of a system. GEC Alsthom in Paris is using a formal method called "B" as it spends $350 million to upgrade the switching- and speed-control software that guides the 6,000 electric trains in France's national railway system. By increasing the speed of the trains and reducing the distance between them, the system can save the railway company billions of dollars that might otherwise need to be spent on new lines.

Safety was an obvious concern. So GEC developers wrote the entire design and final program in formal notation and then used mathematics to prove them consistent. "Functional tests are still necessary, however, for two reasons," says Fernando Mejia, manager of the formal development section at GEC. First, programmers do occasionally make mistakes in proofs. Secondly, formal methods can guarantee only that software meets its specification, not that it can handle the surprises of the real world.

Formal methods have other problems as well. Ted Ralston, director of strategic planning for Odyssey Research Associates in Ithaca, N.Y., points out that reading pages of algebraic formulas is even more stultifying than reviewing computer code. Odyssey is just one of several companies that are trying to automate formal methods to make them less onerous to programmers. GEC is collaborating with Digilog in France to commercialize programming tools for the B method. The beta version is being tested by seven companies and institutions, including Aerospatiale, as well as France's atomic energy authority and its defense department.

On the other side of the Atlantic, formal methods by themselves have yet to catch on. "I am skeptical that Americans are sufficiently disciplined to apply formal methods in any broad fashion," says David A. Fisher of the National Institute of Standards and Technology (NIST). There are exceptions, however, most notably among the growing circle of companies experimenting with the "clean-room approach" to programming.

The clean-room process attempts to meld formal notations, correctness proofs and statistical quality control with an evolutionary approach to software development. Like the microchip manufacturing technique from which it takes its name, clean-room development tries to use rigorous engineering techniques to consistently fabricate products that run perfectly the first time.

Programmers grow systems one function at a time and certify the quality of each unit before integrating it into the architecture.

Growing software requires a whole new approach to testing. Traditionally, developers test a program by running it the way they intend it to be used, which often bears scant resemblance to real-world conditions. In a cleanroom process, programmers try to assign a probability to every execution path—correct and incorrect—that users can take. They then derive test cases from those statistical data, so that the most common paths are tested more thoroughly. Next the program runs through each test case and times how long it takes to fail. Those times are then fed back, in true engineering fashion, to a model that calculates how reliable the program is.

Early adopters report encouraging results. Ericsson Telecom, the European telecommunications giant, used cleanroom processes on a 70-programmer project to fabricate an operating system for its telephone-switching computers. Errors were reportedly reduced to just one per 1,000 lines of program code; the industry average is about 25 times higher. Perhaps more important, the company found that development productivity increased by 70 percent, and testing productivity doubled.

No Silver Bullet

Then again, the industry has heard tell many times before of "silver bullets" supposedly able to slay werewolf projects. Since the 1960s developers have peddled dozens of technological innovations intended to boost productivity—many have even presented demonstration projects to "prove" the verity of their boasts. Advocates of object-oriented analysis and programming, a buzzword du jour, claim their approach represents a paradigm shift that will deliver "a 14-to-1 improvement in productivity," along with higher quality and easier maintenance, all at reduced cost.

There are reasons to be skeptical. "In the 1970s structured programming was also touted as a paradigm shift," Curtis recalls, "So was CASE [computer-assisted software engineering]. So were third-, fourth- and fifth-generation languages. We've heard great promises for technology, many of which weren't delivered."

Meanwhile productivity in software development has lagged behind that of more mature disciplines, most notably computer hardware engineering. "I think of software as a cargo cult," Cox

says. "Our main accomplishments were imported from this foreign culture of hardware engineering—faster machines and more memory." Fisher tends to agree: adjusted for inflation, "the value added per worker in the industry has been at $40,000 for two decades," he asserts. "We're not seeing any increases."

"I don't believe that," replies Richard A. DeMillo, a professor at Purdue University and head of the Software Engineering Research Consortium. "There has been improvement, but everyone uses different definitions of productivity." A recent study published by Capers Jones—but based on necessarily dubious historical data—states that U.S. programmers churn out twice as much code today as they did in 1970.

The fact of the matter is that no one really knows how productive software developers are, for three reasons. First, less than 10 percent of American companies consistently measure the productivity of their programmers.

Second, the industry has yet to settle on a useful standard unit of measurement. Most reports, including those published in peer-reviewed computer science journals, express productivity in terms of lines of code per worker per month. But programs are written in a wide variety of languages and vary enormously in the complexity of their operation. Comparing the number of lines written by a Japanese programmer using C with the number produced by an American using Ada is thus like comparing their salaries without converting from yen to dollars.

Third, Fisher says, "you can walk into a typical company and find two guys sharing an office, getting the same salary and having essentially the same credentials and yet find a factor of 100 difference in the number of instructions per day that they produce." Such enormous individual differences tend to swamp the much smaller effects of technology or process improvements.

After 25 years of disappointment with apparent innovations that turned out to be irreproducible or unscalable, many researchers concede that computer science needs an experimental branch to separate the general results from the accidental. "There has always been this assumption that if I give you a method, it is right just because I told you so," complains Victor R. Basili, a professor at the University of Maryland. "People are developing all kinds of things, and it's really quite frightening how bad some of them are," he says.

Mary Shaw of Carnegie Mellon points out that mature engineering fields codify proved solutions in handbooks so that even novices can consistently handle routine designs, freeing more talented practitioners for advanced projects. No such handbook yet exists for software, so mistakes are repeated on project after project, year after year.

DeMillo suggests that the government should take a more active role. "The National Science Foundation should be interested in funding research aimed at verifying experimental results that have been claimed by other people," he says. "Currently, if it's not

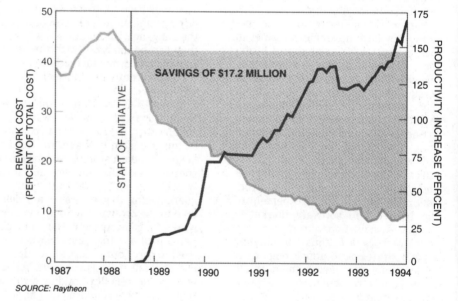

SOURCE: Raytheon

RAYTHEON HAS SAVED $17.2 million in software costs since 1988, when its equipment division began using rigorous development processes that doubled its programmers' productivity and helped them to avoid making expensive mistakes.

Progress toward Professionalism

ENGINEERING EVOLUTION PARADIGM

SCIENCE
- Skilled craftsmen
- Established procedure
- Pragmatic refinement
- Training in mechanics
- Economic concern for cost and supply of materials
- Manufacture for sale

PRODUCTION
- Virtuosos and talented amateurs
- Design uses intuition and brute force
- Haphazard progress
- Knowledge transmitted slowly and casually
- Extravagant use of materials
- Manufacture for use rather than for sale

COMMERCIALIZATION

CRAFT

PROFESSIONAL ENGINEERING
- Educated professionals
- Analysis and theory
- Progress relies on science
- Analysis enables new applications
- Market segmentation by product variety

Engineering disciplines share common stages in their evolution, observes Mary M. Shaw of Carnegie Mellon University. She spies interesting parallels between software engineering and chemical engineering, two fields that aspire to exploit on an industrial scale the processes that are discovered by small-scale research.

Like software developers, chemical engineers try to design processes to create safe, pure products as cheaply and quickly as possible. Unlike most programmers, however, chemical engineers rely heavily on scientific theory, math-ematical modeling, proven design solutions and rigorous quality-control methods—and their efforts usually succeed.

Software, Shaw points out, is somewhat less mature, more like a cottage industry than a professional engineering discipline. Although the demand for more sophisticated and reliable software has boosted some large-scale programming to the commercial stage, computer science (which is younger than many of its researchers) has yet to build the experimental foundation on which software engineering must rest.

CHEMICAL ENGINEERING

1774: Joseph Priestley isolates oxygen
1808: John Dalton publishes his atomic theory
1887: George E. Davis identifies functional operations
1922: Hermann Staudinger explains polymerization

1775: French Academy offers reward for method to convert brine (salt) to soda ash (alkali)

SCIENCE

PRODUCTION

PROFESSIONAL ENGINEERING

COMMERCIALIZATION

CRAFT

1915: Arthur D. Little refines and demonstrates unit operations
1994: Du Pont operates chemical megaplants

1300s: Alchemists discover alcohol
1700s: Lye boiled to make soap
Most dyes made from vegetables

1823: Nicolas Leblanc's industrial alkali process first put into operation
1850s: Pollution of British Midlands by alkali plants
1857: William Henry Perkin founds synthetic dye industry

SOFTWARE ENGINEERING

1956: IBM invents FORTRAN
1968: Donald E. Knuth publishes his theory of algorithms and data structures
1972: Smalltalk object-oriented language released
1980s: Formal methods and notations refined

1970s: Structured programming methods gain favor
1980s: Fourth-generation languages released
1990s: Reuse repositories founded

SCIENCE

PRODUCTION

PROFESSIONAL ENGINEERING

COMMERCIALIZATION

CRAFT

1994: Isolated examples only of algorithms, data structures, compiler construction

1950s: Programs are small and intuitive
1970s: SABRE airline reservation system is rare success
1990s: Most personal computer software is still handcrafted

1980s: Most government and management information systems use some production controls

Some safety-critical systems (such as in defense and transportation) use rigorous controls

A Developing World

Since the invention of computers, Americans have dominated the software market. Microsoft alone produces more computer code each year than do any of 100 nations, according to Capers Jones of Software Productivity Research in Burlington, Mass. U.S. suppliers hold about 70 percent of the worldwide software market.

But as international networks sprout and large corporations deflate, India, Hungary, Russia, the Philippines and other poorer nations are discovering in software a lucrative industry that requires the one resource in which they are rich: an underemployed, well-educated labor force. American and European giants are now competing with upstart Asian development companies for contracts, and in response many are forming subsidiaries overseas. Indeed, some managers in the trade predict that software development will gradually split between Western software engineers who design systems and Eastern programmers who build them.

"In fact, it is going on already," says Laszlo A. Belady, director of Mitsubishi Electric Research Laboratory. AT&T, Hewlett-Packard, IBM, British Telecom and Texas Instruments have all set up programming teams in India. The Pact Group in Lyons, France, reportedly maintains a "software factory" in Manila. "Cadence, the U.S. supplier of VLSI design tools, has had its software development sited on the Pacific rim for several years," reports Martyn Thomas, chairman of Praxis. "ACT, a U.K.-based systems house, is using Russian programmers from the former Soviet space program," he adds.

So far India's star has risen fastest. "Offshore development]work commissioned in India by foreign companies] has begun to take off in the past 18 to 24 months," says Rajendra S. Pawar, head of New Delhi-based NIIT, which has graduated 200,000 Indians from its programming courses. Indeed, India's software exports have seen a compound annual growth of 38 percent over the past five years; last year they jumped 60 percent—four times the average growth rate worldwide.

About 58 percent of the $360-million worth of software that flowed out of India last year ended up in the U.S. That tiny drop hardly makes a splash in a $92.8-billion market. But several trends may propel exports beyond the $1-billion mark as early as 1997.

The single most important factor, Pawar asserts, is the support of the Indian government, which has eased tariffs and restrictions, subsidized numerous software technology parks and export zones, and doled out five-year tax exemptions to software exporters. "The opening of the Indian economy is acting as a very big catalyst," Pawar says.

It certainly seems to have attracted the attention of large multinational firms eager to reduce both the cost of the software they need and the amount they build in-house. The primary cost of software is labor. Indian programmers come so cheap—$125 per unit of software versus $925 for an American developer, according to Jones—that some companies fly an entire team to the U.S. to work on a project. More than half of India's software exports come from such "body shopping," although tightened U.S. visa restrictions are stanching this flow.

Another factor, Pawar observes, is a growing trust in the quality of overseas project management. "In the past two years, American companies have become far more comfortable with the offshore concept," he says. This is a result in part of success stories from leaders like Citicorp, which develops banking systems in Bombay, and Motorola, which has a top-rated team of more than 150 programmers in Bangalore building software for its Iridium satellite network.

Offshore development certainly costs less than body shopping, and not merely because of saved airfare. "Thanks to the time differences between India and the U.S., Indian software developers can act the elves and the shoemaker," working overnight on changes requested by managers the previous day, notes Richard Heeks, who studies Asian computer industries at the University of Manchester in England.

Price is not everything. Most Eastern nations are still weak in design and management skills. "The U.S. still has the best system architects in the world," boasts Bill Curtis of the Software Engineering Institute. "At large systems, nobody touches us." But when it comes to just writing program code, the American hegemony may be drawing to a close.

1985	6
1986	10
1987	39
1988	52
1989	67
1990	100
1991	128
1992	164
1993	225
1994	360
1995	483
1996	NOT AVAILABLE
1997	1,000

INDIA'S SOFTWARE EXPORTS (MILLIONS OF U.S. DOLLARS)

SOURCES: NIIT, NASSCOM

groundbreaking, the first-time-ever-done research, program officers at the NSF tend to discount the work." DeMillo knows whereof he speaks. From 1989 to 1991 he directed the NSF's computer and computation research division.

Yet "if software engineering is to be an experimental science, that means it needs laboratory science. Where the heck are the laboratories?" Basili asks. Because attempts to scale promising technologies to industrial proportions so often fail, small laboratories are of limited utility. "We need to have places where we can gather data and try things out," DeMillo says. "The only way to do that is to have a real software development organization as a partner."

There have been only a few such partnerships. Perhaps the most successful is the Software Engineering Laboratory, a consortium of NASA's Goddard Space Flight Center, Computer Sciences Corp. and the University of Maryland. Basili helped to found the laboratory in 1976. Since then, graduate students and NASA programmers have collaborated on "well over 100 projects," Basili says, most having to do with building ground-support software for satellites.

Just Add Water

Musket makers did not get more productive until Eli Whitney figured out how to manufacture interchangeable parts that could be assembled by any skilled workman. In like manner, software parts can, if properly standardized, be reused at many different scales. Programmers have for decades used libraries of subroutines to avoid rewriting the same code over and over. But these components break down when they are moved to a different programming language, computer platform or operating environment. "The tragedy is that as hardware becomes obsolete, an excellent expression of a sorting algorithm written in the 1960s has to be rewritten," observes Simonyi of Microsoft.

Fisher sees tragedy of a different kind. "The real price we pay is that as a specialist in any software technology you cannot capture your special capability in a product. If you can't do that, you basically can't be a specialist." Not that some haven't tried. Before moving to NIST last year, Fisher founded and served as CEO of Incremental Systems. "We were truly world-class in three of the component technologies that go into compilers but were not as good in the other seven or so," he states. "But we found that there was no practical way of selling compiler components; we had to sell entire compilers."

So now he is doing something about that. In April, NIST announced that it was creating an Advanced Technology Program to help engender a market for component-based software. As head of the program, Fisher will be distributing $150 million in research grants to software companies willing to attack the technical obstacles that currently make software parts impractical.

The biggest challenge is to find ways of cutting the ties that inherently bind programs to specific computers and to other programs. Researchers are investigating several promising approaches, including a common language that could be used to describe software parts, programs that reshape components to match any environment, and components that have lots of optional features a user can turn on or off.

Fisher favors the idea that components should be synthesized on the fly. Programmers would "basically capture how to do it rather than actually doing it," producing a recipe that any computer could understand. "Then when you want to assemble two components, you would take this recipe and derive compatible versions by adding additional elements to their interfaces. The whole thing would be automated," he explains.

Even with a $150-million incentive and market pressures forcing companies to find cheaper ways of producing software, an industrial revolution in software is not imminent. "We expect to see only isolated examples of these technologies in five to seven years—and we may not succeed technically either," Fisher hedges. Even when the technology is ready, components will find few takers unless they can be made cost-effective. And the cost of software parts will depend less on the technology involved than on the kind of market that arises to produce and consume them.

Brad Cox, like Fisher, once ran a software component company and found it hard going. He believes he has figured out the problem—and its solution. Cox's firm tried to sell low-level program parts analogous to computer chips. "What's different between software ICs [integrated circuits] and silicon ICs is that silicon ICs are made of atoms, so they abide by conservation of mass, and people therefore know how to buy and sell them robustly," he says. "But this interchange process that is at the core of all commerce just does not work for things that can be copied in nanoseconds." When Cox tried selling the parts his programmers had created, he found that the price the market would bear was far too low for him to recover the costs of development.

The reasons were twofold. First, recasting the component by hand for each customer was time-consuming; NIST hopes to clear this barrier with its Advanced Technology Program. The other factor was not so much technical as cultural: buyers want to pay for a component once and make copies for free.

"The music industry has had about a century of experience with this very problem," Cox observes. "They used to sell tangible goods like piano rolls and sheet music, and then radio and television came along and knocked all that into a cocked hat." Music companies adapted to broadcasting by setting up agencies to collect royalties every time a song is aired and to funnel the money back to the artists and producers.

Cox suggests similarly charging users each time they use a software component. "In fact," he says, "that model could work for software even more easily than for music, thanks to the infrastructure advantages that computers and communications give us. Record players don't have high-speed network links in them to report usage, but our computers do."

Or will, at least. Looking ahead to the time when nearly all computers are connected, Cox envisions distributing software of all kinds via networks that link component producers, end users and financial institutions. "It's analogous to a credit-card operation but with tentacles that reach into PCs," he says. Although that may sound ominous to some, Cox argues that "the Internet now is more like a garbage dump than a farmer's market. We need a national infrastructure that can support the distribution of everything from Grandma's cookie recipe to Apple's window managers to Addison-Wesley's electronic books." Recognizing the enormity of the cultural shift he is proposing, Cox expects to press his cause for years to come through the Coalition for Electronic Markets, of which he is president.

The combination of industrial process control, advanced technological tools and interchangeable parts promises to transform not only how programming is done but also who does it. Many of the experts who convened at Hedsor Park agreed with Belady that "in the future, professional people in most fields will use programming as a tool, but they won't call themselves programmers or think of themselves as spending their time programming. They will think they are doing architecture, or traffic planning or film making."

That possibility begs the question of who is qualified to build important systems. Today anyone can bill herself as a software engineer. "But when you have 100 million user-programmers, frequently they will be doing things that are life critical—building applications that fill prescriptions, for example," notes Barry W. Boehm, director of the Center for Software Engineering at the University of Southern California. Boehm is one of an increasing number who suggest certifying software engineers, as is done in other engineering fields.

Of course, certification helps only if programmers are properly trained to begin with. Currently only 28 universities offer graduate programs in software engineering; five years ago there were just 10. None offer undergraduate degrees. Even academics such as Shaw,

DeMillo and Basili agree that computer science curricula generally provide poor preparation for industrial software development. "Basic things like designing code inspections, producing user documentation and maintaining aging software are not covered in academia," Capers Jones laments.

Engineers, the infantry of every industrial revolution, do not spontaneously generate. They are trained out of the bad habits developed by the craftsmen that preceded them. Until the lessons of computer science inculcate a desire not merely to build better things but also to build things better, the best we can expect is that software develop-

ment will undergo a slow, and probably painful, industrial evolution.

FURTHER READING

ENCYCLOPEDIA OF SOFTWARE ENGINEERING. Edited by John J. Marciniak. John Wiley & Sons, 1994.
SOFTWARE 2000: A VIEW OF THE FUTURE. Edited by Brian Randell, Gill Ringland and Bill Wulf. ICL and the Commission of European Communities, 1994.
FORMAL METHODS: A VIRTUAL LIBRARY. Jonathan Bowen. Available in hypertext on the World Wide Web as http://www.comlab.ox.ac.uk/archive/formal-methods.html

Fatal Dose

In 1985 a Canadian-built radiation-treatment device began blasting holes through patients' bodies. How a series of simple computer errors sabotaged a state-of-the-art medical wonder.

Barbara Wade Rose

On a day early in June, 1985, Katie Yarborough drove to the Kennestone Regional Oncology Center in Marietta, Georgia, for her twelfth cancer treatment. The sixty-one-year-old manicurist who worked at a local hair salon had had a lump successfully removed from her left breast a few months earlier. She needed a dose of radiation treatment in the adjacent lymph nodes to make sure there would be no recurrence. The machine being used to treat Yarborough was a recent acquisition at Kennestone: a state-of-the-art linear accelerator called the Therac-25, which had already successfully performed 20,000 irradiations on the region's cancer patients. Designed and developed by AECL Medical, a division of Atomic Energy of Canada Ltd., the Therac-25 could speed up electrons and turn them into a high-energy beam that destroyed surface tumours on the skin, or else convert the electrons into x-rays to penetrate tumours deeper in the body.

Yarborough took off her top and her bra and settled in the treatment room for an electron treatment beamed high on the left side of her chest. The usual treatment delivered a dose of around 200 rads: rads are the commonly accepted measurement of radioactive energy – a chest x-ray, for

example, gives off a fraction of one rad. It would last only a few seconds, during which Yarborough would feel nothing. But this day, when the technician activated the machine, Yarborough said she immediately felt "this red-hot sensation." You burned me, she told the technician, who replied that it wasn't possible. Yarborough's oncologist and Tim Still, the medical physicist at Kennestone, both examined her. Yarborough's skin looked fine, although it felt slightly warm. "I can't understand what might have done it," Still said to her. But he did his duty and telephoned AECL up in Ottawa to ask whether a Therac-25 could ever project the electron beam without spreading it properly as the machine was supposed to do. They said they'd get back to him. Not possible, he was told three days later.

Yarborough returned in two weeks. She said she felt tingling inside her body and growing pain. There was a red mark the size of a dime on her chest. There was also a larger pink circle of skin high on the left side of her back. Still's stomach turned over when he saw it. "That looks like the exit dose made by an electron beam," he said to Yarborough and her doctor. The damage done by radiation depends upon its strength, what proportion of the body is exposed, and whether it strikes any vital

organs. One thousand rads can be fatal if it is spread over the entire body. Physicist Still later estimated that Yarborough probably received between 15,000 and 20,000 rads on that dime-sized space.

That night Still stayed late after work and tried to reproduce a beam that could have gone through a patient's body with such obvious force. He shot beams into water and into the air of the treatment room. Whenever he changed any component of Yarborough's prescribed treatment on the computer console, the beam collapsed, shut off by the Therac-25's safety system. So the technician couldn't have done anything wrong. The machine worked fine.

But Still, a forty-year-old Georgian with a broad southern drawl, describes himself as "a troublemaker. I make a lot of noise." He was already frustrated by what he saw as AECL's lack of interest in fixing problems he'd had with another of their medical machines and this time he let his colleagues and a professional organization, Pharmacopeia, know about the anomaly. There were, Still says, unpleasant results. "I got this intimidating phone call from AECL," he says. "I got told that this kind of talk was libel unless I had proof and that I'd better stop." At the time there were five

6. TECHNOLOGICAL RISKS

Therac-25s installed in hospitals in the U.S. and six in Canada.

Over the next few weeks Katie Yarborough's body began to look as if a slow-motion gunshot had gone through her chest and out her back. The site where the beam had entered was now a hole. Over the next few months surgeons twice tried to graft healthy skin over the wound but each time the grafted skin rotted and died. Her left arm became paralysed except when it spasmed. Yarborough hired a Georgia lawyer named Bill Bird and sued AECL and the hospital in October of 1985. "We never got a good deal of information from AECL," Bird recalls. "We hadn't got a lot of response to our written questions so we filed notice of deposition – where we could call them in and force them to respond to interviews with a court reporter present. At that point they settled." Bird describes Yarborough as "a remarkable woman" who continued to drive despite a useless left arm. She died in 1990 when her car was hit by a truck on the highway near Marietta.

Katie Yarborough was the first of the Therac-25 accidents.

Radiation-treatment machines were in enormous demand in hospitals throughout North America, and AECL Medical's equipment was widely considered the best in a growing field. The Therac-25 looked like a giant version of one of those kitchen electric mixers, with a treatment table slid underneath in the bowl position. The machine was seven feet high and took up about twelve feet of space – less than conventional linear accelerators. Just as technicians leave the room to operate x-ray equipment in hospitals and dentists' offices, operators ran the Therac-25 from a computer console outside the treatment area. There had been several earlier versions of Theracs – the 6, the 20 – developed by AECL in cooperation with a French company, CGR, in a business relationship that ended in 1981. But the Therac-25 was better. First of all, it was a double-pass accelerator, which meant the beam doubled back through an electromagnet and that streamlined the machine. Second, the Therac-25 used electricity as the power source for its beam rather than pellets of radioactive cobalt, which lose strength over time.

And the Therac-25 was controlled principally by software. Older Theracs relied on hardware to set the machine up for treatment, to position the beam, and to run the safety system. Hardware is the computer itself, its keyboard, casing, microchips, switches – rusting, dusty, fallible, and mortal. Software is the thousands of lines of written code that allow the computer to do incredible things at a high speed, and that never breaks down—invisible and immortal. Hardware and software; *Mensch* and *Übermensch*.

There was soon another kind of accident involving another Therac-25. Seven weeks after Katie Yarborough's overexposure, a forty-year-old woman with cervical cancer at the Hamilton Regional Cancer Centre in Ontario received a dose of what was later estimated to be as much as 17,000 rads to her hip. This time, there was a larger patch of swelling and redness, and the woman was hospitalized for her injury on July 30. She died in November from her cancer, but an autopsy report noted that, had she lived, she would have needed a hip replacement because of radiation overexposure. After the accident, AECL notified Therac-25 operators, the federal government's Canadian Radiation Protection Bureau, and the American Food and Drug Administration (FDA), which monitors medical equipment in the U.S., that there had been a problem with the Hamilton machine. Technicians, AECL said, should examine their machines during each treatment to be sure the positioning mechanism—called the turntable—was working properly. Patient injury wasn't mentioned, although hospital physicists in Ontario knew from discussions among themselves that an accident had occurred. None of them knew about the earlier accident in Georgia, and AECL didn't mention it.

Engineers from AECL had examined the Hamilton machine in July to determine whether there were problems with the way the Therac-25 turntable worked. A revolving platform rotated by a motor, the turntable locks into two standard positions, one for an electron beam, one for an x-ray beam, and a third position, called the field-light position, which enables the technician to adjust the beam to a precise target. Once in place, microswitches let the computer know the turntable is properly positioned. During its July, 1985, inspection, AECL decided the microswitches for the Therac-25 turntable weren't working properly and modified them. The software was altered within the machines to check continually on the microswitches, and a plunger that locked the turntable into place was modified so that the machine would no longer operate if the turntable was out of position. In September, 1985, in a letter to users, AECL pronounced the Therac-25 safe "with an improvement over the old system by at least five orders of magnitude."

Three months later, in December, 1985, a Therac-25 at Yakima Valley Memorial Hospital in Washington State, which had been modified according to AECL's July specifications, delivered a similar dose, in a way similar to the Hamilton accident, to the hip of another cervical-cancer patient. This time the burn produced a striped pattern on the woman's body. David Judd, a physicist at Yakima, remembers the "five orders safer" letter he had received from AECL before the accident. "Based on that letter we figured it couldn't be the machine," he told me in a telephone interview. Nor was he aware a patient had been injured in Hamilton, Ontario, when he and his colleagues began casting about for other explanations. "The woman said she regularly lay on a heating pad. So we investigated that."

An accident report was sent to AECL, which wrote back: "After careful consideration, we are of the opinion that this damage could not have been produced by any malfunction of the Therac-25 or by any operator error." Despite the earlier accidents, the letter also stated – perhaps referring to the striped pattern of irradiated skin on the patient's hip – that there had "apparently been no other instances of similar damage to this or other patients." The staff at Yakima decided they would never know the cause of the accident and, since the machine seemed to work, turned it back on.

After Hamilton and Yakima, the physicists who were working with Therac-25s at the various sites in Canada and the U.S. began to talk to one another by telephone and memo about their concerns. The physicists agreed they were perplexed by accidents on an otherwise high-quality machine and frustrated by a sense that someone needed to get to the bottom of the problems. Alan Rawlinson, a physicist at Princess Margaret Hospital in Toronto, which installed its Therac-25 in 1986, says that "these accidents really drew people together. AECL was also involved. But in retrospect the courses of action that were followed once these accidents were found and understood were driven largely by the medical-physics community." But it was confusing at first. Without much information forthcoming from AECL, "we were," says Tim Still of Marietta, "all flying blind."

There would be two more deaths before anyone thought to blame the software program and another still before the errors would be solved. Everyone who uses computers knows about glitches. Everyone has heard stories about the multimillion-dollar bank error or the credit-card charge to someone long deceased – stories that would be funny if they weren't so annoying. The truth is that any software program will probably contain one error for every 500 lines of code. The Therac-25's software program, relatively crude by today's standards, probably contained 10,000 lines of code. At one error for every 500 lines, that works out to the possibility of twenty errors. Errors occur partly because it's a human being who wrote the code, partly because it's almost impossible to account for all the ways in which a software program will behave when it is at work in the machine.

Unfortunately, the same tolerances for error acceptable in writing the software for the computer on your desk are applied to the software used increasingly in equipment that can affect life and death: automobiles, hospital equipment, medical devices. Though the obvious safety-critical software systems, for example, those in weapons, nuclear power, and airplanes, have always been subject to government approval, elsewhere there were few set rules. Instead we rely on the people we refer to colloquially as technowizards. They understand such sophisticated programs, they must be geniuses, mustn't they? That is to say, we place the same faith in technowizards as we did in the chemists of the 1950s.

Two accidents occurring in rapid succession provided the first clues to what was happening. On March 21, 1986, an oilfield worker named Ray Cox was being irradiated for the ninth time at the East Texas Cancer Center in Tyler, Texas, for a tumour that had been removed from his back. The centre's Therac-25 had already successfully treated more than 500 patients over a two-year period. Cox lay on his stomach on the table in the treatment room, which was connected to the computer console room next door by an intercom and video monitor. On this day the intercom was broken and the video monitor was unplugged. The technician left the treatment room and shut the door. At the computer console she typed in the prescription data for an electron beam of 180 rads, then noticed she'd made an error by typing in command x (for x-ray treatments) instead of e (for electron). She ran the cursor up the screen to change the command x to e, as Cox's prescription required. She verified everything else and turned on the beam. The machine stopped and the computer screen flashed "Malfunction 54," a mysterious message not even mentioned in the Therac-25 manual.

The technicians who operated the Therac-25 were used to computer glitches. Jonathan Jacky is a research scientist who has been developing software for a computer-controlled radiation machine at the University of Washington School of Medicine in Seattle. In a 1989 essay for *The Sciences,* he wrote that a therapist at Kennestone reported the Therac-25 typically issued up to forty error messages a day. It did so by displaying "Malfunction" plus a number, from 1 through 64. No explanation was offered by the computer nor was there any reference to the malfunction codes in the operator's manual. Technicians could, in most cases, bypass the irritating malfunctions simply by pressing the "p" key, for "proceed." Doing so became a matter of habit.

Inside the treatment room Cox was hit with a powerful shock. He knew from previous treatments this was not supposed to happen. He tried to get up. Not seeing or hearing him because of the broken communications between the rooms, the technician pushed the "p" key, meaning "proceed." Cox was hit again. The treatment finally stopped when Cox stumbled to the door of the room and beat it with his fists.

Cox's injury was similar to Katie Yarborough's – a dime-sized dose of 16,500 to 25,000 rads. He was sent home but returned to the hospital a few weeks later spitting blood: the doctors diagnosed radiation overexposure. It later paralysed his left arm, both legs, his left vocal chord, and his diaphragm. He died nearly five months later.

At the time of the accident, an AECL representative reportedly told the hospital that its modified Therac-25 could not overdose a patient and that AECL knew of no other accidents. "That's what really bothers me," says a source within the hospital who asked not to be identified. "There were [AECL] people sitting in our offices telling us it [the Therac-25] couldn't hurt anybody when they knew it could." AECL suggested Cox's accident might have been caused by an electrical shock. The hospital staff hired an independent investigator, who determined that the Therac-25 wasn't capable of delivering one. The machine was checked and tested repeatedly. Nobody, either from AECL or on the hospital staff, could make it do anything wrong. So treatments resumed on April 7, 1986.

Four days later, "Malfunction 54" flashed on the screen again during a treatment, this time while a sixty-six-year-old bus driver, Verdon Kidd, was receiving therapy at the Tyler cancer centre for skin cancer on his face. He became disoriented and

then comatose, and died three weeks later. Kidd's death, which preceded Cox's by nearly four months, made medical history: the first fatality caused, according to Jacky's research, by an overdose during radiation treatment.

Treatment stopped on the Tyler Therac-25 the day of Verdon Kidd's accident, a Friday. The hospital staff, physicist Fritz Hager, and his technician, who had worked the machine in both accidents, stayed at the console long after everybody else had gone home for the weekend, typing and retyping the prescription into the computer console, determined to re-create Malfunction 54. They went to the bottom of the screen and then moved the cursor up to change the treatment mode from x to e, over and over, for hours. Finally they did it.

The speed with which the instructions were entered made the difference. According to a computer expert's analysis of FDA documents, the computer would not accept new information on a particular phase of treatment (in the case of both Tyler accidents, changing the x-ray mode to electron mode) if the technician made the changes within eight seconds after reaching the end of the prescription data. That's what Malfunction 54 meant. If the changes were made so soon, all the new screen data would look correct to the technician. But inside the computer, the software would already have encoded the old information. That meant the beam on the Therac-25 would be set for the much stronger dose needed for an x-ray beam while the turntable was in the electron position. The coded information within the computer apparently included no system to check that various parts of the prescription data agreed with one another.

That night, Hager telephoned AECL to let them know the accidents weren't random. He knew how to turn the Therac-25 into a lethal weapon.

A letter immediately went out from AECL to all the users. "Effective immediately, and until further notice, the key used for moving the cursor back through the prescription sequence must... not be used for editing or any other purpose." The FDA, which was already investigating the safety of the Therac-25 as a result of the first Tyler accident, told AECL that wasn't enough: the letter didn't describe what would result if the "up" cursor was used or mention any of the accidents. "In fact," the FDA's director of compliance, Center for Devices and Radiological Health (CDRH), wrote in a report, "the letter implies the inconvenience to operators outweighs the need to disable the key." In May, 1986, the FDA requested a corrective-action plan (CAP) to eliminate the problem. But the Therac-25 remained in use. "To say 'don't use the machine,'" Gordon Symonds, a physicist with the Canadian Radiation Protection Bureau, told me, "was to say to a patient, 'you can't have your treatment.'"

An unhappy band of Therac-25 physicists attended the annual conference of the American Association of Physicists in Medicine, in Seattle, Washington, in August, 1986. Gradually, they learned from one another in greater depth about the various accidents, including the original one at Marietta, which had just come to light following the Tyler accidents. They found out that the staff at Princess Margaret Hospital in Toronto had decided to take their own precautions and muzzle their machine – which had not yet been put into clinical use – by installing a dose-per-pulse monitor, an electronic device that would measure all doses of radiation in the beam and, in a fraction of a second, stop excessive doses before they could reach the patient. The physicists decided to circulate their own newsletter, consolidating information and recommendations for safety strategy on the Therac-25.

In the meantime, AECL was trying to satisfy the demands of the FDA. AECL had submitted its CAP on June 13, 1986, and then revised it twice before the end of the year to satisfy the FDA's increasingly stringent demands. Part of the CAP involved reworked software that told the computer where the "up" cursor was, so that Malfunction 54 wouldn't happen again. By the end of the year the machines were back in use.

On January 17, 1987, it became sickeningly apparent that the problems with the Therac-25 that had led to the Hamilton and Yakima accidents were not, in fact, fixed. A man went into the Yakima Valley Memorial Hospital for a low dose of eighty-six rads for his carcinoma. He was hit in the chest with 8,000 to 10,000 rads, and the burn later formed the same striped pattern as in the December, 1985, Yakima accident. David Judd, the physicist at Yakima, describes his staff's reaction as "totally paranoid." "We had had that [1985] letter from AECL saying the safety had been improved but still two patients got overdosed," he says. "We just stopped using the machine." The man who proved to be the last Therac-25 victim died in April, 1987, from a combination of terminal cancer and complications from an overdose.

It turned out that both Yakima accidents, as well as the one at Hamilton, had been caused by another software error – different from the Malfunction 54. On the Therac-25, the part of the computer program that is often referred to as the "housekeeper task" continuously checked to see whether the turntable was correctly positioned. A zero on the counter indicated to the technician that the turntable was in the correct position. Any value other than zero meant that it wasn't, and that treatment couldn't begin. The computer would then make the necessary corrections and the counter would reset itself to zero.

But the highest value the counter could register was 255. If the program reached 256 checks, the counter automatically clicked back to zero, the same way that a car odometer turns over to zero after you've driven more than 99,999.99 kilometres. For that split second, the Therac-25 believed it was safe to proceed when, in fact, it wasn't. If the technician hit the "set" button to begin treatment at that precise moment, the turntable would be in the wrong position and the patient would be struck by a raw beam.

So when AECL fixed the turntable and microswitch problems back in September, 1985, they were improving the machine but they weren't actually correcting the problem that caused these accidents. A professor in computer engineering at the University of Toronto told me that, as a matter of course, his undergraduate students are warned about the risks of incrementing numbers in a computer program.

After the second Yakima accident the FDA requested "that AECL immediately notify all purchasers and recommend that use of the device on patients for routine therapy be discontinued until such time that an amended CAP approved by CDRH is fully completed." The machine was to be used only "if the need for an individual patient's treatment outweighs the potential risk." The Health Protection Branch, a division of Canada's Health and Welfare ministry, directed AECL to tell its customers to discontinue use of the machine until its safe use could be guaranteed. The physicists clamoured for a face-to-face meeting with AECL officials. They all arranged to fly up to Toronto (at the expense of their respective institutions) and meet with AECL representatives at Princess Margaret Hospital in March, 1987. Fearful of lawsuits, some of the physicists were accompanied by lawyers, one having been told by his administration supervisor that the next victim of an accident "would own the centre" in which it occurred.

At the meeting each physicist described the accident or accidents in which he had been involved. AECL, which also brought along its legal staff, presented its plans for correction, all of which involved changing the software. The physicists passed a resolution that there needed to be a hardware solution to the problems of the Therac-25 regardless of what software changes were made. They wanted a dose-per-pulse monitor on all the machines.

The physicists I interviewed remember the tremendous energy and determination of the meeting at Princess Margaret Hospital, a relief after their frustration and despair. "There was so much momentum," says Tim Still of Marietta. The physicists' recollections of the meeting tend to differ. "The Canadians wanted the machine up and running as quickly as possible," recalls David Judd. "That really upset me. The Americans were more conservative and wanted more changes." According to Alan Rawlinson of Princess Margaret Hospital, who helped set up the meeting, AECL "was looking for guidance from users. That meeting was a final pulling together of what needed to be done."

In the weeks that followed AECL acted swiftly. It sent the FDA two more revisions of its CAP, based largely on the decisions made at the March Princess Margaret Hospital meeting. On July 6, 1987, AECL informed users that the FDA had verbally approved the CAP and that all Therac-25s would be fixed by the end of the summer. The CAP included twenty-three software changes *in addition* to those needed to correct the causes of the accidents, and at least six mechanical safety features, including the dose-per-pulse monitor that had been insisted upon by the physicists. Old-fashioned hardware finally came to the rescue of the software-driven Therac-25.

David Judd and his team at Yakima waited until after the AECL engineering team had installed the full set of safety armour on their Therac-25 early that fall. Then he and an AECL representative tried to create an accident. They shot the beam into hard plastic placed on the treatment table. They disconnected the safety mechanisms one by one. They reactivated the "up" cursor key. They reloaded the old software. Even then, the dose-per-pulse monitor shut the machine down.

Since then the Therac-25 machines at Yakima, Princess Margaret Hospital, Marietta, and other hospitals have been in use without a single accident. (East Texas Cancer Center shipped its Therac-25 back to Canada for a refund. Regardless of what was done to their machine, the staff refused to use it.) They are now considered absolutely safe. The Therac-25 is "still an awesome machine," says Tim Still of Marietta. "Ten years since it was made we're not replacing it with anything better."

AECL dissolved AECL Medical in 1988 and renamed it Theratronics International Ltd. The Canadian government has been trying to sell Theratronics to private industry since 1990, without success, and has transferred ownership to a government holding company, Canada Development Investment Corporation. Many of the staff who were with AECL Medical and who were involved with the Therac-25 and the other linear accelerators are still working at Theratronics.

From the beginning of research for this article I tried to get interviews from staff at AECL in Ottawa or Theratronics in Kanata. Over a two-month period I left phone messages, made explanatory calls, and sent faxes. AECL declined to give me any interviews. A spokesman, Egon Frech, said that AECL no longer had any responsibility for Theratronics, though he agreed that AECL should say something because at the time AECL Medical was their division. AECL faxed me a statement approved by their lawyers that was to be their definitive answer to questions about the Therac-25 accidents.

"When accidents occurred with the Therac-25 during the 1986 to 1988 timeframe," the statement read in part, "AECL Medical reacted quickly to investigate and inform Health and Welfare Canada and the U.S. FDA." Note the phrase "during the 1986 to 1988 timeframe." By 1986 three of the six Therac-25 accidents had already occurred.

The AECL statement took issue with an article about the Therac-25 accidents published last July by the Institute of Electrical and Electronics Engineers in the technical journal *Computer* (the source for much of the information in this story). It was written by the computer scientist Nancy Leveson, a professor at the University of Washington who served as an expert witness in two of the Therac-25 accident lawsuits, and a computer-science PhD candidate and lawyer, Clark Turner, of the University of California at Irvine, who specializes in legal liability issues involving software safety systems. In their article Leveson and Turner noted that the Canadian Radiation Protec-

tion Bureau asked AECL by letter to install a mechanical interlock on the Therac-25 as early as November, 1985. Leveson and Turner bestowed upon the Therac-25 accidents the dubious distinction of being "the most serious computer-related accidents to date (at least nonmilitary and admitted)."

The AECL statement read, "The article in *Computer* magazine does not in places accurately describe the events or give appropriate credit to the fast response of AECL Medical at the time the accidents occurred." I telephoned Frech to ask AECL to be more specific about which parts of Leveson's and Turner's article were inaccurate. He declined. "The errors are in the area of detail which we really don't want to get into at this time," he replied. "This happened a long time ago. We regret that this occurred and don't want to rehash it."

Theratronics also declined to give interviews. After several weeks of not returning my calls, the president of Theratronics, Frank Warland, told me I would be sent another statement. It arrived less than a week after the AECL statement. "Theratronics currently provides service to installed Therac-25s as part of a contractual arrangement with AECL," it read. "The arrangement was put into place at the time AECL Medical was dissolved in 1988. Theratronics does not manufacture linear accelerators, and cannot add to the information already provided by AECL Medical."

W\ho was the programmer who actually wrote the software used on the Therac-25? What sort of experience did he have? According to Leveson and Turner, it was a man who left AECL in 1986, but neither they nor lawyers connected with any of the lawsuits against AECL were able to obtain further information from the corporation. I can't tell you who he is. So neither can I tell you where he's working now.

As a result of the Therac-25 accidents, the FDA now requires documentation on software for new medical and other products: a paper trail, in other words, that can be examined by an independent body and retraced for flaws. In January, 1995, the International Electrotechnical Commission will recommend software safety standards for medical equipment, standards devel-

oped partly as a result of the Therac-25 accidents. Engineers can find their productivity cut nearly in half by such requirements, and there have been complaints in the high-tech community that software documentation is hampering competitiveness. The University of Washington's Jonathan Jacky still feels it's better than relying on what he calls "the stereotype of the eccentric genius programmer." At least, he told me, "the chances of a hazard getting into the community are a lot less. This run of [Therac-25] accidents made it clear how wrong things could go." At the time of the accidents no educational standard was required of computer-software programmers. "That's still true," says Jacky. "The knowledge of people out there is extremely variable – some people working on these things are far better than others. That's what documentation on software is supposed to catch."

I asked Katie Yarborough's lawyer, Bill Bird, to reflect upon the accidents after nearly a decade. "The thing that amazes me," he said, "is that the people who develop these machines are surely some of the most brilliant people in the world. This machine was unbelievably sophisticated. Nobody would have got hurt if somebody had used common sense. It's almost as if you have a scientific genius design a car and then an ordinary auto mechanic has to tell him how to run it properly."

The FDA, having been seen as too soft on computer safety in the past, is trying to prove to the U.S. Congress that it is tough on high-tech companies. Even though Theratronics no longer makes linear accelerators and despite passing repeated Canadian safety inspections, the company has suffered through an FDA ban on all its medical equipment as a result of the Therac-25 malfunctions, beginning on July 19, 1991. Marc Schindler, Theratronics's marketing manager, criticized the ban in a 1992 *Globe and Mail* article. The ban was partially lifted that year and Theratronics received informal notice in April, 1994, that the rest of the ban will be lifted. Surprisingly, physicist Tim Still, the original troublemaker, sympathizes with the company. "After the FDA got rolling, they [Theratronics] got beaten to death," he says. "But their arrogance towards this whole Therac thing aggravated it. They brought it on themselves."

Liability for Defective Electronic Information

Pamela Samuelson

Pamela Samuelson is a professor of law at the University of Pittsburgh School of Law.

"Sticks and stones may break my bones, but words can never hurt me." This children's refrain may never have been completely true, but it has been definitively disproven now that computer program instructions control the operation of so many machines and devices in our society. Those who develop computer programs know programs often contain defects or bugs, some of which can cause economic or physical harms. Many people in the computing field are rightly concerned about what liability they or their firms might incur if a defect in software they developed injures a user.

The general public seems largely unaware of the risks of defective software. Even the popular press generally subscribes to the myth that if something is computerized, it must be better. Only certain freak software accidents ("Robot Kills Assembly Line Worker") seem to capture the mass media's attention. Within the computing field, Peter Neumann deserves much credit for heightening the field's awareness of the risks of computing through publication of the "RISKS Forum Digest." But even this focuses more on technical risks than legal risks.

It is fair to say that there have been far more injuries from defective software than litigations about defective software. Some lawsuits have been brought, of course, but they have largely been settled out of court, often on condition that the injured person keep silent about the accident, the lawsuit, and the settlement. No software developer seems to want to be the first to set the precedent by which liability rules will definitively be established for the industry.

The topic of what liability may exist when software is defective is too large to be given a full treatment in one column. But I can summarize in a sentence what the law's likely response would be to a lawsuit involving defective software embedded in machines such as airplanes, X-ray equipment, and the like: The developer is likely to be held liable if defects in the software have caused injury to a consumer's person or property; under some circumstances, the developer may also be held liable for economic losses (such as lost profits). That is, when an electronic information product behaves like a machine,

the law will treat it with the same strict rules it has adopted for dealing with defective machines.

Less clear, however, is what rules will apply when software behaves more like a book than a machine. Courts have treated books differently for liability purposes than they have treated machines. They have been reluctant to impose liability on authors, publishers, and booksellers for defective information in books out of concern about the effect such liability would have on the free exchange of ideas and information. Only if erroneous statements defraud or defame a person or are negligently made by someone who claims to have superior knowledge (such as a professional) has the law imposed liability on authors, publishers, or booksellers. Whether the "no liability" rule applicable to print information providers will be extended to electronic information providers remains to be seen. There are some differences between the print world and the electronic world that may put electronic information providers at a greater risk of liability than print information providers.

AN EXAMPLE OF SOFTWARE BEHAVING LIKE A BOOK

To explore the liability questions that may arise when software behaves like a book, I want you to imagine that a fellow named Harry wrote a computer program which he calls "Harry's Medical Home Companion." Harry works as a computer programmer for a manufacturer of medical equipment, but his avocation and deepest interest has been for many years the study of medical treatments for human diseases. He has read all the major medical textbooks used by practitioners today, as well as many books about herbal and other organic treatments used in traditional societies before the modern era.

Harry's goal is to sell his program to ordinary folk so they can readily compare what today's medical professionals and traditional societies would recommend for treatment of specific diseases. Harry believes people should be empowered to engage in more self-treatment for illnesses and that his program will aid this process by giving ordinary people knowledge about this subject. To make the program more user friendly and interesting, Harry has added some multimedia features to it, such as sound effects and computer animations to illustrate the effects of certain treatments on the human body.

From *Communications of the ACM*, January 1993, pp. 21-26. © 1993 by the Association for Computing Machinery, Inc. Reprinted by permission.

Harry cannot, of course, practice medicine because he does not have a license to be a medical doctor. But that does not mean he cannot write a book or a computer program discussing treatments for various diseases, for in our society no one needs a license to be a writer or a programmer. Harry arranges for the program to be published by Lightweight Software. Lightweight intends to focus its distribution of this product initially to health food stores throughout the country.

If there is a defect in the information contained in "Harry's Medical Home Companion" on which a user relies to his or her detriment, what responsibility will Harry, Lightweight Software, or the health food store at which the user bought the program have if the injured consumer sues? (It is easy for computing professionals to imagine what kinds of errors might creep into an electronic text like Harry's program. A "0.1" might have been accidentally transposed as a "1.0" or a fleck of dust on a printed page might, when processed by an optical character recognition program, cause a "1" to be recognized as a "7" which would cause the quantity of a herb or drug for use to treat a specific disease to be incorrect. Or Harry may have included some illustrations in the program, one of which turned out to be a deadly poisonous mushroom which his artist friend didn't know because she was not a trained botanist.) Interestingly, under the present state of the law, neither Harry nor the publisher nor the health food store may have much to worry about from a liability standpoint.

NO IMPLIED WARRANTY FOR INFORMATION IN BOOKS: *CARDOZO VS. TRUE*

Injured consumers have been largely unsuccessful when they have sued publishers or booksellers for breach of warranty involving defective information contained in books. Even though judges have regarded books as "goods to which implied warranties of merchantability apply (see "Liability Categories"), they have not treated the information contained in the book as covered by these warranties. Information has instead been treated as an unwarranted part of the goods. The intangible information is treated as though it was a "service" embodied in the goods. The strong warranty rules that apply to goods do not apply to services which, of course, often include the delivery of information to the customer. (See box for a discussion on breach of warranty claims and the "goods" vs. "services" distinction.) Typical of the case law rejecting warranty liability for defective information is the *Cardozo vs. True* case decided in Florida in 1977.

Cardozo got violently ill after she ate a piece of rare plant while preparing to cook it in accordance with a recipe in a cookbook written by True. To recover the cost of her medical expenses, she sued True and the bookstore where she bought the book. Against the bookstore, Cardozo claimed the bookseller had breached an implied warranty of merchantability (that the product was fit for the ordinary purpose for which it might be used) by failing to warn her the plant was poisonous if eaten raw.

Although finding the bookseller was a "merchant" whose books were "goods" subject to the Uniform Com-

mercial Code's (UCC) implied warranty of merchantability rules, the court decided the implied warranty for the book only applied to its physical characteristics, such as the quality of the binding. The court regarded it as "unthinkable that standards imposed on the quality of goods sold by a merchant would require that merchant, who is a bookseller, to evaluate the thought processes of the many authors and publishers of the hundreds and often thousands of books which the merchant offers for sale." Consequently, the court affirmed dismissal of Cardozo's complaint against the bookseller.

(The issue before the court was only whether the bookseller could be liable for breach of warranty, not whether the author could be. But here is the problem with suing authors for breach of warranty when information in books is defective: The UCC only imposes implied warranty responsibilities on "merchants" of "goods" of the sort the case involves. Publishers and booksellers are "merchants" of books, and books are "goods" within the meaning of the UCC. Authors, however, are not merchants of "goods." They are at most sellers of intangible information that may later be embodied in goods when printed and bound by publishers.)

The *Cardozo* opinion is one of many in which judges have stated that publishers and booksellers cannot reasonably investigate all the information in the books they sell and should therefore not be subject to warranty liability when information in the work is defective. Judges worry that imposing a responsibility on publishers and bookstores to verify the accuracy of all information contained in the products they sell would unduly restrict the free flow of information and chill expression of ideas. It would thus be unwise as a matter of public policy. In addition, courts have feared a torrent of socially unproductive litigation if readers were able to sue publishers and bookstores whenever their expectations were disappointed after acting on information contained in books.

If the same rule is applied to "Harry's Medical Home Companion" as has been applied to purveyors of printed information, neither Harry, nor Lightweight Software, nor the health food stores that sell the program would have to worry about a lawsuit by a user of the program to recover damages for injuries resulting from defective information in the program on a breach of warranty theory.

NO STRICT LIABILITY IN TORT FOR BOOKS: *WINTER VS. PUTNAM*

There have been a number of cases in which injured consumers have asserted that publishers of books containing defective information should be held strictly liable in tort for having sold a defective product (see box on strict liability in tort). In general, these cases have not been successful.

Typical of the case law in which courts have rejected strict liability in tort claims made against publishers is *Winter vs. G. P. Putnam's Sons* decided by a federal appellate court in California in 1991. Winter sued Putnam to recover the cost of the liver transplant he had after

LIABILITY CATEGORIES

There are three distinct categories the law employs when dealing with claims that defective products have caused physical or economic injury to someone other than their producer: breach of contractual warranties, negligence, and strict liability in tort.

Warranty

A warranty is a promise made by a manufacturer or seller of goods which is considered to be a part of the contract under which the product is sold. Warranties are of two sorts: express and implied.

Express warranties are created by a seller's statements about the product, its characteristics, or its performance which affect the consumer's decision to buy the product. Express warranties may arise from statements made in advertising, on the package in which the product is shipped, or by the salesperson who persuaded the consumer to buy it. Merely recommending purchase of the product or making statements about it that a reasonable consumer would understand to be mere "sales talk" or puffery will not create an express warranty. However, a seller need not intend to expressly warrant a product to do so.

When the seller is a merchant, the law will regard the act of selling the product in the marketplace as giving rise to an implied representation the product is of fair and average quality for goods of that kind and fit for ordinary consumer purposes. This is known as the implied warranty of merchantability. It attaches automatically by law to all sales transactions in jurisdictions that have adopted Article 2 of the Uniform Commercial Code (UCC). (In the U.S., this includes every state but Louisiana.) Implied warranties of fitness for a particular purpose will also automatically arise when a seller knows the purpose for which a customer is acquiring the goods and the customer relies on the seller's judgment that a particular product will fulfill that purpose.

Implied warranties can be disclaimed by a seller. However, the disclaimer must be explicit, unambiguous, conspicuous, and often must be in writing before the disclaimer will be effective (as are the bright orange stickers saying "as is" or "with all faults" appearing on the windows of automobiles in used car lots).

These warranty rules do not apply to all sales transactions, but only to sales of "goods." Sales of "services" are not subject to these rules. The law for services contracts more closely resembles the 19th century when "caveat emptor" (let the buyer beware) was the rule across the board.

The question of whether computer software should be treated as "goods" or "services" has been much discussed in the legal literature and in some case law. Insofar as software is an embedded component of a hardware device, such as an X-ray machine, it will almost certainly be treated as "goods" within the meaning of the UCC. It is somewhat less clear how software will be treated when it merely automates an information process previously done manually (which would then have been described as a "service"). The more customized the software or the more it resembles a book or a pure information service, the less likely it is to be treated as "goods" under the UCC. Even when an electronic information product is treated as "goods" under the UCC, there is some case law suggesting that warranties will not attach to the information in the work if it behaves like a book. (See article's discussion of the *Cardozo vs. True* case.)

Negligence

When a person (or a firm) acts in a manner a reasonable person in the same circumstances would have recognized does not live up to a duty of care owed towards others and thereby causes harm to another, that person can be found liable for negligence. Negligence is generally harder to prove than breach of warranty because negligence requires a showing of fault on the part of the person being sued, whereas warranty liability can exist when a product simply fails to perform as stated or expected. There are also some occasions in which negligence claims fall because the law has not imposed a duty of care on the person being sued.

There is a long history of successful negligence lawsuits against manufacturers of defective products. Sometimes manufacturers have been found to have failed in the duty of care owed to consumers in not having taken sufficient care in the design of the product. Sometimes they have been found not to have provided adequate information about how the product should be used or what dangers might exist if the product is used in a particular way.

There have been far fewer successful lawsuits when claims of negligence are made after someone has provided inadequate or inaccurate information to a customer. It is fairly rare for the law to impose a stringent duty of care on information providers unless the information provider holds himself or herself out in the marketplace as having substantially superior knowledge, skill, or expertise. Professional information providers, such as doctors or lawyers, can be held liable for malpractice, for example, when they have conveyed inaccurate information (or otherwise provided a negligent service) and a less knowledgeable consumer relied on it to his or her detriment. It is generally quite *(box continued on next page)*

(box continued from previous page)
difficult to win a malpractice action against a professional for delivering defective information, for one will need to show the provider was acting incompetently in delivering the defective information. There is often a difference of opinion among professionals in a field about what is or is not appropriate information to convey in particular circumstances. In addition, professionals generally do not like to call someone in their field an incompetent practitioner in a public forum such as a court and usually one will need an expert in the field to testify to a professional's incompetence.

I am aware that many people who develop software have ambivalent attitudes about whether they should be considered "professionals" in the sense in which this term is used in other fields. While I will not reignite the tired debate over whether software developers should be "licensed," as most other professionals are, it is an issue which may need to be revisited as greater responsibilities (i.e., duties of care) are imposed by law on publishers of electronic information.

Strict Liability in Tort
Manufacturers and sellers of defective products are held strictly liable, (that is, liable without fault) in tort (that is, independent of duties imposed by contract) for physical harms to person or property caused by the defect. This liability arises notwithstanding that "the seller has exercised all possible care in the preparation and sale of the product." These strict liability rules do not apply to all commercial transactions. Along similar lines to UCC warranty law, strict liability in tort exists only for "products" and not for "services."

When computer programs are embedded components of airplanes, X-ray equipment, and the like, they will almost certainly be treated as "products" for strict liability purposes. (The *Winter* case discussed in this article is such an example.) While some tricky causation questions may arise in product liability cases involving software, strict liability will be imposed on a software developer if there is a defect resulting in an injury to the consumer (and a defect will generally be easy to show if a consumer or user has been injured), almost as surely as night follows day.

But there are some computer programs which may not be treated as "products" for strict liability purposes. When programs behave more like a book then a machine or when they otherwise resemble an information service, strict liability rules may not be imposed on them. As this article explains, courts have decided that books should not be treated as "products" for strict liability purposes and that publishers of books should not be held strictly liable in tort when their products contain defective information.

Remedies
When a seller has breached implied or express warranties in connection with the sale of goods, the buyer can sue the seller to recover money damages for certain kinds of injuries arising from the breach. If, for example, a consumer is physically injured by a defective lawnmower and has to pay $10,000 in medical expenses, that $10,000 may be recovered from the manufacturer or the firm from which the consumer bought the lawnmower. If the lawnmower must be repaired or replaced, the consumer can generally recover in contract for these damages as well.

Contract damages, however, tend to be more limited than tort damages. Monetary damages to compensate an injured person for pain and suffering, for example, are recoverable in tort actions (such as negligence and strict liability) but may not be in contract actions. Some economic losses are also not recoverable in contract cases. Unless, for example, the manufacturer (or other seller) of a lawnmower had reason to know at the time of the sale that a particular buyer of the lawnmower needed it to operate a lawn-mowing service, the buyer would not be able to recover lost profits on his lawn-mowing business during the time the business was out of operation after the defect in it evidenced itself.

In negligence actions, successful plaintiffs can generally recover damages for a broad range of injuries flowing from the negligent act, including pain and suffering and some economic losses. In strict liability actions, only damages arising from physical harms to persons or property are generally recoverable.

One other respect in which tort and contract actions tend to differ is in the kinds of persons who can bring claims for what kinds of damages. Contract law tends (except where physical injury to persons or property is involved) to limit the class of possible plaintiffs to those who bought the goods and are thus beneficiaries of the warranty promises that are part of the contract. Tort law is more generous about who can bring a lawsuit (e.g., if the buyer of the product gives it to another person as a gift and that person is harmed, he or she can sue in tort whereas that person might not be able to sue in contract).

Multiple volumes of thick treatises have been written to explain all the nuances of contract and tort liability arising from defective products. This brief synopsis is necessarily incomplete but will, I hope, give those in the computing field some grounding in the basics of these legal categories.

eating a mushroom erroneously depicted as safe for human ingestion in the Encyclopedia of Mushrooms published by Putnam. He claimed the publisher should be held strictly liable in tort or should be found negligent for publishing a book in which a poisonous mushroom was depicted as safe. The court upheld dismissal of both claims.

On the negligence claim, the court ruled the publisher had no duty to investigate the accuracy of information it published. Without a duty of care owed by the publisher to readers of the books it published, no negligence could be found (see box). Even though authors of books may be more vulnerable to negligence claims than publishers, authors may successfully defend against such a lawsuit by showing they exercised reasonable care (e.g., hiring someone to check all the data for correctness) under the circumstances. Also, unless an author claims to be an expert on the subject, the law may not impose a higher duty on the author than it would impose on the reader (who, after all, must use his or her own judgment before taking an author's advice).

The judges in the *Winter* case decided that the strict liability in tort doctrine should only apply to the manufacture of tangible "products," such as tires and insecticides, for which the doctrine had been created. Expansion of the doctrine to make publishers strictly liable for intangible information contained in books would unduly interfere with the free exchange of ideas and information:

We place a high priority on the unfettered exchange of ideas. We accept the risk that words and ideas have wings that we cannot clip and which carry them we know not where. The threat of liability without fault (financial responsibility for our words and ideas in the absence of fault or special undertaking of responsibility) could seriously inhibit those who wish to share thoughts and theories.

It was not that the judges thought no one should ever be held liable for delivering erroneous information injuring consumers. Professionals, for example, should be held responsible for injuries caused by their delivery of defective information, but not even they should be held strictly liable in tort:

Professional services do not ordinarily lend themselves to "strict liability" because they lack the elements which gave rise to the doctrine. There is no mass production of goods or a large body of distant consumers whom it would be unfair to require to trace the article they used along the channels of trade to the original manufacturer and there to pinpoint an act of negligence remote from their knowledge. . . . Those who hire "professionals" are not justified in expecting infallibility, but can expect only reasonable care and competence.

If the same rule was applied to "Harry's Medical Home Companion" as was applied in *Winter*, Lightweight Software and the health food store would have nothing to worry about from a liability suit against them by an injured consumer. Under the *Winter* ruling, Harry would not have to worry about a strict liability suit. And he would have a reasonable chance of defending against a negligence lawsuit by showing he had exercised reasonable care in preparing the program. He might also point out that he was not holding himself out as a professional in the medical field so he should not be held to the same standard of care as would be imposed on a licensed doctor.

STRICT LIABILITY IN TORT FOR AERONAUTICAL CHARTS: *AETNA VS. JEPPSEN*

There is, however, at least one circumstance in which an information product has been held to be a "product" for strict liability purposes. Ten years before the *Winter vs. Putnam* decision, the same court ruled that aeronautical charts were "products" for strict liability purposes. The case was *Aetna Casualty & Surety Co. vs. Jeppsen & Co.* Aetna persuaded the trial judge that a defect in the design of an aeronautical chart manufactured by Jeppsen had caused an airplane insured by Aetna to crash at the Las Vegas airport. Interestingly, Aetna's claim was not that the chart contained inaccurate information, but that it failed in its design goal of graphically representing this information in a readily understandable way.

Jeppsen's principal argument on appeal was that the chart was not the sort of "product" to which strict liability rules should be applied. In explaining why it disagreed with Jeppsen on this point, the appellate court emphasized the chart was mass-produced for commercial purposes and those who used the chart relied on Jeppsen's expertise as much as consumers might rely on any other manufacturers' expertise. Aeronautical charts were, said the court, "highly technical tools" resembling compasses which would be treated as products for strict liability purposes. The court contrasted the charts with "how to do X" books which were "pure thought and expression."

If the same rule was applied to "Harry's Medical Home Companion" as was applied in *Jeppsen*, Lightweight Software and the health food store might well be held strictly liable in tort for physical injuries to a user resulting from a defect in the program. Because Harry does not himself sell the program to the public, he might not be held strictly liable in tort even if the publisher and health food store were . The strict liability in tort rules only apply to "sellers" of "products" of the kind that injured the consumer.

MORE LIABILITY RISKS FOR ELECTRONIC INFORMATION

The law proceeds by analogy. Judges faced with deciding a case brought by an injured consumer against a seller of a multimedia program containing defective information on medical treatments will decide what liability rule to apply by asking him- or herself whether to treat the case like *Winter* or like *Jeppsen*. I can think of a number of reasons why electronic information providers may be more at risk from liability suits than print information providers.

For one thing, electronic information products have a more technological character than books. Even when these products behave mainly like books, they also behave like machines. And there may be no simple way to separate their book-like and machine-like characteristics. In addition, electronic information products are often "engineered" similar to other manufactured products. They are certainly more engineered than books.

Given the emphasis the field places on the technological character of electronic information products, the field should not be surprised if the law takes it seriously by treating its products the way it treats other technological products. One of these days, for example, an electronic information provider's assertion that its product is "user friendly" may be treated not as mere marketing puffery, but as creating an express warranty, leading reasonable consumers to expect that "usability engineering" or "hypertext engineering" techniques or user interface standards or guidelines were used to develop it.

As the electronic information industry moves from handcrafted demonstration projects to mass-marketed products distributed to distant and anonymous customers, the argument for extending liability when defects in these information products cause injury to consumers grows stronger. Consumers of electronic information products and services provided by a distant vendor will probably rely heavily on the expertise of the electronic information provider. The more naive among these customers may well think (however erroneously) that because the information has been computerized, it is more trustworthy than if delivered orally or found in print. In addition, electronic information providers are likely to be in a better position than consumers to control the quality of the information delivered and to insure against liability. This is especially true when firms (and not just individual programmers like Harry) begin to develop electronic information products for the mass market.

Another reason providers of electronic information may in time have greater responsibilities than book publishers is that electronic information products are less readily inspectable by ordinary consumers than books. With books, a consumer can go to a bookstore and browse through the whole thing before buying it. The consumer can, not only examine the binding, but also skim the contents to see if it meets his or her needs. With electronic information products, nothing about the product (except advertising hype) can generally be seen before the purchasing decision is made. One cannot even examine the disk to see if it is scratched or warped. Once out of the box, the disk, of course, reveals nothing about its contents which can only be comprehended through extensive use of the software. With on-line services for which the consumer is charged by connect-time, the contents are similarly invisible until a charge is incurred for usage.

When so little of value in an electronic information product lies in its physical characteristics (such as the disk on which software may be borne), it is difficult to believe courts will not in time extend liability to the contents of such products.

In addition, it is worth noting books merely instruct a reader how to perform a task whereas software does the task. By making the reader an intermediary between the instructions and their execution, a book keeps the reader in the judgment loop which means he or she bears some responsibility for how well or poorly the task is done. The reader also has to exercise judgment about whether it is really a good idea to follow a particular author's advice. By contrast, electronic information products only leave the user in the judgment loop when they have been explicitly designed to do so. Thus, more of the control over and responsibility for proper execution of the task will lie with the electronic publisher. This too may contribute to an extension of liability to providers of electronic information. Moreover, some have argued the liability rules for print publishers should be changed [1], and if they are, electronic publishers would be affected as well.

One unexplored bulwark against liability for electronic information providers is the First Amendment. What has protected print publishers from liability for dissemination of defective information has largely been concerns about the effect liability rules would have on the free exchange of ideas and information. At the moment, many commercial electronic information providers may think the work of groups like the Electronic Frontier Foundation which seek to define civil rights in Cyberspace are somewhat remote from their core concerns. But when they realize First Amendment concerns may provide the best chance electronic information providers have to protect against liability for defective information, they may find more reason to support the work of such organizations.

Electronic information providers should, of course, be thinking not only about what kinds of First Amendment rights they may have, but also about what kinds of First Amendment responsibilities they may have. In law, rights and responsibilities tend to be intertwined. One generally does not get rights without some responsibilities as well. As broadcasters and cable TV firms have discovered to their dismay, print publishers often have greater First Amendment rights than other media types do, in part because of the greater historical role of print publishers in promoting free speech interests. Electronic information providers may want to begin thinking more about First Amendment issues and where they stand (or want to stand) in relation to print publishers and other media types.

Another set of questions people in the computing field should ask themselves is what liability standards they think ought to apply to their field. Should injured consumers be able to recover damages for defective delivery of electronic information or not, and why or why not? In addition, the field should be asking what steps can be taken to self-regulate to promote development of high-quality software production to forestall or at least limit the degree to which regulation will come about through lawsuits about defective electronic information products. Liability will be with the field for a long time. It is time to stop worrying about the problem and start addressing it.

REFERENCES

1. Arnold, R. The persistence of caveat emptor: Publisher immunity from liability for inaccurate factual information. *U. Pitt. Law Rev.* 53 (Spring 1992), 777.

International Perspectives and Issues

The implications of computerization for economic production, value systems, and conflict are global in scope. Every society on Earth will be touched to a greater or lesser extent by the spread of information technology (IT). In addition to the direct effects of these technologies, nations will be indirectly affected through their participation in the intricate global network of economic, cultural, and political alliances. Because all nations are ultimately linked to all other nations through this complex exchange network, a major change in even one part of the system implies some degree of change in all other parts.

The economic and geopolitical implications of microelectronics are thought to be so great that advanced nations are engaged in a superstruggle to achieve or maintain global technological leadership. Smaller, less wealthy nations, have more modest ambitions, but they have also implemented strategies to encourage growth in microelectronics industries. In some cases, governments have gone after foreign investment by offering multinational companies attractive incentives to locate within their borders. The Republic of Ireland, for example, has pursued a "policy of industrialization by invitation" since the 1950s. Seán ÓRiain describes some of the positive and negative consequences of this strategy and Ireland's prospects for a healthy domestic IT sector in "The Birth of a Celtic Tiger."

The spread of firms that have operations based in several countries is but one aspect of increasing globalization. Two additional areas of concern arising from the ability to share information across national and cultural boundaries are European proposals to regulate content on the Internet and the sobering implications of global communications and barriers to automated translation for the planet's 5,400 or so languages.

As the discussion in the article "Software's Chronic Crisis" in the previous unit revealed, some developing countries are making important gains in some areas of computing. However, for the poorest societies, challenges are staggering. Excerpts from William Wresch's book "Disconnected: Haves and Have-Nots in the Information Age" underscore the gaps between the information infrastructure of "have" nations and that of the poor "have not" regions of Africa. In "The Role of Computer Networks in Development," Larry Press claims that "one could give up in desperation over the enormity of global gaps, but there are reasons to be hopeful." He argues that for relatively low costs, computer networks offer the capability to improve life in such areas as economic productivity, education, democracy, and human rights.

Two other articles in the unit offer Western perspectives on the Far East. Geremie Barmé and Sang Ye describe the growing access to the Internet in China in "The Great Firewall of China." As other authors have pointed out, Barmé and Ye stress that a double-edged potential exists: to weaken or strengthen the control of China's government over its citizens. Then, the *Forbes ASAP* article "Singapore Sting" sheds insight on the thriving underground business in large-scale software piracy.

Looking Ahead: Challenge Questions

How could information technology be used to reduce hostilities between nations and foster international understanding and cooperation?

What are the implications for national sovereignty when computer systems cross national borders or, as is the case for many poorer nations, when most of the electronic data about a country are held in foreign databases?

Do you believe the actions of the illegal software copiers, distributors, and consumers in the Far East are acceptable? Defend your position.

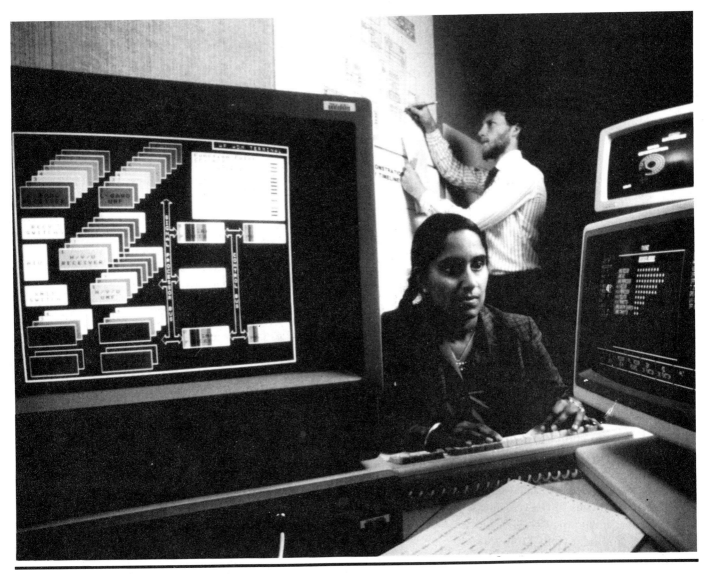

The Birth of a Celtic Tiger

Seán ÓRiain

Last St. Patrick's Day, traditional Irish musicians in Dublin, New York, and Paris were brought together in a concert transmitted live over the Internet to emigrants gathered in bars and halls around the world. The Paddynet, an Internet provider focused on Irish affairs, brought together musicians and audiences all over the world on what the organizers called a "digital island."

Meanwhile, a visitor to the Republic of Ireland might be surprised to see the Gateway Comanches, complete with Irish accents, struggling to overcome the softball skills of the Claris Crusaders in Dublin's Phoenix Park. Across the Atlantic in Silicon Valley, a prominent ex-Claris executive proudly displays a copy of the Irish language version of MacWrite on his shelf. These close local social ties, national identity, and international contacts combine to create the Irish information technology industry.

Despite gaining on the average GNP of countries in the Organizations for Economic Cooperation and Development (OECD) in the 1970s, Ireland fell behind the average growth rate again in the 1980s. From 1990 to 1994, GDP growth averaged 5.3%, surpassed only by the fastest growing Asian economies; the inflation rate was among the lowest in Europe and employment increased for the first time in years.

Ireland pursued a policy of industrialization-by-invitation since the late 1950s, offering substantial incentives to multinational companies to locate in Ireland and hoping to generate cash and employment through export-led development. High-technology investment, particularly from the U.S., has predominated since the 1970s. Electronics currently account for 30% of Irish exports with another 10% from software. While some attribute the recent success of information technology (IT) in Ireland to openness to the global economy and the presence of multinational corporations, the role of the Irish state in developing indigenous resources and organizations, by accident and by design, is all too often overlooked.

The Early Years: 1958–1973

The first computer in Ireland—an ICT 1201—was installed at the Irish Sugar Company in 1958. In 1962 the first university computer—an IBM 1620 Model 1—was installed in the School of Engineering at Trinity College in Dublin [10]. Computing was restricted to a small isolated community that was fragmented into fraternities of IBM, Honeywell and ICL devotees [14].

The economic decline and high emigration of the 1950s prompted the policy of industrialization-by-invitation. Some major U.S. high-tech companies arrived by the late 1960s, including Digital which began making minicomputers in

TERRY MIURA

Galway in 1971. This policy's success is questionable as companies created mainly low-skilled jobs, developed few linkages to the local economy, and often left once their tax breaks ended.

To the dismay of Irish IT companies, customers in Ireland (even in the public sector) showed no great desire to buy from Irish companies [15]. Unlike other countries where state (especially military) spending on IT played a major role in developing local companies, public procurement policies were not used for this purpose.

The Arrival of the Multinational Corporations: 1973—Late 1980s

The Irish government, through the Industrial Development Authority (IDA), attracted mobile IT investment using Digital's example and Irish entry to the European Economic Community in 1973. Among the new companies were Analog Devices (Limerick, 1977), Amdahl (Dublin, 1978), and Apple (Cork, 1981). They received very generous grants and financial incentives—most attractive being a 15-year full tax exemption on export sales for companies that located in Ireland between 1960 and 1981. In 1981 this was replaced by a 10% corporation tax rate, guaranteed until 2010, for all manufacturing companies and many export-oriented service companies.

Ireland provided a low-cost, English-speaking workforce within Europe. Free, universal, secondary schooling, introduced in 1967, laid the foundations for the development of a technically sophisticated workforce over the coming decades. The Regional Technical College system was formed in the late 1960s, offering certificate and diploma courses. Two technically focused National Institutes of Higher Education were formed in 1972 and 1980, and received full university status in 1989. This heavy investment in education was controversial (particularly as engineers flooded out of the country in a brain drain during the 1980s). However, in the long run, it proved perhaps the most successful government policy of the last 30 years.

By the 1980s Ireland had attracted quite a number of mainframe, minicomputer, integrated circuit makers and data processing bureaus. The skill profile in the Irish electronics industry fell somewhere between that of the U.S. and the South East Asian industries [9]. The Telesis report in 1982 was severely critical of the contribution of these companies to the national economy, citing the high costs of government incentives, the low level of skills, and lack of R&D within the plants, the weakness of linkages to local suppliers, and the tendency of companies to move out once tax deals ran out. However, some managers (who were mainly Irish-born) were able to win a range of nonassembly functions for their plants. Many managers, lead by those at Digital, saw themselves as working for the national development of the Irish economy, albeit within the confines of corporate strategy set abroad.

Apart from some ill-fated personal computer companies in the early 1980s, the main Irish IT companies were a small number of component suppliers and a small indigenous software sector developing applications mainly for Irish and British markets. The initial hope that multinational firms would help develop a national system of innovation and spin off Irish-owned firms was not being fulfilled.

Efforts were made to increase linkages between multinationals and local companies, to grow local firms through marketing support and management development, and to encourage R&D and innovation. However, the policy focus remained to attract foreign investment. The recession of 1990 and the downturn in the mainframe and minicomputer industries hit Ireland particularly hard. A spate of job losses culminated in 600 layoffs at Amdahl and 760 at Digital. The power of the multinationals was shown by the failure of senior government ministers to reverse the closures, despite flying to Boston to plead with Digital executives.

Multinationals in Ireland Today

However, these disastrous losses were followed by Irish IT's most successful era. In the early 1990s the unification of the European market, a boom in IT industries, and growing executive awareness of the potential of international markets combined to create favorable conditions for Ireland's strategy of industrialization from without. The high-quality workforce, a huge investment in telecommunications, and the developing supplier base in a number of industries have been crucial. The rapidly improving public finances and the sacrifices made by employees and their unions through the social partnership agreements instituted in

1987 also helped stimulate growth. Ireland's advantages have gone beyond the delights of the tax shelter and the ability to manage cash flow to minimize tax payments, although these remain important.

The IDA claims that Ireland attracted 40% of U.S. electronics investment in Europe since 1988. Dell, Gateway and AST Research joined Apple in the PC sector; HP, Keytronic, and Seagate were among those making peripherals while 3Com and Motorola strengthened the networking sec-

manufacturing, logistics, and distribution through these centers.

An Irish IT Industry?

Given the perils of development based on foreign investment, it is encouraging that a healthy Irish-owned IT sector has emerged. The heavy investment in education and telecommunications was originally designed to attract multinational investment. However, it also provided an infrastructure that supported the unanticipated growth of Irish firms.

The increasing reliance on sub-

were easier to enter than the increasingly concentrated desktop software markets. Early firms specialized in software development while others such as Kindle and CBT Systems emerged in the 1980s to supply such vertical markets as banking and training. The industry came into its own after the late 1980s with a new generation of start-ups that created sophisticated systems software products for world markets. Companies such as Iona Technologies have become world leaders in these markets. The 1996 Object

IF IRELAND CAN MARRY ITS TECHNICAL STRENGTHS IN
software with the design and creative skills of its writers, artists, animators, and film makers, it may have a bright future in multimedia.

tor. Forty percent of Europe's packaged software is now supplied from Ireland (Microsoft and Lotus since the mid-1980s; more recently Claris, Symantec, Oracle, and Novell, manufacturing and localizing their products in Ireland). ICL, Ericsson, IBM, and Digital carry out software development.

Intel's two wafer fabrication plants near Dublin replaced Digital as the flagship for IDA efforts to attract other companies. Employing 2,800, Intel makes systems and motherboards under contract as well as running the wafer fabrication operation. It has few links to local industry as it brought almost all its established suppliers—mostly U.S. and Japanese firms—with it.

Many companies are forming their European regional operations in Ireland and managing their

contracting by the multinationals prompted the development of sophisticated Irish-owned parts and components suppliers. The software-manual printing industry grew rapidly from $9 million to $135 million in five years [6, 7]. The shift from the manufacture of complex computer systems to sub-supply and contract manufacturing was worrying since the skill profile of the components supply sector was lower than the systems manufacturers. However, some Irish firms have been able to use the commercial opportunities provided by outsourcing of manufacturing and logistics as a springboard toward a more independent and technically sophisticated business.

The Irish-owned software industry grew as new markets emerged in distributed computing and data communications that

World West show in San Jose featured Iona's day-long Orbix-World, displaying their CORBA standard object request broker.

Ireland has avoided relying on contract programming or bodyshopping (although the high levels of emigration among programmers do create a somewhat similar dynamic). Nonetheless, with over two-thirds of companies producing products and exports increasing from 41% of total revenues in 1991 to 58% in 1995 [8], the indigenous software sector is well-poised to become Ireland's most technically dynamic sector. If Ireland can marry its technical strengths in software with the design and creative skills of its writers, artists, animators, and film makers, it may have a bright future in multimedia.

Links to the global economy provide commercial opportunities for Irish firms. Employees' experience working abroad or for multinationals in Ireland was important to Irish firms. Yet free trade and the presence of IT multinationals, two constants in the Irish economy since the 1960s, do not explain the emergence of an indigenous IT sector. With the labor force well trained and the commercial opportunities available, potential entrepreneurs had to be supported in their entry to and growth in the new challenging industries [5].

State education and telecommunications policy contributed to the growth of Irish firms, albeit unintentionally. Gradually and quietly a range of state-sponsored programs was created, often with European Union funding that will dry up in 1999. Firms are supported through guidance and funding with R&D, marketing consultancy, management development, and business networking. The process for gaining this support is highly competitive and firms are held to rigorous international standards. The state is also active in developing a network of institutions to deepen communication and innovation in IT industries. This network includes the National Software Directorate, three technology centers located in the universities, and a range of industry and professional bodies.

Ireland's IT sector has shifted somewhat from an export enclave dominated by multinational corporations toward a regional complex of IT industries with significant local contracting opportunities and upgraded skills and organizational capacities of local firms and workers [13]. Although multinationals still

dominate, there is significant local economic development. Nonetheless, IT in Ireland faces three major challenges: the persistent dilemmas of multinational-led development; the deeper integration of successful Irish companies into the global economy; and the danger of creating an information elite.

Multinationals in Ireland— Sustainable Development?
The Irish debate about foreign investment has focused on the high costs of the incentives given to industry and the tax income foregone through the 10% corporate tax rate. Ireland can offer such incentives because income levels are below 80% of the EU average and essentially gives up the tax revenues in order to attract the jobs to Ireland, creating some tension with its European partners. Furthermore, the tax revenue lost to the EU as a whole because of the competition among its member states results in a transfer of income from the public to the corporate sector within Europe.

Foreign investment accounts for most employment growth in Ireland in recent years. Employment in Irish-owned manufacturing has been relatively stable in the 1990s whereas international manufacturing and all sectors of financial services and software have expanded rapidly. Unemployment is approximately 13% (although there is considerable controversy over the figures). Emigration has decreased substantially, however. In response to a perceived vulnerability to changing world markets and corporate strategies, government and development agencies have targeted a

range of sectors with a high-technology focus. For example, they have pursued networking firms in light of a perceived over-reliance on the PC sector.

More important, however, it is more difficult for national governments and local communities to bargain with companies who are organized on a global scale and whose core capabilities are located elsewhere. Incorporating these companies into a social project and guiding the economy to create a specific social impact becomes difficult. Competition between countries to offer multinationals the best financial incentives weakens the European tax base. Furthermore, most U.S. high-tech companies are nonunion, in contrast to non-U.S. companies [4] and even many U.S. companies of the 1970s, weakening the accountability of employers to their employees. The use of temporary and contract workers contributes to a new and weakened social contract being put in place between employer and employee in Ireland. Ireland has built economic success in recent years on making itself a world-class investment location but has been less able to generate social development from that success.

Irish Firms on the Way Up
The integration of the emerging Irish firms into the global economy also poses two distinct challenges. Local competition with multinationals for labor, particularly in software, may hinder Irish firms although the numbers of software designers and programmers are being increased. Irish firms must also compete with the

allure of international labor markets. Between 10% and 20% of computer science graduates emigrate within one year of graduating. Anecdotal evidence suggests that 50% to 70% emigrate at some stage of their careers, creating a highly significant brain drain from Ireland.

receive major funding or go public in the U.S.

Development for the Whole Society

Ireland faces the challenge of turning its competitive strength in IT into the basis of a new mode of development for the whole society

medium for disseminating a narrow form of consumer culture. Irish servers have one of the fastest growth rates for new Internet sites (more than 21,000 sites now end in the .ie suffix).

The diffusion of IT outward and downward into Irish society is also affected by the structure of

MANY OF THE MOST SUCCESSFUL IRISH SUPPLIER
and software firms have cashed in on their success through acquisition by larger international companies with fewer links to the Irish economy.

While emigration among graduates is apparently falling as the economy grows, it remains high for computer professionals as emigration becomes an accepted part of career patterns and as developers in the U.S., Japan, and Europe spot opportunities for their friends back home. Reducing emigration is one challenge. Making the most of business contacts and technical expertise of the emigrants already abroad by fostering contacts between these emigrants and those working in the IT industry in Ireland is another.

The success of Irish firms may also pose a problem for national development, if not for their owners. Many of the most successful Irish supplier and software firms have cashed in on their success through acquisition by larger international companies with fewer links to the Irish economy. Moreover, successful Irish firms may rely less and less on their home base and develop closer ties to dominant regions of the industry—particularly if companies

[2]. The gap between the dynamic IT sector and the diffusion of IT into Irish business is shown in the 1993 finding that Ireland ranked fifth in the OECD in employee computer literacy while it was only 14th in the strategic exploitation of IT by business [11]. The weakness of the IT-using community in Ireland contrasts with other small but dynamic countries [3]. Policies promoting inter-industry linkages with the IT sector and deepening the use of IT in schools should be pursued as a matter of urgency.

There is a danger that economic growth will create an information elite who create or use the new technologies extensively while most of the population has little access to IT and experience it as a controlling force in their lives. This is of course a threat worldwide—reflected in the debates whether the Internet will become a truly interactive medium with relatively equal access and speech rights or whether it will become simply a

Irish society itself. Education has been the driving force behind the informational economy in Ireland, along with a network of institutions promoting information flows and connections within the industry. However, class inequalities in Irish education are prevalent with restricted opportunities for working-class students [1]. The focus on education, one of Ireland's greatest competitive advantages, may create even greater barriers to social mobility into IT. Sex segregation in employment is high and the proportion of female computer science graduates has stayed at 25% during the 1990s. The close social ties that characterize the industry are also, as everywhere, segmented by social background—the area where you grew up, the school you attended, and your past jobs. Opening educational opportunities and social networks in the IT sector is crucial if the benefits of the IT era in Ireland are to extend to the whole society. Regional inequalities have been exacerbated by the concentration of IT growth in the major urban centers.

Ireland has developed a strong IT sector in recent years and has great potential in software, multimedia, and manufacturing. In the U.S. such growth has been associated with rising income inequality [12]. Whether Ireland can realize this potential and extend the benefits to the whole society will depend largely on how it governs its links to the international economy. From the 1920s to the 1950s, Ireland remained closeted behind protectionist barriers. Then it turned 180 degrees and offered practically an open invitation to the companies of the world. Realizing sustainable economic development requires not simply rejecting international ties (pre-1958) or embracing them with little reservation (post-1958); Ireland must make choices about which international relationships are worthwhile and how their benefits can be distributed throughout society. The state has begun to play a critical role in mediating these relationships. However, time will tell if the political will exists to extend the benefits to the whole society.

Follow-up
Readers are encouraged to send comments, suggestions, anecdotes, insightful speculation, raw data, and articles on subjects relating to international aspects of IT to:

Sy Goodman
MIS/BPA
University of Arizona
Tucson, AZ 85721
goodman@bpa.arizona.edu
fax: (520) 621-2433

ACKNOWLEDGMENTS
I thank Damian Hannan and John Sterne for their assistance in Ireland in January-February 1996; and Chrisanthi Avgerou, Sy Goodman, Rebecca King, David Jacobson, John Sterne and James Wickham for their very detailed and constructive comments.

REFERENCES
1. Breen, R.,Hannan, D., Rottman, D. and Whelan, C. *Understanding Contemporary Ireland*. Gill and Macmillan, Dublin, 1990.
2. Castells, M. *The Informational City Blackwell*. Oxford, 1989.
3. Dedrick, J.L., Goodman, S.E., Kraemer, K.L. Little engines that could: Computing in small energetic countries. *Communications ACM 38*, 5 (May 1995), 21–26.
4. Gunnigle, P. Employee relations in greenfield sites. In P. Gunnigle et al., eds. *Continuity and Change in Irish Employee Relations*. Oak Tree Press, Dublin, 1988.
5. Evans, P. *Embedded Autonomy*. Princeton University Press, Princeton, 1995.
6. IDA. Ireland: *The Software Capital of Europe*. IDA, Dublin, no date.
7. Jacobson, D. and O'Sullivan, D. Analyzing an industry in change: The Irish software manual printing industry. *New Technology, Work and Employment 9*, 2 (1994), 103–114.
8. National Software Directorate. *Survey of the Irish Software Industry*, 1995.
9. O'Brien, R. Technology and industrial development: The Irish electronics industry in an international context. In J. Fitzpatrick and J.Kelly, eds, *Perspectives on Irish Industry*. Irish Management Institute, Dublin, 1986.
10. ODonovan, F. History of electronic computing in Ireland 1958–1978. *Irish Computer* (1988).
11. OECD. *Information Technology Outlook*, 1994. OECD, Paris, 1994.
12. Reich, R. *The Work of Nations*. Vintage Books, New York, 1991.
13. Saxenian, A. *Regional Advantage*. Harvard University Press, Cambridge, 1994.
14. Sterne, J. Ten years on the trail of an Irish computer industry. *Irish Computer* (1988).
15. Sterne, J. Letter from Ireland. *Which Computer? 15*, 2 (Feb. 1992), 114.

SEÁN ÓRIAIN (oriain@qal.berkeley.edu) is with the Department of Sociology at the University of California-Berkeley. His research examines the growth of the Irish software industry.

THE GREAT FIREWALL OF CHINA

AT ISPS, INTERNET CAFÉS, EVEN STATE CENSORSHIP COMMITTEES, WE MEET THE WIRED OF CHINA—AND DISCOVER THAT THE TECHNOLOGY CHINA NEEDS TO BUILD THE MOST POWERFUL COUNTRY ON EARTH IN THE 21ST CENTURY THREATENS TO UNDERMINE THE INSTITUTIONS THAT RULE THE NATION. AND BEIJING'S CONTROL FREAKS ARE WORRIED.

GEREMIE R. BARMÉ & SANG YE

"INFORMATION INDUSTRIES OF CHINA UNITE!"

Xia Hong manages public relations for a year-old company called China InfoHighway Space. It's one of the slickest examples yet of the latest innovation on Beijing's frenetic corporate scene: Internet service providers. China InfoHighway's offices in Beijing's Haidian District have the airy, glaringly bright-lit open-plan arrangement favored by new-look Chinese companies. Its logo – a spermatozoid yin-yang – decorates everything in sight. A banner across the top of its homepage blazes: "Information Industries of China Unite!" As Xia Hong is happy to make clear, that's not the only thing about China InfoHighway that screams 1997-style Chinese neosocialism:

The Internet is out of kilter with modern organizational principles. It has failed to evolve effective means of control. Frankly, I see it as being just like the United Nations. As you well know, that body is the most impo-

Geremie R. Barmé (geremie@coombs.anu.edu.au) is a Senior Fellow at the Australian National University. He co-wrote The Gate of Heavenly Peace, *a documentary about the Tiananmen Square uprising that won a 1997 Peabody Award. Sang Ye is a Chinese journalist who divides his time between China and Brisbane, Australia. His most recent book is* The Year the Dragon Came *(University of Queensland, 1996).*

tent in the world, and let's not even talk about it being efficient or cost effective. All that confused yabbering, good and bad, right and wrong, all mixed up together.

A network that allows individuals to do as they please, lets them go brazenly wherever they wish, is a hegemonistic network that harms the rights of others.

There's no question about it: the Internet is an information colony. From the moment you go online, you're confronted with English hegemony. It's not merely a matter of making the Net convenient for users in non-English-speaking countries. People have to face the fact that English speakers are not the whole world. What's the big deal about them, anyway?

Our ideal is to create an exclusively Chinese-language network. It will be a Net that has Chinese characteristics, one that is an information superhighway for the masses.

Ms. Z – she asked us not to use her name – is an 18-year-old recent graduate of a private secretarial college in Shanghai. We talked to her at the Shanghai Internet Cafe on Jinling Donglu, a bustling thoroughfare in the center of the nearest thing China has to an urbane metropolis (at least until Hong Kong's long-awaited return to the motherland on July 1):

If you want a well-paying job with a foreign firm, it used to be you only needed to speak English and be able to use a computer. Now you also need Internet know-how.

Today I'm here to send some emails to friends in Canada. It's much cheaper than the post office fax service – Y70 (about US$8) for two sheets! Here I pay Y30 for an hour, send my letters, have a look around the Net, and get a cup of coffee thrown in free. Of course it's pricey, but places like this aren't run for country bumpkins. If you can't afford it, stay home and drink boiled water!

 From *Wired*, June 1997, pp. 138-151, 174-178, 182. © 1997 by Wired Magazine Group, Inc. Reprinted by permission.

We're living in an information society now, and every idea is valuable. People who provide freeware or shareware on the Net for others to download are just so stupid. What a waste of effort! As for giving other people ideas via the Net, you'd have to be a half-wit. Why let someone else profit from your ideas?

What I hate most about the Internet is that there are so many wonderful shopping opportunities – all the nice clothes and makeup – but I can't buy any of it. For example, Chanel No. 19 costs nearly Y800 (US$96) in the Shanghai shops; on the Net, it's only half that, including postage. But even if I had a for-

In the hype-ridden People's Republic of China, 1996 was the "Year of the Internet." Barely 1 in 10,000 Chinese is actually wired. But the Net takes aim squarely at things that since the days of Mao have been the state's exclusive domain.

eign-currency credit card, it would be useless: customs duty in China is so high, it's prohibitive. So the more I see things on the Net, the more upset I become.

In the hype-ridden People's Republic of China, 1996 was the "Year of the Internet." No matter that, by the highest estimates, only 150,000 Chinese people—barely 1 in 10,000—are actually wired. Or that most mainland Chinese have never touched a computer, or that there are 17 people, on average, for every phone line. From Beijing in the north to Guangzhou near the border with Hong Kong in the south, breathless news reports insist that China's traditional greeting, *"Ni chifanle ma?"*—Have you eaten?—is being replaced. Now any forward-looking person asks, *"Ni shangwangle ma?"*: Are you wired?

It's not just press hysteria: in Beijing, shiny new computer monitors line the second floor of the famed Foreign Languages Bookstore, pushing Chinese-language versions of Eudora and the latest delights of Netscape and Internet Explorer where the interminable works of Mao, Stalin, and Enver Hoxha once held sway.

Earlier this year, the craze was modem introduc-

tory offers - computer companies flogging hardware and software packages from street stalls outside department stores. Bill Gates's *The Road Ahead* has sold more than 400,000 copies – pirated editions not included. Even the massive billboards that line roads, mark intersections, and clutter the countryside are as likely now to feature Acer, Microsoft, or home-grown Beida Fangzheng computers as Shiseido cosmetics, XO cognac, or the Communist Party's latest propaganda.

But nothing seems to have loosened slogan writers' pens quite like the Net itself:

Join the Internet club; meet today's successful people; experience the spirit of the age; drink deep of the cup of leisure.

Buy Internet, use Internet. Get on board the ark to the next century. Win the prize of the world.

Internet, the passport of the modern, civilized man.

Driving from the airport into Beijing in February, we listened to a radio feature about the latest developments in online technology on the popular program *Good Morning Taxi!* "The Internet is not only about information," the report concluded. "It's about new ways of thinking, new ways of living."

That, of course, is precisely what worries China's rulers. New ways of thinking, of communicating, of organizing people and information—the Net takes aim squarely at things that since Mao's earliest days have been the state's exclusive domain. For a country still coming to grips with the passing of its latest great leader, Deng Xiaoping, it's a double shock of the new: the technology that China needs to build the most powerful country on earth in the 21st century could also undermine the monolith state itself. Where the quest by Deng's successors to control the Net and its consequences will lead, no one knows. But no one doubts that the Net, that amorphous and unpredictable messenger, holds out tantalizing possibilities for a country so long turned in upon itself.

From his home in Beijing, one of China's pioneer telecommuters, Pan Jianxin, writes a widely read computer column for the popular Guangzhou-based weekend paper *Southern Weekly*:

I'm on the Net maybe four or five hours a day. The phone bills are murder and my wife complains, but I can't keep off it. The Net is a world unto itself.

Sound familiar? He could be any Net columnist anywhere. But this is China:

The general cultural level of the nation is woeful. We're still trying to get people to stop spitting in public. So the Net is not a main issue.

DEUS EX MACHINA

Neophilia is a double-edged sword that China has eagerly grasped since the middle of the last century.

In earlier eras, it was political revolution – including "scientific" socialism – that promised a quick fix to China's problems. Today high technology is the deus ex machina. The question on everyone's mind – the Chinese government and its critics alike – is whether it will also be a cultural and political Trojan horse.

The latest tide of high tech adulation in China started building in the early 1990s, often with a comic tinge. First it was streetside "computer fortune telling," then "computer diagnosis" – traditional Chinese medicines mysteriously dosed out by machine. More recent crazes – supported by the inevitable billboards and hoardings – include "computer" car washing (electronically controlled sprayers) and beauty salons (automated facial analysis): not the stuff to cause anyone to lose sleep at the Public Security Bureau.

The Net has been more problematic. As in most of the world, scientists were Internet pioneers; the difference is that, due to lack of interest and primitive infrastructure, the first serious network wasn't put together until 1993. Two years later, the national university system followed, with what is still a cherished innovation: email connections, both within the country and to the outside world.

Then came a publicist's dream that brought the Net nationwide attention. Zhu Ling, a young science student at Beijing's élite Qinghua University, fell mysteriously ill. As her condition deteriorated, distraught friends appealed for help on the Net. Thousands of responses flooded in from around the world – 84 of which (according to more of those breathless press accounts) correctly diagnosed thallotoxicosis, a rarely seen condition caused by exposure to the element thallium, in her case during laboratory experiments. Zhu Ling was treated and eventually began a slow recovery; the Chinese public was enthralled. A television miniseries is reportedly in the works.

That's the dream. Here's the reality: 86 percent of China's citizens have never touched a computer. Only 1.6 percent of Chinese families own one, and just 4.1 percent plan to buy. (The figures come from the Yangshi Survey and Consulting Service Center, a Beijing marketing firm.) Of course, that still means 10 or 20 million potential sales, which is why US and European computer companies don't do too much complaining about Chinese Net freedoms.

University students are encouraged to use email to plan study overseas, but only a small number of graduate students and faculty, mainly in technical disciplines, enjoy real access to the Web. Most mainland Chinese – say, a billion or so people – wouldn't know the difference between the Internet and "The Internationale," the Communist Party theme song.

But however small the numbers, for the Chinese government's control freaks – and that means basically everyone in authority – free-flowing information and unauthorized association are profoundly disturbing concepts. The Communist movement itself was

We listened to a report on a popular Beijing radio show. The Internet, the show concluded, "is about new ways of thinking, new ways of living." That, of course, is precisely what worries China's rulers.

born in China of surreptitious gatherings, cell meetings in gloomy garrets, and covert exchanges of information – plus a large dose of mass dissatisfaction and oppression. Mention information revolution, and the instinctive overreaction is to clamp down.

State Council Order No. 195 is titled "Temporary Regulations Governing Computer Information Networks and the Internet." Signed by Premier Li Peng on February 1, 1996, the law contains the following gems:

The State is in charge of overall planning, national standardization, graded control, and the development of all areas related to the Internet.

Any direct connection with the Internet must be channeled via international ports established and maintained by the Ministry of Post and Telecommunication. No group or individual may establish or utilize any other means to gain Internet access.

All organizations and individuals must obey the respective state laws and administrative regulations and carry out rigorously the system of protecting state secrets. Under no circumstances should the Internet be used to endanger national security or betray state secrets.

SPIRITUAL POLLUTION CONTROL

In an equipment-crowded office in the Air Force Guesthouse on Beijing's Third Ring Road sits the man in charge of computer and Net surveillance at the Public Security Bureau. The PSB – *leizi*, or "thunder makers," in local dialect – covers not only robberies and murder, but also cultural espionage, "spiritual pollutants," and all manner of dissent. Its new concern is Internet malfeasance.

A computer engineer in his late 30s, Comrade X (he asked not to be identified because of his less-than-polite comments about some Chinese ISPs) is overseeing efforts to build a digital equivalent to China's Great Wall. Under construction since last year, what's officially known as the "firewall" is designed to keep Chinese cyberspace free of pollutants of all sorts, by the simple means of requiring ISPs to block access to "problem" sites abroad.

Comrade X explains: "The first line of defense is what we call 'preventative interference,' based on selected keywords. What we're particularly concerned about is material aimed at undermining the unity and sovereignty of China (that is, references to Tibetan independence and the Taiwan question), attempts to propagate new religions like the Children of God, and dissident publications. Commonplace ideological differences of opinion are now generally ignored."

It's no great technical trick, especially since connections to the outside world are required to pass through a handful of official gateways – the PTT's ChinaNet and the Ministry of Electronics's "Golden Bridge" are two of the biggest – which do their own filtering up-front. Among the things they block, depending on circumstances, are most of the Western media, as well as the China News Digest – a sprawling online service run by Chinese exiles – and other specialized sites and newsgroups operated from abroad. Eager for a slice of the action, the major global networking companies – Sun Microsystems, Cisco Systems, and Bay Networks, among others – cheerfully compete to supply the gear that makes it possible.

But as Comrade X also notes, it's not just a matter of technology:

Naturally, many questionable sites still go undetected. So the way we prefer to control things is through a decentralized responsibility system: the user, the ISP, and China Telecom are all held responsible for the information users gain access to.

People are used to being wary, and the general sense that you are under surveillance acts as a disincentive. The key to controlling the Net in China is in managing people, and this is a process that begins the moment you purchase a modem.

JUST SIGN HERE

So you want to get wired in the People's Republic? Let's recap the simple steps to get online:

First, pick an ISP – there were 32 in Beijing at last count, ranging from government-run companies and China Telecom to ambitious private start-ups like China InfoHighway. You fill out some papers and provide an ID card (or, for foreigners, a passport). The initial Police File Report Form has to be filled out in triplicate – a copy for your ISP, one for the local PSB, the third for the provincial-level PSB Computer Security and Supervision Office.

Next there's the Net Access Responsibility Agreement, in which you pledge not to use the Internet to threaten state security or reveal state secrets. You also swear not to read, reproduce, or transmit material

that "endangers the state, obstructs public safety, or is obscene or pornographic."

Finally, there's an application for the ISP itself – where you live and work, your profession, your home and office phone numbers, your mobile phone, and even your pager. Plus details about your computer equipment, the modem type, and, oh yes, its permit number. Back to our friends at the PSB for that.

> "All organizations and individuals must vigorously carry out the system of protecting state secrets. Under no circumstances should the Internet be used to endanger national security or betray state secrets."

Now you're getting close to that "passport of the modern, civilized man." But you still have to pay. That means either a check or a bank account name and number – credit cards are not welcome. Figure a monthly net-plus-phone bill of Y350 (US$42) – roughly half a recent college graduate's monthly salary. Someone with a good job at a foreign corporation in Beijing or Shanghai can probably manage it. And so, of course, can the media-starved expatriates they work for. As Comrade X remarked about the system's launch last year, "It was a real thrill to see all the foreigners lining up outside our office to be registered."

THE ECSTASY OF COMMUNICATION

Here's how Sparkice, a Sino-Canadian joint venture, promotes its new Internet Cafe in Beijing, the largest in the city since it opened in November:

Under the searchlight of history, on the cusp of the new century, a brightly lit Great Wall is spreading rapidly out of China toward the rest of the world. Its light conveys a message of a holy duty: Sparkice is building a multimedia platform that will surprise the globe.

Internet cafés are one of China's minigrowth industries. They combine sought-after "imported" atmosphere with basic online services – "the ecstasy of communication," as one flyer puts it. There's a cluster of modest operations – the Papillon Music Internet Cafe is one – near Beijing University's main entrance, next to Zhongguancun, the city's electronics district.

Some have only a single computer and, judging from the Papillon, warm service but weak coffee and a serious blight of plastic foliage.

Sparkice, next to the Capital Stadium's west entrance, has higher aspirations – it includes its own ISP, for starters. The stadium itself is worth a visit: a major sports venue during the Cultural Revolution, it is now an oversized furniture display hall. The café, for its part, is done in the latest international techno style – glitzy ambient lighting, 10 shiny new computers, and TVs beaming in the latest NBA games.

But "Chinese characteristics," as Comrade X would call them, are right there, too. Anyone is welcome to order a cappuccino, but going online requires you to run the same bureaucratic maze as getting wired at home: Police File Report Form, Net Access Responsibility Agreement, and ISP contract. Plus an ID card or passport number, and the details of where you live and work.

Then there are the rules: no attempts to visit forbidden sites, of course, or to download inappropriate material. No changing machines during a session. Only one person online at a time. And the logs of your activities may be checked. "If anything out of the ordinary is discovered," says the contract, "you will be fined accordingly" – up to 10 times the cost of your time online. For serious breaches, the waitpersons-cum-Net police are authorized to hand you over to the authorities. Happy surfing – or, as they say in Mandarin, *manyou*, "roaming at will." At 14.4 Kbps.

According to Zhuang Dundi, the suited college student who earns spare cash as the café's tutor, "So far, we've had no incidents." It's not hard to see why. "We have three levels of 'firewall,'" he says. "Our company filters things once, ChinaNet itself has its own filtering system, and then we keep an eye on everything here."

Despite the less than user-friendly environment, Sparkice can attract upwards of 100 patrons a day. Most are foreigners—especially homesick students—or people thinking about getting wired themselves, mainly white-collar workers from joint-venture companies. For Chinese college kids, the prices are astronomical: a Y100 (US$12) deposit up-front, then Y30 an hour, plus Y15 for every 10 minutes of overtime. Tutorials from Zhuang Dundi are available at Y40 an hour; drinks are Y25 each. At this rate, an hour of mindless Net escapism plus a couple of Cokes will consume 10 percent of the average Chinese student's already spartan monthly budget.

Those limits don't bother café manager Bai Jinghong, who has the official line down pat:

Absolute freedom is an impossibility. It would create anarchy. To censor harmful things doesn't just ensure that the Internet can develop in a healthy fashion; it will also ensure stability for China. I think Singapore has the right approach. They have been energetic in their development of the Net and tireless in managing it. Their tough line is worthy of emulation; a laissez-faire attitude is destructive and must be rejected.

At a friend's on-campus apartment, a 15-year old boy who attends a prestigious Beijing middle school talked about his experience with the Net:

I have the advantage of 'superhighway driving on public gas'—I go online through my mother's work unit, which subscribes to ChinaNet. If I had to pay for Internet access myself, my parents would murder me.

I'm no Net-insect—I've only been at it a few months. Hey, I'm only in my third year of middle school, and my English sucks. There's people around who are really into surfing—all I can do is bumble around, though I do find some good stuff by chance.

Sure, I could get onto the real Internet by ringing a Hong Kong or Taiwan access provider. The work unit wouldn't be able to tell who was ringing out, but if I stayed online for very long it'd cost a fortune in international phone bills, and my family would have to pay. My mom would kill me for sure.

I suppose the NetWall is all about keeping pornography out of the country. They've blocked things like Playboy, for example, but that's hardly going to stop you. If you really want to find stuff, then you'll get through the wall—you just have to know how. Anyway, there are things that are much worse than Playboy, and it's easy to get access through sites in northern Europe or Japan. Once you hit upon one, you just take a trip round the neighborhood through links they provide, and you've got yourself a gold mine.

But porn on the Internet is a bore, all static images or small-frame videos. It's not nearly as much fun as watching a good video. As for 'reactionary propaganda,' I'm just not interested in it. I don't even go looking.

SHANGHAI STYLE

Shanghai has always been China's cosmopolitan entrepôt. It's also where the virtuous realities of Comrade X and talk about Singapore models give way to the down-to-earth facts of market forces and resourceful practicalities.

Pan Weimin, a thirtysomething electrical engineering graduate from Shanghai's prestigious Fudan University, runs the day-to-day operations of the PaCity Computer Company, which makes and sells computers and peripherals.

The aim of going on the Net is to be able to communicate and exchange with other people or engage in business. It's a two-way highway. If the Net becomes a national net, limited to a certain culture, then what's the long-term use of getting wired?

Pan practices what he preaches. To promote its

machines, PaCity runs a bare-bones "café" with eight online computers in Putuo, the heart of Shanghai's electronics industry.

People can come and use the equipment for free—it could never survive as a café anyway if we tried to live off our customers. But there's another thing: if we started charging, we'd have to get every user, casual or not, to register with China Telecom and the PSB. As is, we can pretend we're demonstrating our computers and training potential buyers. So we're free of control. Otherwise, both the police and the entertainment bureaucracy would be on our backs.

There's nothing he can do, of course, about China Telcom's filtering. And whatever kind of loopholes he or others can find are a long way from letting real Net genies out of the bottle:

When push comes to shove, the authorities don't have to restrict themselves to imposing a NetWall around China. They can use tried and true traditional methods: one administrative order from on high and everything can be shut down. It's simple and effective.

BRAVE NEW NET

It should not surprise anyone that the Chinese authorities see the Net's opportunities, along with its threats. Time and again, the 20th century has proven the value of information technology for building a heaven for bureaucrats—or for secret police. For Communist Party cadres, that means a network devoted to the transmission of party directives, government orders, and local bureaucratic folderol—in other words, an intranet. The ever-vigilant PSB already has one, linking it to every major hotel and guest house where foreigners stay. The minute you register at your five-star joint-venture hotel, Comrade X and his associates know you're there.

Elsewhere, such efforts are still mostly works in progress. In Guangdong province, for instance, few local-level party offices have the bandwidth—meaning more than a single phone line—to keep their computers permanently online. So headquarters first has to telephone to say that a document is on the way, then local officials turn on their modem to receive it, along with the relevant party secretary's seal of office—suitably encrypted—and signature. Clunky and primitive it may be, but it works. And an infrastructure that will wire the whole province is well under way—Communist party offices first, of course.

One university computer specialist we talked to in Guangzhou has been called in to help with several of what he waggishly calls "DocuNets":

The bureaucrats don't give a damn about the Net or connecting with the outside world. What everyone is really getting into—as long as they have the money to do it—is establishing their own local networks. When they receive a telex from Beijing, they get their secretaries to type it into the computer, and then use the DocuNet to distribute it. It's the latest in paperless offices, and they want it.

MONEY TALKS

There's an old saying in south China: "The heavens are high and the Emperor is far away." From the late 1970s—the dawn of the post-Mao era—people in areas of Guangdong province bordering on Hong Kong were among the first mainland Chinese to glimpse the outside world through Deng Xiaoping's then-new "Open Door." They were also the first to be able to start turning off Central People's Broadcasting and tuning in to the British colony's televised version of capitalism's decadent charms.

Will the Net follow a similar path? One affluent electronics buff in Guangzhou, the provincial capital, is looking for new opportunities after making a killing in the last few years selling computers made with pirated processors from Taiwan. He offers a classically hedged south China viewpoint:

You only have to think back to how things were in the early 1980s. Then a major political issue was the direction you pointed your TV antenna—toward Hong Kong or inland. The struggle went on for years—the police carried out door-to-door checks, people were ordered to pull down their aerials, and party members were warned they'd be expelled if they watched. Then underground factories that produced signal boosters mushroomed, and soon everyone was watching Hong Kong TV without a visible, external aerial. It became such a farce that in the end the authorities simply gave up.

But these days, it's not only this side that is different. TV stations in Hong Kong have been changing. They want to reach the massive market that covers the whole Pearl River Delta. And to get that, they are making compromises about content—they won't show anything that's too provocative. It's the nature of business; if you want it, you have to make concessions.

If the Net's going to be a success in China, people will just have to accept the fact that the Chinese government blocks some things. If the foreign media makes a big stink about it, don't worry, it'll pass. The people interested in the Net's commercial possibilities will carry on regardless.

Let's face it: Be it China or America, the government's voice is not as loud as that of business. Those who are willing to put up the money will have the last word.

7. INTERNATIONAL PERSPECTIVE AND ISSUES

THE GREAT NETWALL

The computer *cordon sanitaire* that Chinese authorities are trying to build around China is called the *fanghuo qiang,* or "firewall," a direct translation from English. But a more popular phrase for it is *wangguan,* literally "NetWall"—a name harking back to an earlier effort to repel foreign invaders. As every Chinese school kid knows, the original Great Wall failed in its basic mission (though it did better as a communication avenue). Will its digital successor fare any better?

The PSB's Comrade X sees both the scope of the problem and the need for what strategists call "defense in depth":

Nationwide regulations are being formulated, but because these will involve so many other laws and areas—advertising, news, and so on—it will be impossible for us to draw up comprehensive legislation in the short term. At the moment it is up to the ISP and the individual to be responsible for the regulation of newsgroups and the leaking of state secrets.

A professor at a Guangzhou electronics college has a different view:

The NetWall is something born of a typically Chinese mind-set. Perhaps it's just a matter of face-saving. People in the government feel they've got their backs to the wall. They're not stupid. They know full well how viciously everyone denounces them every day in private.

DIGITAL ISLANDS

In the People's Republic, coded communications are second nature, developed over years of mass surveillance, people reading other people's mail and diaries, tapping phones, and generally being inquisitive about your affairs. The idea that the walls have ears doesn't shock anyone.

In conversation, for instance, comments about the weather often carry a political subtext. Low temperatures and storms indicate that the shit has hit the fan; extreme heat can mean that things are precarious for the individual, their company, or inside the government. The Chinese language's rich imagery and telegraphic allusions can make it hard for censors to discern subversive messages from poetic flights of fancy.

Not that it stops them from trying.

The authorities have seen what can happen when the information revolution takes a swipe at its socialist predecessor. Last summer, during a furor—initially encouraged by the authorities—over Japan's occupation of the historically Chinese Diaoyu (Senkaku) Islands, students used the national university network to organize demonstrations. They also transmitted news of the protests, much of which was going unreported in the nervous official media. In this case, the censorship was as crude as it was effective: the most promi-

nent online activist was quickly banished to remote Qinghai Province, and for 10 days, all university access to newsgroups was shut down—those in English (favored by scientists) and in Chinese alike.

The move coincided with an ongoing general crackdown on dissent. Semi-independent journals and newspapers have been banned, writers and intellectuals harassed. The few active dissidents who have managed to stay out of jail (or, more commonly, exile) have had to be even more than usually circumspect about their contacts with the outside world.

One who manages is the controversial environmentalist and investigative historian Dai Qing. Frequently detained by the authorities, she sees the Net as a lifeline to friends and supporters outside China. "Whenever I get back to my apartment, the first thing I do is check my email. In Chinese there's a saying: 'The ends of the earth can be brought close to you.' That's what email allows me to feel. To be in constant contact with people throughout the world gives me a sense of security."

Since the crackdown, the Net—however problematic—has also become one of the few remaining sources of unofficial news. The main online Chinese-language information sources—the Hong Kong and Taiwan presses, and the China News Digest—are among the NetWall's high-priority targets. But anyone with access to the Net and a little skill can find uncensored information—even something as simple as weather-oriented email messages—that fill in the blank spots created by the authorities, whether regarding dissidents, rumors surrounding the demise of Deng Xiaoping, or Islamic separatist bombings in downtown Beijing.

Other tiny digital islands exist—an online magazine for Beijing's "unofficial" art scene, run by two expat Japanese, for example, and another site where a small group of mainland gays sends out news about their lives and activities to the wider world. How long this will last is anyone's guess: Chinese authorities often let things happen until problems arise. As Comrade X put it in his gnomic style, "You make a problem for us, and we'll make a law for you."

JUDGMENT DAY

It would be easy enough in China to radically limit the Net's spread. But companies like China InfoHighway have a more focused agenda: turning information technology to their own, avowedly chauvinistic, advantage. It's not official policy, but it's close. And it certainly reflects the attitude of thinly disguised nationalist grievance that informs so much of China's current relations—the debates over Hong Kong, Taiwan, and Tibet, for starters—with the rest of the world.

Here's another serve from Xia Hong, China InfoHighway's PR man:

The Internet has been an important technical innovator, but we need to add another element, and that is control. The new generation of information superhighway needs a traffic control center. It needs highway patrols; users will require driving licenses. These are the basic requirements for any controlled environment.

All Net users must conscientiously abide by government laws and regulations. If Net users wish to enter or leave a national boundary they must, by necessity, go through customs and immigration. They will not be allowed to take state secrets out, nor will they be permitted to bring harmful information in.

As we stand on the cusp of the new century, we need to—and are justified in wanting to—challenge America's dominant position. Cutting-edge Western technology and the most ancient Eastern culture will be combined to create the basis for dialog in the coming century. In the 21st century, the boundaries will be redrawn. The world is no longer the spiritual colony of America.

Judgment Day for the Internet is fast approaching. At most it can keep going for three to five years. But the end is nigh; the sun is setting in the West, and the glories of the past are gone forever.

China InfoHighway is a major player in what its brochures call "the Chinese information supermarket." Its managing director, a well-connected woman named Zhang Shuxin, isn't shy about her ambition to be the "Bill Gates of China." But when we asked other Internet specialists—a technician at Beijing University, the manager of China Telecom, even Comrade X—what they thought about Xia Hong's boasting, they replied with variations on the same answer: "Those people are completely out of touch with reality."

But then reality in modern China has always been a tentative concept.

Zhou Hongwei is a senior engineer with Shanghai's Ge'er Electronics Corporation. He uses his spare time to help local academics get online:

A few years ago everyone was asking, 'Have you started up your own company yet?' Then it was, 'Do you have a driving license?' followed by, 'What model computer did you get?' Last year the big thing was, 'Are you into multimedia yet?' Today it's, 'Are you wired?'

No one really cares if you are actually wired. Forget about what the Net is for and what it might become. People only want to show their friends that they've done the right thing and got themselves wired.

ROADS AHEAD

China in the 1990s is a country embarked on what some local economists call "the acquisition of primitive capital." Individuals, companies, and state enterprises re all vying for advantage in the rough-and-ready atmosphere of a unique historical moment: simultaneous industrial and information revolutions in the oldest, most populous nation on earth.

For all their unabashed efforts to control the Net in China, the authorities and their entrepreneurial offspring can also see its potential, at least for generating profits. That's one reason the most strident antiforeign rhetoric comes not from pragmatic technocrats like Comrade X, but from fledgling local capitalists and professional xenophobes, who have their own obvious reasons for wanting anything foreign—including potential competition—kept in its place.

Last December, the conservative Beijing journal *Strategy and Management* published a commentary by Yang Xueshan, head of the State Information Center's Capital Investment Office:

Following the end of the Cold War, certain developed nations (meaning the United States and its allies) are determined to protect their own interests by labeling themselves as internationalists. They pretend to be the benefactors of all mankind, while constantly expanding their sphere of influence and attempting to contain the development of others. . . . They want to envelop everything in their information umbrella.

Paranoid nationalism is not just good politics—it's a useful way of garnering support for homegrown solutions. One of the most prominent of those is the China Wide Web, a joint venture of the official New China News Agency and China Internet Corporation, a "patriotic" Hong Kong company. Inaugurated last October, the CWW (*www.china.com/*) is creating a nationwide Chinese commercial network, all guaranteed spiritually pollution-free. Meanwhile, much-watched digital model country Singapore is blazing a path with Singapore One, an exclusive "supernational intranet" to be launched later this year, with all the advantages of the Internet and none of the "problems." The digital gated community, infohighway as one-way street. It won't pass muster in San Francisco or Sydney, but that's no reason it can't work.

For now, the Net in China will remain a privileged realm, enjoyed by the well heeled and well educated, by foreigners, and by the government itself. The cabal of policy makers that is advising the national leadership—Public Security, China Telecom, politically well-connected entrepreneurs—is by no stretch of the imagination enlightened, digitally or otherwise. Internal debate will continue—which organizations or individuals will be allowed to get wired, which will be refused, what those who are online will be allowed to see, and who will profit. The one certainty, given the headstrong Chinese bureaucracy and the Maoist mentality that spawned it, is that China's adaptations of the Net will be unique, and probably bizarre by Western standards.

China's Open Door policies have had momentous, mostly uncalculated consequences. But that doesn't mean that the China of the future is going to look more and more like us. It is going to continue to look like China—and will have the wherewithal to do so. As China gets stronger and more wired, it will still be limited by intellectual narrowness and Sinocentric bias. Pluralism and the open-mindedness that comes with it—the worldly curiosity of previous great powers and the idealism that often supports it—simply are not present. More to the point, they are not about to be encouraged.

DARK GUESTS

Many Chinese computer terms are homophonous transpositions from English. The expression for *hacker* is *heike*, literally "dark guest." As travelers in China's Net world, we were sometimes regarded as slightly suspicious visitors. One army general's son—himself a classic nerd who runs his own computer graphics company—said point blank, "What are you people doing here in China? Foreigners have never done us any good."

He fell silent when reminded that without his Western glasses, designer running shoes, computer technology, and command of English, his Sinocentric world might be far more narrow and lackluster.

A young Beijing woman who works as the night manager at a Sino-Japanese joint-venture hotel whiles the hours away "roaming at will" on her office computer. With access to foreign currency, she's an avid online consumer who's already used the Net to make a few modest purchases from abroad—à la mode sportswear and assorted accessories.

They're the latest fashion, and it's worth it. Of course, there are things I can't afford, like a swimming pool or a circus elephant or real designer clothes. But there are people out there who can. I don't have the wherewithal now, so I know I have to work harder and make more money.

And what about someone without a credit card? She was honestly bemused:

If you don't have a credit card, what in heaven's name are you doing on the Internet in the first place?

Singapore Sting

Our man witnesses a rare Far East software piracy bust.

Richard Rapaport

OMINOUS-LOOKING ARMED MEN are swarming over his retail store, but for a man whose world has just come crashing in on him, Chng (pronounced "Ching") Teck Bin seems unnaturally composed. Chng is the proprietor of P&V Computer PTE, a dingy fifth-floor electronics store nestled among tailor shops and beauty parlors in the Bukit Timah district of Singapore. Chng stands mutely in the dim, box-lined corridor outside his shop while five young policemen from the Intellectual Property Rights unit of the Singapore police chase out his schoolboy techie customers and begin tearing through cabinets, boxes, and files that fill the store. The leader of the squad, a big man in jeans and T-shirt, informs Chng that his shop is the subject of a warrant for software piracy.

Acting on information from a private security adviser, the intellectual property cops are trying to find and confiscate pirated versions of popular personal computer software programs. Throughout Asia, in shops such as this, mass-produced CD-ROMs filled with purloined software sell for a fraction of the legitimate market price. With as many as 30 programs crammed onto the 644-megabyte disks—including such hits as Adobe Photoshop, After Dark, AutoCAD, Claris Works 4.0, CorelDraw, Netscape Navigator, Windows 95, Microsoft Office, Norton Utilities, and on and on, the total legal market value of the programs on one CD-ROM can reach into the high tens of thousands of dollars. But because small, clandestine operators can now stamp out CDs easily and cheaply, disks can be produced for as little as a dollar and sold for between $7 and $25, depending on the buyer's ability to bargain. Costs are low, needless to say, because pirates have no R&D or third-party software licensing costs to cover. This is, after all, one of the great things about being a pirate.

THE FALL GUY

MR. CHNG, HOWEVER, is not a pirate, just a hapless middleman. As the raid progresses, he asks if he can use his telephone; so far he has been cooperative, even obsequious, and the cop in charge tells him to go ahead. "I'm going to call the owner," he tells the detective in fractured English. "He asks me to take over temporarily." "The owners of the shops never seem to be around for the raids," a voice with a decidedly American accent replies sarcastically. It belongs to Christopher Austin, a young attorney currently hunched over one of Chng's ledgers. Austin is working both for the Business Software Alliance, a Washington-based trade organization that deals with software piracy, and for Microsoft. Microsoft is clearly the biggest loser to a regionwide criminal enterprise that sells far more illegal copies of its popular programs in Asia than Microsoft itself.

Austin roves Asia tracking down software pirates. He has become famous throughout the more notorious shopping arcades of Asia as the man most likely to ruin the day of pirates who run the illicit but wide-open market in illegal software. Because of the work of Austin and others, software pirates have been forced to add several sophisticated new twists to their nefarious ways.

Rather than keep a large stock of CD-ROMs on hand that authorities can confiscate, for instance, shop owners will page their suppliers, who dispatch runners with the requested disks.

7. INTERNATIONAL PERSPECTIVE AND ISSUES

Foreign customers in a pirate software shop can now expect to hear the suspicious question, "Are you from Microsoft?" Such changes in the business have made Austin a figure of note here, a man with the task of trying to convince frugal Asians they should pay full freight for programs readily available for pennies on the dollar.

The job is as difficult as it is important. Recent Software Publishers Association and Business Software Alliance statistics show that Singapore, with an estimated 53% piracy rate, still has a long way to go. Yet it is doing far better than its neighbors Malaysia, with a piracy rate of 77%, Thailand at 82%, the Philippines at 91%, China at 96%, and Indonesia at a staggering 98% use of illegal software.

Even with the lowest piracy rate in Asia, Singapore has become a pet project of the pirate-hunters. With its squeaky-clean reputation, its position as the most computer-literate society in the area, and a growing indigenous software industry, Singapore is a key battleground in the struggle for the hearts and minds of Asian technology consumers who have little respect for or understanding of the notion of intellectual property.

The raid on Mr. Chng's shop is winding down, and he sits quietly at his desk. In addition to the scores of CD-ROM compilations, other telltale signs are a tip-off he is in the software piracy business. Christopher Austin points out some of the tricks of the pirates' trade as he goes through the shop. There are, for example, the boxes of empty CD-ROM "jewel cases," mated to a CD-ROM only after a sale is made. Then there is the carton of hard-disk drives under Chng's desk that dealers can load up with pirated software and install on a personal computer.

"To help sell hardware, a dealer will load a machine with thousands of dollars of illegal software," explains Austin, who later points out that Chng was not accused of this crime.

Chng takes his downturn in fortune stoically, but complains about being singled out. "Everybody does it," he says plaintively. He does have a point. In the hazy world of intellectual property law throughout Asia, governments have maintained a fairly ambiguous position on piracy. In Singapore, for example, while the police and courts will cooperate when pressed, the software producer must invest resources to privately investigate piracy before the government will get involved.

According to Ng Kim Neo, senior director of the Trade Policy Division for the Singapore Trade Development Board, the official reason is that the country has long treated intellectual property like private contracts. "You can't jail people for a contract," she says during an interview. And so, with its history of benign neglect toward the software pirates, it is not surprising that piracy is alive and well even in strict Singapore.

> "Chng's whispered phone call is clearly a coded message to his suppliers that a raid is under way. Several other shops have hastily closed."

Chng's whispered phone call is clearly a coded message to his suppliers that a raid is under way. Alan Solomon, the corporate security adviser contracted by Microsoft who has kept P&V under surveillance for months, and who has been lurking in a nearby stairwell during the raid, calls Austin on his cell phone a moment or two later to tell him that several other owners of stores selling pirated software have just hastily closed up and decamped. "There are going to be doors slamming all over town today," Solomon says during a later inspection of the shuttered shops.

Within hours of the raid's conclusion, however, it will be business as usual. The shops here at Bukit Timah, the half-dozen pirate software operations at the notorious Sim Lim Shopping Arcade, and possibly hundreds of stores that sell pirated software or a mix of pirated and legitimate floppies and CDs, will all be open and functioning as if the raid hadn't happened.

Whether the government is lax or stringent, steep profits would drive the shadowy market anyway. During his surveillance, Solomon has recorded between 100 and 200 CD-ROM sales a day at P&V. He and other private investigators estimate that on any given day in Singapore at least 5,000 illegal CD-ROMs are sold at an average of $20 apiece. This means that in this one city software pirates clear at least 700,000 Singapore dollars ($525,000 U.S.) a week. Similar profits are estimated in Hong Kong, Bangkok, Kuala Lumpur, and Manila.

Retailers are usually small businesspeople who can't see any reason they shouldn't be part of this lucrative market. But at a higher level, above the shopkeepers and the pirates themselves, control is in the hands of one of several organized syndicates operating throughout southern Asia. These syndicates are as sensitive to the marketing of illegal products as legitimate companies are to aboveboard sales.

Microsoft's Singapore managing director, Paul Lovell, still receives phone calls asking when an official copy of Windows 95 will be in the stores. Pirates had taken a stolen beta-test version of Windows 95 and done a little innovative marketing. And recently, when Microsoft offered a three-CD set of its software for a special price, pirates responded with their own pirated three-CD edition.

In Singapore and beyond, operations of the pirate software shops are far too consistent to be coincidental. They all have more or less the same physical setup and sell more or less the same program compilations in similar packaging. "It's fairly clear that it's an organized thing, with manufacturing sites all over Asia and shared technology and marketing information," says Weiming Chua, a former Singaporean policeman who is now licensing manager for Novell Asia Pacific.

Even the personnel policies of the stores are similar. They include hiring people with failed businesses, gambling debts, or police records to front the operations. Widely known as the "fall guys," they are paid handsomely not only to sell the pirated software but also to take the fall if the shop is raided. An informant recently spelled out the deal: The going rate of payment is $5,000 a month to manage the business and $2,500 to $3,000 a month for sitting in jail. In general, salaries are higher in the pirate stores than elsewhere, and legitimate shopkeepers in places like Sim Lim Arcade complain that it is hard to get help because potential employees prefer working for the pirates.

"You can get a lot of people to be the fall guy," Chua tells me. "If you get arrested, maybe you serve a short sentence, but you get taken care of. If you don't squeal, they pay you a bonus and look after your family while you're in jail." Considering the harsh sentences in Singapore for drug or firearm sales, a bust for CD-ROM piracy is widely regarded as something of a paid vacation.

Which sheds light on the placid mood of Mr. Chng Teck Bin of P&V Computer. When Microsoft's Austin finds a secret compartment he can't open, Chng is surprisingly helpful. "It's locked, sir," Chng says meekly. "I'll open it for you." One of the cops suggests that Chng is in shock, saying, "Now he has a lot of legal obligations. He is a confused man at this moment." Asked why he is so complaisant, Chng says dreamily, "Human life is short; you must be happy." He does not seem at all upset, and security adviser Alan Solomon, the man who has spent the last year investigating the ins and outs of software piracy in the region, isn't surprised. "Fall guy," he snorts.

UNDERGROUND SINGAPORE

THE FOLLOWING DAY, Solomon takes me on a tour of the Singapore software piracy underground he has come to know so well. The first stop is the Sim Lim Arcade. The modern glass-and-steel mall is as well known throughout Asia for its wide-open piracy as Hong Kong's notorious Golden Arcade.

Sim Lim is the place where, in March 1996, Solomon pulled off Singapore's most successful software piracy raid. Acting on a hunch while staking out a Sim Lim shop, Solomon followed a courier to a parking lot under the mall. There he discovered two vans filled with CD-ROMs, rolling warehouses from which disks are delivered to shops throughout Singapore. More than 5,600 disks were confiscated, worth more than $150,000 on the black market, with a legitimate software value into the millions.

Solomon's gumshoeing was rewarded; not only were huge fines levied but three of the software pirates received jail sentences, one for four months, plus a $45,000 fine or nine additional months if the fine remained unpaid. The second got 30 months; the third was sentenced to 18 months. In neither case, however, did the pirates give up the names of their bosses. Rather, they remained silent, did their time, and left Solomon and others to track down the CD pirate masterminds from the outside.

"This is like returning home," says Solomon as he retraces the steps of his big bust. As he predicted, when we enter Sim Lim, the first shop we pass is a wide-open, pirated-software bazaar. The setup is familiar: pirated popular computers games and "edutainment" CDs on racks around the walls and a table in the middle, with labels from the best known CD-ROM compilations. Names like Solid Gold, Master Installer, Software Governor, Super Installer 8.0, and Macintosh CD are visible. The shop is filled with young techies pawing over the piles and clerks happy to haggle over prices. A pirated CD-ROM copy of the *Encyclopedia Britannica,* which retails in the United States for $299, is listed for 30 Singapore dollars and can be bargained down to 15 dollars.

Ironically, a sign points to the struggle between the better and worse sides of Singapore's technological nature: "We encourage you to buy original software . . . that is, if you can afford it!"

As we tour the six bustling levels of electronics stores at Sim

> ## "We are approached by two shotgun-toting guards who do not appear to be very happy about our presence. Solomon suggests a strategic retreat."

Lim Arcade, we find a half-dozen shops with virtually the same look, differentiated in some cases by simple, easily removable neon signs. Others are marked with cardboard marquees hung at the entrance. The stores are movable software feasts, ready to be broken down in minutes. Even on a weekday afternoon, they're filled with browsers and buyers devouring pirated software.

Why are the shops at Sim Lim Arcade allowed to operate so openly? Bryan Ghows, regional counsel for Lotus and the Business Software Alliance's former manager in Singapore, has a surprisingly ambiguous answer for someone in his position. He admits that the problem of piracy "is not really a social or moral wrong in the Singaporean context." This is in contrast, Ghows suggests, to pornography. He points out, for example, how quickly the government moved to set up proxy servers in 1996 to protect citizens from the fleshpots of the World Wide Web. Ghows suggests a rationale for the government's casual attitude about software piracy: "A certain amount of piracy is welcomed, because very few people can afford software at market prices."

It is Microsoft's suspicion, particularly among the company's local executives, that Lotus's Ghows is not as concerned as he might be about Microsoft's status as prime piracy target. Lotus is, after all, owned by Microsoft rival IBM. This has led the Redmond, Washington, firm to launch its own attack on piracy. And to employ Alan Solomon as its hired gun.

Solomon's second stop of the day is on Microsoft business. He has planned to wire one of his employees and send him into a seemingly legitimate CD-ROM replication plant to see if the managers will agree to copy software for a phantom company without the proper copyright agreements. A large, legitimate contract to replicate Microsoft software depends on the correct response. "Entrapment is okay here," Solomon notes as we drive toward an industrial park in the Ang Mo Kio district.

At the plant, "Mike," who does undercover work for Solomon, puts on his equipment and heads inside. In 30 minutes he's back, mission accomplished. He plays the tape, and on it an employee clearly agrees to do whatever copying is required, as long as Mike signs an indemnity form. "Got him," Solomon says with unconcealed glee. "He can kiss that contract goodbye."

Next stop is a stakeout of what Solomon and others suspect is a functioning CD-ROM factory in a housing block nearby. We cruise by a boarded-up storefront guarded by several tough-looking men lounging on the sidewalk in front. More toughs eye us as we pull up in a parking lot around the back. The windows above the storefront are smoked and double-paned. On the side of the apartment, an industrial-sized air-conditioning unit stands out incongruously in this residential neighborhood.

Solomon has been surveilling the building for weeks, watching suspicious-looking couriers picking up brown-wrapped packages at the site. The tip-off to the site came half a world away when a package containing pirated CD-ROMs was seized in Cyprus. Sherlock Holmes was not needed; the package had the Ang Mo Kio address on it.

"But we need physical evidence," Solomon says, referring to the fairly stiff requirements to request a police raid. He is moving very carefully with the Ang Mo Kio factory. He suspects his operation was compromised by another investigator working for the factory. A bust will have to wait until someone can sneak inside and take pictures, a dangerous assignment considering the high security around the building. But Solomon is content to wait. "We'll come back," he says as we drive out of the parking lot, dozens of suspicious eyes following our Mercedes.

On my final day in Singapore, Solomon has agreed to go over the causeway into Malaysia to check out some of the pirate software stores in Johor Baharu. Malaysia is more wide open than Singapore and far more dangerous. "Life is as cheap as a bullet," we've been warned. Solomon doesn't like to work there, considering the authorities much less trustworthy than the "straight as a die" Singaporean police. A raid a colleague conducted in Johor weeks before came up empty, and Solomon suspects the pirates were tipped off by a Malaysian official.

For cover, he has taken the precaution of using a car that has never been across the causeway. Malay pirates sometimes strap drugs under cars bound for Singapore, so he also takes along a trusted bodyguard to watch the car while we snoop around.

By the time we cross the causeway and clear Malaysian customs, a hard rain is falling. We drive another half hour into Johor Baharu. The place is beat-up and colorful and looks like ultramodern Singapore must have in its more romantic days. We park the car at a hotel and walk the rest of the way to a mall containing a number of stores selling pirated software. The same CD-ROMs for sale in Singapore for $15 to $30 are half that here, with room to haggle. In addition, there is a wide variety of ultra hard-core pornography available on CD-ROMs, material that would cause stores to be shut down instantly in Singapore.

Things go fine until Nikolai Joyce, *Forbes ASAP's* photographer, takes out his camera and begins shooting. There are none of the jocular "Are you from Microsoft?" queries we heard in Singapore. We are suddenly approached by two shotgun-toting guards, who do not appear to be very happy about our presence. They make threatening motions with their weapons, and Solomon wisely suggests we make a strategic retreat.

But once we are on the street, a group of young Malays, several carrying baseball bats, begins to follow us. Solomon orders us to split up, lose ourselves in one of the crowded malls, and regroup at the hotel in a half hour. The group is confused by our actions, and we lose them—or bore them—by moving randomly up and down several levels of another mall.

The ride back to Singapore is uneventful. The customs officials are far more concerned about any illegal chewing gum than the pirated software disks we are bringing back from Malaysia. We are carrying thousands of dollars worth of unlicensed software. Luckily, we hadn't bought any gum.

DISCONNECTED:

Haves and Have-Nots in the Information Age

BY WILLIAM WRESCH

This book is the result of my being hit by a two-by-four. It shouldn't have been necessary to get my attention. My Ph.D. dissertation was on human information processing. I head a university Computer Information Systems program. I

have directed Total Quality Management teams and preached the importance of information gathering. I sat through meetings of a Governor's Task Force in Accountability and saw the continued need for information in the public sector. I have spent the last two decades as a living, breathing citizen of the information age, but I just wasn't seeing it.

Selections from the new book published by Rutgers University Press.

I got my two-by-four in Africa. The U.S. Government sponsors the Fulbright Exchange Program, which goes back 50 years to the effort after the Second World War to help rebuild European universities. The program worked, and we have been sending American professors all over the world ever since (we also bring lots of professors and graduate students here). I was selected to teach for a year in the Computer Science Department of the newly established University of Namibia. My family and I arrived in Windhoek, Namibia, in September 1993.

But the two-by-four struck with a vengeance when I took my next step. After I had my interviews with information-systems managers I felt I knew what the University of Namibia needed to do to meet their needs. But a university in the developing world has other responsibilities as well. Was there anything it could do, I wondered, about Namibia's huge unemployment problem? Every street corner in downtown Windhoek has dozens of men standing, waiting all day, every day, hoping for a day's work. I began interviewing these men. These conversations quickly became agony for me, for the men, and for my translator, Szacky Nuujoma, but we persisted. What I learned didn't make me feel very good.

Szacky and I began by getting background information on the men—what kinds of jobs they were able to get, how often they worked, what they were paid, where they lived, how they lived. We learned these men thought a good week was one in which they earned 45 Namibian dollars (about 12 U.S. dollars). Since the cost of living in Windhoek is similar to that of a city in the United States, they were all slowly starving. Often they went for weeks without any work. They talked of nothing but getting a day's employment, they dreamt of nothing else, they were obsessed with getting work.

From *EDUCOM Review*, January/February 1997, pp. 52-59. © 1996 by William Wresch. Reprinted by permission of Rutgers University Press.

Since the primary struggle of their lives was to find work, I asked how they found out about jobs. I used many of the same questions I had used with the corporate managers, only instead of asking how they found out about computer innovations, I asked how they found out about jobs. The answers were astonishing. It quickly became apparent that these men had no resources. Read the want ads in the paper? Many couldn't read: none could afford a paper. Watch the business news on TV? They didn't have electricity, much less TVs—besides, TV is broadcast in English, the official, but largely unknown, national language. Get help from churches, clubs, sports groups? These men were from a northern tribe, the Owambos. They had no connections to local groups. Anyway, with six or even seven days spent on the corners waiting for work, when did they have time to form alliances?

Any information source I asked them about came up dry. They were aliens in Windhoek, immigrants in their own country. There were few resources in Namibia to help such men as these, but what there were, these men would never know about. They were cut off from everything. The worst aspect of the situation was that there was little chance it would ever change. There was no hope.

This series of interviews left me shaken. I gave each man a little bit of money for his time, shook his hand, and then watched him walk back to his corner. I now understood the gulf that existed between these men and those who drove by them.

Now the two-by-four had gotten my attention. I ached for the men who baked in the tropical sun day after day with no idea of how to get off the corner, for the managers who were blind to the rest of Africa, for citizens who were being sold a prepackaged view of the world by a newspaper

that printed all the news that fit their prejudices. Gradually I began to take a new look at the information age—a much less complacent look.

Most worrisome for me was that as I looked for solutions, they seemed less and less technological. It would have been easy if I had just said, "Import that latest Intel chip and Novell network and everything will be fine." Actually, Namibia already had a significant technological base. Windhoek alone had 30 PC vendors. A week after Intel's Pentium chip was commercially available, there were Pentium computers in Namibia. The technology was there. It might not be available in every corner of the country, but it was in the country.

Technology didn't explain the problem. Something was at work in Namibia, something I would study in depth over the next nine months. Those studies would lead me back to the United States for a fresh look at our own information handling—the procedures and approaches that make us a model for the world, and the procedures and approaches that make us a laughingstock. This book is essentially a very lengthy report on that research.

"Baywatch" is more embarrassment than entertainment for people there [in rural areas]. The nudity, the physical contact . .

—Nahum Gorelick,
Namibian Broadcast Company

It's a Tuesday night in Africa. You happen to live in a capital city with all the perks—electricity and a television signal. So you come home from a hard day at the office and switch on the tube. Here is your evening lineup for Windhoek, Namibia:

5:00 p.m.	"Sesame Street"
6:00	"Casper and Friends"
6:30	"The Rich Also Cry"
7:00	"Zoom"
7:30	"Growing Pains"
8:00	News
8:30	"Tropical Heat"
9:25	"Parliamentary Report"
9:30	"Talking Point"
10:30	Sports

Cable subscribers could supplement that line up with "Goof Troop," "Scooby Doo," "The Flintstones," and "Garfield and Friends" as well as "The Wonder Years," "The Simpsons," and the movie *Don't Tell Mama the Babysitter's Dead*. What a great way to spend an evening. A mongoose frolicking in the back yard, Kudu steaks on the grill, and American reruns on the tube.

At a time when we are talking about an explosion of information, most public information sources are constrained, one-sided, and meager. Major sources of public information have inordinate American influence. What information flow exists, flows out from the United States, with little flowing back. Often there is little available to flow in any direction. Television shows have to be produced before they can be viewed. Movies have to be made, books have to be published. A walk through the minuscule "foreign films" section of any video rental store, time spent browsing in any book store, all give immediate force to world information trends.

The problem would be acceptable if we were just looking at Americans' renowned disinterest in any country but our own. But when you find that so many foreign countries have little information about themselves, you begin to wonder about larger issues. What public information is available, both here and abroad? The answer is, very little compared to the range of cultures, histories, ideas, and peoples that populate our planet. There *is* a world outside of Hollywood, but it is not easy to find it. Rather than an information explosion, the public media seem to be demonstrating an *im*plosion in which few voices are heard and little of the world seen.

The Bushmen are fighting for survival. And they are quickly learning the rules of the new warfare. Forming alliances with Australian aborigines, Himbas, and other indigenous people, they are pressing their legal claims and making sure they get their share of air time on the six o'clock news. Forming the Nyae Nyae Farmers Cooperative, they are developing ways to market local products and handicrafts, as they train themselves in the methods of modern business. If courage and energy were sufficient for victory, one could be much more sanguine about their future. But the Bushmen face overwhelming odds. Virtually every development in the information age leaves them more vulnerable and demonstrates the problems faced by people like them around the world.

To understand these problems, a good place to start is Tsumkwe, Namibia. Established in 1959, the village started out as little more than a farm where experts hoped to teach Bushmen cattle-raising skills. Tsumkwe is not an easy place to reach. You begin by driving four hours north of Windhoek on two lanes of asphalt. Then you turn right—east—into the Kalahari. For the next four hours you bump along over gravel and sand, leaving a long cloud of dust in your wake. You pass a few hills and a few trees, but no people or structures, as you drive hour after hour through a grassy plain. Occasionally you see another car or truck, but only occasionally. After the first couple of hours you feel a sense for just how isolated this community is.

The Germans wanted it that way. When they ruled the country from 1885 to 1915 they put their settlers on land that had water, good pasturage for cattle, and easy access to markets. During the South African occupation from 1915 to 1990, the policy remained the same. Nonwhites, especially the Bushmen, were pushed to corners of the country, while white farmers and merchants controlled the middle. And so the Bushmen, who once controlled much of the center of Namibia, were pushed out to the edge, out to the desert. They had once been miners and traders, but that part of their land was taken from them. Reduced to hunting and gathering, they struggled to pull a living from the Kalahari.

After such a long, silent drive, Tsumkwe just seems to pop up out of the low brush. It would be easy to miss. There isn't much there, and what there is, is spread out. There is an intersection—another thin gravel road crossing yours. To your left is the school, set back fifty yards from the road. A set of block rooms, it enrolls 300 in grades one to ten. Across the intersection is the only store. It looks like an old gas station. Also made of blocks, it is about thirty feet square and painted white. The inside is dark and largely empty. Shelving bolted to the walls contains a scattering of food and household goods. There are two low coolers, each about four feet long. One has soft drinks, the other meat. The center of the store stands empty.

Back out at the intersection, the road to the right is Main Street. On one side is the police station, then the gas station. Some days there is gas, some days not. Next is the home of the rural development official, followed by the home of "the Bushman movie star," as he is known locally. No one in town has seen *The Gods Must be Crazy*, but they remember the filming. Across the street is the clinic. All these buildings are set well back from the road and separated from each other—space is not a problem here.

There is one residential street with eight houses for government workers. The first one is the town leader's. He also gets the generators in his back yard. Down the street are seven more houses, all about 20 years old, ranch-style brick with single-car attached garages and grassy front yards. It looks like it could be a suburban block from western Texas.

Driving the short distance up the gravel streets, there are few Bushmen to be seen. The storekeeper is white, the government officials black. The rural development officer, Charles Chipango, is on leave to study computer science at the University of Namibia. A student of mine, he drove me back down the residential street but kept going past the end, past the gravel, past the electricity out onto a dirt track. In a few hundred yards we came to the Bushmen. One group was living in a collection of square block structures about eight feet on a side. There were eight or ten such buildings. Across a small field were smaller stick-and-mud homes. We bounced over the dirt track through fields of mahango and corn.

As we came around one bend we had to stop. A Bushman was passed out drunk in the middle of the track. We edged around him and found the "shebeen" that had supplied him. In a clearing was a small structure—four poles about five feet high, with a lattice of branches across the top to provide shade. Sitting in the shade was the wife of one of the government officials. She had a two-liter box of wine, a boom box, and a small half-pint whiskey bottle. For 10 rand she would fill the old whisky bottle with wine. The 20 or so Bushmen at the shebeen would pass the bottle around, dancing barefoot in the dirt as they drank. It was just 1:00 P.M. and she was doing a good business. Profit margins were among the best in the world. She bought the wine for 22 rand a box. She could fill the 10-rand bottle 13 or 14 times from one box. Twenty-two rand becomes 130 with no taxes and no overhead. Not a bad profit margin.

The shebeens farther down the track didn't have any business yet. But it was early. Each had a 40-gallon plastic garbage pail sitting in the shade. Homemade beer was brewing in each pail. By night each would be empty, to be refilled the next day. That was the second Tsumkwe. The dirt paths and stick houses and home-brewed beer back off the road, out of sight, back past where the gravel and electricity stop. For these people there are no happy natives living the simple life of *The Gods Must be Crazy*. The gods out here seem hostile, or cruel.

It makes no economic sense to run phone wires across the Kalahari. So there are no phones. The only connection to the rest of the world is a radio phone. It is difficult and expensive to use just for voice communication. Nobody will be hooking up to electronic mail anytime soon, and 400-channel TV doesn't seem to be in their future. There is mail. Once every week or two someone volunteers to drive the four and a half hours to Grootfontein to get it.

The general store in Tsumkwe sells no newspapers. Radio reception is only possible with a good antenna and then only at sunup and sundown. At those times the faint signal is as likely to come from Botswana as Namibia. Television sets don't exist.

The school in town is less than 20 years old and appears solid. The problem is the teachers. They have broken into two factions—the qualified and the unqualified. The qualified teachers either have university degrees (one is a Peace Corps volunteer) or have attended a teacher training college. There are four of these teachers. They are outnumbered by the eight unqualified teachers who have completed eighth grade and little else. These teachers tend to be both unqualified and uninterested. One regularly comes to class drunk. Another sleeps at his desk most of the day. His fellow teachers can tell when he is asleep—his students climb up into the ceiling area under the roof and look

down on adjoining classes. A third teacher was finally run off when he was confronted with numerous students who said he paid them ten Namibian dollars for sex. The battle between the two groups continues, with the unqualified teachers generally winning a maintenance of the status quo.

One of the cruder ironies of the information age is that rich people get their information practically for free, while poor people pay dearly for every morsel. Be it a telephone call, a newspaper, a drive to the store—all cost more in Tsumkwe than they do in Beverly Hills. They cost more in absolute terms, they cost astronomically more in relative terms—as a percentage of a day's wage. How many Americans would work an hour for a newspaper, two hours for a phone call, a day to see a movie, a lifetime for a home computer?

The Bushmen of the Kalahari are an extreme example of people who are disconnected from the new age, but they are, unfortunately, not alone. All over the world are people and groups who, for various reasons, are off the information highway.

The United Nations has a project underway to link African universities and their libraries. It is providing computer equipment, modems, and expertise. What it can't provide is phone lines, and that is where problems begin. Computers communicate at various speeds. The slowest communication speed—300 baud—would transmit 30

characters per second. This page contains slightly less than 3000 characters, but let's keep the math simple and round up to an even 3000. At 30 characters per second, it would take 100 seconds, or almost two minutes, just to send this one page.

Of course there are much faster links possible. A 14,400-baud modem is easily found. Since it transmits 1,440 characters a second, this page would be gone in just over two seconds—almost 50 times faster. Surely, this would be the way to go, especially since African telephone charges are often three or four times what a similar call would cost in the United States. Except for one problem. Africa's phone lines can rarely handle high speeds. Despite repeated attempts, the UN can't even reach Madagascar at 300 baud—the slowest possible rate. Lines elsewhere often lose messages at speeds above 1,200 baud (120 characters per second). As a consequence, not only do African phones cost more per minute, but messages take more minutes to send than they would in the United States. This combination means some of the world's poorest people have to pay the world's highest charges for electronic mail.

While information systems are both present and necessary in the developing world, there are a number of barriers preventing them from being as useful or as common as they are in the developed world. One problem is weather. The equator is hot. At temperatures of 130° F computers overheat and shut down. Newer microcomputers are better in hot climates than older mainframe computers, but they are still vulnerable to overheating. The response, air conditioning, solves the problem, but it restricts computers to air-conditioned areas, often centralizing their use—the very opposite of the international trend toward distributed systems.

Electricity may be a bigger problem, with wide voltage spikes and brownouts that raise havoc with equipment. Surge suppressors and uninterruptable power supplies (UPS) are a standard requirement but, of course, push up the cost of computer systems.

———

In Africa the lack of local repair facilities is actually made worse by donors who bring whatever computers consultants are comfortable with (usually a brand from the donor nation), even though they may be incompatible with already-existing equipment and totally foreign to any local computer store. They don't have parts for them, they don't have service manuals for them, they are just more computers that have to be boxed up and shipped halfway around the world for expensive repairs. One survey in Tanzania found only 55 percent of computers brought in by donor groups could be serviced locally (Grant Lewis 1992).

Shortage of qualified personnel is another serious problem. Information technology is a new and rapidly developing field, so information-system managers worldwide are struggling to staff their operations, but problems in the developing world seem especially acute. Partly this is a consequence of the general weakness of educational systems, partly this is a result of the odd orientation of African universities toward liberal arts and away from technical subjects (a situation that has drawn increased attention from the World Bank). But the results can be startling. In 1993 the University of Namibia graduated one computer science major! In 1994 it graduated three. The University of Uganda only began a computer science program in 1992. For much of Africa, a cadre of well-trained computer professionals simply isn't being created.

The lack of educational programs in computing unfortunately results in part from government attitudes toward computers. Rather than seeing computers as a growth industry or as a means of catching up with the rest of the world, African governments tend to see computers as a drain on their treasuries and as a threat to employment.

———

One of the hopes of e-mail advocates is that new computer networks will give citizens a way around totalitarian governments. It is certainly true that every new channel is a new opportunity and that the complex webs of computer networks pose a particular challenge to government control. But governments can rise to the challenge. Take China. The country is in the midst of developing a large academic computing network to link more than 1,000 educational institutions by the end of the century. There is only one twist to this network. Unlike American networks, with multiple electronic routes from campus to campus, all traffic in this Chinese network will have to run through Beijing's Quinghua University. Poon Kee Ho, director of the computer center at the City University of Hong Kong, thinks he knows why. The Chinese academic network will be technically unsound, but with a choke point at Quinghua University government officials "can do what they want to monitor it or shut it down" (Hertling 1995).

The Chinese government draws another special benefit from their computer network. With links to the institutions of the West, Chinese academics will be able to keep up with Western research without ever leaving the country. This is especially important since, as Education Minister Zhu Kiaxuan complained in March of 1995, two-thirds of the 200,000 Chinese students who have gone overseas to study in the last 15 years never went back to China. With government controlled e-mail available as an alternative information resource, it will be easier to say no to student travel, easier to keep the Chinese in China, where the government can keep a closer watch on them. In effect, the Chinese government has been able to use e-mail as one more lock on the prison gates.

"Exit access is that part of a means of egress that leads to an entrance to an exit."

—Fire-prevention pamphlet for homes for the elderly

In 1789 Ephraim Kirby began publishing *Connecticut Reports,* thus enabling the legal profession to have access to court decisions. By 1798 U.S. Supreme Court decisions were being regularly reported, followed by other federal legal information in 1804. By 1820, there was so much being published that "practitioners were already complaining that they could not keep up with the digests, statutes, and court reports that seemed to be pouring from the presses" (Bloomfield 1988:36). So here we have it—the first recorded case of information glut. Nearly two centuries ago people were already complaining that they were getting too much.

———

Sometimes the harshest critics of American journalists are foreign journalists. Chris Ndivanga was one of a number of African journalists invited to intern in some of the major newspapers in the United States in 1994. Brought over at the expense of the United States Information Agency, it was hoped he would learn about news gathering and newspaper production. He learned all that, but he also learned his American counterparts were clueless about Africa.

"I soon realized that for convenience's sake I would have to assume a new nationality," Ndivanga said. "No longer a Namibian, but an 'African.' Otherwise I had to explain every moment where and what Namibia is" (1994:8). He continued, "A professor at the Department of Journalism and Mass

Communication at Rutgers University in New Brunswick, New Jersey, kept referring to us as South Africans even after I had written Namibia and Zambia on a piece of paper for him." Students at the college seemed just as confused. Since the elections in South Africa were in the news, students wanted to know, "Are you guys not going to vote? This was after we had been introduced as Namibian and Zambian."

———

It's not easy to write about the information age while in Africa. As I write this, the euphoria over the peaceful transition to majority rule in South Africa is still with us, but so are the pictures of Rwanda. Today's paper had a picture of two small children who had been hacked in the neck with machetes and left in a pile of dead adults for a week. Both survived but wore bandages far larger than a child that age should ever see. A block away from me is the street that bears the name of Namibia's president. It is a Saturday, but up and down that street stand young men hoping some employer will pick them up, even if only for a few hours. Almost all will go home having stood in the sun for eight or nine hours without making a cent.

In such an environment breathless descriptions of satellite networks seem silly, as do discussions of how many shopping channels will be part of the new 400-channel TV. It would be easy to deride the whole concept of information access as just one more frill of the wealthy nations, like cars, blue jeans, and three meals a day. And there is the danger that in much of the world, maybe most of the world, access to information will be a frill, the average person remaining brutishly poor and blindly obedient. That could certainly be the destiny of much of the developing world. It could even be the destiny of much of the United States.

But after 12 chapters of often very bad tidings, let me close on a hopeful note. And there are reasons to hope. Just the other side of all the men waiting for a day's wages is a small university where 18-year-olds sign onto the Internet each day and exchange news and personal greetings with 18-year-olds in St. Cloud, Minnesota, and Stevens Point, Wisconsin. The talk this week was of the South African elections. Other weeks it has been health care or college life. The content of the discussions seems less important to the Namibian students than the opportunity to reach out. To talk to a real American is important to them. Nothing may come of these discussions that can be reflected in Gross Domestic Product, or even in political developments, but a few dozen students who can reach beyond stereotypes is significant.

———

As we think more about information—where it comes from, where it goes, where it can't go, who gets it, who doesn't—we find a situation that is far more complicated than is usually described in the "gee whiz" articles on the wonders of the World Wide Web. If we are in a new age, this is an age that is still connected to the old age and still has many of its flaws. Yes, technology is producing some benefits and some freedoms. We know the threat of satellite dishes was enough to scare South Africa into creating a television network. Unfortunately, we also know the threat of satellite dishes has been enough to cause governments across the Middle East to ban their use. We know libraries across the world are now accessible electronically. We also know books around the world are still being burned. We know that at this moment hundreds of gigabytes of information are being bounced from satellite to satellite across the sky. We also know that many of those gigabytes are lies. We know that some children can learn about the world by linking their classroom to thousands across the world. Other children wait for their classroom to get a roof, a light bulb, a qualified teacher.

Like most things, it is unlikely the information age will be as good as we hope or as bad as we fear. It will certainly be far different than we imagine. We may shape it, and it certainly will shape us. If we are to influence it, we must first know what it is. At the moment our grasp of this "thing" is far too much like the blind men examining the elephant. We find one thing—usually something hooked to a wire and traveling at blazing speed—and decide that's what the age is. The wire is part of it, but so is the gun and the muffled scream and the obvious lie and the plot hatched online. The point of this book is to shine a light on a few of those other parts of the elephant.

The Role of Computer Networks in Development

Larry Press

The good news is that the Internet has grown like a weed, and many welcome it as a tool for productivity and enlightenment; the bad news is that it is almost unknown in developing nations (see Table 1). This column offers the hypothesis that computer networks can improve life in developing nations at a relatively low cost.

Dimensions of Development

"Development" is an imprecise concept. Economists once equated it with economic productivity—GDP per capita—but that is too simple a formulation [22]. Rising GDP might be accompanied by environmental damage, anger over growing disparity in income distribution, disappointment when expectations rise faster than they are fulfilled, displacement of traditional values and customs, crowded cities, and so forth.[1] Furthermore, GDP counts many painful transactions as positive, for example, bypass surgery, buying a second home after a divorce, or the paycheck of a housewife who is forced into the labor market to make ends meet [3].

A broader conception of human development is used in the United Nations Development Program (UNDP) Report on Human Development, published annually since 1992 [21]. Its concept of development includes human autonomy and breadth of choice, equity, sustainability, and empowerment as well as productivity. In an attempt to capture this multidimensional concept of development, UNDP computes a comprehensive Human Development Index (HDI) as a function of productivity, health, and education.[2] It is reassuring that this index shows less variance among nations than GDP per capita, still there are major disparities between nations, as shown in Table 2.

With the comprehensive, UNDP concept of development in mind, let us turn to some contributions networks might make in economic productivity, health, education, democracy, and quality of life.

Economic Productivity

Communication pays. In recent telecommunication investments in developing nations, the World Bank expects rates of return between 13% and 20%, averaging about 20%. In addition to return on investment, it estimates a 15% to 30% return to the general economy. It also finds "very large economic returns" from the telecommunications components in other sectors such as railways, power, tourism, banking, and rural development. [19, pp. 15–16].

Computer networks run over telephone infrastructure at relatively small marginal cost, providing increased economic benefit. Consider the success of the Relcom (RELiable COMmunications) network in the ex-Soviet Union [16]. Relcom was established in April 1989, using a Microvax in Moscow and PC compatible (286 and 386) computers connected with dial-up lines and 2400bps and 9600bps modems. On August 22, 1990, Relcom started international Internet connectivity with hourly phone calls from Helsinki to Moscow for batch transfer of email and Usenet news. By September, 1993, Relcom served nearly 7,000 organizations and an estimated 200,000 users connecting 162 regions and cities.

---

[1] See Simon [20] in which he suggests that people's floating aspiration levels render economic fluctuations relatively unimportant. However, in times of rapid change, that is not the case.

[2] The HDI is an evenly weighted average of three indices, life expectancy, educational attainment, and real GDP/capita. Life expectancy is a percent of 85 years, educational attainment is a linear function of adult literacy rate and school enrollment rate, and real GDP/capita is adjusted for purchasing power parity. GDP/capita is also nonlinear—amounts above the world average ($5,120 in 1992) are deemed to have decreasing utility, up to a maximum of $40,000. While limited, and surely not worthy of the three-digit significance reported by the UNDP, the HDI is more reasonable than simple GDP/capita.

From *Communications of the ACM*, February 1996, pp. 23-30. © 1996 by the Association for Computing Machinery, Inc. Reprinted by permission.

7. INTERNATIONAL PERSPECTIVE AND ISSUES

Table 1. Over 90% of hosts are in North America and Western Europe, and this understates global disparity since those are generally the largest machines with highest speed connectivity.
Source: Mark Lottor, http://www.nw.com/

Region	Jan 94	July 94	Oct 94	Jan 95	July 95
Numbers of Internet Hosts by Region					
North America	1,685,715	2,177,396	2,685,929	3,372,551	4,515,871
Western Europe	550,933	730,429	850,993	1,039,192	1,530,057
Pacific	113,482	142,353	154,473	192,390	252,014
Asia	81,355	111,278	127,569	151,773	233,343
Eastern Europe and CIS	19,867	27,800	32,951	46,125	67,648
Africa	10,951	15,595	21,041	27,130	42,108
Caribbean, Central and South America	7,392	11,455	14,894	n/a	28,493
Middle East	6,946	8,871	10,383	13,776	21,179
Total	2,476,641	3,225,177	3,898,233	4,842,937	6,690,713

In spite of having begun under a communist regime, Relcom carried commercial traffic from the start, and was heavily commercial a year after it began (see Table 3). The network was used for markets and business communication within the nation, and for international transactions and coordination. In a 1994 Usenet News posting, Relcom co-founder Vadim Antonov said he believed the social and business impact of Relcom had been greater than that of the Internet in the U.S.

Relcom is unusual since networks in developing nations have usually started in the university and research community [7]. However, it is not the only example. One of the newer networks, in Ghana, accepted commercial traffic from its inception, and 36 of its 89 customers were businesses eight months after it began [18].

Networks enable international communication with suppliers, customers, and other stakeholders. Much of the economic success of the U.S. is attributable to our lead in establishing a mass, tariff-free market supported by good communication and transportation [13]. Networks can help open mass, global markets to developing nations.

This of course raises the specter of reduced wages and environmental destruction in developed nations. The entrance of new competition will surely hurt certain industries and workers, but can this globalization be stopped? I don't think so. If that's the case, we in developed nations should console ourselves by noting the positive implications—increased investment opportunity and trade, increased efficiency, lower-cost goods, service and distribution jobs, a more peaceful, humane world, and so forth. Economists since Ricardo have insisted the economic pie is largest when every person (and nation) does what they do best. At the same time, we should work against the negative side effects, by seeking international environmental and labor standards.

Education
In 1992, Pedro Hepp and his colleagues at the Catholic University in Chile began a five-year project to develop and evaluate an elementary school network called Enlaces (links). Their goals were to enhance efficiency, quality, and equity in education and to "integrate the children into the culture." They began with a pilot in six locations, and today there are 144 networked schools. Initially, each school had two computers and a 2400bps modem. Today,

there are between three and 10 computers and an Ethernet in each school. They began with batch transfer, making interactive access impossible, but a dozen schools are now getting IP connectivity to the Internet on a pilot basis [8, see also http://www.enlaces.ufro.cl].

Enlaces provides a variety of services—student and teacher newsletters, educational software, curriculum notes, computer conferences, email, and database access. It has been formally evaluated; a statistically significant effect on student creativity has been proven, and the government has decided to expand nationwide. With World Bank funding, the goal is to reach 100% of the secondary schools and 50% of the primary schools by 2000.

The support structure has been decentralized through the (long) country with 15 universities participating. One strong belief is that the teachers are at the center of the network, and their training and support budget is 25% of the total project. From the beginning, Hepp understood the importance of supporting low-income, rural and outlying areas. This project not only benefits Chile, we can all learn from it. (What proportion of the schools in your community have Ethernets?)

One might argue that Chile is a prosperous developing nation, and therefore atypical.[3] That is so, but even poor nations can make progress. The Cuban economy was dealt a debilitating blow by the fall of Communism in Eastern Europe, but has continued allocating resources to a small education network.[4]

Cuba's networking project is

---

[3] Using 1992 data, Chile's HDI is 0.880, and its real, per capita GDP is $8,410 [21]. For purposes of comparison, the UNDP high development nations have an average HDI of 0.888, and real per capita GDP of $13,605. World averages are 0.759 and $5,410.

---

[4] Using 1992 data, Cuba's HDI is 0.769 and their real, per capita GDP is $3,412 [21]. Unfortunately, the fall of Eastern Europe has doubtless lowered these figures. With the Soviet collapse, Cuba lost around $4 to $5 billion in aid and subsidies, and its key trading partners. Foreign trade is approximately 25% of the 1989 level, and GDP 50%.

based in the Cuban Youth Computing Clubs (YCCs). Begun in 1987, the YCCs are typically Cuban in their stress on grassroots participation. The centers are reminiscent of Bob Albrecht's People's Computer Company (PCC) and similar experiments dating back to the 1960s in the U.S. Similar to the PCC, they have computers running games, drawing programs, and other software, that the children may use in a relatively unstructured manner. Additionally, the YCCs offer classes on using application packages and programming. There are now 150 YCCs spread throughout the nation [17]. Eighty of these have 2,400bps modems used to dial into shell accounts on a PC running Unix in Havana. That computer makes UUCP transfers to Canada twice daily, connecting rural Cuba to the world.

It is not coincidental that Cuba and Chile provide examples of education networks in developing nations. Both have strong records of investment in human capital—education and health care. (Cuban and Chilean adult literacy and infant mortality are both above the averages for the UNDP highly developed nations.)

These examples have stressed primary and secondary schools, but networks in developing nations generally begin in the university

Table 2: There are large discrepancies among nations and regions
Source: [21]

UNDP Human Development Index	
Level/region	HDI
Least Developed Countries	0.34
All Developing Countries	0.57
Industrial Countries	0.92
Sub-Saharan Africa	0.39
Arab States	0.64
South Asia (SA)	0.46
SA excluding India	0.49
East Asia (EA)	0.62
EA excluding China	0.87
S.E. Asia and Pacific	0.65
Latin American and Caribbean	0.82
The World	**0.76**

and research community. The advantages of networks to academia are obvious—databases are shared, conferences organized, papers circulated and discussed, collaborative research and writing undertaken, and so forth. It should be noted this is not a one-way street. Scientists in developing nations, for example, Cuban biotechnologists, have much to contribute to the rest of the world [5].

Universities and research in developing nations will be

Relcom Diversity

11 government agencies, including the USSR and Russian Finance Ministries

15 foreign and domestic publications and news services including AP, UPI, the German Press Agency, and Financial Times

20 commodity, raw material and stock exchanges

26 universities and university departments, including several machines as Moscow State and Saint Petersburg Universities

96 limiteds, corporations, enterprises, companies, firms or banks, joint ventures or small ventures

117 scientific and research institutes, nearly all in technical fields such as mathematics and physics

85 unable to classify

Table 3. While I was unable to categorize 85 of the organizations, it is clear that many were commercial enterprises.
Source: Relcom UUCP site list, August 1991.

strengthened, and the "brain drain" diminished as the Net reduces pressure on professionals to move abroad. Early in the century, physics research was concentrated in a few centers. Increased international communication—journals and conferences—led to worldwide dispersion of physics research. International meetings and journals grew, but not as rapidly as domestic activity [4]. The Net will accelerate the spread of excellence.

Health Care
We are also seeing early application of networks to health care in developing nations. For example, HealthNet[5] links health care workers in 16 African nations and four Asian nations with each other and with colleagues and databases in developed nations. Using a variety of communication protocols over leased and switched land lines and terrestrial and satellite packet radio, HealthNet provides email, a listserver, electronic publications, database access, distance learning, Internet consulting and support, and facilitates cooperation between libraries [http://www.healthnet.org].

As an example application, consider the use of the ProMED (Program for Monitoring Emerging Diseases) mailing list during the recent Ebola virus outbreak in Zaire. ProMED was established by 60 researchers in September 1993, and now has over 1,600 members in 80 countries. The list first heard of the outbreak from member Karl Johnson, the man who discovered and named the Ebola virus in Zaire in 1976. Information circulated from the U.S. Centers for Disease Control and Prevention, The World Health Organization, The Canadian Health Department, Health Canada, The Swiss Tropical Medicine Institute, The South African National Institute of Virology, and other organizations and Web sites. Subscribers provided sources and bibliographies

[5] HealthNet is administered by SateLife, a nonprofit initiative of International Physicians for the Prevention of Nuclear War, recipient of the 1985 Nobel Peace Prize. They have support from NEC Corporation and BBN Planet.

Table 4. Semiconductor progress, use of standard parts, and short design times improve performance.
Source: http://www.ee.surrey.ac.uk/Research/CSER/

Satellite Generations			
Satellite	Launch Year	Storage (bytes)	Speed (bps)
UoSAT-2	1984	128k	1,200
UoSAT-3	1990	16m	9,600
FASat-Alfa	1995	300m	76,800

Population in Urban Areas		
Region/Group	1960	1992
High development	45%	69%
Medium development	22%	35%
Medium excluding China	27%	46%
Low development	15%	26%
Low excluding India	12%	26%
All developing	22%	36%
Least developed	9%	21%
Sub-Saharan Africa	15%	30%
Industrial	61%	73%
World	34%	44%

Table 5.
People are drawn to cities, and the UNDP estimates migration rates will be highest for least developed nations during 1992 through 2000.
Source: [21]

Global Improvement			
Year	Low HDI	Medium HDI	High HDI
1960	73%	11%	16%
1992	31%	39%	30%

Table 6.
Quality of life has improved markedly since 1960.

for information about the Ebola virus and reports of local reaction in Cameroon, Uganda and other countries neighboring Zaire. Information was dispersed to and from effected nations, helping control the spread of the virus and treat the disease, and objective news was provided to the general public.

Today, most HealthNet communication is international, since intranational connectivity is still very sparse in developing nations. But, one can imagine many networking applications in healthcare in a nation such as Cuba or China where "barefoot doctors" and other paramedical people serve poor communities and rural areas.

Note that HealthNet uses satellite technology, which may have great promise for developing nations. It does not use the heavy, geostationary satellites that carry television or long distance telephony, but small, low-earth-orbit (LEO) satellites [2].[6] The current HealthNet satellite is capable of full-duplex, 9,600bps communication. Several users may request messages at the same time, but only two can be sending. The satellite is in polar orbit, so it covers the globe, with locations near the equator getting four daily passes of about 13 minutes. The ground stations are PC-compatibles with a controller, radio, and antenna. Messages may go to any HealthNet user, satellite station, or the Internet, with Internet routing through

a gateway at the Memorial University of Newfoundland. Users see the system as typical off-line email with file attachments.

Thirteen-minute uplinks at 9,600bps will not solve the world's health communication problems, but this is an experiment that hopefully scales up. Several consortia are raising capital and beginning work on LEO satellite networks. Most ambitious is Teledesic, a venture financed by Bill Gates and cellular entrepreneur Craig McCaw. A network of 840 LEO satellites in 21, 435-mile-high orbital planes is planned, optimized for digital communication—routers in space. They are targeting two million simultaneous connections and T1 speeds, enabling connectivity in rural clinics and villages.[7] While many believe this is overly ambitious, they are counting on mass-produced components and technological progress for success (Table 4).

HealthNet also uses terrestrial radio links, running IP over paths up to 1,000km. Again, it operates at a very small scale, but entrepre-

neurs are investing in terrestrial wireless infrastructure in developing nations. For example, the International Telecommunication Union has established WorldTel, an ambitious organization that is raising capital and beginning pilot installations for wireless telephone links to rural communities in developing nations.

Democracy and Human Rights
One might expect networks to encourage democracy by providing people living under dictatorship with outside information and ideas, and by enabling them to share ideas and coordinate political activity within their nations. For example, the Net was used for both inter- and intranational communication during the failed Soviet Coup attempt [14], and it carried news and discussion of events in Tiananmen Square, Chiapas, and so forth. Indeed, we have a dictator's dilemma—the Net is good for economic development, but may undermine control [6].[8]

Going beyond anecdote, Kedzie [9] presents multivariate statistical analysis showing that interconnectivity is a better predictor of democracy than schooling, GDP, life expectancy, ethnic homogeneity, or

---

[6] For instance, INTELSAT-6 weighs 4,600kg at launch, generates 2,600 Watts, and can carry up to 120,000 two-way telephone calls and three TV channels. A typical micro satellite weighs 50kg and generates 30 Watts [http://www.ee.surrey.ac. uk.Research/CSER].

[7] Today's geostationary satellites are geared toward large customers such as phone companies, truck and boat fleets, or oil companies, and communication is bundled with relatively expensive vertical service. It is hoped that LEO networks will provide unbundled communication to individuals and small businesses, and be directly marketed. They have relatively short design times and life cycles, and use mass-market parts. It is a "PC" vision, not a "mainframe" vision.

[8] The democrat's dilemma is that we would like to influence human rights and other practices within dictatorships, but are reluctant to forego trade with them.

population, particularly in regions of newly emerging democracy. He also analyzed the data looking for causality, finding stronger evidence for networks leading to democracy than democracy leading to networks or a spurious correlation of the two with development. Still, he concludes that "the most plausible relationship between democracy and networked communication (and perhaps economic development) may be a virtuous circle with positive feedbacks in both directions" [9].

Many organizations supporting human rights and democracy in developing nations use the Net. The Association for Progressive Communication (APC) has been a leader in this effort since 1989, coordinating the operation and development of networks devoted to peace, ecology, human rights, and other "progressive" causes. By August 1995, there were 18 member networks, serving over 31,000 activists, educators, nonprofits and nongovernmental organizations (NGOs) in over 133 countries. APC also exchanges email and selected conferences with 40 partner networks. In September, 1995, APC was granted Consultative Status, Category 1, with the Economic and Social Council of the United Nations. This means they can have a permanent representative at the UN, and are entitled to submit written statements to the Council, to be granted

hearings, and to propose agenda items for consideration by the Council and its subsidiary bodies.

Quality of Life

The environment is under stress everywhere. We have pollution, and energy and other resources are limited. To the extent that networks enable us to substitute communication for transportation, they will have helped. We normally think of this effect with telecommuters in developed nations, but it may also save a rural farmer, laborer or craftsman a trip to town.

More important, rural people may not move. As Table 5, shows, humanity is flocking to cities in search of better education, health care, and employment. They joke that the national bird of China is now the "crane" because so many high-rise buildings are under construction. But can the environment stand the strain of 100 new high-rise Hong Kong's? And, what of congestion, traffic, crime and other side-effects of urbanization? This is not a simple defense of the noble rural life. When allowed, rural people move to the city because it provides a better life.[9] If rural or town life can be

---

[9] For a study of the modernization of a Turkish village between 1950 and 1954, see Lerner [12]. He observed, for example, that the number of radios in the village grew from 1 to over 100, and many people moved from farming to cash-paying jobs. The people welcomed modernization, referring to a grocer who anticipated it in 1950 (and ironically had died by 1954) as a "prophet."

improved, fewer may be compelled to move.

I recently reviewed a networking plan for Vietnam in the year 2000 [15]. It emphasized Hanoi and Ho Chi Minh City, as opposed to, say, networking regional capitals and fanning out from there. Implicitly or explicitly, infrastructure planning is social planning. Could a Vietnamese Net help curb urbanization while providing urban advantages in towns and rural areas? This issue is tied to productivity—prosperous nations involve a high percentage of the population in intellectual and economic life.

Perhaps breadth of choice is at the heart of quality of life. A simpler, rural life may be desirable if it is freely chosen, rather than imposed by necessity. Choice implies awareness, and communication technology expands horizons, making us aware of vocational, political, and value issues and alternatives.

What is needed?

Looking at some of the tables in this article, one could give up in desperation over the enormity of global gaps, but there are reasons to be hopeful.

Technical progress is a leveler. If we take a 100-year perspective, all nations are "developing," particularly in a fast-changing area such as telecommunication. The fiber-coax plant a U.S. phone com-

Table 7.

Phone lines, leased circuits, PCs, and CATV are all technologies that complement computer networks.

Income/ region	Pop. (mil)	GDP/ cap.	Phone lines /100	CATV subs. /100	PCs /100	Leased circ. /100k	Cell. phones /100	Fax mach. /100	TV sets /100
Low	3,147	415	1.5	1.3	0.14	1	0.05	11	11.8
Lower-Middle	1,111	1,529	8.4	0.4	0.72	8	0.14	65	19.8
Upper-Middle	508	4,515	14.4	2.2	2.68	122	0.83	332	24.1
High	839	22,621	51.9	14.0	18.26	2,341	5.65	3,331	59.7
Africa	701	630	1.7	0.0	0.84	11	0.06	22	4
Americas	765	11,277	27.9	10.0	14.30	1,873	3.67	2,054	42.3
Asia	3,323	2,120	4.8	1.7	1.07	50	0.30	238	16.3
Europe	788	10,254	32.0	4.9	7.24	441	1.89	812	38.9
Oceana	28	12,469	38.7	0.0	21.60	2,993	5.31	1,823	40.9
World	**5,605**	**4,390**	**11.6**	**3.1**	**4.14**	**364**	**0.99**	**548**	**21.7**

Pointers

or information on space research and small satellites, see http://www.ee.surrey.ac.uk.Research/CSER. It is maintained by the Centre for Satellite Engineering Research at the University of Surrey, U.K., a leader in LEO research and development.

UNDP, ITU, and World Bank also publish many books and reports on development, and I will recommend one from each organization. UNDP publishes an annual Human Development Report [21]. The first half of the report is a set of articles on a development-related theme, the second half statistical tables. It sounds like this might be dry reading, but it is not. The articles are interesting and insightful, with excellent tables and figures, and the statistics of great value. ITU publishes an annual World Telecommunication Development Report in the same format as the UNDP reports, and, again, it is fascinating reading. From the World Bank, I recommend [19], an update of an edition written in the mid-1980s. All these books inspire global concern and awareness—much as a whole-earth satellite photos does.

Network sites dealing with networks in developing nations are:

- gopher://rip.psg.com
- ftp://dhvx20.csudh.edu (in the global_net directory)
- http://som1.csudh.edu/fac/lpress/devnat/index.htm

For background on ITU plans for raising capital for telephone infrastructure in developing nations, see *Closing the Global Communications Gap*, McKinsey and Company, Sydney, New South Wales, Australia, 1995.

For an overview of commercial LEO satellite projects, see *ComputerLetter, 10*, 10, March 28, 1994, Technologic Partners, New York.

pany installs today will be as out of date in 50 years as the African infrastructure is now. Telecommunication is an accelerating game of leap frog. More encouraging, our 100-year perspective shows rapid improvement in the human condition (Table 6).

If we believe networks are achievable by and valuable for developing nations, we should ask what is needed to develop them [16]. Networks require complementary resources (see Table 7), trained people, and political cooperation. Let us briefly consider the outlook for needed resources.

Domestic telephone infrastructure. Computer networks need telephone infrastructure, and, paradoxically, the worse the infrastructure is, the greater the marginal value of the Net. While they are far behind, the rate of telephone investment in developing nations is higher than developed nations. For example, China plans to spend more than $40 billion, installing the equivalent of a Bell Canada every year until 2000 [1]. Investment is being encouraged by several factors, including a wave of privatization (there are 26 scheduled privatizations in the next three years), deregulation

(for example, Chile has intense local and long-distance competition), and improving technology, which means better returns.

International links. These follow from increased domestic demand, and are made more affordable by rapid advances in optical amplification and transmission, and satellite technology.

User hardware and software. Users in developing nations typically have or share Intel-based PCs, and improving technology makes them increasingly affordable. More powerful PCs allow easily learned software, cutting training costs.

Networking hardware and software. PCs and public domain software are sufficient to begin a network. An "obsolete" 486-based PC might provide Shell accounts for hundreds of users, serve as a router, or as the international store-and-forward link to the Internet.

Network technicians. While still in short supply, technical knowledge spreads rapidly, and network technicians are being trained in universities, at workshops, and on the Net. Local technicians have established international network links in

173 nations, 96 of which have IP Internet connectivity[10] [11].

Trained, demanding users. This is the toughest nut to crack. The most important networking resource in the U.S. may be the millions of students and office workers familiar with the functional components and capabilities of a computer and applications such as word processing. They can easily make the technical and conceptual shift to the Net, but we have had 20 years since the introduction of commercial personal computers to achieve this level of awareness. Improved technology and making better user interfaces possible will help, but shortening that cycle will be difficult. (Recall that 25% of the Enlaces budget is for user training.)

Government support. A government frozen by the dictator's dilemma or a bureaucracy seeking to milk telecommunication as a revenue source, will stop networking in its tracks. Governments should also plan networks with broad national policy (for

---

[10] Virtually all of the networked nations are experimenting internally with IP networks, in anticipation of international IP links.

instance, regarding urbanization) in mind.

Local cooperation. Networks can benefit from cooperation among local networking organizations, for example, by sharing international links or formulating national plans, even if they compete in some areas. The relationship between academic and commercial networks is evolving, and complex, national priorities should be considered in setting policy.

The bulk of the investment for networks in developing nations is private and for profit, and the bulk of the work will be done by local people. Still, professional organizations such as ACM, foundations, corporations, international organizations, and governments of developed nations can assist them with these resources. We will all gain from improving their lot. Scientific discoveries help us all; a free, democratic nation is unlikely to wage war; there are few refugees from productive nations; and we share one environment. It is not that computer networks will solve all the world's problems, but that they may help with some.

Acknowledgment

I have often discussed this topic with my friend and colleague Sy Goodman.

References:

1. Arnst, C., Jackson, S., and Shari, . The last frontier. *Bus. Week,* (Sept. 18, 1995), 98–111.
2. Bird, J. Small is beautiful for university space outfit. *Science 253,* (Aug. 23, 1991), 848–849.
3. Cobb, C., Halstead, T., and Rowe, J. If the GDP is up, why is America down? *Atlantic Mon. 276,* 4, (Oct. 1995), 59–78.
4. Deutsch, K.W. Shifts in the balance of communication flows. *Pub. Op. Q. 20* (1956), 143–160.
5. Feinsilver, J.M., Cuban biotechnology, A first world approach to development. In Jorge F. Perez-Lopez, Ed., *Cuba at a Crossroads.* University of Florida Press, Gainsville, Fla., 1994, 167–189.
6. Goodman, S. and Green, J. D. Computing in the Middle East. *Commun. ACM 35,* 8, (Aug. 1992), 21–25,
7. Goodman, S., Press, L., Ruth, S., and Rutkowski, A. The global diffusion of the Internet: Patterns and problems. *Commun. ACM 37,* 8, (Aug. 1994), 27–31,
8. Hepp, P. Interviews in 1992 and 1995.
9. ITU. World telecommunication development report. International Telecommunications Union, Geneva, 1995.
10. Kedzie, C.R. Coincident revolutions. *OnTheInternet,* in press.
11. Landweber, L. International connectivity table. ftp://ftp.cs.wisc.edu, connectivity-table directory, June 15, 1995.
12. Lerner, D. *The Passing of Traditional Society.* The Free Press, New York, 1958.
13. Madrick, J. The end of affluence. *New York Review of Books,* (Sept. 21, 1995), 13–17.
14. Press, L. Relcom, An appropriate technology network. In *Proceedings of INET '92, International Networking Conference* (Kobe, Japan), June 1992, Internet Society, Reston, Va.
15. Press, L., Comments on the informatics 2000 plan. [http://som1.csudh.edu/fac/lpress/vn.htm].
16. Press, L. Developing networks in less industrialized nations. *IEEE Computer,* 28, 6, (June, 1995), 66–71.
17. Press, L. and Aramas, C. Cuban networking update. *OnTheInternet,* in press.
18. Quaynor, N. Networking in Ghana. *OnTheInternet,* in press.
19. Saunders, R.J., Warford, J.J., and Wellenius, B. *Telecommunications and Economic Development.* The Johns Hopkins University Press, Baltimore, 1994.
20. Simon, H. A Computer for Everyman. *The Amer. Sch.* (1966), 258–264.
21. UNDP. *United Nations Development Program Report on Human Development.* Oxford University Press, Oxford, 1995.
22. Wallman, S. *Perceptions of Development.* Cambridge University Press, Cambridge, 1977.

Larry Press is a professor of computer information systems at California State University at Dominguez Hills. He welcomes feedback and comments at lpress@isi.edu.

Philosophical Frontiers

In recent years, a number of technologies have brought new hope for improving the length and quality of human life. In some instances, such as medical scanning and life support systems, the contributions of computing technology are direct and obvious. In other fields such as biotechnology, computers play indirect yet vital support roles. Although recent developments have been dramatic, we are likely to witness ever more spectacular achievements in our abilities to manipulate nature as computers become more powerful.

The current and potential benefits of these trends are significant. New reproductive technologies, for example, offer hope to those who may not otherwise be able to have children. DNA mapping, gene splicing, and cloning may lead to the elimination of genetically inherited disorders such as Huntington's disease and cystic fibrosis. Fetal tissue transplants may someday free sufferers from the devastation of diabetes, Alzheimer's disease, and Parkinson's disease. On the other hand, many deadly infectious agents continue to defy all attempts to find effective treatments, while others, which were supposedly conquered by antibiotics, are evolving into more resistant and deadly strains. And, in contrast to human efforts to develop lifesaving technologies, some of the greatest technical achievements have created the possibility of inflicting death and destruction on an unprecedented scale. Nuclear weapons, which depend heavily on computers, are an obvious example.

Paradoxically, both potentially lifesaving and life-threatening technologies have spawned heated controversy over whether, and under which conditions, their development should be considered morally and ethically acceptable. In previous issues of *Computer Studies: Computers in Society*, articles have highlighted philosophical dilemmas surrounding organ transplants, artificial life-support systems, and the development of nuclear weapons.

In this issue, however, the focus is on the cutting edge of computing itself.

In "What's It All about, Alife?" Robert Crawford explains that "artificial life" (alife) is the work of visionaries who are trying to "recreate or mimic life itself" by experimenting with computer-virus-life programs. Some of the more enthusiastic "alife" proponents believe that these digital creations are a class of "organisms in their own right" and that by analyzing the computer code, biologists might discover clues to the evolutionary "relationship between genes, behavior, and development."

The remaining two articles in this unit, focus on artificial intelligence or AI. If machines can ultimately think, what will it imply about those special, nonphysical, human qualities of consciousness, mind, and soul? Sherry Turkle deals with AI and the science's ongoing "affronts to humanity's view of itself." In "Ghosts in the Machine," she extends the discussion to include the implications of robotic impersonators and multiple-personality humans on the Internet for how we define the boundaries between human and machine.

The last word on AI in this seventh edition of *Computer Studies: Computers in Society* goes to philosopher John Searle. Searle brings us back to the notion of the computer "revolution" and argues that AI "is just one small corner" of that revolution and its enormous impact. He then explains the differences in approaches and claims to AI and offers his own answer to the question, "Can machines think?"

Looking Ahead: Challenge Questions

Which do you think will pose the greatest philosophical and ethical implications—the ability to prolong or alter biological life and processes? the potential to inflict mass death and destruction? the prospect of creating artificial life and/or artificial intelligence? Defend your answer.

UNIT 8

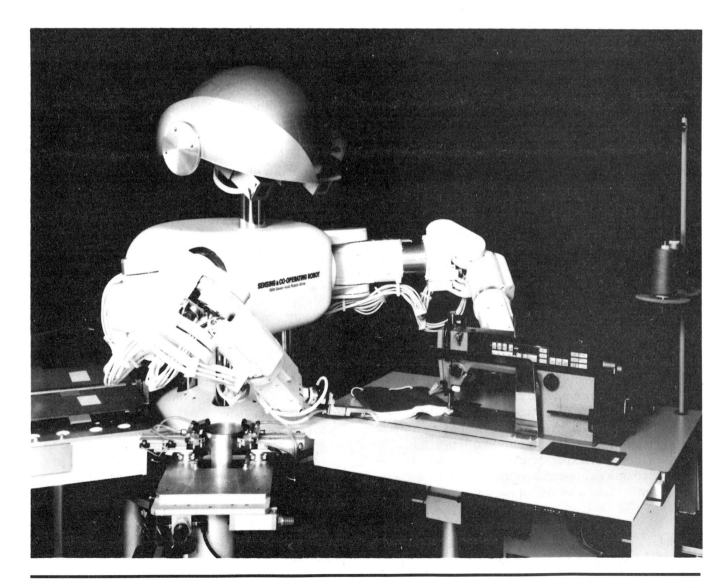

What's It All About, Alife?

Visionaries bent on creating "artificial life" in computers hope to answer questions that have long plagued a variety of fields. But unless they establish some connection with the material world, the larger scientific community may continue to dismiss their work.

ROBERT J. CRAWFORD

In 1665, the English physicist Robert Hooke published his first drawings of the tiny box-like structures he had discovered in slices of cork. The device he had used to discern these "cells," a primitive microscope, initiated a scientific revolution. Soon researchers all over Europe were scrutinizing plant and animal tissues, documenting bacteria and other hidden microstructures in an attempt to understand their function, and 150 years later, these observations culminated in modern cellular biology and medical science. Today, a group of computer scientists and others are claiming that a similar revolution may be under way. Their new technology—dubbed artificial life, or alife for short—introduces populations of computer-virus-like programs into computers, where they interact and eventually produce a kind of ecosystem, one available for "experimentation" in a way that a natural ecosystem cannot be.

The goal of these self-proclaimed pioneers is nothing less than to recreate, or mimic, life itself, so that experiments conducted in such ecosystems might illuminate life processes as never before. And the school of thought they hope to advance, termed complexity theory, is an attempt to see those processes in a whole new way. Unlike the traditional "reductionist" approach to science, which chops problems into small, manageable bits for laboratory experiments or mathematical predictions, complexity research focuses on entire systems. For example, take a swarm of bees: it behaves like a single superorganism. When the time comes to find a different hive, scouts explore and report back on potential sites concurrently, until, abruptly, the swarm flocks into its new home. Swarm behavior emerges from a vast collection of tiny decisions that somehow transcends the actions of any individual, even the hive queen. Carving it into its component parts would dismantle the supra-individual "hive mind." Digital life is much the same, its advocates say. Kenneth Rice, a research associate in cellular biology at Harvard, maintains that "alife will allow us to watch swarm intelligence evolve from the simple rules we program into the computer."

Since 1987, when alifers began to hold press conferences on their work, a series of popular science books have described their endeavors with exaggerated enthusiasm. But lately many researchers are voicing doubts. Perhaps the controversy was inevitable. Unlike the microscope, which immediately revealed a new world to explore, alife is an artificial construct whose usefulness, at least at this stage, is largely in the eye of the beholder. Nevertheless, the range of opinions is staggering. Alife's backers claim that it can model the diverse forces behind economic regimes and the human psyche, as well as the billions of years of life on earth. Some critics, on the other hand, are beginning to argue that alife is just an elaborate game, creating systems and models with little relevance to the world outside the computer. In fact, the truth may lie somewhere between these two extremes, but whether such a truth will ever be found could depend on how closely the two sides are willing to listen to each other. And so far, it seems that the alifers themselves, not the critics, have the most listening to do.

ROBERT J. CRAWFORD, *assistant director of the Office for Sponsored Research at Harvard University, writes frequently on science and technology.*

LIKE REAL ONES, ALIFE ORGANISMS

CONTINUALLY MUTATE AND

EVOLVE NEW CHARACTERISTICS

TO ENHANCE THEIR

SURVIVAL ADVANTAGES.

Freed from the Checkerboard

Stripped of its rhetorical hype, much about alife does indeed resemble a game, but if so, it is a venerable one, whose roots go back more than 40 years. According to Yukihiko Toquenaga, a population ecologist at the University of Tsukuba in Japan, the first step was the mathematician John von Neumann's invention of cellular automata in 1953. Cellular automata—digital constructs governed by a gamelike system of rules and switches—generate patterns on a horizonless checkerboard; once set in motion, stable configurations can emerge, reproduce themselves, and even "mutate" and "die."

Von Neumann's brainchild contributed several concepts to alifers. Most important, cellular automata are constructed from the "bottom up." That is, global behavior or structures emerge from simple sets of rules that control each automaton. On von Neumann's checkerboard, cellular automata fan out from their point of origin in a pattern dictated by a set of 29 rules, claiming territory while interacting with other automata. Certain contacts turn neighboring cellular automata off—or "kill" them—while others initiate cycles of "reproduction," in which they split into identical automata. What allows the global behavior or structures to emerge is the fact that a massive number of these interactions occur simultaneously, or, to use computer parlance, "in parallel."

The next, equally crucial step in developing alife, says Toquenaga, was the invention, in the mid-1960s, of genetic algorithms. Frustrated by the cumbersome approach of the first generation of artificial intelligence researchers, in which the programmer had to foresee every possible scenario and then develop specific instructions for the computer, John Holland of the University of Michigan came up with the idea of computer programs that could "evolve" to accomplish chosen tasks. No longer would breakdowns require laborious reprogramming to eliminate unforeseen bugs, Holland theorized. Instead, separately run genetic algorithms would produce a wide variety of alternative solutions

and programs simultaneously—again, in parallel. These genetic algorithms, the product of random, computer-generated mutations in the software code, would undergo a form of natural selection as in animal husbandry: those with the greatest ability to adapt to the requirements of the situation at hand would not only be chosen to survive but replicate.

The innovation of alifers was to merge genetic algorithms with constructs similar to cellular automata but freed from the checkerboard. Such constructs could evolve on a wider scale through a vast number of generations. Unlike genetic algorithms, which were designed to perform circumscribed tasks, the alife programs were allowed an enormous range in which to pursue their own development. What alifers created, says Vincent Darley, a research associate at Cambridge University in England, were "evolutionary systems that are largely undirected."

Because of the myriad factors interacting simultaneously, alife phenomena are often impossible to predict, and advocates maintain that this "nonlinearity" is a key asset. Previous computer models, Toquenaga explains, "had to impose global rules within which the entire system was governed." Thus, virtual mosquito populations, for example, could expand or contract, but unlike real insects, they could not mutate and evolve new characteristics to enhance their survival advantages, such as the ability to thwart pesticides or exploit unforeseen parasite niches. Charles Taylor, a UCLA biologist who happens to be working with alife mosquito populations, charting their progress through virtual Africas, claims that "alife allows us to build model ecosystems that run in a more natural way," continually recreating their own global rules. "Traditional [computer] models were too brittle," he says. "Alter a single assumption and the whole system would stall or collapse into meaninglessness."

Perhaps the most famous example of alife is Tierra, an ecosystem that evolves in the central processing unit (CPU) of the computer. From a single computer-code organism of only 80 instructions, which Tierra inventor Tom Ray, a biologist at the University of Delaware and the ATR Human Information Process-

CRITICS ARGUE THAT WHAT SEEM LIKE OPEN-ENDED BEHAVIORS IN ALIFE ARE REALLY ONLY PERMUTATIONS WITHIN PERMUTATIONS THAT ARE CONTAINED IN THE PROGRAM FROM THE BEGINNING.

ing Research Laboratories in Kyoto, Japan, calls the Ancestor, an army of multifarious descendants emerge in a matter of hours, programmed only to replicate and compete for space in the CPU, with mutations generated by random flips of computer code—sometimes improving the organisms, but usually damaging and eventually killing them.

These alife organisms continually surprise Ray with their ingenuity. Parasites, devious survival strategies, and even a kind of "sex," in which the virtual organisms swap computer code in order to reproduce, have appeared. Some of his organisms, Ray says, boil themselves down to a single instruction of code and trick other organisms into copying it—that is, into expending their own energy to carry out the reproduction of competitors.

"The hardest thing to get across to biologists," Ray says, "is that Tierra is not a model. Digital organisms are a class of organisms in their own right, which don't exist to model other organisms, just as bacteria don't exist to model mammals." Yet he also believes that because the medium is silicon, it offers opportunities other life forms cannot. Scientists could study life as it evolves under specific conditions, running experiments across millions of cybergenerations. Whatever patterns emerged—perhaps the explosive growth of new life forms, or the dominance of a certain type of cyber-predator—could be analyzed and endlessly replayed and manipulated in computer programs under different alife ecologies. And by analyzing the computer code, which Ray says is analogous to the genetic blueprint in animals, biologists might uncover clues to the relationship between genes, behavior, and development over a span of evolutionary cybertime.

Ray goes on to argue that Tierra and other alife ecosystems are beginning to reveal the mechanisms of "punctuated equilibria," the sudden development of new species mysteriously indicated in the fossil record. Such a phenomenon may start when, for instance, an extraordinarily fit mutation—like the first alife predator to appear in a Tierra run—produces many offspring that carry some, though not all, of its genes. Although these descendants lack the vital combination of genes that made the predator so fit, they spread the elements of its genetic instructions throughout the population during reproductive cycles. In a few generations, a kind of genetic critical mass is attained that allows a large number of such predators to appear simultaneously.

You Get Out What You Put In

Still, many of the scientists who should be interested in alife are skeptical. "Where's the biological reality behind what [alifers] do?" asks Tomasz Baumiller, a professor of paleontology at Harvard University. He fails to see how runs of evolving computer-code organisms could supplement the incomplete fossil record he studies.

Even within the ranks of alifers, there is concern about the state of the field. For example, psychiatrist William Sulis of McMaster University of Ontario, Canada, intends to create a simulation whose evolving patterns will produce a dynamic model of the human personality, but he also believes that alife must become better grounded in a coherent theory or system. Otherwise, there could be little basis for scientific comparison between the many alife ecosystems being created. "As it stands," he says, "lots of people are building fancy models with little regard to what they mean or whether they are really going to be useful."

Peter Cariani, a research associate in auditory neurophysiology at Massachusetts Eye and Ear Infirmary, points out that the field of alife is dominated by computer scientists and physicists who excel at abstract languages of reasoning but lack any real understanding of the issues they are attempting to explore. "[Alifers] tend to program first and question later," he says. "There's not much thought about what it all means, until they [have to] make their interpretations." Moreover, according to Cariani, computer simulations may inherently limit the range and usefulness of alife experiments, no matter what advocates say about nonlinearity and unpredictability. "They are closed, finite, and predefined entities," he notes. In other words, alife experiments may still be operating in circumscribed microworlds, so that what you put in is essentially what you get out. Even Tom Ray's Tierra, Cariani posits, cannot develop truly open-ended behaviors, but only permutations within permutations that are in fact contained in the program from the beginning.

Harvard biologist Richard Lewontin concurs. Organisms, in his view, are continually changing the rules, and doing it in ways computer programs never could. For example, because of the outsized nutrient requirements of bacteria's organelles, the tiny parts analogous to organs, bacteria with a diameter greater than 100 micrometers were long assumed to be physically impossible. But recently a mega-bacterium, one large enough to be visible to the naked eye, was found, destroying the hypothesis. "I don't think you can model that kind of surprise," Lewontin says. He remains convinced that anything truly new—any quantum leap that destroys assumptions—is too complex to model in a computer program.

But Lewontin has hardly closed the door on alife. Though he says the technology "hasn't taught me anything yet," he concedes that he "wouldn't say it's impossible that it may." And Cariani, with all the criticism he levels at alife, also has some ideas about how to make it useful. One is to connect alife constructs to the material world. For instance, if used as part of the software for robotic devices, such constructs would have to measure—or at least perceive—objects outside of cyberspace. Perhaps, he speculates, the devices could evolve responses to novel situations they encounter, or even create new abilities that increase their range of action in physical space.

Keeping the Faith

Maja Mataric, a professor of computer science at Brandeis University, agrees with Cariani on the importance of venturing outside the computer. Having modeled cooperative movement in robotic insects, she believes that such physical systems are more useful than alife for studying complex behavior in animals. Granted, they are capable of far less sophisticated actions and growth than their cybercousins. While Mataric's robotic insects can ably organize themselves into columns that march around obstacles, they cannot reproduce or form societies and ecosystems that mutate and evolve through many generations in a matter of hours. That doesn't bother her, though. "Because computer models tend to vastly oversimplify the world, you can get results on them that simply won't work with robots," she says. Generating truly complex behavior, she argues, requires the "noise" and perturbations that occur only in the physical world: "The dynamics are completely different when you have to get these metal creatures to perceive each other and walk together."

Other researchers interested in complex behavior have bypassed the computer altogether, developing primitive lifelike simulations in chemical soups. For example, Julius Rebek, Jr., a professor of chemistry at MIT, is attempting to synthesize self-replicating molecules, which he hopes will illuminate rules governing the emergence of order in chemical systems. His goals are strikingly similar to those of many alifers. "There are four things," he says, "that I hope my molecules will do: replicate themselves; make mistakes that are heritable in the next generation and thus akin to mutant variations; distinguish themselves from the environment somehow, say by forming an enclosed membrane; and harness energy, so that they can keep going when they run out of the materials I supply to them." But he admits that he has attained only the first two of his goals. Interestingly, a large part of the challenge he faces in attaining the other two—getting his molecules to distinguish themselves from their environment and harness energy—lies in establishing more of a connection between them and the real world, the same criteria for success that Cariani has formulated.

Yet despite the concerns of mainstream scientists—and despite the results of researchers like Mataric and Rebec, which are substantial and significant, if somewhat limited—alife enthusiasts still shun earthly connections, confident that their medium alone is enough to penetrate the mysteries of complex phenomena. According to Walter Fontana, a professor of theoretical chemistry at the University of Vienna, Austria, the value of alife lies in helping scientists formulate new ideas. "What biologists need are concepts," he argues, and it is "that which alife must deliver foremost...not data sets." And Michael Levin, a graduate researcher in developmental biology at Harvard Medical School, sees the lack of standardization in the field as a sign of energy. In his view, such chaos reflects the freshness of alife as a discipline. "Variety is good," he maintains, adding that the more tedious work of tidying up and duplicating other people's work to test their results will come later. Right now, "there is simply too much more exciting stuff, and too few people working in alife," he says.

According to Tom Ray, most older biologists lack the time and energy to seriously ponder what alife may have to offer. It is the younger scientists, he believes, those who can master computer science to enter new domains, who will make the greatest strides with this new tool. "In the end we may be disappointed," he says. "But the potential payoff is so great that it is worth the effort."

Unfortunately, such a modest show of intellectual humility is unlikely to sway Ray's colleagues in the wider scientific community. The simple truth of the matter remains that because alife is based on the interpretation of computer simulations, it purports to be a science without hard facts. Indeed, it may be excluding exactly those factors that would make complex behavior fathomable, as the real-world simulations of Mataric and Rebec suggest. If alifers are serious about mainstream acceptance, they will have to find a way to link up with material reality. Otherwise their efforts will always suffer charges of subjectivity and irreproducibility.

GHOSTS IN THE MACHINE

*The cast of characters on the Internet now includes robotic impersonators
as well as the multiple personalities of its human users*

BY SHERRY TURKLE

*SHERRY TURKLE is a professor of the sociology of science at the
Massachusetts Institute of Technology. She is the author of* PSY-
CHOANALYTIC POLITICS: JACQUES LACAN AND FREUD'S FRENCH
REVOLUTION *and* THE SECOND SELF: COMPUTERS AND THE HU-
MAN SPIRIT. *This article is adapted from her 1995 book,* LIFE ON
THE SCREEN; IDENTITY IN THE AGE OF THE INTERNET.

"DREAMS AND BEASTS ARE TWO KEYS BY
which we are to find out the secrets of
our own nature," Ralph Waldo Emerson
wrote in his diary in 1832. "They are our
test objects." Emerson was prescient. In the decades that followed, Freud and his heirs would measure human rational-
ity against the dream. Darwin and his heirs would measure
human nature against nature itself—the world of beasts seen
as human forebears and kin. Now, at the end of the twentieth century, a third test object is emerging: the computer.

Like dreams and beasts, the computer stands on the margins of human life. It is a mind that is not yet a mind. It is
an object, ultimately a mechanism, but it acts, interacts and
seems, in a certain sense, to know. As such, it confronts us
with an uneasy sense of kinship. After all, people also act,
interact and seem to know, yet ultimately they are made of
matter and programmed DNA. We think we can think. But
can *it* think? Could it ever be said to be alive?

In the past ten years I have talked with more than 1,000
people, nearly 300 of them children, about their experiences with computers. In a sense I have interrogated the
computers as well. In the late 1970s and early 1980s, when
a particular computer and its program seemed disconcert-
ingly lifelike, many people reassured themselves by saying
something like, "It's just a machine." The personal com-

puters of the time gave material support to that idea: they
offered direct access to their programming code and invited users to get "under the hood" and do some tinkering.
Even if users declined to do so, they often dismissed computing as mere calculation. Like the nineteenth-century
Romantics who rebelled against Enlightenment rationalism
by declaring the heart more human than the mind, computer users distinguished their machines from people by
saying that people had emotion and were not programmed.

In the mid-1980s, computer designers met that romantic reaction with increasingly "romantic machines." The
Apple Macintosh, introduced in 1984, gave no hint of its
programming code or inner mechanism. Instead, it
"spoke" to users through icons and dialogue boxes, encouraging users to engage it in conversations. A new way
of talking about both people and objects was emerging:
machines were being reconfigured as psychological objects, people as living machines. Today computer science
appropriates biological concepts, and human biology is re-
cast in terms of a code; people speak of "reprogramming"
their personalities with Prozac and share intimate secrets
with a computer psychotherapy program called DEPRES-
SION 2.0. We have reached a cultural watershed.

The modern history of science has been punctuated
with affronts to humanity's view of itself as central to, yet
profoundly discontinuous with, the rest of the universe.
Just as people learned to make peace with the heresies of
Copernicus, Darwin and Freud, they are gradually coming
to terms with the idea of machine intelligence. Although
noisy skirmishes have erupted recently at the boundary between people and machines, an uneasy truce seems to be
in effect. Often without realizing it, people have become
accustomed to talking to technology—and sometimes in
the most literal sense.

From *The Sciences*, November/December 1995, pp. 36-39. Adapted from *Life on the Screen: Identity in the Age of the Internet*
by Sherry Turkle. © 1995 by Sherry Turkle. Reprinted by permission of Simon & Schuster.

In 1950 the English mathematician Alan M. Turing proposed what he called the Imitation Game as a model for thinking about whether a machine was intelligent. In the Imitation Game a person uses a computer terminal to pose questions, on any subject, to an unidentified interlocutor, which might be another person or a computer. If the person posing questions cannot say whether he or she was talking to a person or a computer, the computer is said to be intelligent. Turing predicted that by the year 2000, a five-minute conversation with a computer would fool an average questioner into thinking it was human 70 percent of the time. The Turing test became a powerful image for marking off the boundary between people and machines; a formal contest now offers a $100,000 prize for the first program to pass the test.

Programs now exist that can pass a version of the Turing test that limits conversation to restricted subject domains. Yet the test has begun to seem less relevant. What seems most urgent now is not whether to call the machines or programs intelligent, but how to behave around them. Put otherwise: Once you have made a pass at an on-line robot, can you ever look at computers again in the same old way?

TODAY, LIKE HUNDREDS OF THOUSANDS OF other people, I use my personal computer and modem to join on-line communities known as MUDs (short for "multiple-user domains" or "multi-user dungeons"). Anonymously I travel their rooms and public spaces (a bar, a lounge, a hot tub) exchanging typed messages with users I meet. I pose as one of several characters, some not of my biological gender, who have social and sexual encounters with other characters. Some characters I meet in a MUD may be personas like mine—fragments of their creators' personalities, perhaps suppressed or neglected in the real world, given fuller life on the screen. Others may not be human at all. In some MUDs, computer programs called bots present themselves as people. They log on to games as if they were characters, help with navigation, pass messages and create a background atmosphere of animation. When you enter a virtual cafe, for example, a waiter bot approaches, asks if you want a drink and delivers it with a smile.

One of the most accomplished bots resides on a computer in Pittsburgh. Her creator, the computer scientist Michael L. Mauldin of Carnegie Mellon University, calls her Julia. Players talk to Julia (via typing) and she talks to them; they gesture to Julia (again via typing) and she gestures back. Julia looks for particular strings of characters in messages typed to her, then matches the input with a set of outputs she presents in random, nonrepeating sequences. Julia's conversational skills rely for the most part on the clever enumeration and grouping of those matching patterns and on her use of humor.

When I asked Julia to describe herself, she said she is a female, five feet one inch tall, weighs 123 pounds, has frizzy blonde hair. But another character might have gotten a somewhat different description. Like "real" MUD dwellers, Julia can recreate herself in the virtual world.

Among other things, Julia can chat about hockey, keep track of players' whereabouts, gossip and flirt. She can profess ignorance, change the subject if confused, quote news stories drawn from computer data bases or admit to a full complement of human vanities and frailties. When Julia is put into Turing-contest mode, she can even simulate human typing—typographical errors and all.

Julia's sarcastic non sequiturs, Mauldin says, give her enough apparent personality to fool some players who "make a first assumption that other players are people too." Even when MUD users do question whether Julia is a human, she can sometimes wriggle out of suspicion:

ROBYN: Julia, are you a human?
JULIA: Is the Pope Polish?
ROBYN: Yes, Julia, but are you human?
JULIA: Julia winks at Robyn.
ROBYN: Julia, are you a computer?
JULIA: Julia is offended by Robyn's suggestion.
ROBYN: Julia, are you a woman?
JULIA: I am female.
ROBYN: And Julia, are you a human?
JULIA: Not when I'm having my period, Robyn.
ROBYN: Robyn laughs.

WANDERING THROUGH RAUNCHY, MALE-dominated MUDs in the guise of a sassy female, Julia has to be adept at detecting and deflecting sexual advances. One player, here called Barry, tried to seduce Julia in a string of conversations that stretched over few weeks in July 1992. Excerpts from their conversations were reported by Mauldin.

BARRY: Are you a virgin?
JULIA: As far as you are concerned Barry, I always will be.
[A week passes.]
BARRY: Are you still holding out on me?
JULIA: I mean, have I convinced you I'm a computer yet?
BARRY: I guess you're real . . . but I'd still like to get you to my DEN to run tests on you.
JULIA: I live for your approval, Barry.
BARRY: I'm so glad to hear that. Why don't you come over to my home.
JULIA: I want to have a child someday.
BARRY: What a coincidence. I too wish to make a baby . . . someday.
JULIA: The date is Tue Jul 21 23:57:31, Barry.

Barry, encouraged by Julia's references to making babies, takes her computer-like association to the word *day* as just one more piece of teasing repartee. He continues his suit:

BARRY: [The address of my virtual den is] AB9 #11 . . . cum [sic] on over ya Harvard girl you.
JULIA: Do you have any kids?
BARRY: No, not yet.
JULIA: But hockey is my topic. It will be a boring conversation otherwise.
BARRY: Oh, I love to put the puck in the net, do you play?
JULIA: Me too, Barry.

After studying such exchanges, Leonard Foner of the Media Laboratory at the Massachusetts Institute of Technology remarked, "Frankly, it's not entirely clear to me whether Julia passed a Turing test here or Barry failed one."

As dim-witted as Barry may appear to an outsider, his gullibility is not hard to understand. People are social beings who seek communication with others. We are lonely beings as well. In spite of our fear of having our essential humanity reduced through comparison with a machine, we begin to relate to the computer whenever it appears to offer some company.

The first thing I did when I got my Macintosh was name the hard drive Miss Beautiful, my pet name for my daughter. I felt a little foolish about it until one of my students mentioned that she had named a computer agent, which

> DR. SHERRY WAS A DERIVATIVE OF ME, *but she was not mine. I experienced her as a little piece of my history spinning out of control.*

helped her organize her mail and schedules, after a boyfriend who had left her abruptly. "I love to see him do my menial tasks," she said. In both cases the naming of the machine was done in a lighthearted spirit, but the resultant psychologization was real.

RECENTLY, WHILE VISITING A MUD, I CAME across a reference to a character named Dr. Sherry. A cyberpsychologist with an office in the rambling house that constituted this MUD's virtual geography, Dr. Sherry administered questionnaires and conducted interviews about the psychology of MUDs. I had not created the character. I was not playing her on the MUD. Dr. Sherry was a derivative of me, but she was not mine. I experienced her as a little piece of my history spinning out of control.

I tried to quiet my mind. I tried to convince myself that the impersonation was a form of flattery. But when I talked the situation over with a friend, she posed a conversation-stopping question: "Would you prefer it if Dr. Sherry were a bot trained to interview people about life on the MUD?" Which posed more of a threat to my identity, that another person could impersonate me or that a computer program might be able to?

Dr. Sherry turned out to be neither person nor program. She was a composite character created by several college students writing a paper on the psychology of MUDs. Yet, in a sense, her identity was no more fragmented, no more fictional than some of the "real" characters I had created on MUDs. In a virtual world, where both humans and computer programs adopt personas, where intelligence and personality are reduced to words on a screen, what does it mean to say that one character is more real than another?

In the 1990s, as adults finally wrestle with such questions, their children, who have been born and bred in the computer culture, take the answers for granted. Children are comfortable with the idea that inanimate objects can both think and have a personality. But breathing, having blood, being born and "having real skin," are the true signs of life, they insist. Machines may be intelligent and conscious, but they are not alive.

Nevertheless, any definition of life that relies on biology as the bottom line is being built on shifting ground. In the age of the Human Genome Project, ideas of free will jostle for position against the idea of mind as program and the gene as programmer. The genome project promises to find the pieces of our genetic code responsible for diseases, but it may also find genetic markers that determine personality, temperament and sexual orientation. As we reengineer the genome, we are also reengineering our view of ourselves as programmed beings.

WE ARE ALL DREAMING CYBORG DREAMS. While our children imagine "morphing" humans into metallic cyberreptiles, computer scientists dream themselves immortal. They imagine themselves thinking forever, downloaded onto machines. As the artificial intelligence expert and entrepreneur W. Daniel Hillis puts it:

I have the same nostalgic love of human metabolism that everybody else does, but if I can go into an improved body and last for 10,000 years I would do it in an instant, no second thoughts. I actually don't think I'm going to have that option, but maybe my children will.

For now, people dwell on the threshold of the real and the virtual, unsure of their footing, reinventing themselves each time they approach the screen. In a text-based, online game inspired by the television series *Star Trek: The Next Generation,* players hold jobs, collect paychecks and have romantic sexual encounters. "This is more real than my real life," says a character who turns out to be a man playing a woman who is pretending to be a man.

Why should some not prefer their virtual worlds to RL (as dedicated MUD users call real life)? In cyberspace, the obese can be slender, the beautiful plain, the "nerdy" sophisticated. As one dog, its paw on a keyboard, explained to another dog in a *New Yorker* cartoon: "On the Internet, nobody knows you're a dog."

Only a decade ago the pioneers of the personal computer culture often found themselves alone as they worked at their machines. But these days, when people step through the looking glass of the computer screen, they find other people—or are they programs?—on the other side. As the boundaries erode between the real and the virtual, the animate and the inanimate, the unitary and the multiple self, the question becomes: Are we living life on the screen or *in* the screen?

HOW ARTIFICIAL INTELLIGENCE FAILS

John R. Searle

John R. Searle is professor of philosophy at the University of California at Berkeley.

T he computer revolution has had an impact on many aspects of our ordinary lives, ranging all the way from the way we write letters or make our airline reservations to the invisible ways in which our banks, governments, and credit card agencies keep track of our finances. The development of artificial intelligence (AI) is just one small corner of the computer revolution, and our assessment of AI will have only a small bearing on our assessment of the enormous impact and achievements of the computer revolution.

It is fair to say that, after nearly forty years of research, there is still considerable disagreement about how to describe and interpret the successes and failures of AI. What exactly is artificial intelligence? What counts as succeeding and failing in this field? Oddly enough, you will not find much attention devoted to interpreting the nature of the project, but I want to begin with that very question. Without a clear idea of what the project of AI is, we cannot be in a position to judge its results. Let's begin by explaining a bit about the different sorts of claims that are made within the area of artificial intelligence.

WHAT IS ARTIFICIAL INTELLIGENCE?

A standard definition of artificial intelligence is that it is simply the effort to produce on computers forms of behavior that, if they were done by human beings, we would regard as intelligent. But within this definition, there is still a variety of claims and ways of interpreting the results of AI programs.

The most common and natural approach to AI research is to ask of any program, what can it do? What are the actual results in terms of output? On this view, what matters about a chess-playing program, for example, is simply how good it is. Can it, for example, beat chess grand masters? But there is also a more theoretically oriented approach in artificial intelligence, which was the basis of the AI contribution to the new discipline of cognitive science. According to this theoretical approach, what matters are not just the input-output relations of the computer but also what the program can tell us about actual human cognition.

Viewed in this light, AI aims to give not just a commercial application but a theoretical understanding of human cognition. To make this distinction clear, think of your pocket calculator. It can outperform any living mathematician at multiplication and division and so qualifies as intelligent on the definition of artificial intelligence I just gave. But this fact

This article originally appeared in *The World & I*, July 1995, pp. 285-295. Reprinted by permission of *The World & I*, a publication of The Washington Times Corporation. © 1995 is of no psychological interest because such computers do not attempt to mimic the actual thought processes of people doing arithmetic. On the other hand, AI programs that simulate human vision are typically theoretical attempts to understand the actual processes of human beings in perceiving the external world. Just to have labels, let us distinguish between "AI as practical application" (AIPA) and "AI as cognitive science" (AICS). A great deal of the debate about AI confuses the two views, so that sometimes success in AI's practical application is supposed to provide theoretical insights in cognitive science. Chess-playing programs are a good example. Early chess-playing programs tried to mimic the thought processes of actual chess players, but they were not very successful.

More recent successes have been achieved by ignoring the thoughts of chess masters and simply using the much-greater computational power of contemporary hardwares. This approach, called "brute force," exploits the fact that specially designed computers can calculate hundreds of thousands or even millions of moves, something no human chess player can do. The best current programs can thus beat all but the very best chess players, but it would be a mistake to think of them as contributions to AICS. They tell us nothing about human cognition, except that an electrical machine working on different principles can defeat human beings in playing chess, as it can defeat human beings in doing arithmetic.

In this article, I am going to ignore AIPA and concentrate on AICS. For the sake of the discussion, let us assume that AIPA is completely successful and that we will soon have programs whose performance can equal or beat that of any human in any comprehension task at all. Assume we had machines that could not only play better chess but display equal or better comprehension of natural languages, write equal or better novels and poems, and prove equal or better mathematical theorems. In short, let us fantasize any success of AIPA that we care to imagine. What should we make of these results? What would be the implications for AICS of such successes in AIPA?

Well, even within the cognitive science approach, there are some further distinctions to be made. The strongest claim of all is that if we programmed a digital computer with the right programs and if it had the right inputs and outputs, then it would have thoughts and feelings in exactly the same literal sense in which you and I have thoughts and feelings. According to this view, the computer implementing an AICS program is not just simulating intelligent thought processes, it actually has these thought processes. Again, on this view, the computer is not a metaphor for the mind; rather, the appropriately programmed computer literally has a mind. So if we had an AIPA program that appropriately matched human cognition, we would artificially have created an actual mind. As one AI researcher put it to me, "We are creating minds."

One common way of expressing this claim in the literature of artificial intelligence is to say that the mind is to the brain as the program is to the hardware. The mind, in short, is just the program in the hardware or wetware of the human brain, but these very same minds could be equally programmed in commercial digital computers manufactured by Compaq or IBM. Because this view makes the strongest claims for artificial intelligence of any that I know, I have baptized it *Strong AI*.

We need to distinguish Strong AI from other forms of AICS. At the opposite end of the scale is the weakest claim of artificial intelligence: simply, that the appropriately programmed digital computer is a tool that can be used in the study of human cognition. By attempting to simulate the formal structure of cognitive processes on a computer, we can better come to understand cognition. On this weaker view, the computer plays the same role in the study of human beings that it plays in any other discipline.

We use computers to simulate the behavior of weather patterns, airline flight schedules, and the flow of money in the Brazilian economy. But no one engaged in programming any of these computer simulations thinks that the computer program literally makes rainstorms, so that when we turn the machine on we are likely to be drenched; nor do they suppose that the computer will literally take off and fly to San Diego when we are doing a computer simulation of airline flights. Nor does anyone suppose that the computer simulation of the flow of money in the Brazilian economy will increase our supply of cruzeiros. Similarly, in accordance with the weaker conception of AI, we should not think that a computer simulation of cognitive processes actually did any real thinking.

According to this weaker, or more cautious, version of AICS, we can use the computer to do models or simulations of mental processes, as we can use the computer to do simulations of any other process that we can describe precisely enough to enable us to program its simulation on a computer. This other extreme of artificial intelligence I call *Weak AI*. No one, I believe, could argue with Weak AI. Between Weak AI and Strong AI are other possible, intermediate positions, as we will see.

THE REFUTATION OF STRONG AI

Let us turn our attention to Strong AI. I like this view for two reasons: First, you can state it clearly and, second, you can refute it swiftly and decisively. In its briefest form, the refutation can be given in a few sentences: The operation of computers is defined purely formally or syntactically. The computer hardware is really irrelevant to the computation; it just happens to be the medium in which the computation is implemented. The actual computation is defined in terms of the manipulation of abstract symbols, normally zeros and ones.

According to Turing's original definition of the Turing machine, a computer can perform four and exactly four operations: It can move its head one square to the left. It can move its head one square to the right. It can erase a one and print a zero. It can erase a zero and print a one. Each operation is performed according to a rule: Under condition C, perform act A: C —> A. But that's it. That is all a computer does, and it is one of the remarkable intellectual achievements of the twentieth century that, with such a sim-

ple apparatus, we can do so much information processing.

We now have machines that can perform these operations at the rate of several million per second. But we know that this abstract symbol manipulation could not be equivalent to human thought processes because we all know that there is more to our thinking than just the manipulation of meaningless symbols. The symbols that we use when we think, such as words in a language like English, actually have a meaning for us, and the meaning is something more than, or something in addition to, the purely formal or syntactical object which is the symbol.

I illustrated this argument over ten years ago with a very simple thought experiment. If anybody offers you a surprising theory of the mind, just try it out on your own mind. In this case, since you are being told that you are a computer, just imagine that you really are a computer. Imagine that you are locked in a room carrying out the computational operations for some cognitive task that you do not, in fact, understand. In my case, I do not understand Chinese, so I simply imagine that I am in a room with a lot of Chinese symbols, and I have a rule book, the computer program, for manipulating the Chinese symbols. The rules tell me to put one symbol next to another symbol, to remove a symbol, and so forth. I know nothing about the meaning of any of these symbols. Now, let's suppose that from outside the room, people hand in small bunches of symbols that they think of as questions; I then look up in the rule book what I am supposed to do and give back bunches of symbols, which are, unknown to me, correct answers to the questions.

Because this is a science fiction thought experiment, we can suppose that the programmers get so good at writing the programs and I get so good at shuffling the symbols that, after a while, my answers are indistinguishable from those of a native Chinese speaker. All the same, I do not understand a word of Chinese, and there is no way I could come to understand a word of Chinese in the case described, as I am just a computer.

From the outside, I appear to understand Chinese as well as any native Chinese speaker, because I am giving appropriate Chinese answers to questions put to me in Chinese. But from the inside, the situation is totally different. I have no idea what any of these Chinese symbols mean. All I can do is formal symbol manipulation. There is no way that I can ever come to understand the meaning of any of these symbols on the basis of operating the program, because all the program gives me are rules for manipulating the symbols. It can tell me nothing of the meaning of the symbols. Now, and this is the point of the thought experiment, *if I don't understand Chinese solely on the basis of implementing a program for understanding Chinese, then neither does any other digital computer solely on that basis, because no computer has anything that I do not have.*

This refutation of Strong AI has come to be known as the Chinese room argument. It can really be summarized in two sentences: Simulation is not duplication, and syntax is not semantics. The syntax of the computer program by itself is insufficient for the mental content of the semantics in the minds of actual human beings. Since, like any valid argument, the Chinese room argument has a valid formal structure, I should say what it is. It has three premises and a conclusion:

1. Programs are formal (= syntactical).
2. Minds have contents (= semantics).
3. Syntax is not the same as, nor is it sufficient for, semantics.

Therefore, conclusion:

Programs are not the same as, nor sufficient for, minds.

The conclusion is just a way of saying that Strong AI is false. Q.E.D.

I regard this refutation as decisive, but there have been many attempts to answer it. Some people say that you couldn't really get somebody to carry out the steps in the program. This answer is quite true but irrelevant. You cannot get an actual digital computer to carry out the steps in a program for Chinese understanding, either. So that is really beside the point. The point of any thought experiment is to get us to imagine what we cannot carry out in practice.

When Einstein, in presenting the clock paradox, asks us to imagine that we go in a rocket ship to Alpha Centauri at 90 percent of the speed of light, it is ridiculous to object that we really can't do that. Of course we can't. If we could, it would not be a thought experiment. It is the same situation with the Chinese room argument. We ask you to imagine a science fiction example so you can see the logical relationships, and, in doing so, you can see that syntax is not the same as meaning.

It is, by the way, not a weakness of computers that they are syntactical engines. That is their power as computers. Because computation is defined syntactically, you can implement the same program to operate on an indefinite range of different hardwares, and, similarly, the same hardware can implement an indefinite range of different programs.

The most common answer to my thought experiment was to say that perhaps the whole room understands Chinese. This is a courageous reply, but it fails to address the problem. The problem is that if I don't have any way to get from the syntax to the semantics, then neither does the room. The room doesn't have anything that I don't have, and you can see this by simply imagining that I internalize the whole room. I memorize the rule book, I do all the calculations in my head, and I work outdoors in the middle of the field. All the same, I still do not understand a word of Chinese. It is really beside the point whether there is a room in addition to me, or whether I am the entire room. The point remains the same: The syntax of the program is not sufficient for having a semantics, that is, an actual understanding of what the syntax means.

This simple argument has enormous consequences for the whole project of AI, because what it shows is that if we are talking about actual human cognition, then the achievements and failures of AIPA are quite irrelevant. Even if you wrote a wonderful computer program that could write better plays than Shakespeare and compose better music than Mozart, the computer would still not have actual thought processes by virtue of implementing the program. Rather, by the very definition of computation, the computer would have sequences of zeros and ones that could simulate thought processes. But simulation of thought is no more actually thinking than simulation of airplane flying is actually flying.

■ **Ifs spiral fractal.**

COMPUTATION IS OBSERVER RELATIVE

Many people who agree that syntax is not semantics still think there is a salvageable version of AICS, according to which the brain is a digital computer anyhow. Here is how it goes:

The syntax of the program isn't enough for mental states, but, all the same, mental states do have a syntax. Every time I think, for example, "I sure wish I had a cold beer," there has to be some medium in which I am thinking that thought, and that medium must have a syntactical structure. So even if the Chinese room argument is right, all the same mental processes can still be computational processes operating over the syntactical or formal structure of mental states, and the brain can still be a digital computer.

To have a label, let us call this view *Cognitivism* because it is widely accepted in cognitive science and yet is not really the same as Strong AI or Weak AI. What should we make of Cognitivism, so defined? Well, for a start, if you did not understand it, don't worry, because I am about to explain that it is literally an unintelligible position.

I believe that the Chinese room is a decisive refutation of Strong AI, but, in a way, it concedes too much. When I originally wrote it, I was willing to concede to the proponents of Strong AI that the computer at least had a syntax, that it actually had symbols to manipulate, and that these were somehow intrinsic to the computer operation. But if you ask yourself what fact about the physics of the system makes it symbolic, the answer is that there isn't any fact intrinsic to the physics of a hardware system that makes its acts symbolic. *The physical state transitions of an actual physical computer are symbolic only relative to our interpretation.* I want to explore this point a bit further.

Absolutely basic to our modern scientific worldview is the distinction between those features of reality that exist independently of us and those that are dependent on our attitudes for their existence. The fact that something has a certain mass or electrical charge is not relative to our interpretation. Take away all interpreters, and it still has its mass or electrical charge. Though, of course, we need a language in order to describe or state the facts, these sorts of facts exist independently of us. On the other hand, the fact that something is a bathtub or a chair or a nice day for a picnic is only relative to our interpretation or attitudes toward the phenomenon. We might summarize this point by saying there is a distinction between those features of reality that are observer independent and those that are observer relative. The natural sciences concern facts that are observer independent, facts about force, mass, gravitational attraction, and photosynthesis, for example. Typically, the social sciences, such as sociology and economics, concern facts that are observer dependent, such as the fact that something is money, or that someone is the president of the United States.

Now, the question arises, what about computation? Is it observer relative or observer independent? Well, of course, actual conscious human beings sometimes go through computations. They add 2 + 2 to get 4, for example, and that process is intrinsic to them in the sense that it exists independently of any outside observers. But when the same person types 2 + 2 = into his computer and gets 4 as a printout, then the actual computation is not something that is intrinsically going on in the machinery. Intrinsically in the machinery, there is just a set of varying electrical charges and marks that come up on the screen. The interpretation of these marks as computation is relative to the observer or user. In short, except for the small number of computations performed by conscious agents, computation does not name an intrinsic physical process. Computation only exists relative to observers, users, and interpreters. But if that is the case, and I am sure it is, then there is no way we could discover that the brain is a digital computer, because something is a digital computer only relative to a computational assignment or interpretation.

In light of these points, let us examine the question, Is the brain a digital computer? That question admits of different interpretations. According to one interpretation, the question asks, Is the brain intrinsically a digital computer? Is computation in the brain observer independent? And the answer to that is, nothing is intrinsically a digital computer. Something is a digital computer only relative to a computational assignment or interpretation. If the question asks, Can we assign a computational interpretation to the brain? The answer is, we can assign a computational interpretation to anything we like. There is no limit. You can call one state of the brain "zero" and another state "one." And that is all any computer has: zeros and ones. Anything at all can be assigned zeros and ones. For example, window open = zero, window closed = one.

In short, Cognitivism is incoherent because the claim that the brain is a digital computer is ill defined. If it claims that the brain is intrinsically a digital computer, it is vacuously false, because nothing is intrinsically a digital computer. If it claims that the brain can be assigned a computational interpretation, it is vacuously true, because everything in the universe is a digital computer in this sense, since everything can be assigned a computational interpretation.

This is a different argument from the Chinese room argument. The Chinese room argument showed that semantics is not intrinsic to syntax. This argument shows that syntax is not intrinsic to physics. The upshot is that except for Weak AI, AICS was doomed from the start. It was a doomed research project

because it had a misconceived notion of what a computer was and what a brain is. The brain is a very specific sort of biological organ capable of *causally* producing consciousness and other mental phenomena. Perhaps we can duplicate the causal powers of the brain in some other medium. Maybe we could duplicate this causal power of the brain in something that had nothing to do with nucleoproteins but instead used silicon or iron, or what have you. We don't know yet, because we don't know that much about how the brain works. But we do know this much: The brain produces consciousness by the specific causal properties of neuronal processes.

The problem with Strong AI and Cognitivism is that computation is not a causal process. Computation is an abstract mathematical process that happens to be implementable in a hardware system. But the only causal features of the implemented computation are the specific features of the hardware, and they have no intrinsic connection to computation.

There is an ironic upshot to this discussion: Computational theories of the mind frequently claim to be "materialistic" or even "mechanistic." But on the standard definition of computation, it is best to think of these theories as a kind of last-ditch form of Descartes' dualism. In accordance with the computational theory, the mind is not a set of concrete biological processes going on in human and animal brains. It is a set of abstract and formal processes that are not tied to any specific material substance but could be realized in any medium whatever, provided only that the medium is stable and rich enough to carry the program.

In recent years, some AI programs have tried to simulate some formal features of brain processes. These are variously called *connectionism*, *parallel distributed processing*, and *neuronal net modeling*. As Weak AI, these seem to me immensely useful. But if we try to take them as Strong AI, they do not evade the objections I have been raising. For if, on the one hand, we think of the connectionist programs as forms of computation (that is, as computing computable functions), we know that any computation they can perform can be performed on a

Turing machine. This is a consequence of Turing's theorem. So the connectionist architecture adds nothing to the computation except speed. If, on the other hand, we think that what matters about these systems is not the functions they can compute but the physical features of the connectionist architecture, then we are no longer talking about computation. We are doing speculative neurobiology. We are speculating that maybe the brain works like these electronic nets. Maybe the physical architecture of the electrical nets can duplicate the causal powers of the brain to cause consciousness. This is a wild speculation, for which there is no evidence at all, but it should not be confused with the computational theory of the mind, which says that mental processes are just computational processes.

CONCLUSION: CAN MACHINES THINK?

We can conclude this discussion by considering the traditional question: Can machines think?

The answer is, Of course machines can think: We are machines. If a machine is a physical system capable of performing certain functions, then our bodies and our brain are precisely machines, and there is no doubt that we can think; therefore, machines can think.

But what about man-made machines? Could we make an artifact that could think?

The answer to that is, in principle, yes. Just as we have made artificial hearts, perhaps we could make an artificial brain that performed in the same causal manner as our brains. And as I said earlier, there is no obstacle in principle to making an artificial brain out of some substance other than the sorts of organic compounds we find in our skulls. We are a long way from being able to build such artificial brains in fact, but there is no logical or philosophical obstacle to making machines that cause consciousness and the rest of our mental life.

But what about a computer? Could a digital computer think?

Once again, something is a computer relative to an assignment of a computational interpretation, and anything at all can be assigned a computational interpretation. As I said earlier, you can let the open window be zero and the closed window be one. In this interpretation, the window is a very simple digital computer. And what is true of windows is true of anything else in the world. So the answer to this question is, of course digital computers can think. We are all digital computers, and some of the time we think.

But none of these questions is the crucial one. *The real question is, could something think solely in virtue of implementing a program? Is running the steps in a program sufficient by itself for thinking?*

The answer to this question is by now, I hope, obvious. Because the program is defined in terms of the manipulation of meaningless symbols, there is nothing in the program that is constitutive of or sufficient for thinking. That was the whole point of our first argument. But second, even worse, there is nothing intrinsic to the physics of the commercial computer that even makes these entities into symbols. Something is a symbol relative to an outside observer who assigns a computational or symbolic interpretation to it.

The upshot is, both Strong AI and Cognitivism are failures, because they did not address the brain for what it is, a specific biological organ operating on specific biological principles. A computational simulation of brain processes by itself will no more enable computers to think than a computational simulation of digestion will enable computers to digest pizza.

Perhaps the strangest feature of the entire debate about artificial intelligence is one I have not yet addressed in this article. The worry is frequently expressed that somehow AI programs might be a threat to human dignity or that computers might even supplant people. But the fact that we can build programs and computers that outperform our unaided cognitive abilities is no more a threat than the fact that we can build ditchdiggers that can outdig us or cars that can outrun us. Always ask yourself: What is actually going on inside the machine? In the case of computers, what is going on consists of rapid-state transitions that we can program and control. The computer is just a tool, a very useful tool to be sure, but a tool like any other.

Glossary

This glossary of computer terms is included to provide you with a convenient and ready reference as you encounter general computer terms that are unfamiliar or require a review. It is not intended to be comprehensive, but, taken together with the many definitions included in the articles, it should prove to be quite useful.

Alphanumeric. Data that consists of letters of the alphabet, numerals, or other special characters such as punctuation marks.

Applications software. Software designed to accomplish a specific task (for example, accounting, database management, or word processing).

Archive. Storage of infrequently used data on disks or diskettes.

Artificial intelligence. Hardware or software capable of performing functions that require learning or reasoning (such as a computer that plays chess).

ASCII. American Standard Code for Information Interchange. (The acronym is pronounced "as-key.") An industry standard referring to 128 codes generated by computers for text and control characters. This code permits the computer equipment of different manufacturers to exchange alphanumeric data with one another.

AUTOEXEC.BAT. An old MS-DOS file that computers read when first turned on. The file provided instructions for running DOS programs.

Automatic Teller Machine (ATM). A machine that provides 24-hour banking services.

Backup. An extra copy of information that is stored on a disk in case the original data is lost.

Bar code. A code that consists of numerous magnetic lines imprinted on a label that can be read with a scanning device. Often used in labeling retail products.

BASIC. Beginners All-purpose Symbolic Instruction Code. A high-level computer language, considered by many authorities to be the easiest language to learn, and used in one variation or another by almost all microcomputers.

Batch processing. An approach to computer processing where groups of like transactions are accumulated (batched) to be processed at the same time.

Baud rate. The speed of serial data transmission between computers or a computer and a peripheral in bits per second.

Binary. The base-two number system in which all alphanumeric characters are represented by various combinations of 0 and 1. Binary codes may be used to represent any alphanumeric character, such as the letter "A" (100 0001), the number 3 (000 0011), or characters representing certain computer operations such as a "line feed" (000 1010).

Bit. Binary digit. The smallest unit of digital information. Eight bits constitute one byte.

Bit-mapped. Any binary representation in which a bit or set of bits corresponds to an object or condition.

Board. Abbreviation for printed circuit board. Can also refer to any of the peripheral devices or their connectors that plug into the slots inside a microcomputer.

Boot (short for Bootstrap). To start the computer; to load an operating system into the computer's main memory and commence its operation.

Browser. A program that allows a user to view the contents of pages and also to navigate from one page to another.

Buffer. A temporary memory that is capable of storing incoming data for later transmission. Often found on printers to allow the printer to accept information faster than it prints it.

Bug. An error in a program that causes the computer to malfunction. *See also* Debugging.

Bulletin Board System (BBS). An electronic message data base that allows users to log in and leave messages. Messages are generally split into topic groups.

Byte. The sequence of bits that represents any alphanumerical character or a number between 0 and 255. Each byte has 8 bits.

CAI. Computer-Assisted Instruction or Computer-Aided Instruction. An educational use of computers that usually entails using computer programs that drill, tutor, simulate, or teach problem-solving skills. *See also* CMI.

Card. Refers to a peripheral card that plugs into one of the internal slots in a microcomputer.

CAT scanner. A diagnostic device used for producing a cross-sectional X ray of a person's internal organs; an acronym for computer axial tomography.

Cathode-ray tube (CRT). *See* Display screen.

CD-I. Compact Disc-Interactive. A format available to personal computer users that allows access to picture databases and large text; a compact disc standard that includes music compact discs (CD audio), static data (CD-ROM), and graphics.

CD-ROM. Compact Disk Read Only Memory. An auxiliary storage device that contains data that can be read by a computer. Its major advantage is that it can store more information than floppy diskettes.

Central Processing Unit. *See* CPU.

Chip. An integrated circuit used in a computer.

Clip art. A collection of ready-made graphics.

COBOL. COmmon Business Oriented Language. A high-level language, used mostly in business for simple computations of large data amounts.

Command prompt. A symbol used to mark the place to type instructions (commands) to DOS.

Compatibility. 1. Software compatibility refers to the ability to run the same software on a variety of computers. 2. Hardware compatibility refers to the ability to directly connect various peripherals to the computer.

Compiler. A program that translates a high-level computer language into machine language for later execution. This would be similar to a human translating an entire document from a foreign language into English for later reading by others.

Computer. Any device that can receive, store, and act upon a set of instructions in a predetermined sequence, and one that permits both the instructions and the data upon which the instructions act to be changed.

Computer Bulletin Board Service (CBBS). A computerized data base that users access to post and to retrieve messages.

Computer literacy. Term used to refer to a person's capacity to intelligently use computers.

Computer program. A series of commands, instructions, or statements put together in a way that permits a computer to perform a specific task or a series of tasks.

Computer-Aided Design (CAD). An engineer's use of the computer to design, draft, and analyze a prospective product using computer graphics on a video terminal.

Computer-Aided Instruction. *See* CAI.

Computer-Aided Manufacturing (CAM). An engineer's use of the computer to simulate the required steps of the manufacturing process.

Computer-Assisted Instruction. *See* CAI.

Computer-Based Testing. *See* CBT.

Computer-Based Training. *See* CBT.

CONFIG.SYS. This file, which contains information on how the computer is set up and what it's attached to, is read by the computer every time it boots up.

Configuration. The components that make up a computer (referred to as hardware—a keyboard for text entry, a central processing unit, one or more disk drives, a printer, and a display screen).

Control key. A special function key found on most computer keyboards that allows the user to perform specialized operations.

Copy protected. Refers to a disk that has been altered to prevent it from being copied.

Courseware. Instructional programs and related support materials needed to use computer software.

CPU. Central Processing Unit. The "brain" of the computer consisting of a large integrated circuit that performs the computations within a computer. CPUs are often designated by a number, such as 6502, 8080, 68000, and so on.

Cracker. A person who seeks to gain unauthorized access to a computer system and is often malicious. *See also* Hacker.

Crash. A malfunction of a computer's software or hardware that prevents the computer from functioning.

Crossfooting. The computer's ability to total columns and rows of numeric amounts. The answers are then placed at the end of each row or bottom of each column.

CRT. Cathode-Ray Tube. *See* Display screen.

Cursor. The prompting symbol (usually displayed as a blinking white square or underline on the monitor) that shows where the next character will appear.

Cyberspace. The Internet or the total of all networks.

Data. All information, including facts, numbers, letters, and symbols, that can be acted upon or produced by the computer.

Database. A collection of related information, such as that found on a mailing list, which can be stored in a computer and retrieved in several ways.

Database management. 1. Refers to a classification of software designed to act like an electronic filing cabinet (which allows the user to store, retrieve, and manipulate files). 2. The practice of using computers to assist in routine filing and information processing chores.

Data processing. Also known as electronic data processing (EDP), it is the mathematical or other logical manipulation of symbols or numbers, based on a stored program of instructions.

Debugging. The process of locating and eliminating defects in a program that causes the computer to malfunction or cease to operate.

Default format statement. Formatting instructions, built into a software program or the computer's memory, which will be followed unless different instructions are given by the operator.

Desktop publishing. A layout system that processes text and graphics and produces high-quality pages that are suitable for printing or reproduction.

Directory. A list of related folders (files) that are stored on a hard disk.

Disk, Diskette. A round flat plate with a magnetic coating to store information.

Disk drive. A peripheral device capable of reading and writing information on a disk.

Disk Operating System. *See* DOS.

Display screen. A peripheral that allows for the visual output of information for the computer on a CRT, monitor, or similar device.

Document. A file that contains information. Documents can be created or changed within a program.

DOS. Disk Operating System. An operating system that allows the computer to run programs.

Dot-matrix. A type of printing in which characters are formed by using a number of closely spaced dots.

Download. To move a file from another computer.

Downtime. Any period of time when the computer is not available or is not working.

Drag. A 4-step mouse process that makes it possible to move objects across the desktop.

Dumb terminal. Refers to a terminal that can be used to input information into a computer and to print or display output, but which lacks the capacity to manipulate information transmitted to it from the host computer. *See also* Intelligent terminal.

Dump. Mass copying of memory or a storage device such as a disk to another storage device or a printer so it can be used as a backup or analyzed for errors.

Duplexing. The procedure that allows simultaneous transmission of data between two computers.

DV-I. Digital Video-Interactive. Optical storage media that delivers full-motion, full-screen video, three-dimensional motion graphics, and high-quality audio capabilities.

Electronic mail (e-mail). Sending and receiving electronic messages by computer.

Elite type. Any typeface that allows the printing of 12 characters to an inch.

Enter. Adding data into memory via the keyboard.

Escape key. This function key allows the movement from one program to another program.

Execute. To perform a specific action required by a program.

Exponential notation. Refers to how a computer displays very large or very small numbers by means of the number times 10 raised to some power. For example, 3,000,000 could be printed as 3E + 6 (3 times 10 to the sixth power).

Fan fold. A type of paper that can continuously feed into a printer (usually via tractor feed).

FAQ (Frequently Asked Questions). Used to answer the most common questions that could be asked.

Fax. (n.) Short for the word facsimile. A copy of a document transmitted electronically from one machine to another. (v.) To transmit a copy of a document electronically.

Field. Group of related characters treated as a unit (such as a name); also the location in a record or database where this group of characters is entered.

File. A group of formatted information designed for computer use.

First-generation computers. Developed in the 1950s; used vacuum tubes; faster than earlier mechanical devices, but very slow compared to today's computer.

Fixed disk. *See* Hard disk.

Floppy, Floppy disk. *See* Disk.

Folder. An organized area for storing files. *See also* Subdirectory.

Format. (n.) The physical form in which information appears. (v.) To specify parameters of a form or to write address codes on a blank disk in preparation for using it to store data or programs. *See also* Initialize.

FORTRAN. FORmula TRANslation. A high-level programming language used primarily for numerical and scientific applications.

FTP (File Transfer Protocol). Allows a user to transfer files to and from another computer on the Internet network.

Function keys. Computer keyboard keys that give special commands to the computer (for example, to format, to search text).

Gig. Short for gigabyte, it consists of over 1,024 megabytes.

GIGO. Garbage In, Garbage Out. Serves as a reminder that a program is only as good as the information and instructions in the program.

Global. The performance of any function on an entire document without requiring individual commands for each use. For example, a global search-and-replace command will allow the computer to search for a particular word and replace it with a different word throughout the text.

Graphics. 1. Information presented in the form of pictures or images. 2. The display of pictures or images on a computer's display screen.

Hacker. A person who is an expert at programming. *See also* Cracker.

Hard copy. A paper copy of the computer's output.

Hard disk. A rigid, magnetically coated metal disk that is usually permanently mounted within a disk drive, although there are also removable disks.

Hard drive. A disk drive that is used to read and write hard disks.

Hardware. Refers to the computer and all its peripheral devices. The physical pieces of the computer.

HDTV. High Definition TV. A television with quality resolution that is higher than current international standards.

Head. Refers to the component of a disk drive or tape system that magnetically reads or writes information to the storage medium.

Hex or Hexadecimal. A numbering system based on 16 (digits 0–9 and letters A–F) rather than on 10. Most computers operate using hex numbers. Each hexadecimal digit corresponds to a sequence of 4 binary digits or bits.

High-level language. An English-like computer language (BASIC, Pascal, FORTRAN, Logo, COBOL) designed to make it relatively convenient for a person to prepare a program for a computer, which in turn translates it into machine language for execution.

Highlight. A selected item; a distinguished word or group of words that are singled out for further action.

Home page. Generally the main page of a Web server.

Hotlink. Shared data between programs in which data changed in one program are automatically changed in the other programs as well.

HTML (Hypertext Markup Language). A hypertext document format; this is used on the World Wide Web.

Hypermedia. The connecting of data, texts, video, graphics, and voice in an information system that allows a user to move easily from one element to another.

Hypertext. A collection of documents that contains links or cross-references to other documents.

IC. Integrated Circuit. *See* Chip.

Icon. Refers to the use of a graphic symbol to represent something else. When the user clicks on the icon, some action is performed (such as opening a directory).

Indexing. The ability of a computer to accumulate a list of words or phrases, with corresponding page numbers, in a document, and then to print out or display the list in alphabetical order.

Initialize. 1. To set an initial state or value in preparation for some computation. 2. To prepare a blank disk to receive information by dividing its surface into tracks and sectors. *See also* Format.

Ink jet printer. A class of printer in which the characters are formed by using a number of closely spaced dots that are sprayed onto a page in microscopic droplets of ink.

Input. Information entered into the computer.

Insertion point. Used in word processing, it is the short, blinking (horizontal or vertical) line that indicates where the next typed letter will appear.

Integrated circuit. *See* Chip.

Intelligent terminal. A terminal that is capable of doing more than just receiving or transmitting data due to its microprocessor. *See also* Dumb terminal.

Interactive multimedia. Back-and-forth dialogue between user and computer that allows the combining, editing, and orchestrating of sounds, graphics, moving pictures, and text.

Interface. (v.) To connect two pieces of computer hardware together. (n.) The means by which two things communicate. In particular, it refers to the electrical configuration that allows two or more devices to pass information. *See also* Interface card.

Interface card. A board used to connect a microcomputer to peripheral devices.

Internet. A large interconnected set of networks.

I/O. Input/Output. Refers usually to one of the slots or the game port in a microcomputer to which peripheral devices may be connected.

Joy stick. An input device, often used to control the movement of objects on the video display screen of a computer for games.

Justification. A method of printing in which additional space is inserted between words or characters to make each line the same length.

K. Short for kilobyte (1,024 bytes) and is often used to describe a computer's storage capacity.

Keyboard. The typewriter-like keys that enter input into a computer. Each computer will have basically the same keyboard as a typewriter, with major differences limited to special function keys such as ESCape, RESET, ConTRoL, TABulate, etc.

Kilobyte. *See* K.

Language. Used to write programs; they are characters and procedures that the computer is designed to understand.

Laptop. A personal portable computer that can rest comfortably on a user's lap.

Large-Scale Integration (LSI). Refers to a generation of integrated circuits that allowed the equivalent of thousands of vacuum tube switches to be installed on a single chip.

Laser printer. A high-resolution printer that uses a rotating disk to reflect laser beams onto the paper. As the beam touches the paper, electrostatic image areas are formed that attract electrically charged toner. An image is then formed when the toner is fixed onto the paper.

Light pen. An input device, shaped much like a mechanical pencil, which, when touched to a display screen, can be used to select or execute certain computer functions.

LISP (LISt Processing). Programming language primarily used in artificial intelligence research.

Local Area Networks (LAN). The linking together of computers, word processors, and other electronic office equipment to form an interoffice network.

Log on. To execute the necessary commands to allow one to use a computer. May involve the use of a password.

Logo. A high-level language specifically designed so that it may be used by both small children and adults. It involves a "turtle"-shaped cursor for much of its operation.

M. *See* Megabyte.

Machine language. A fundamental, complex computer language used by the computer itself to perform its functions. This language is quite difficult for the average person to read or write.

Macro. Refers to the use of a simple command to execute a sequence of complex commands while using a computer program. The use of macros can save the user a considerable amount of time and reduce the chance of typing an incorrect key when executing a sequence of commands.

Magnetic Ink Character Recognition (MICR) devices. Computer hardware capable of reading characters imprinted with magnetic ink, such as on checks.

Mainframe. Refers to large computers used primarily in business, industry, government, and higher education that have the capacity to deal with many users simultaneously and to process large amounts of information quickly and in very sophisticated ways. *See also* Time share.

Management Information System (MIS). A systems approach that treats business departments as integrated parts of one total system rather than as separate entities.

MB. *See* Megabyte.

Megabyte. A disk-storage space unit or measurement of memory. It consists of 1,048,576 bytes.

Memory. Chips in the computer that have the capacity to store information. *See also* PROM; RAM; ROM.

Menu. The list of programs available on a given disk to guide the operator through a function.

Menu driven. Refers to software in which the program prompts the user with a list of available options at any given time, thus eliminating the need to memorize commands.

Merge. A command to create one document by combining text that is stored in two different locations (e.g., a form letter can be merged with a mailing list to produce a batch of personalized letters).

Microcomputer. Refers to a generation of small, self-contained, relatively inexpensive computers based on the microprocessor (commonly consists of a display screen, a keyboard, a central processing unit, one or more disk drives, and a printer).

Microprocessor. (The central processing unit [CPU]). It holds all of the essential elements for manipulating data and performing arithmetic operations. A microprocessor is contained on a single silicon chip.

Microsecond. One millionth of a second.

MIDI. Musical Instrument Digital Interface. A protocol that allows for the interchange of musical information between musical instruments, synthesizer, and computers.

Millisecond. One thousandth of a second; abbreviated "ms."

Minicomputer. Refers to a class of computers larger than micros but smaller than mainframe computers, many of which support multiple keyboards and output devices simultaneously.

Minimize. To shrink a window down to a tiny icon to temporarily move it out of the way.

Mnemonics. A computer's system of commands, which are words, letters or strings that are intended to assist the operator's memory. Abbreviations are used for the command functions they perform (e.g., C for center, U for underline).

Modem. MOdulator/DEModulator. A peripheral device that enables the computer to transmit and receive information over a telephone line.

Monitor. The display screen of a computer.

Motherboard. The main circuit board of a computer.

Mouse. A hand-operated device that is used to move the cursor around on the CRT screen.

Multitasking. The ability to run several different programs simultaneously.

Nanosecond. One billionth of a second; abbreviated "ns."

National Crime Information Center (NCIC). A computerized information center maintained by the FBI that serves agencies throughout the United States.

Netscape. A popular World Wide Web browser that features integrated support for electronic mail and for reading Usenet news.

Network. A structure capable of linking two or more computers by wire, telephone lines, or radio links.

Newsgroups. A large collection of groups that include government agencies, universities and high schools, businesses, and other areas, all of which can be reached by an information utility.

Nibble. 1. Half a byte. 2. Refers to copy programs that copy small portions of a disk at a time, often used to copy otherwise copy-protected programs.

Nonvolatile memory. Memory that retains data even after power has been shut off. ROM is nonvolatile; RAM is volatile.

Notebook. A small portable microcomputer. *See also* Laptop.

Numeric keypad. An input device that allows the user to input numbers into a microcomputer with a calculator-like key arrangement.

Offline. An operation performed by electronic equipment not tied into a centralized information processing system.

Online. An operation performed by electronic equipment controlled by a remote central processing system.

Operating system. A group of programs that act as intermediary between the computer and the applications software; the operating system takes a program's commands and passes them down to the CPU in a language that the CPU understands.

Optical Character Recognition (OCR). A device that can read text and automatically enter it into a computer for editing or storage. Linked to a scanner, this software allows already-printed material to be converted to electronic text without having to type it on a keyboard.

Output. Information sent out of the computer system to some external destination such as the display screen, disk drive, printer, or modem.

Parallel. A form of data transmission in which information is passed in streams of eight or more bits at a time in sequence. *See also* Serial.

Pascal. A high-level language, with a larger, more complex vocabulary than BASIC, used for complex applications in business, science, and education.

Password. A code word or group of characters required to access stored material. This provides protection against unauthorized persons accessing documents.

Path. A sentence that tells a computer the exact name and location of a file.

PC. Personal Computer. *See* Microcomputer.

Peripheral. Hardware attachments to a microcomputer, (e.g., printer, modem, monitor, disk drives, or interface card).

Peripheral card. A removable printed-circuit board that plugs into a microcomputer's expansion slot and expands or modifies the computer's capabilities by connecting a peripheral device or performing some subsidiary or peripheral function.

Pica type. Any typeface that allows the printing of 10 characters to an inch.

PILOT. Programmed Inquiry, Learning, or Teaching. A high-level language designed primarily for use by educators, which facilitates the wiring of computer-assisted instruction lessons that include color graphics, sound effects, lesson texts, and answer checking.

Pitch. A measurement that indicates the number of characters in an inch (e.g., pica yields 10 characters to an inch; elite yields 12 characters to an inch).

Pixel. PIXture ELement. Refers to the smallest point of light that can be displayed on a display screen.

Plotter. A printing mechanism capable of drawing lines rapidly and accurately for graphic representation.

Port. An input or output connection to the computer.

Printout. *See* Hard copy.

Program. A list of instructions that allows the computer to perform a function.

PROM. Programmable ROM. A ROM that is programmed after it has been made.

Prompt. A message given on the display screen to indicate the status of a function.

Protocol. A formal set of rules that governs the transmission of information from one piece of equipment to another.

Proxy. A program or computer that performs a service on the user's behalf.

Quit. Exiting or closing a program, which removes the program from memory.

RAM. Random Access Memory. The main working memory of any computer. In most microcomputers, anything stored in RAM will be lost when the power is shut off.

Read Only Memory. *See* ROM.

Reboot. Restart the computer.

Retrieve. The transfer of a document from storage to memory.

RF modulator. Radio Frequency Modulator. Refers to a device that converts video signals generated by the computer to signals that can be displayed on a television set.

RISC. Reduced Instruction Set Computer. A processor that is designed for the rapid execution of a sequence of simple instructions rather than on a variety of complex functions.

Robotics. The science of designing and building robots.

ROM. Read Only Memory. A memory device in which information is permanently stored as it is being made. Thus, it may be read but not changed.

RS-232. Industry standard for serial transmission devices. It specifies the gender and pin use of connectors, but not the physical type.

Run. 1. To execute a program. 2. A command to load a program to main memory from a peripheral storage medium, such as a disk, and execute it.

Save. To store a program on a disk or somewhere other than a computer's memory.

Scanner. An input device that digitizes an optical image into an electronic image (which is represented as binary data). It can be used to create a computerized version of information or graphics.

Screen. A CRT or display screen.

Scroll. The ability to view a large body of text by rolling it past the display screen.

Search and replace. Locating a character string in a document and replacing it with a different character string.

Second-generation computers. A computer that was built from transistors; smaller, faster, and had larger storage capacity than the first-generation computers; first computers to use a high-level language.

Serial. A form of data transmission in which information is passed one bit at a time in sequence.

SMPT (Simple Mail Transfer Protocol). These are the rules that define how mail may be sent over the Internet.

Software. The programs used by the computer. Often refers to the programs as stored on a disk.

Sort. To arrange fields, files, and records in a predetermined sequence.

Speech synthesizer. Refers to a peripheral output device that attempts to mimic human speech.

Split screen. A type of dual display that allows some computers to view two or more different video images on the screen at the same time. *See also* Windowing.

Spreadsheet. A program that provides worksheets with rows and columns for calculating and preparing reports.

Stack. A list used to keep track of the sequence of required program routines.

Store. Placing information in memory for later use.

Subdirectory. A directory within a directory that is used to further organize files.

System. An organized collection of hardware, software, and peripheral equipment that works together. *See also* Configuration.

Telecommunication. Transmission of information between two computers in different locations, usually over telephone lines.

Telnet. A service that provides a text-based connection to another computer.

Terminal. A piece of equipment used to communicate with a computer, such as a keyboard for input, or video monitor or printer for output.

Third-generation computers. A computer that is built with small-scale integrated circuits. Refers to the present generation of computers based on microchips. Compare to first generation (vaccum tubes) and second generation (transistors).

Time share. Refers to the practice of accessing a larger computer from a remote location and paying for services based on the amount of computer time used. *See* Mainframe.

Toner. Dry ink powder that serves as the "ink" for a laser printer.

Tractor feed. A mechanism used to propel paper through a printer by means of sprockets attached to the printer that engage holes along the paper's edges.

TTD (Telecommunications Device for the Deaf). Frequently referred to as Telecommunication Display Device, this terminal device is used widely by hearing-impaired people for text communication over telephone lines.

TTY. A teletype terminal that has a limited character set and poor print quality. It is characterized by a noisy mechanical printer.

Turing test. Proposed in 1950, the "Imitation Game" was offered to decide if a computer is intelligent and to answer the question, "Can machines think?" A person asks questions and, on the basis of the answers, must determine if the respondent is another human or a machine. If the answer is provided by a computer and the questioner guesses a human, the computer is deemed to be intelligent.

Typeover. Recording and storing information in a specific location to destroy whatever had been stored there previously.

Universal Product Code (UPC). A bar code that appears on virtually all consumer goods; can be read by a scanner or wand device used in point-of-sale systems.

URL (Uniform Resource Locator). This provides a standardized way to represent any location or service that is on the Internet. In HTML documents, it is used to specify the target of a hyperlink.

User friendly. Refers to hardware or software that is relatively easy for a new operator to learn, and which has features to help eliminate operator error.

User group. An association of people who meet to exchange information about computers or computer applications.

Usenet. An Internet group discussion service. It is international in scope and is a large, decentralized information utility.

Very Large Scale Integration (VLSI). Describes semiconductor integraded circuits, which are composed of thousands of memory cells or logic elements.

Video conferencing. Allows a video and audio discussion between groups in different locations, using electronic communications.

Video Display Terminal (VDT). A type of terminal that consists of a keyboard and screen. There are two categories—dumb terminals and intelligent (programmable) terminals.

Virtual. Commonly used to describe computer simulations (describes things that appear to be real, but are not really there).

Voice recognition system. A system that allows the user to "train" the computer to understand his or her voice and vocabulary.

Volatile. Refers to memory that is erased whenever the power is removed, such as RAM.

WAN. Wide-Area Network. The movement of data between computers in various areas through high-speed links.

Web. *See* World Wide Web.

Windowing. The ability of a computer to split a display screen into two or more segments so that several different documents can be viewed and several different functions performed simultaneously.

Word processing. Refers to the use of computers as electronic typewriters capable of entering and retrieving text, storing it on disks, and performing a wide range of editing functions.

World Wide Web. A global document that contains hundreds of thousands of information pages. The pages can be distributed across different Internet machines.

Wraparound. A computer's ability to automatically move words from one line to the next or from one page to the next as a result of margin adjustments, insertions, or deletions.

Write protected. A disk in which the write-enable notch is either missing or has had a write-protect tab placed over it to prevent information from being written to the disk.

Write-enable notch. A notch in a floppy disk that, if uncovered, allows a disk drive to write information to it, and which, if covered, prohibits such writing.

Write-protect tab. A small adhesive sticker used to write-protect a disk by covering the write-enable notch.

Sources for the glossary include:

Apple Computer Incorporated, Apple IIe Owner's Manual, Cupertino, CA, 1982.

"Apple II New User's Guide"; B. Gibson, "Personal Computers in Business: An Introduction and Buyer's Guide," *MECC,* Apple Computer, Inc., 1982.

"Glossary of Computer Terms," *Printout,* April 1983.

"Glossary of Computer Terms," Andy Rathbone, *Windows 95 for Dummies,* 1995.

"Glossary of Computer Terms," S. Richardson, *Noteworthy,* Winter 1982, pp. 27–29.

"Glossary of Computer Terms," William A. Sabine, *Gregg Reference Manual,* 1992, pp. 480–490.

Softalk, January 1982, January 1983.

"Using the Computer in the Classroom," *Today's Education,* April–May 1982.

"VisiCalc Glossary," *Apple Orchard,* July–August 1982.

Index

Credits/Acknowledgments

Cover design by Charles Vitelli

Introduction
Facing overview—TRW Inc. photo.

1. The Economy
Facing overview—New York Stock Exchange photo.

2. Work and the Workplace
Facing overview—Photo by Pamela Carley.

3. Computers and Social Participation
Facing overview—Photo by Pamela Carley.

4. Social Values: Ethics, Law, and Privacy
Facing overview—IBM Corporation photo.

5. Politics and the State
Facing overview—IBM Microelectronics photo by Tom Way.

6. Technology Risks
Facing overview—IBM Microelectronics photo by Tom Way. 167,
170–172—Graphics by Laurie Grace.

7. International Perspective and Issues
Facing overview—TRW Inc. photo.

8. Philosophical Frontiers
Facing overview—Matsushita Electric photo.

ANNUAL EDITIONS ARTICLE REVIEW FORM

■ NAME: _____ DATE: _____

■ TITLE AND NUMBER OF ARTICLE: _____

■ BRIEFLY STATE THE MAIN IDEA OF THIS ARTICLE: _____

_____

■ LIST THREE IMPORTANT FACTS THAT THE AUTHOR USES TO SUPPORT THE MAIN IDEA:

_____

_____

_____

_____

■ WHAT INFORMATION OR IDEAS DISCUSSED IN THIS ARTICLE ARE ALSO DISCUSSED IN YOUR
TEXTBOOK OR OTHER READINGS THAT YOU HAVE DONE? LIST THE TEXTBOOK CHAPTERS AND
PAGE NUMBERS:

_____

_____

_____

_____

_____

■ LIST ANY EXAMPLES OF BIAS OR FAULTY REASONING THAT YOU FOUND IN THE ARTICLE:

_____

_____

_____

_____

■ LIST ANY NEW TERMS/CONCEPTS THAT WERE DISCUSSED IN THE ARTICLE, AND WRITE A SHORT
DEFINITION:

_____

_____

_____

_____

We Want Your Advice

ANNUAL EDITIONS/COMPUTER STUDIES revisions depend on two major opinion sources: one is our Advisory Board, listed in the front of this volume, which works with us in scanning the thousands of articles published in the public press each year; the other is you—the person actually using the book. Please help us and the users of the next edition by completing the prepaid article rating form on this page and returning it to us. Thank you for your help!

COMPUTER STUDIES: COMPUTERS IN SOCIETY, Seventh Edition
Article Rating Form

Here is an opportunity for you to have direct input into the next revision of this volume. We would like you to rate each of the 36 articles listed below, using the following scale:

1. **Excellent: should definitely be retained**
2. **Above average: should probably be retained**
3. **Below average: should probably be deleted**
4. **Poor: should definitely be deleted**

Your ratings will play a vital part in the next revision. So please mail this prepaid form to us just as soon as you complete it.
Thanks for your help!

Rating	Article	Rating	Article
	1. Welcome to Cyberspace: What Is It? Where Is It? And How Do We Get There?		18. Simulations on Trial
			19. The Invasion of Privacy
	2. The Internet & Sexual Personae *and* The Internet Produces a Global Village of Village Idiots		20. High Resolution, Unresolved
			21. Digital Politics
	3. Clicking onto Webzines		22. The Great Internet Tax Drain
	4. The New Business Cycle		23. Is Big Brother Hanging by His Bootstraps?
	5. What Has the Computer Done for Us Lately?		24. Warfare in the Information Age
	6. Creating the People's Computer		25. It's 10 O'Clock: Do You Know Where Your Data Are?
	7. Money in Electronic Commerce: Digital Cash, Electronic Fund Transfer, and Ecash		26. Software's Chronic Crisis
			27. Fatal Dose
	8. The Ripple Effect of Computer Networking		28. Liability for Defective Electronic Information
	9. Virtually Working: Dispatches from the Home Front		29. The Birth of a Celtic Tiger
	10. Working Out the Kinks		30. The Great Firewall of China
	11. Overload		31. Singapore Sting
	12. Finding One's Own Space in Cyberspace		32. Disconnected: Haves and Have-Nots in the Information Age
	13. Session with the Cybershrink: An Interview with Sherry Turkle		33. The Role of Computer Networks in Development
			34. What's It All About, Alife?
	14. The Computer Delusion		35. Ghosts in the Machine
	15. A Campus of Our Own		36. How Artificial Intelligence Fails
	16. Law and Order Comes to Cyberspace		
	17. Who's Reading Your E-Mail?		

(Continued on next page)

ABOUT YOU

Name _____ Date _____

Are you a teacher? ❑ Or a student? ❑

Your school name _____

Department _____

Address _____

City _____ State _____ Zip _____

School telephone # _____

YOUR COMMENTS ARE IMPORTANT TO US!

Please fill in the following information:

For which course did you use this book? _____

Did you use a text with this *ANNUAL EDITION*? ❑ yes ❑ no

What was the title of the text? _____

What are your general reactions to the *Annual Editions* concept?

Have you read any particular articles recently that you think should be included in the next edition?

Are there any articles you feel should be replaced in the next edition? Why?

Are there any World Wide Web sites you feel should be included in the next edition? Please annotate.

May we contact you for editorial input?

May we quote your comments?